Intuition, Imagination, ~~...~~philical
Methodology

Concerns about philosophical methodology have emerged as a central issue in contemporary philosophical discussions. In this volume, Tamar Gendler draws together fourteen essays that illuminate this topic.

Three intertwined themes connect the essays. First, each of the chapters focuses, in one way or another, on how we engage with subject matter that we take to be *imaginary*. This theme is explored in a wide range of cases, including scientific thought experiments, early childhood pretense, thought experiments concerning personal identity, fictional emotions, self-deception, Gettier and fake barn cases, the relation of belief to other attitudes, and the connection between conceivability and possibility. Second, each of the chapters explores, in one way or another, the implications of this for how *thought experiments and appeals to intuition* can serve as mechanisms for supporting or refuting scientific or philosophical claims. Third, each of the chapters self-consciously exhibits a particular *philosophical methodology*: that of drawing both on empirical findings from contemporary psychology, and on classic texts in the philosophical tradition (particularly the work of Aristotle and Hume). By exploring and exhibiting the fruitfulness of these interactions, Gendler promotes the value of engaging in such cross-disciplinary conversations to illuminate philosophical questions.

Tamar Szabó Gendler is the Vincent J. Scully Professor of Philosophy and Professor of Psychology and Cognitive Science at Yale University.

Intuition, Imagination, and Philosophical Methodology

By Tamar Szabó Gendler

OXFORD
UNIVERSITY PRESS

OXFORD
UNIVERSITY PRESS

Great Clarendon Street, Oxford, OX2 6DP,

Oxford University Press is a department of the University of Oxford.
It furthers the University's objective of excellence in research, scholarship,
and education by publishing worldwide.

Oxford is a registered trade mark of Oxford University Press
in the UK and in certain other countries

First published 2010
First published in paperback 2013

British Library Cataloguing in Publication Data

Data available

Library of Congress Cataloging in Publication Data

Data available

ISBN 978-0-19-958976-0 (Hbk)
ISBN 978-0-19-968315-4 (Pbk)

Preface

The fourteen essays collected in this volume explore a trio of interrelated themes. The first is *intuition*: what are the powers and limits of appeals to intuition in supporting or refuting various sorts of claims? The second is *imagination*: what are the cognitive consequences of engaging with content that is represented as unreal? The third is *philosophical methodology*: what are the implications of these issues for the methodology of philosophy more generally? These themes are explored in a variety of cases, including thought experiments in science and philosophy, early childhood pretense, self-deception, cognitive and emotional engagement with fiction, mental and motor imagery, automatic and habitual behavior, and social categorization. The essays are organized into two large sections. Those that appear in Part I—six in all—explore the role of intuition and thought experiment in science and philosophy; those that appear in Part II—the remaining eight—look more generally at the role of imagination in a range of domains. Within each section, the essays are grouped into pairs. In Part I, the first two essays look at the role of thought experiments in science; the next two at the role of thought experiments in exploring philosophical questions about personal identity; and the final two at a number of issues concerning intuitions and philosophical methodology more generally. In Part II, the first two essays explore the relation between pretense and belief; the next two look at the phenomenon of imaginative resistance; the next two consider issues of imagination and emotion; and the final two introduce and discuss an attitude that I call *alief*.

In addition to the thematic connections, the essays also share a methodological outlook. Each draws not only on traditional and contemporary philosophical work, but also on related work in empirical psychology. One of the volume's main goals is to demonstrate the numerous ways in which these approaches can be mutually illuminating.

The pieces themselves were composed over a fifteen-year period: a preliminary version of the earliest essay was delivered as a conference presentation in 1993; the final version of the most recent appeared in print in late

2008. Original publication information for each essay, along with information about revisions introduced in the context of the volume, can be found in the opening pages of each chapter.

In the remainder of this preface, it is my pleasure to express some of the many debts that I have incurred in the course of composing the writings that are included in the pages below.

During my graduate and professional career, I have been fortunate enough to have received support from the Mellon Foundation (1989–90, 1994–5, 2009–10), the National Science Foundation (1991–4), the Collegium Budapest (2003–4), and the American Council for Learned Societies (2003–4). I am enormously grateful to all of these organizations for their financial and professional assistance; without it I would never have been able to have written these essays.

My initial training in philosophy took place at Yale University (1983–7), and I spent my first year of graduate school at the University of California at Berkeley (1989–90). Among the teachers who supported me most at the beginning of my academic career, I owe special thanks to Karsten Harries, Jonathan Lear, and Ruth Barcan Marcus from the Yale Philosophy Department; Neil Ribe from the Yale Geology Department; Louis Dupré, Cyrus Hamlin, and Ralph Hexter from the Yale Humanities Program; Hannah Ginsborg and Lisa Lloyd from the University of California at Berkeley Philosophy Department; and John Dupré from the Stanford University Philosophy Department. During the years that these essays were conceived and composed, I had the privilege of being part of the Departments of Philosophy at Harvard University (1990–6), Yale University (1996–7 and 2006–present), Syracuse University (1997–2003), and Cornell University (2003–6). I am grateful to all of these departments—and to the faculty, students, and staff that composed them—for providing such supportive and exciting places for learning, work, and philosophical conversation.

It was Lisa Lloyd and Robert Nozick who first prompted me to think about the philosophical implications of empirical psychology, and Robert Nozick, who, when I expressed an interest in investigating the topic of thought experiments, introduced me personally to two figures whose work on the subject has influenced mine in countless ways: Thomas Kuhn and Roger Shepard. During the fall term of 1994, I had the good fortune to attend Roger's William James lectures at Harvard University, which were on the topic of thought experiment, and from the interactions that ensued emerged my introduction—in person and in writing—to the wider world of cognitive psychology. Since then, I have had the opportunity to interact with some of the most interesting and generous people working in psychology today. Among those who have been kind enough to discuss some of the ideas in this volume are Woo-Kyoung Ahn, John Bargh, Paul Bloom, Jack Dovidio, Frank Keil, Laurie Santos, and Brian Scholl at Yale; Susan Carey, Paul Harris, Steven Pinker, and Liz Spelke at Harvard; Leda Cosmides and John Tooby at the University of California at San Diego; James Cutting, Carol Krumhansl, David Pizarro, and Michael Spivey at Cornell; Alan Leslie and Deena Skolnick Weisberg at Rutgers; Tania Lombrozo at the University of California at Berkeley; Jaak Panskepp at the University of Washington; and Rebecca Saxe and Josh Tenenbaum at MIT.

Numerous people provided the infrastructure support that made composition of these papers possible. Most of them touched my life in indirect ways: I am grateful to the maintenance, clerical, and technical staff at the institutions enumerated for all that they do to make these communities run so smoothly. Others supported my work more directly: I am grateful to the office staff at the institutions with which I have been affiliated—particularly to Lisa Farnsworth and Sue McDougal at Syracuse University; Vera Kempa at the Collegium Budapest; Marlene Reitz and Sarah Weibly at Cornell University; and Monique Boney, Linda Ceneri, Vicki D'Agostino, and Pat Slatter at Yale University—for their professionalism and good cheer. Yet others have provided extraordinary care for my children: Sharon Grace (1997–8), Katalin Laczkó (2003–4), and the staff at Ithaca Community Child Care Center at Kendal (1998–2000, 2004–6), the Early Childhood Center at Cornell (2000–2), the Cayuga Heights Elementary School (2002–3 and 2004–6), the Akadémiai Óvoda of Budapest (2003–4), the Cold Spring School of New Haven (2006–present), and numerous wonderful summer programs in Ithaca, Budapest, and New Haven. Finally, for friendship throughout the years that has made the process of writing manageable, I am grateful to Charles and Harriet Brittain and to Heidi and Rick Brooks.

Individual acknowledgements for each of the papers express my gratitude to those who played a role in their composition. But a special debt is owed to a number of people for sustained support over many projects. My three graduate school advisors—Robert Nozick, Derek Parfit, and Hilary Putnam—were extraordinarily generous in their mentorship throughout my graduate career; their confidence that my interests in intuition, imagination, and philosophical methodology "counted" as something worth exploring in a dissertation was what kept me in the field. My early Syracuse colleagues—John Hawthorne, Daniel Nolan, Ted Sider, Brian Weatherson, and Dean Zimmerman—provided me with a new way of thinking about philosophy; while my work will never approach theirs in precision and exactitude, their questions and comments changed the ways that I think about nearly everything. Since I began working on the topic of imagination, I have had the opportunity to attend a number of workshops and conferences on the topic: seven colleagues whom I got to know in these settings have influenced my work more than I suspect they realize: Greg Currie, Alvin Goldman, Paul Harris, Alan Leslie, Shaun Nichols, Steve Stich, and Kendall Walton. Three additional colleagues have been primary conversation partners in various settings: Tim Crane, who was my fellow Fellow during the year that I spent at the Collegium Budapest (2003–4); Jason Stanley, who has been one of my most stalwart philosophical interlocutors for nearly two decades; and Paul Bloom, who has been an extraordinarily generous colleague, friend, and intellectual resource during my time in New Haven. Finally, over the years I have been fortunate enough to have a number of highly gifted students as research assistants; four of those stand out for special mention here: Carolyn Caine, Roald Nashi, Aaron Norby, and Elliot Paul.

For encouragement over the decades, I am extremely grateful to the members of my family. To my parents, Everett and Mary Gendler, and my sister, Naomi Gendler Camper, thank you for your good sense, sympathy, and support. To my husband and colleague Zoltán Gendler Szabó, eternal gratitude for your help—philosophical, editorial, and emotional: nearly every page bears the imprint of your advice, and those that do not are the worse for it. To my children László and Jonah, whose patience has been extraordinary throughout: dudes, you're the best!

This volume would never have come into existence were it not for the encouragement of Peter Momtchiloff, editor extraordinaire. Thanks to Peter, and to the entire staff at Oxford University Press (especially Catherine Berry, Daniel Bourner, Abi Coulson, and Sarah Parker) for their patience and professionalism. Thanks also to Katherine Alcauskas at the Yale University Art Gallery for help in obtaining the cover image, to the amazing Bonnie Blackburn for outstanding copy-editing, and to Clifford Willis for careful proofreading. Finally, for supererogatory efforts in preparing the bibliography and index—as well as sage philosophical advice throughout the volume's assembly—I am indebted to the talented Aaron Norby.

For production help on the paperback edition, I offer thanks to Production Controller Cherry Brooker. For extraordinary skill in proofreading this edition, identifying errors both typographical and substantive, I offer my gratitude to the gifted Cameron McCulloch.

T.S.G., New Haven, Connecticut,
December 2009 (updated May 2013)

Contents

Contents

Introduction

Three intertwined themes connect the papers collected in this volume. As the title suggests, these are *intuition, imagination*, and *philosophical methodology*. Each of the essays in Part I addresses, in one way or another, the question of how thought experiments and appeals to intuition can serve as mechanisms for supporting or refuting scientific or philosophical claims. Each of the essays in Part II explores, more generally, how engagement with subject matter that we take to be imaginary may affect our actions and perceptions. And each of the essays in the volume both explicitly concerns itself with philosophical methodology as a subject of investigation, and self-consciously exhibits a particular philosophical methodology: one that recognizes a continuity between classic texts in the Western philosophical tradition—particularly the work of Aristotle and Hume—and contemporary empirical findings in psychology and neuroscience.

In the remainder of this introduction, I offer some additional thoughts about how these three themes unify the essays that have been selected for inclusion in the pages below.

1. Thought Experiments, Intuitions, and Philosophical Methodology

The method of thought experiment is employed in nearly every field of human investigation: in legal reasoning, philosophical inquiry, scientific exploration, and ordinary conversation. But what exactly does the method amount to? This question is less straightforward than it might seem. In the broadest usage of the term, to perform a thought experiment is simply to work through the implications of a scenario. On this sort of account, nearly any instance of hypothetical or counterfactual reasoning would count as a thought experiment: "Would the pasta taste better if I added more salt?" "If I hadn't pushed the snooze button three times, would I have missed the bus?" Though these questions are not without interest, they do not wear their philosophical import on their sleeves. (Of course, general issues concerning hypotheticals and counterfactuals arise here as elsewhere. But that's not the central topic in debates about scientific or philosophical thought experiments—at least, not directly.)

So the first task of the essays in this volume is to try to articulate a conception of thought experiments that helps focus attention on the distinctive issues to which they seem to give rise. One way to do this is to think about thought experiments in contrast with actual experiments: the former are conducted by engaging in an imaginative act, the latter by manipulating features of the observed world. So if to perform an (actual) experiment is to conduct an empirical test under controlled conditions with the aim of illustrating, supporting, or refuting some hypothesis or theory, then to perform a thought experiment is to reason about an imaginary scenario with a similar aim. In the case of actual experiments, the theory-relevant evidence generally takes the form of data concerning the behavior of the physical world under specific conditions; in the case of thought experiments, the theory-relevant evidence generally takes the form of intuitions (or predictions) concerning such behavior. And in both instances, imagining or performing the experiment ostensibly results in new knowledge, often about contingent features of the natural world.

In light of this characterization, a number of questions naturally arise: How could thinking about a purely imaginary scenario provide us with new knowledge about the world or about our concepts? Are there certain sorts of imaginary scenarios that are likely to be especially illuminating or especially problematic? And what, if anything, can be said systematically about circumstances where the technique is likely to be particularly effective or ineffective?

Each of the chapters in Part I of the volume is devoted to answering one or more of these questions.

1.1. Scientific Thought Experiments

In "Galileo and the Indispensability of Scientific Thought Experiment" (1998b; Ch. 1) and "Thought Experiments Rethought—and Reperceived" (2004; Ch. 2), I examine the role of thought experiments in science. In both chapters, I consider the question of whether reasoning about specific entities within the context of an imaginary scenario could lead to rationally justified conclusions that—given the same initial information—would not be rationally justifiable on the basis of a straightforward argument. And in both chapters, I contend that the answer is *yes*.

In "Galileo," I argue against what I call the *Dispensability Thesis*: the view that any good scientific thought experiment can be replaced, without loss of epistemically significant demonstrative force, by a non-thought-experimental argument. The bulk of the chapter is devoted to looking closely at the famous thought experiment by which Galileo is credited with having refuted the Aristotelian theory that the speed with which a body falls is directly proportional to its weight. I contend that what allows the Aristotelian to have novel justified true beliefs about the empirical world is not that he has (whether he knows it or not) followed along the path of a recognized argument form; rather, it is that he has performed an act of introspection that has brought to light heretofore inarticulated and—because he lacked a theoretical framework in which to make sense of them—heretofore implausible tacit beliefs.

I suggest that the new knowledge that the thought experiment provides comes from a reconfiguration of conceptual commitments that enables the Aristotelian to see old phenomena in a new way. Prior to this conceptual reconfiguration, the Aristotelian considers aberrant what the Galilean takes as typical: that the rate of fall of bodies of radically different weights is sometimes (nearly) identical. Part of the power of Galileo's thought experiment comes in helping the Aristotelian to see that the cases he has been taking as anomalous are in fact the norm, and that what cries out for explanation is precisely the opposite of what he initially thought; the cases that require explanation are those where heavier objects fall faster than lighter ones.

A related argument can be found in the second essay, "Thought Experiments Rethought" (Ch. 2). There, I consider the question of how contemplation of an imaginary scenario can provide us with true beliefs about contingent features of the natural world that are simultaneously *novel* and *justified*. I suggest that focused attention to a specific scenario (as opposed to a general schema) may give rise to quasi-sensory intuitions that may, in turn, lead to and justify new beliefs about the natural world. The process is a quasi-observational one: the presence of the relevant mental image may play a crucial cognitive role not only in producing but also in justifying the belief in question.

Two core claims lie at the heart of the picture presented and defended in this pair of essays. The first is that our tacit commitments are often detached from our explicit beliefs, and that bringing these tacit commitments to light may provide us with fresh epistemically significant insights. The second is that contemplation of a paradigmatic imaginary case may generate a novel theoretical framework, and that apprehending things in its light may radically redirect our attention to heretofore unnnoticed patterns in the world.

Aspects of both of these themes are explored in a number of other essays in the volume. The first theme plays a pivotal role in Chapters 7, 11, 12, 13, and 14, all of which look at another consequence of the fact that our tacit commitments are often detached from our explicit understanding, namely, the apparently perplexing behavior that arises in cases involving what I call "imaginative contagion" and "alief." And the second theme is centrally at play in Chapters 6, 9, 10, 13, and 14, all of which consider some of the ways that vivid contemplation of particular imaginary scenarios may lead to more general reconfigurations of our understanding. I return to these issues below.

1.2. Thought Experiments and Personal Identity

In contrast to the papers on scientific thought experiment (Chs. 1 and 2), which are generally sanguine about the ways that the contemplation of imaginary cases may help generate new knowledge about the content under investigation, the papers on philosophical thought experiment (Chs. 3, 4, 5, and 6) strike a more cautionary note. In particular, the two chapters on thought experiments and personal identity—"Exceptional Persons: On the Limits of Imaginary Cases" (1998a; Ch. 3) and "Personal Identity and Thought Experiments" (2002b; Ch. 4)—argue that our ability to make *sense* of certain sorts of imaginary scenarios far outruns our ability to make informative *judgments* about them, and hence that arguments based on judgments about such scenarios may be based on shaky premises.

A good deal of philosophical literature on personal identity—particularly work of the last two decades of the last century—has focused on providing systematic accounts of subjects' judgments about a wide range of often far-fetched imaginary cases. But one might wonder when we should expect such judgments to offer reliable guides to our genuine commitments. In "Exceptional Persons" (Ch. 3), I offer a specific proposal: I suggest that if the imaginary scenario is adduced to illuminate a concept structured around a set of necessary and sufficient conditions, *and* if these conditions play a role in how we identify candidates as falling under that concept, then our judgments about the far-fetched imaginary case may help us to separate essential features of the concept from accidental ones. But if the concept is not structured in that way, or if the features in question do not govern our application of the concept, then our judgments about imaginary cases are likely to be misleading. I go on to argue that the concept of personal identity falls into the second of these classes, and hence that far-fetched thought experiments may not illuminate the concept in the way that they have been purported to.

In "Personal Identity and Thought Experiments" (Ch. 4), I offer a related argument, defending what I call "the merits of provincialism": the value of recognizing that certain patterns of features that coincide only fortuitously may nonetheless play a central role in the organization of our concepts. In particular, I suggest that our understanding and employment of the concept of *person* rests on the assumption that actual human beings come into existence only through a predictable sequence of events—even though we can imagine circumstances (such as fission or teletransportation) where this assumption would be violated. The core of the essay consists of a detailed assessment and critique of Derek Parfit's widely discussed contention that fission cases reveal that "personal identity is not what matters." I suggest that Parfit's argument rests on a subtle confounding of two kinds of features: *explanatory features* (those that explain or justify the holding of a relation) and *common factor features* (those that underpin it as necessary conditions). With this distinction in place,

I concede that there are conceivable circumstances where it might be rational to bear a relation of prudential concern towards a continuer with whom one is not identical; Parfit is right that personal identity is not what—in the common-factor sense—matters. But, I contend, this does not show what Parfit needs for his larger argument to go through, which is that that personal identity is not what matters in the explanatory sense.

These two essays (Chs. 3 and 4) also offer some more general thoughts about how thinking about imaginary exceptions might help us to refine our (understanding of our) concepts. Suppose that entities that fall under a concept *C* normally have characteristics *a, b, c, d*, and *e*, and that we are presented with a case of an entity that has only *b* and *d*, but that seems to fall under *C*. What I call the *exception-as-scalpel* strategy uses such cases to isolate essential features from those that are merely ordinarily correlative; what is taken to matter about normal cases is whatever they have in common with the exceptional cases, namely the presence of *b* and *d*. By contrast, the *exception-as-cantilever* strategy views the category-membership of exceptional cases as essentially reliant on the ordinary instances with respect to which they can be seen as exceptions. On this view, the conclusion to be drawn is that the *b-d* entity falls under *C* only because it is similar in certain crucial ways to more typical instances of the entities that *C* ordinarily describes.

One way to test whether exception-as-scalpel or exception-as-cantilever is the appropriate strategy is to ask whether if there were only *b-d* entities, we would still have the concept *C*. Where the answer is "yes," there is no reason to doubt that the conditions of concept-application for *C* are organized around a set of necessary and sufficient conditions; hence, the traditional analytical method of exception-as-scalpel is appropriate. But where the answer is "no," there is reason to think that the conditions of concept-application for *C* are organized around what psychologists refer to as a *paradigm* or *prototype*; hence, the appropriate method is exception-as-cantilever. In "Exceptional Persons" (Ch. 3) and "Personal Identity and Thought Experiments" (Ch. 4), I use the distinction to argue against a number of specific arguments that have been made in the personal identity literature.

1.3. Intuitions and Philosophical Methodology

The remaining two essays in Part I of the volume look at the role of intuitions in additional domains of philosophical inquiry. "The Real Guide to Fake Barns: A Catalogue of Gifts for Your Epistemic Enemies," co-authored with John Hawthorne (Gendler and Hawthorne 2005; Ch. 5), presents a series of cases designed to convince the reader that a particular intuition in epistemology is highly unstable. This is the intuition that, in so-called fake barn cases, the subject does not know that he is seeing a barn. By presenting a range of cases that share the structural features of the original fake barn case, but that differ from it in the details of their content, we attempt to show that the fake barn intuition is not one around which a theory of knowledge can be aptly built.

In "Philosophical Thought Experiments, Intuitions, and Cognitive Equilibrium" (2007; Ch. 6), I address the role of thought experiments in philosophy more generally. Drawing on literature from the dual processing tradition in psychology, I try to explain why contemplation of an imaginary particular may have cognitive and motivational effects different from those evoked by an abstract description of the same content, and hence, why thought experiments may be effective devices for conceptual reconfiguration. I suggest that by presenting content in a suitably concrete way, thought experiments recruit representational schemas that were otherwise inactive, thereby evoking responses that may run counter to those evoked by alternative presentations of relevantly similar content. This echoes one of the themes of the two scientific thought experiment essays (Chs. 1 and 2), which looked at some of the ways this process might occur in scientific reasoning.

At the same time, because the contemplation of particular cases may recruit heretofore uninvolved processing mechanisms, thought experiments can be expected to produce responses to the target material that remain in disequilibrium with responses to the same material under alternative presentations. This means that a theory may be correct even if we consistently and resiliently react to specific cases in ways that run counter to the theory's predictions. This introduction of an additional degree of freedom into the enterprise of philosophical explanation may introduce a feeling of vertigo. This echoes a theme elicited by the cases presented in Chapter 5.

What role, then, could thought experiments possibly play? In the closing section of Chapter 6, I suggest that when thought experiments succeed as devices of persuasion, it is because the evoked response becomes dominant, so that the subject comes (either reflectively or unreflectively) to represent relevant non-thought experimental content in light of the thought experimental conclusion. The thought experiment provides the subject with a powerful frame through which the target can be reconceptualized. Again, this echoes one of the central themes of Chapter 2, and foreshadows some of the issues that are addressed in Chapters 13 and 14.

2. Imagination, Pretense, and Belief

Each of the essays in Part II of the volume is concerned, in one way or another, with the ways that imagined content may affect our actions and perceptions. Together, these essays provide a more comprehensive framework within which the particular claims of the earlier essays can be understood.

2.1. Imagination: Overview

Our perceptions and memories of what we take to be real are typically linked up to our actions and responses in ways that our representations of what we take to be imaginary are typically not. Other things being equal, my perception of a snowstorm will motivate me to put on my boots, whereas my imagining a snowstorm will not; my memory of having lost my gloves will cause me to buy a new pair, whereas my imagining having lost them will not. In some contexts, however, the differences are less apparent. The sorts of emotions that are evoked by the contemplation of what we know to be imaginary are remarkably like those evoked by what we know to be real. And the imaginative rehearsal of the outcomes of certain decisions is one of the central tools of practical reasoning.

In "On the Relation between Pretense and Belief" (2003; Ch. 7), I explore some of the implications of the fact that this complex interplay between responses to imagined content and actual experience develops at a very early age. Before the age of two, typically developing toddlers are able to engage in highly elaborate games of symbolic pretense—in which objects and actions in the actual world are taken to stand for objects and actions in a realm of make-believe (cf. Harris 2000). These games of pretense are marked by the presence of two central features, which I call *quarantining* and *mirroring*. Quarantining is manifest to the extent that causes within the pretense-episode are taken to have effects only within the pretense-episode. So, for example, if a child "spills the lemonade" (in the pretense) she does not expect the table *really* to be wet. Mirroring is manifest to the extent that features of the imaginary situation that have not been explicitly stipulated are derivable via features of their real-world analogues. So, for example, if the child up-ends a toy pitcher that is "full of lemonade" (in the pretense), she *does* expect the table beneath it to become "wet" (in the pretense).

At the same time, from the same early age, both quarantining and mirroring are violated in crucial ways. Quarantining gives way to *contagion* in cases of what I call *affective* or *cognitive transmission*: A child who imagines that there is a monster in the closet may be reluctant to open its door; a person who has been playing at "birdwatching" may perceive a partially hidden squirrel in a nearby tree as having birdlike features. And mirroring gives way to *disparity* as a result of the fundamental incompleteness and potential incoherence of the imaginary: There may be no fact of the matter (in the pretense) just how much "tea" there is left in the teapot; and the same teacup may (in the pretense) simultaneously contain both "banana milkshake" and "root beer float" (just as a character may—in a dream—simultaneously be both your ex-wife and your third-grade teacher).

2.2. Imagination and Contagion

Although quarantining and mirroring are the central norms governing imagination and pretense, disparity and contagion are often evident, for both conceptual and architectural reasons. A number of the chapters—particularly Chapters 11 and 12—focus specifically on the issue of contagion, examining both its sources and its philosophical implications.

2.2.1. IMAGINATION AND EMOTION

So, for example, "Genuine Rational Fictional Emotions" (Gendler and Kovakovich 2005; Ch. 11) explores the phenomenon of contagion in the context of what is sometimes called *the paradox of fictional emotions*: the puzzle of why we seem to feel genuine emotions in response to descriptions of characters that we know to be fictional. I begin the chapter with an overview of work by neuroscientist Antonio Damasio showing that patients with damage to the ventromedial prefrontal cortex typically show a pair of deficits: they lack autonomic responses to emotionally disturbing images (though they have no cognitive difficulty identifying such images, nor do they lack autonomic responses in general) and they reveal a marked tendency to engage in high-risk behavior (despite describing themselves as fully aware of its inadvisability) (cf. Damasio 1994). What this seems to suggest is that subjects who lack somatized emotional responses to imagined courses of action are unable to translate knowledge of their advantages and disadvantages into action-guiding behavior. And this in turn suggests that without the capacity to respond emotionally to merely imagined situations, we would be unable to engage in practical reasoning. This means that a certain degree of contagion is inevitable, indeed desirable, in a well-functioning mind: Even when content is explicitly and consciously represented as imaginary or hypothetical, a vivid emotional response is to be expected.

But how widespread are contagion phenomena, and what does their distribution reveal about the structure of the imagination? These are the questions that I explore in "Imaginative Contagion" (2006a; Ch. 12), the bulk of which is devoted to presenting examples where merely imagining or pretending P has effects that one might expect would come only from believing or perceiving P. So, for example, visual imagination can be contagious: merely imagining a figure of a certain size and shape can sometimes produce a corresponding afterimage. So too can motor planning: simply imagining performing a motor sequence may produce effects akin to those that would result from its actual performance. The same is true of the activation of social categories: merely imagining being in the presence of others may instigate corresponding behavioral tendencies. And so on. In the chapter, I offer a general way of thinking about these phenomena: I suggest that imaginative contagion arises because certain features of our mental architecture are *source-indifferent*, in the sense that they process externally generated (perceived) and internally generated (imagined) content in similar ways. Moreover, this source-indifference persists even in the face of explicit recognition via other features of our mental architecture that the content in question is the result of a reality-insensitive process. Simply "marking" something as imaginary through some higher-level cognitive route does nothing to guarantee that the rest of our mind will hear the news and respond to it as such. (I return to this theme in the two Alief papers; Chs. 13 and 14.)

2.2.2. IMAGINATIVE RESISTANCE

The idea that imaginary content may be processed in "leaky" ways also plays a role in my diagnosis of what I call *the puzzle of imaginative resistance*: that while we typically have no difficulty fictionally entertaining all sorts of far-fetched and implausible scenarios (including those that invoke impossible situations), we seem to encounter striking impediments when we are asked to imagine situations that require us to suspend or invert our ordinary moral judgments. In both "The Puzzle of Imaginative Resistance" (2000a; Ch. 9) and "Imaginative Resistance Revisited" (2006b; Ch. 10) I offer reasons for thinking that the primary source of such imaginative resistance lies not in our *inability* to imagine morally deviant situations, but in our *unwillingness* to do so.

In the earlier paper—"Puzzle" (2000a; Ch. 9)—I explore the phenomenon of imaginative resistance by focusing on the ways that imagination involves engaged participation of a sort that mere supposition does not. I point out that when we allow an author to direct us towards certain ways of experiencing and evaluating an imaginary world, those ways of attending and responding become more readily available in our non-imaginary lives. Although this process happens without conscious awareness and beyond the range of intentional control, we are nonetheless tacitly aware of the dangers of this sort of leakage. I argue that it is fundamentally because of this that we may find ourselves hesitant or unwilling to engage imaginatively in ways that call for the suspension or inversion of our ordinary moral judgments.

In the later paper—"Revisited" (2006b; Ch. 10)—I partially defend and partially refine the account presented in the earlier paper. In contrast to "Puzzle," which looks at imaginative resistance as a *sui generis* phenomenon, "Revisited" explores imaginative resistance as a special case of a more general puzzle that I call the *puzzle of authoritative breakdown*: that when an author follows standard conventions for fictionally asserting P, engaged readers typically imagine P— but in some cases this relation falls apart. The bulk of the chapter is devoted to systematically identifying and explaining where and why this breakdown occurs.

Although they differ in certain details, both of the chapters defend four main claims, the earlier chapter implicitly, the later chapter explicitly. First, both argue that a crucial component in bringing about resistance-like phenomena is the engagement that distinguishes imagination from mere supposition. Second, while the later chapter also looks at a wider range of resistance phenomena, both chapters defend the view that the most interesting resistance cases are those that arise when the reader takes the author to be making simultaneous claims about the fictional and the non-fictional world. Third, both chapters argue that there is an important class of resistance cases where our failure to imagine can be traced to a degree of unwillingness that amplifies—in subtle and complicated ways—other sources of difficulty in imaginatively engaging with the content presented. And, finally, both chapters provide reasons for thinking that a successful characterization of the resistance-family needs to explain not only our specific resistance to accepting as fictional the contents of certain stories, but also our more general reluctance to adopt metaphoric perspectives that emphasize similarities we prefer to overlook.

2.2.3. OVERVIEW: CONTAGION

Together, these five chapters—Chapters 7, 9, 10, 11, and 12—provide an extended exploration of the ways in which imagined content and imaginary attitudes may seep into the domain of the non-imaginary in ways over which we have little control. Though there is some redundancy among the papers (Chapters 7, 11, and 12 all discuss the topic of fictional emotions from similar perspectives), and some backtracking in a couple of them (Chapters 9 and 10 offer somewhat different accounts of the phenomenon of imaginative resistance), overall, they provide a fairly coherent picture of a range of ways that contagion plays a role in our mental lives.

The core ideas in these chapters foreshadow some of the central themes of the two Alief papers (discussed in §4 below). In those papers (Chs. 13 and 14), additional lessons are drawn from the fact that contagion may occur even in the face of our explicit recognition that a certain class of content is mistaken or imaginary.

2.3. Imagination and Action

Before turning to the issue of disparity, it is worth briefly mentioning a chapter where I look from a slightly different perspective at the role of imagination in bringing about action. In "Self-Deception as Pretense" (2008c; Ch. 8), I try to show that attitudes such as pretense or make-belief can motivate action in ways traditionally credited to belief alone. A special instance of this phenomenon, I suggest, can be seen in cases of self-deception, for which I propose an analysis that I call *self-deception as pretense*.

The analysis is addressed to paradigmatic cases of self-deception: cases where a subject who believes P brings herself to act and speak and (in many ways) think in the manner that one would expect from someone who believed not-P. So, for example, a subject who believes that she is suffering from some dreaded disease, or that her child is guilty of some terrible crime, may bring herself to act and speak and (in many ways) think in the manner that one would expect from someone who believed the contrary. Crediting the subject in such cases with both believing and not believing P, or with believing both P and not-P, is problematic, for reasons that I discuss in detail in the course of the chapter. Instead, I suggest, what is going on in such cases of self-deception is that the person pretends (in the sense of *makes-believe* or *imagines* or *fantasizes*) that not-P is the case, and the pretense that not-P comes to play many of the roles normally played by belief. So while the self-deceived patient believes that she is ill, she pretends or imagines that she is not—and her actions and her speech and (many of) her thoughts accord with that content.

As in the cases of contagion described above, this process exploits the ways that imaginative pretense may come to play a central role in one's mental life—both introspectively and in the regulation of one's actions—despite one's residual awareness of its self-generated provenance, and despite one's consequent unwillingness to endorse its content as fully reflective of reality. But while the other papers focus largely on the mechanisms by which contagion comes about (Chs. 7, 11, and 12), or on a particular largely unconscious strategy we seem to have for dealing with one sort of situation in which contagion seems to occur (Chs. 9 and 10), "Self-Deception" examines some of the consequences of allowing a *projective* attitude (such as pretense) to play a role that only a *receptive* attitude (such as belief) could actually fulfill.

The self-deceived subject's attitude towards not-P is, in important ways, reality-indifferent: she holds not-P not because it is (taken to be) true, but because she wishes to be (or to have the experience of being) in a not-P world. Although the evidence that is in principle available to her supports the hypothesis that P (else this would not be a case of *self*-deception), and although she has a general topic-neutral reason for letting her thoughts and actions be P-directed (namely, that she will thereby be better able to satisfy her world-directed desires), she has a *topic-specific* reason for wanting to occupy herself with thoughts of not-P, and (perhaps independently, perhaps consequently) for letting her actions reflect an apparent belief to that effect.

The analysis predicts that there will be certain sorts of cases where it should be possible to bring the subject's commitment to reality-sensitivity to the fore, so that her belief rather than her make-belief comes to govern her responses: I call these cases of *motivation occlusion, evidential override*, and *trumped incentive*. In the final section of the essay, I offer further defense of this analysis by adverting to empirical psychological work on a quasi-automatic mechanism that exhibits precisely this trio of features.

This brings us back full circle to one of the themes in §2.1 above, namely that in order for intentional action to be possible, our perceptions and memories of what we take to be real must be linked up to our actions and responses in ways that our representations of what we take to be imaginary are not. Despite the many important and interesting violations that the phenomenon of contagion reveals, this norm of quarantining must largely govern imagined content, lest we lose hold of our status as purposive agents in a world that is not of our own making.

2.4. Imagination and Disparity

The counterpart of my work on contagion is my work on disparity, which explores the ways in which imagined content may diverge radically from content that is believed or perceived. The degree to which it is possible for us to imagine content that is incomplete or incoherent is addressed explicitly in "On the Relation between Pretense and Belief" (Ch. 7) and is a central theme of both the original "Puzzle of Imaginative Resistance" paper (Ch. 9) and of "Imaginative Resistance Revisited" (Ch. 10).

One of the key claims of those chapters is that we can—in the sense of *imagine* that is relevant for understanding fiction and our responses to it—imagine things that are impossible. This is in part because imagination and pretense involve what I call *partial mapping* (Ch. 7): entities in stories and imagined aspects in games of prop-based make-believe may have some but not all of the properties of their actual-world analogues, or they may have an incoherent amalgam of them. So, while it is arguable that conceivability under ideal rational reflection tracks conceptual possibility (for detailed discussion see Gendler and Hawthorne 2002), this kind of possibility-tracking is a non-starter when the issue is imaginability of the sort we are concerned with in games of make-believe and pretense and fictional engagement. For unlike ideal rational reflection, these sorts of attitudes depend upon precisely the sort of abstraction that leaves out conceptually relevant features of the situation at hand. (Indeed one of the main *points* of pretense and make-believe and reading fiction and viewing art is to take on various ways of seeing things—ways that focus on certain elements of the situation, while ignoring others.)

This observation plays a particular role in the arguments in the two imaginative resistance papers (Chs. 9 and 10), where it is used to rule out what I call the *impossibility hypothesis*: the view that what explains imaginative resistance is the impossibility of the situations that we are called upon to imagine. I contend that imaginability in the sense relevant to the understanding of fiction simply isn't governed by the sorts of consistency constraints that underpin possibility. But the observation also plays a more general role in the essays' broader reflections about the nature of the imagination. Certain strands in the Anglo-American tradition have, I think, restricted their focus to cases where we imaginatively entertain content as a way of limning the bounds of the possible. Though this is an important aspect of imagination (and one that I discuss in the context of "Thought Experiments Rethought—and Reperceived" (Ch. 3), as well as in Gendler and Hawthorne 2002), one should not lose track of the otherwise obvious fact that we can bear such attitudes towards contents that are not regulated by requirements of consistency and completeness.

This also helps to explain why intellectual contemplation of merely imaginary cases may, in certain cases, produce importantly different responses than actual experience would. This is a central theme of Chapters 3 through 6, as noted above.

3. Philosophical Methodology and Empirical Psychology

In addition to the explicit concern with philosophical methodology as a topic of philosophical reflection, each of the papers in the volume also exhibits a commitment to a particular philosophical methodology. All of the chapters draw deliberately both on empirical findings from contemporary psychology and on classic texts in the philosophical tradition.

"Galileo" (Ch. 1) and "Thought Experiments Rethought" (Ch. 2) make explicit use of empirical psychological work on mental models, contextual prerequisites for understanding, and mental imagery. "Exceptional Persons" (Ch. 3) and "Personal Identity and Thought Experiments" (Ch. 4) draw extensively on empirical psychological literature on concepts. "Exceptional Persons" (Ch. 3), "The Real Guide to Fake Barns" (Ch. 5), "Philosophical Thought Experiments" (Ch. 6), "Alief and Belief" (Ch. 13), and "Alief in Action" (Ch. 14) all make explicit use of recent empirical work on reasoning and rationality, and "Philosophical Thought Experiments" (Ch. 6) and the two "Alief" papers (Chs. 13 and 14) also draw extensively on traditional and recent work in the dual processing tradition.

"On the Relation between Pretense and Belief" (Ch. 7) bases much of its argument on work in developmental psychology, and "Self-Deception as Pretense" (Ch. 8) bases a key step in its argument on work on mindset and the illusion of control. Work on the neuroscience of emotion plays a central role in arguments in "Pretense and Belief" (Ch. 7), "Genuine Rational Fictional Emotions" (Ch. 11) and "Imaginative Contagion" (Ch. 12), while studies of automatic processing are a focal point of discussions in "Imaginative Contagion" (Ch. 12), "Alief and Belief" (Ch. 13), and "Alief in Action" (Ch. 14). And work on implicit attitudes, aversive racism, and the regulation of habit are central to the discussion of "Alief in Action" (Ch. 14).

This empirical work is not intended to supplant philosophical argument: I see the two domains as genuinely continuous. Philosophers concerned with the cluster of topics that I try to explore in this volume—topics that lie within the domains of epistemology, philosophy of mind, action theory, and aesthetics—have always made use of the best empirical psychology of their time. Aristotle and Hume, two thinkers whose influence can be found on nearly every page, were among the most brilliant psychologists ever to have lived. That psychology has, in the last century or so, become a discipline governed by a certain sort of experimental method does nothing to impugn its philosophical significance. Or so I try to demonstrate in the pages below.

4. Bringing the Strands Together: Alief

The two final chapters in the volume ("Alief and Belief" (2008a; Ch. 13) and "Alief in Action (and Reaction)" (2008b; Ch. 14)) bring together the themes of the earlier chapters. Both of these chapters focus on the nature and role of a cognitive state that I have dubbed *alief*. Aliefs are, roughly speaking, innate or habitual propensities to respond to (possibly accurate) apparent stimuli in ways that are associative and automatic. (By contrast, beliefs are, roughly speaking, evidentially sensitive commitments to content.) When aliefs activate behavioral propensities that accord with our beliefs, I call them *belief-concordant aliefs*; when they activate propensities that run counter to those evoked by our beliefs, I call them *belief-discordant aliefs*.

So, for example, when you (without conscious attention) shift your car from first to second gear at just the moment when you should, or when a tennis player moves to the right location on the tennis court to return the ball, or when Miss Manners says "thank you" in response to your handing her a pencil, each exhibits behaviors that result from belief-concordant aliefs. The notion of belief-concordant alief, I think, lies at the heart of virtue ethics. In "Alief in Action" (Ch. 14), I offer some remarks suggesting that Aristotle's *phronimos* is one in whom morally relevant beliefs and aliefs coincide.

By contrast, when a sports fan watching a televised rerun of a baseball game loudly encourages her favorite player to remain on second base, or when a cinema-goer watching a horror film shrieks and clutches her chair, or when a person walking across a transparent glass balcony trembles as she walks out to the railing, each of them displays behaviors that result from belief-discordant aliefs. Appeal to the notion of belief-discordant alief can explain phenomena ranging from superstitious hesitation (refusing to tear up a photograph of a loved one despite believing the action to be harmless), to externalized self-deception (rushing when my watch shows that it is 12:05 despite believing that I have set the watch five minutes fast), to lagging habits (walking towards the location where the wastebasket used to be despite believing that I moved it to another corner when I rearranged the room). I discuss such cases in detail in the two "alief" papers (Chs. 13 and 14).

In some cases, we deliberately take advantage of the fact that our beliefs and aliefs activate contrary associative repertoires: theater, cinema, novel-reading, video games, board games, poetry, metaphor, circumlocution, daydreaming, therapy, roller-coasters, and bungee jumping all exploit—in various ways—our tendency to respond to merely apparent stimuli in habitual ways without thereby forming the relevant associated beliefs. But for the most part, discord between alief and belief is an undesirable state. Since reflective beliefs (in conjunction with endorsed desires) must, by definition, activate propensities to act and react in ways that we (think we) should, belief-discordant aliefs must, by definition, activate propensities to act and react in ways that we (think we) shouldn't. How, in such cases, can alief and belief be brought into accord?

This is the challenge that ancient and medieval philosophers explored when they considered the problem of *harmonizing the parts of the soul,* and that early modern philosophers discussed when they examined the *conflict between reason and the passions.* And it is one that contemporary cognitive and social psychology (among other disciplines) have been exploring under many rubrics—both behavioral and neurological. As I point out in "Alief in Action" (Ch. 14), there are two main strategies for regulating alief. One—stressed by Aristotle among others (especially in the *Nicomachean Ethics*)—involves the cultivation of alternative habits through deliberate rehearsal. The other—stressed by Descartes among others (especially in the *Passions of the Soul*)—involves the refocusing of attention through directed imagination.

In the closing pages of "Alief in Action" (Ch. 14), I consider this question in the context of what psychologists call "aversive racism" (Dovidio and Gaertner 2004)—the situation faced by subjects who consciously endorse egalitarian values, but who exhibit unconscious reactions associated with negative feelings towards the relevant racial group. For more than two decades, the literature on implicit prejudice has explored the question of whether—and if so, how—automatic activation of such stereotypical responses can be controlled. It turns out that purposeful suppression of such responses is cognitively costly: when aversive racists engage in interracial interaction with a deliberate goal of egalitarianism, they show increased activation of areas in the prefrontal cortex associated with executive function and self-regulation, resulting in exhaustion that causes them subsequently to perform poorly on tasks (such as the Stroop color-naming task) that measure executive control (Richeson and Shelton 2003). That is, subjects whose racial aliefs are out of line with their conscious goal of acting in a non-discriminatory fashion must expend significant cognitive effort to suppress the response-tendencies activated through these associations.

This phenomenon results from the ways in which our implicit and explicit attitudes may reflect different contents and different commitments, a theme that is present in every one of the papers included in the volume. It helps to explain the effectiveness of thought experimental reasoning both in science (Chs. 1 and 2) and philosophy (Ch. 6), as well as the challenges posed by such reasoning in certain philosophical domains (Ch. 3, 4, 5, and 6). It lies behind the apparently perplexing responses that arise in cases involving various sorts of imaginative contagion (Chs. 7, 9, 10, 11, 12, 13, and 14), and it helps explain the apparent irrationality of certain ways of relating to the world (Chs. 7, 8, and 14).

The idea of the modular or "divided soul" has played a central role in philosophical discussions in Western and non-Western traditions for nearly two millennia, and its contemporary counterpart underpins nearly every domain of present-day empirical and clinical psychology. But despite this enormous attention, its philosophical import in the domains of intuition, imagination, and philosophical methodology has not, I think, been fully appreciated. The essays collected in this volume represent my own small attempt to partially rectify this omission.

5. Reader's Guide

In closing, a few remarks about what the reader can expect to find in the book itself. In addition to the overviews provided above, I have provided brief introductions to each of the essays in the body of the volume, including a summary of the essay's main claims and—where relevant—an indication of the relation between the essay and its immediate predecessor or successor. Throughout the text, points of connection across the various chapters are offered in parenthetical remarks and cross-referencing footnotes.

As in any collection, the papers vary in quality. While there may be some readers with both the will and the temporal resources to tackle them all, most, I suspect, will engage with only a subset. Such readers may be interested in knowing which of the papers included here are most likely to repay close attention.

In my opinion (which you ought to trust, since I just spent more than a month closely rereading all of them), the four weakest papers in the volume are "Thought Experiments Rethought" (Ch. 2), "Philosophical Thought Experiments, Intuitions, and Cognitive Equilibrium" (Ch. 6), "Genuine Rational Fictional Emotions" (Ch. 11), and "Imaginative Contagion" (Ch. 12). (Each of them has some redeeming quality, of course, or I wouldn't have included it here. But they are not as rich, philosophically speaking, as the remaining essays.) Four other papers compose the volume's middle class: these are "Galileo and the Indispensability of Scientific Thought Experiment" (Ch. 1), "Exceptional Persons: On the Limits of Imaginary Cases" (Ch. 3), "On the Relation between Pretense and Belief" (Ch. 7), and "Imaginative Resistance Revisited" (Ch. 10).

Finally, in its own paragraph so that the casual reader can easily find it, a list of the five most philosophically rewarding papers in the collection: "Personal

Identity and Thought Experiments" (Ch. 4), "Self-Deception as Pretense" (Ch. 8), "The Puzzle of Imaginative Resistance" (Ch. 9), and the two "Alief" essays (Chs. 13 and 14). Plus, a special bonus for getting to the end of the Introduction (even if you just started reading at §5): the essay with the highest ratio of jokes to pages is, by considerable measure, "The Real Guide to Fake Barns" (Ch. 5).[1]

---

[1] *Acknowledgements*: For comments on previous drafts of this introduction, I am grateful to Aaron Norby and Zoltán Gendler Szabó.

Part I

Thought Experiments, Intuitions, and Philosophical Methodology

1

Galileo and the Indispensability of Scientific Thought Experiment

In this chapter, I attempt to show that thought experiments play a distinctive role in scientific inquiry. I contend that reasoning about particular entities within the context of an imaginary scenario can lead to rationally justified conclusions that—given the same initial information—would not be rationally justifiable on the basis of a straightforward argument.

Though the bulk of the essay involves a careful reconstruction of one of the most famous thought experiments in the history of science—that by which Galileo is said to have refuted the Aristotelian theory that heavy bodies fall faster than lighter ones—the conclusion it offers is supposed to be a general one.

I show that the standard argumentative reconstruction of Galileo's thought experiment fails to capture its justificatory power, and I suggest reasons to think that any other argumentative reconstruction would fail in similar ways. I then argue that even if one were to provide an argumentative reconstruction that did almost perfectly capture the thought experiment's demonstrative force, this would not show that the *reason* the thought experiment is successful is because, deep down, it is nothing more than an argument in disguise. I suggest that, to the contrary, the success of the thought experiment is a result of the way in which it invites the reader's constructive participation, describes particulars in ways that make manifest practical knowledge, and presents an imaginary scenario wherein relevant features can be separated from those that are inessential to the question at issue.

This essay and its successor—"Thought Experiments Rethought—and Reperceived" (Ch. 2)—form a natural pair. For those who prefer to read only one of them, this essay, which is more substantive and detailed, can be read as a self-standing piece.

***

This essay was first published in the *British Journal for the Philosophy of Science*, 49/3 (1998), 397–424 and is reprinted with the kind permission of Oxford University Press. The version below omits one section of the original article (§3.4, pp. 415–20), which contains a detailed reconstruction of and response to arguments offered by John Norton and James Robert Brown. (Interested readers can, of course, find that discussion in the original published version.) The remainder of the text is unaltered except for the correction of minor typographical errors and stylistic infelicities, and the addition of some bibliographical and supplementary material to certain footnotes (noted as such). As a result of reformatting, several footnote numbers have changed. The original number of each footnote is noted in [square brackets].

1. Argumentative Reconstruction

Philosophers who are opposed to all things spooky tend to think that thought experiments in science are (at least in principle) eliminable, and that whatever demonstrative force they have is the result of their being sound arguments dressed up in heuristically appealing clothing. On such a view, a scientific thought experiment's justificatory force comes from the fact that it can be reconstructed as an argument with explicit premises that make no reference to imaginary particulars.

My goal in this paper is to challenge this view by carefully examining one of the most famous thought experiments in the history of science: that by which Galileo is said to have refuted the Aristotelian theory that heavier bodies fall faster than lighter ones. I will try to show that the thought-experimental format of Galileo's presentation plays an indispensable role in the persuasiveness of his case against the Aristotelian, and that a similar degree of persuasiveness could not be obtained on the grounds of explicit argument alone.

1.1. The Elimination Thesis

The view that thought experiments lead to justified conclusions because they are arguments finds clear articulation and powerful defense in a pair of papers by John Norton.[1] In those papers, Norton puts forth a hypothesis about thought experiments that he calls the *Elimination Thesis*. Paraphrasing slightly, his thesis is this:

The Elimination Thesis: Any conclusion reached by a (successful) scientific thought experiment will also be demonstrable by a non-thought-experimental argument.[2]

As initially formulated, the thesis is ambiguous; it is compatible with both a weaker reading, which I will call the *Dispensability Thesis*, and a stronger reading, which I will call the *Derivativity Thesis* (cf. Norton 1996: 354–8). In order to formulate these versions, however, I need first to clarify what a number

---

[1] [1] Norton 1991, 1996. [*Note added in 2009*: Norton continues to defend this view; cf. Norton 2004a, 2004b.]

[2] [2] Cf. Norton 1991: 131 and Norton 1996: 336. Note that although I am using Norton's articulation and defense of this thesis as a convenient jumping-off point, the specifics of his position are not my target.

of terms in the thesis mean, and to describe briefly the sorts of arguments which might be offered in its favor.

1.2. Clarification of Terminology

A number of terms in the thesis require further elaboration. Let me begin with "thought experiment" and "non-thought-experimental argument." To draw a conclusion on the basis of a *thought experiment* is to make a judgment about what would happen if the particular state of affairs described in some imaginary scenario were actually to obtain.[3] One might then use that judgment in developing a more general theory, just as one might use the result of an actual experiment. By contrast, to draw a conclusion on the basis of a *non-thought-experimental argument* is to be led by a process of inductive or deductive reasoning from a set of explicit premises which make no reference to particular hypothetical or counterfactual states of affairs to a correspondingly general conclusion. Again, one might use that conclusion as the basis for endorsing one or another general theory about the phenomena in question. So thought experiments differ from non-thought-experimental arguments in two crucial respects: first, they are not presented as arguments, but rather as invitations to contemplate a way that the world might (have) be(en); and second, they make essential reference to particular hypothetical or counterfactual states of affairs (cf. Norton 1991: 229; Norton 1996: 336).

What the Elimination Thesis says is that any good scientific thought experiment can be transformed into a non-thought-experimental argument without loss of demonstrative force. Given the characterization just offered, what an elimination will involve is first a process of argumentative reconstruction in which the narrative presentation is replaced by a series of explicit premises sufficient to establish the desired result, and then a process in which those premises that make reference to hypotheticals, counterfactuals, and particulars are replaced by premises in which no such reference is made. If the Elimination Thesis is correct, such a process will preserve completely the thought experiment's demonstrative force.

What is meant by "demonstrative force"? I will suggest two problematic readings and then one that I will endorse. If the claim that "any conclusion

---

[3] [4] For other recent characterizations of (scientific) thought experiments see, for instance: Bealer 1998; Brown 1986, Brown 1991a, 1991b, 1993a, 1993b, 1995; Carrier 1993; Gooding 1990, 1992, 1993, 1994; Hacking 1993; Humphreys 1993; Irvine 1991; Janis 1991; Kujundzic 1993; Laymon 1991; Lipton 1993; Massey 1991; Nersessian 1984, 1992, 1993; Norton 1991, 1993, 1996; Prudovsky 1989; Shepard 1994; Sorensen 1992a, 1992b; Wilkes 1988; as well as other articles in Horowitz and Massey 1991. The *locus classicus* is, of course, Mach 1883/1960, 1897/1976; for other early discussions cf. also Hesse 1966; Koyré 1960/1968; Kuhn 1964; Popper 1959/1992. [*Added in 2009*: For additional recent discussions, see Atkinson 2003; Brendel 2004; Brown 2004a, 2004b; Davies 2007; DeMey 2006; Norton 2004a, 2004b; Palmieri 2003, 2008; Peijnenburg and Atkinson 2003.]

reached by a good thought experiment will also be demonstrable by a non-thought-experimental argument" means no more than that in the reconstruction of a mature science, the conclusions that were (as a matter of fact) reached by thought experiments can be derived from more fundamental principles by means of inference schemes licensed within the science, then the thesis is trivially true. Even if the development of Newtonian mechanics relied on a series of crucial thought experiments, its textbook presentation might well establish particular conclusions on the basis of more conventional forms of argument.

On the other hand, there is a reading of "demonstrative force" according to which the thesis is trivially false. If the claim is taken to mean that—as a matter of psychological fact—any conclusion that was reached by a good thought experiment might also have been demonstrated to the person who reached the conclusion by means of a non-thought-experimental argument, then the Elimination Thesis is certainly untrue. None would doubt the important heuristic and illustrative role played by thought experiments in scientific exploration, and the crucial tasks they play in instruction and informal demonstration.

The proper reading of "demonstrative force" makes the Elimination Thesis epistemologically interesting. On this reading, demonstrative force concerns the role that thought experiments play in living bodies of knowledge: after the moment of discovery and before the end of inquiry. It concerns whether a particular conclusion based on a particular process of reasoning (thought experiment) is thereby *justified*—whether if such a process leads to true beliefs, those beliefs should count as knowledge. So the issue raised by the Elimination Thesis is this: can reasoning about (reasonably) specific entities within the context of an imaginary scenario lead to rationally justified conclusions that—given the same initial information—would not be rationally justifiable on the basis of a straightforward argument? In the next section, I consider two reasons that one might think such eliminations are possible.

1.3. The Negative Argument and the Positive Argument

The Elimination Thesis (that is, the thesis that thought experiments are dispensable) can be defended with two arguments, one negative, one positive. So, for instance, John Norton argues (negatively) as follows: thought experiments must be arguments because there is nothing else for them to be: "Thought experiments in physics provide or purport to provide us information about the physical world. Since they are *thought* experiments rather than *physical* experiments, this information does not come from the reporting of new physical data. Thus there is only one non-controversial source from which the information can come: it is elicited from information we already have by an identifiable argument" (Norton 1991: 129). Norton considers this position almost trivial: "the alternative," he writes, "is to suppose that thought experiments provide some new and even mysterious route to knowledge of the physical world" (Norton 1991: 129).[4] So the negative argument contends that if we have obtained new information about the empirical world without having obtained new *empirical* information about the empirical world, the only way we *could* have done so is by means of an argument.

The positive reason that one might think that thought experiments are just arguments in disguise is that "the *analysis* and *appraisal* of a thought experiment will involve reconstructing it explicitly as an argument," so that "a good thought experiment is a good argument, a bad thought experiment is a bad argument" (Norton 1991: 131; Norton 1996: 335). So the positive argument amounts to saying that if a thought experiment can be *reconstructed* as an argument, then what it was all along *was* an argument.[5] Even if the reason I come to know something by contemplating a thought-experimental scenario doesn't *seem* to be because there is an argument into which the thought experiment can be reconstructed, it is. The reason my belief is *justified* is because, in the end, the thought experiment *was* a disguised argument all along.

1.4. The Dispensability Thesis and the Derivativity Thesis

We are now in a position to recognize that the Elimination Thesis as originally formulated and defended actually involves two distinct claims. These might be stated as follows:

The Dispensability Thesis: Any good scientific thought experiment can be replaced, without loss of demonstrative force, by a non-thought-experimental argument.

The Derivativity Thesis: The justificatory force of any good scientific thought experiment can only be explained by the fact that it can be replaced, without loss of demonstrative force, by a non-thought-experimental argument.

Loosely put, the Dispensability Thesis says that we can always get from here to there without appeal to a thought experiment. If a thought experiment legitimately transports us from one state of belief to another, a non-thought-experimental argument could too. Thought experiments may be convenient and efficient ways of reaching conclusions about the physical world, but they have only the advantage that a car has over walking; they get us where we want to go much more quickly, but they don't get us anywhere we couldn't reach by more pedestrian means.

---

[4] [6] For an endorsement of this alternative, cf. Brown 1991a, 1991b, 1993a, 1993b, 1995. [*Added in 2009*: Brown continues to defend this view; see Brown 2004a, 2004b.]

[5] [7] "The workings and achievements of any thought experiment can be revealed and captured fully in an explicit argument which employs the same resources" (Norton 1996: 339). Cf. also Norton 1996: 357–8.

The Derivativity Thesis says that not only can any good scientific thought experiment be replaced, without loss of demonstrative force, by a non-thought-experimental argument, but that to the extent that a good scientific thought experiment has demonstrative force, it is *because*, deep down, the thought experiment *is* an argument. We may be misled by the surface features of the case to think that something non-argumentative is doing justificatory work, but we are wrong. The *reason* the Dispensability Thesis is true is that all that was *ever* justificatorily at play was something argumentative. What looked like a car turned out to be propelled by foot power all along (like a child's go-car, or one of the vehicles on *The Flintstones*). So the Dispensability Thesis says we *can* get by without what we commonly call thought experiments; the Derivativity Thesis tells us that we already *do*.

In the next section, I challenge the Dispensability Thesis by showing that it does not hold true of a widely acclaimed thought experiment of Galileo's. I choose this case for two reasons. First, since this particular example is generally treated as the paradigm of an effective thought experiment, diagnosing the source of its success is itself a worthwhile endeavor.[6] Second, challenging the Dispensability Thesis in this way allows me to shed light on the Derivativity Thesis as well. Obviously, if the Dispensability Thesis is false, the Derivativity Thesis is too; the more interesting question is whether some alternative explanation can be offered of the thought experiment's success. I try to say something positive about this question in §§3 and 4.

2. Galileo's Thought Experiment and its Reconstruction

2.1. Galileo's Thought Experiment

Perhaps the most famous thought experiment in the history of Western science is the thought experiment with which Galileo is credited with having refuted the Aristotelian view that the speed with which a body falls is directly

---

[6] [8] For some of the many discussions of this and related thought experiments of Galileo, cf. Brown 1986, 1991a, 1991b, 1993a, 1993b, 1995; Cargile 1987; Clement 1983; Koyré 1939/1979, 1960/1968; Kuhn 1964; Norton 1996; Prudovsky 1989; Sorensen 1992a. [*Added in 2009*: See also the detailed discussions in Palmieri 2005a, 2005b, 2008. Thanks to David M. Miller for alerting me to this work.] In my discussion below, I follow the somewhat unfortunate practice of considering this thought experiment outside of both its historical and textual contexts. As a partial remedy to this misleading presentation, I refer the reader to some of the many general discussions of Galileo's work and its context; one might fruitfully begin with: Butts and Pitt 1978; Claggett 1959; Clavelin 1974; Cooper 1935; Damerow et al. 1992; E. J. Dijksterhuis 1961; Drake 1978, 1989, 1990. See also sources listed in the next three footnotes. [*Added in 2009*: For recent meticulous discussion and extensive references, see Palmieri 2008.]

proportional to its weight.[7] The thought experiment appears in his last and most mature work, the *Discourse Concerning Two New Sciences*, in the context of a more general discussion of the possibility and nature of motion in a void.[8] Galileo's goal in the section as a whole is to establish that "if one were to remove entirely the resistance of the medium, all materials would descend with equal speed" (Galilei 1638/1989: 116);[9] the thought experiment in question leads to the weaker conclusion that "both great and small bodies, *of the same [material]*, are moved with like speeds" (Galilei 1638/1989: 109, italics added, bracketed word replaced).

The view that Galileo is challenging is that "moveables differing in heaviness are moved in the same medium with unequal speeds, which maintain to one another the same ratio as their weights [*gravità*]" (Galilei 1638/1989: 106). That is, he is challenging the view that heavier bodies fall faster than lighter ones, and that they do so in direct proportion to their heaviness. On the version Galileo takes himself to be opposing, the proportionality is linear: "a moveable ten times as heavy as another, is moved ten times as fast" as the other (Galilei 1638/1989: 106).[10]

The famous thought experiment, rephrased slightly, is the following. Imagine that a heavy and a light body are strapped together and dropped from a significant height.[11] What would the Aristotelian expect to be the natural speed of their combination? On the one hand, the lighter body should slow down the heavier one while the heavier body speeds up the lighter one, so their combination should fall with a speed that lies between the natural speeds of its components. (That is, if the heavy body falls at a rate of 8, and the light body

---

[7] [9] Challenges to the Aristotelian thesis—both empirical and conceptual—had appeared in a number of mid- and late 16th-c. works. (For relevant passages, see: [for Cardan] L. Cooper 1935: 7–77; Damerow et al. 1992: 365; [for Tartaglia] Drake and Drabkin 1969: 63–143, esp. 120 ff.; Damerow et al. 1992: 378; [for Benedetti] Drake and Drabkin 1969: 147–237, esp. 206, and 31–41; E. J. Dijksterhuis 1961: 269–71; Drake 1989: 27–30; [for Stevin] L. Cooper 1935: 77–80; E. J. Dijksterhuis 1961: 324–9.)

[8] [10] Galileo himself had produced a less conclusive version of the famous thought experiment as early as 1590 in an unfinished and unpublished dialogue on motion; cf. L. Cooper 1935: 80–90; Drake and Drabkin 1969: 331–77; Galilei 1590/1960: 26–38, esp. 29 (National Edition, p. 265). For an interesting discussion of whether Galileo ever actually performed such an experiment, cf. L. Cooper 1935; Drake 1978, 1989, 1990; Drake and Drabkin 1969; Koyré 1960/1968; Segre 1989. Since my primary purpose in this essay is not historical, I will focus only on Galileo's 1638 presentation of the refutation, bracketing the interesting question (a question not without philosophical interest) of why it was that such a simple and obvious mistake apparently remained part of the West's scientific world view for nearly 2,000 years.

[9] [11] Here and elsewhere, I have made use of Drake's 1974/1989 translation of the *Discorsi*. For easy cross-referencing with the more widely available (though less reliable) Crew and De Salvio translation, page references are to the National Edition (except where noted).

[10] [12] Cf. Aristotle *Physics* 215ᵃ24–216ᵃ21; *On the Heavens* 301ᵇ.

[11] [13] Note that in the remarks that follow, all references to bodies should be understood as referring to bodies of the same material. For the purposes of my discussion, this constraint is irrelevant.

at a rate of 4, then their combination should fall at a rate between the two (cf. Galilei 1638/1989: 107).) On the other hand, since the weight of the two bodies combined is greater than the weight of the heavy body alone, their combination should fall with a natural speed greater than that of the heavy body. (That is, if the heavy body falls at a rate of 8 and the light body at a rate of 4, their combination should fall at a rate greater than 8.) But then the combined body is predicted to fall both more quickly, and more slowly, than the heavy body alone (cf. Galilei 1638/1989: 107–8). The way out of this paradox is to assume that the natural speed with which a body falls is independent of its weight: "both great and small bodies . . . are moved with like speeds" (Galilei 1638/1989: 109).

2.2. Reconstruction of the Galileo Case

Transformed into an argument that conforms to the strictures of the Elimination Thesis, Galileo's reasoning can be reconstructed as follows.[12] The first claim of the Aristotelian is that:

(1)   Natural speed is mediative.

That is, natural speed is a property such that if a body A has natural speed s_1, and a body B has natural speed s_2, the natural speed of the combined body A-B will fall between s_1 and s_2.

The second premise of the reconstruction is that:

(2)   Weight is additive.

That is, weight is a property such that if body A has weight w_1, and body B has weight w_2, the weight of the combined body A-B will be equal to the sum of w_1 and w_2.

From these two premises (plus the assumption that not all weights and natural speeds are either zero or infinite), it follows that:

(3)   Natural speed is not directly proportional to weight.

For the first is a mediative property, whereas the second is an additive property, and a mediative property cannot be directly proportional to one that is additive. Furthermore, the only way to maintain (1), (2), and (3) simultaneously is to assume that all natural speeds are the same. Then weight might be additive and natural speed (in a vacuous sense) mediative, with no contradiction thereby implied. Thus natural speed is shown to be independent of weight.

---

[12] [14] For Norton's reconstruction of this case, cf. Norton 1996: 340–5.

2.3. *Four Ways Out for the Aristotelian*

If the Dispensability Thesis is true, then Galileo's thought experiment should be replaceable by some non-thought-experimental argument without loss of demonstrative force. My goal in the next two sections (2.3 and 2.4) is to show that the reconstruction presented in §2.2 is not such an argument.[13]

I begin my case by pointing out that there are a number of "ways out" for the defender of the view that natural speed is directly correlated with weight—a view which, for the sake of convenience, I will call the Aristotelian view. These ways out involve denying premises (1) and (2) by proposing a series of alternative hypotheses about the physical properties of strapped-bodies, that is, bodies of the sort described by the thought experiment. The point of talking about these ways out is to show that there are ways to maintain the negation of (3) by adopting alternatives to (1) and (2), and adopting these may well be less disruptive to the Aristotelian picture than giving up (3). What I will suggest below is that these ways out, though logically available, run counter to certain tacit knowledge about the physical world. It is for this reason that, when the case is presented as a thought experiment, they do not even occur to us. To block them as moves in a straight argument, however, requires metaphysical commitments that seem not to be at play in the thought experiment itself. What these commitments are, and what role I think they *actually* play in Galileo's reasoning is a point I will turn to after presenting the four ways out.

The first two ways out for the Aristotelian would correspond to denying that the properties in question are *determinate* for strapped-together bodies in one of the following two ways.

(4) Natural speed is not physically determinate for strapped-bodies.[14]
(5) Weight is not physically determinate for strapped-bodies.

That is, she might reject (1) or (2) on the grounds that they presuppose that natural speed and weight are properties that apply universally, even to bodies that are in some way monstrous.[15] Since strapped-bodies are odd entities, she might say, they need not be governed by the sorts of laws that govern ordinary objects. In particular, they need not have determinate natural speeds or weights.

---

[13] [15] Below I suggest reasons for thinking that this will be true for *any* argumentative reconstruction that conforms to the strictures of the elimination thesis.

[14] [16] For a version of this "way out," cf. Koyré 1960/1968: 51.

[15] [17] Galileo preemptively deals with this by getting a concession from Simplicio straight away that "for every heavy falling body there is a speed determined by nature such that this cannot be increased or diminished except by using force or opposing some impediment to it" (Galilei 1638/1989: 107); cf. also Drake's n. 40 in Galilei 1638/1989 at (modern pagination) p. 66.

The third way out for the Aristotelian would be to avoid the conflict between (1) and (2) by saying that there *is* a fact of the matter about whether a strapped-body is one body or two, and that its physical properties in falling will depend on the answer to this question. She might say:

(6)   Natural speed and weight are mediative for strapped-bodies that are *united*.
      Natural speed and weight are additive for strapped-bodies that are *unified*.

That is, sometimes when two bodies are strapped together, they are merely *united* and remain, as a matter of fact, two objects; sometimes, when they are strapped together, they are *unified* and form, as a matter of fact, a single object. In the first case, both weight and speed will be mediative; the combined body will have a weight intermediate between those of the two original bodies, and fall with a natural speed that lies between the two original speeds. In the second case, both properties will be additive; the weight of the unified body will be equal to the sum of the weights of its component parts, and its natural speed correspondingly equal to the natural speeds of the two combined. Since the mediativity of the properties holds only with respect to united pairs of objects, and the additivity only with respect to unified single objects, there is no way that the Aristotelian can be forced to a contradiction. What she *is* forced to accept, however, are radical discontinuities in nature. A body, united, might be falling steadily at a rate of, say, 6, and suddenly, should its parts happen to become unified, begin falling at a rate of, say, 12.

But the Aristotelian can avoid the problem of discontinuity. A fourth way would be for her to say that, given two bodies that fall together, there is a fact of the matter about their degree of connectedness, and that this determines their physical properties when falling. The claim would be:

(7)   Natural speed and weight for strapped-bodies are determined by a *degree of connectedness* (C) such that the speed/weight of B_1-strapped-to-B_2 where B_1 has w_1 and B_2 has w_2 will be: $(C)(w_1+w_2) + (1-C)(w_1+w_2)/2$.[16]

We let C measure the degree of connectedness between the two bodies; that is, we let it be a number between zero and one that corresponds to the degree to which two bodies that fall together are unified: if the bodies are completely unified, C will take a value of 1; if the bodies are completely disunified (that is, united), C will take a value of 0. For intermediate cases, the value will be between these two, and the speed and weight of the combined body will lie between the mean and the sum of the two initial values. So if the two bodies are completely unified, the

---

[16] [18] To keep the equation minimally complicated, I have made a number of trivial simplifying assumptions. I have assumed that the units for measuring weight and natural speed correspond so that the number representing an object's weight is the same as the number representing its natural speed; and I have assumed that the natural speed of two merely unified bodies is the mean of their individual natural speeds.

additive law will apply completely; if the bodies are merely united, the mediative law will apply throughout; and for intermediate cases, some proportional average will be found between them. Thus the assumption that natural speed is a function of weight can be maintained, and it can be maintained without violation of continuity. How can this be done? It can be done under the assumption that degree of connectedness is a relevant physical property.

That this way out too seems not to be a live option brings us to the point where I will suggest my alternative explanation of what is going on.

2.4. What the Reconstruction Misses

Let's begin by thinking about ways in which the four ways out might be blocked. And let's start with the most obvious: we might make appeal to two broad, defeasible, tacit assumptions, each of which captures an important feature of our representation of experienced reality. One is that, for any body that one might encounter, there is a determinate fact concerning its weight and natural speed. That is:

(8) Natural speed and weight are physically determined.

The other is that there is *no* determinate fact whether strapped-bodies are one object or two. That is:

(9) Entification is not physically determined.

What (8) says is that a particular question about natural properties has a determinate answer. Any body, no matter how oddly shaped, will have a particular weight and a particular natural speed that are fixed by the world. What (9) says is that a particular question of entification has an indeterminate answer. Whether we consider a strapped-together body to be a single object, or two objects held together by a strap, or indefinitely many objects held together by internal forces, is merely a question of the aspect under which we choose to view that object. The answer to the question "how many objects?" does not follow from any *physical* property we might discover; it is a question about our words, not a question about the world.

These two premises are sufficient to eliminate the "ways out" enumerated above. If (8) holds, then (4) and (5) are not available as lines of escape; if (9) holds, then neither (6) nor (7) can be appealed to as a means of avoiding the Galilean conclusion. And the *way* in which they eliminate (4)–(7) is very different from the way that a simple reassertion of (1) and (2) would. They show not only *that* there is something wrong with (4)–(7) as descriptions of the way the world is, but *why* there is something wrong with them. They show *what* it is about our tacit understanding of physical reality, and about our instincts concerning plausible candidates for physically relevant and irrelevant properties, that is missed by someone who appeals to (4) or (5) or (6) or even (7).

What this reveals is that the initial reconstruction of the Galilean thought experiment (as presented in §2.2) fails to capture what is really doing the work in the case. As hypotheses about the ways strapped-bodies might behave in fall, (4), (5), (6), and especially (7) are in principle available as alternatives to (1) and (2); just as natural speed might be mediative and weight additive, it might be that both natural speed and weight depend on the degree to which the two bodies are connected. So if (1)–(3) were truly capturing what is going on in the Galilean thought experiment, there would be ways out for the Aristotelian that would allow her at least to shift the burden of proof back to the Galilean.

That these ways out do not seem available when the thought experiment is presented in its unreconstructed form shows that this eliminative reconstruction has failed to capture its original demonstrative force. (What has been lost is the way in which, by evoking tacit knowledge about how falling bodies actually behave, the thought experiment preemptively precludes such ways out.) Accordingly, I tried to come up with a reconstruction sufficiently strong to rule out (4)–(7) in a similarly categorical and decisive manner. This involved appeal to two rather comprehensive and metaphysical-sounding principles, (8) and (9). (8) and (9) give background support to (1) and (2) and thereby help to establish (3).

But just as (1) and (2) are too weak to capture the way in which alternative hypotheses concerning fall are ruled out by the thought experiment, (8) and (9) are too strong. They represent approximate articulations of defeasible assumptions about the physical world. But as they stand, they articulate principles that have less certainty than the conclusion they are taken to support. Prior to contemplation of the case Galileo describes, the Aristotelian may be committed to *something* like (8) and *something* like (9), but he is certainly not committed to them unmodified. To reconstruct the case as an explicit argument with some version of (8) and (9) among the premises would require enumerating outright their defeasability conditions. But this is something he does not know how to do. Contemplation of the case Galileo describes *brings him to see* that these principles are not defeated in *this* case. And it is this recognition that serves as the basis for the case's power. No austere argumentative reconstruction will be able to do this, because part of the thought experiment's function is to bring the Aristotelian to accept certain *premises*. In the next section, I will discuss what makes belief in these premises *new*, and what makes it *justified*.

3. Denying the Dispensability and Derivativity Theses

3.1. Rejecting Reconstruction: What the Thought Experiment Does

If the Dispensability Thesis were correct, then the conclusion established by Galileo's thought experiment—that "both great and small bodies . . . are moved with like speeds" (Galilei 1638/1989: 109)--*should* be demonstrable by means of a non-thought-experimental argument. "Demonstrable" here means: rationally justifiable on the basis of the same background conditions. So let us spell out what the background conditions in question are.

For the Aristotelian, daily experience seems to confirm the theory that heavier bodies fall faster than lighter ones. Just as the Galilean sees cases where lighter bodies fall more slowly than heavy ones as exceptional, so the Aristotelian sees as crying out for explanation those cases where the rate of fall is (nearly) simultaneous. So, when gold beaten into a very thin leaf reaches the ground more slowly than a solid lump of the same material, the Galilean must posit some factor that explains the divergence of this result from the generally expected outcome (Galilei 1638/1989: 109). Similarly, when the Aristotelian sees two stones of very different weights fall to the ground with like speeds, the circumstance requires diagnosis and explanation.

So far all I have pointed out is the possibility of maintaining theoretical commitments in the face of apparent counter-evidence. This can be done by appealing to additional principles that explain away anomalous data by showing that the phenomena at issue are subject to the fundamental principle in question, but that the world's complexity has prevented them from manifesting this. So the Galilean might appeal to air resistance, the Aristotelian to the fact that the bodies have not been dropped from a height sufficiently great.[17] Such explaining-away of recalcitrant exceptions is not a desperate move by a failing paradigm; it is a fundamental element of doing normal science in a non-ideal world.[18]

The point of this discussion is to give a better sense of the background conditions under which the argumentative reconstruction must be demonstratively forceful if the Dispensability Thesis is to be shown to hold in this case. The thesis tells us that some non-thought-experimental reconstruction of the case Galileo presents should be able to do the same thing that the thought-experimental

---

[17] [20] In Galileo's dialogue, when Salviati points out that a rock of two pounds and a rock of twenty pounds will strike the ground nearly simultaneously when dropped from a height of one or two hundred feet, Simplicio retorts that this may just be a result of not having given the objects enough falling-time for the differences to become apparent (see Galilei 1638/1989: 109–10). Simplicio says: "Perhaps from very great heights, of thousands of bracchia, [discrepancies] would follow which [are] not seen at these lesser heights." That is, Simplicio suggests that perhaps the reason we do not observe the sorts of differences which Aristotle's theory predicts is that we are making observations under non-idealized circumstances, and that were we to eliminate distorting elements—like the fact that the fall is only a few hundred feet—the true phenomena would reveal themselves. Galileo provides Salviati with a rather sharp retort (Galilei 1638/1989: 110). See also (pagination here refers to the modern text) Galilei 1638/1989: 69 n. 44.

[18] [21] Of course, it is a commonplace in the history of science that at a certain point the burden of positing literal or metaphoric epicycles becomes too great, and the theory—especially when there is a simpler alternative available—collapses under the weight of its own internal complexity. But it is a similarly well-established commonplace in philosophy that theories are underdetermined by evidence, and that extra-scientific considerations do some of the work in determining theory choice.

version does: lead the Aristotelian *from the same background assumptions to the same rationally justified conclusions*. The standard reconstruction presented in §2.2 fails in this regard, as does the strengthened version presented in §2.4. And, I contend, *any* argument satisfying the Elimination Thesis is likely to fail in the same way.

Why? Because prior to the thought experiment, the Aristotelian is explicitly committed to the *negation* of (3), and this background commitment serves as a filter through which apparently contrary evidence will inevitably be reinterpreted. Any argument which satisfies the Elimination Thesis (that is, any argument with explicit premises which make no reference to particular hypothetical or counterfactual states of affairs) can be reframed by the Aristotelian as a *reductio*. (1) or (2) or (8) or (9) will simply be *denied*, once their implications are made evident. What is remarkable about the thought-experimental presentation is that it is able to undermine this framework-shaping assumption.

So I conclude, tentatively, that the Dispensability Thesis (and *a fortiori* the Derivativity Thesis) is false. Suppose, however, that somehow it were possible to come up with an argumentative reconstruction that almost exactly captures the strength and limits I have attributed to Galileo's thought experiment.[19] Would we then be justified in accepting the deeper methodological claim put forth in the Derivativity Thesis: that the *justificatory force* of whatever beliefs I hold via thought experiment is a function of the thought experiment's argumentational essence? In the next section (3.2), I offer reasons for thinking that the answer to this question is "no."

3.2 Rejecting the Positive Argument: What Makes these Beliefs New?

The Derivativity Thesis says that the justificatory force of any good scientific thought experiment can only be explained by the fact that it can be replaced, without loss of demonstrative force, by a non-thought-experimental argument. So rejection of the thesis can take two forms: denying that the justificatory force of a particular scientific thought experiment *can* be explained this way, and denying that it can *only* be explained this way. The simplest way of doing the former, of course, would be to show that the Dispensability Thesis is not true of some thought experiment; obviously, if there is no non-thought-experimental argument with which the thought experiment can be replaced without loss of demonstrative force, then the justificatory force of the thought experiment cannot be explained by the possibility of such replacement. But for the sake of argument, I am supposing that the Dispensability Thesis is (at least approximately) true. This leaves two avenues for denying the Derivativity Thesis: denying that the argumentative reconstruction explains the justificatory force

---

[19] [22] Suppose, for instance, we were to enumerate the defeasibility conditions of (8) and (9), and we included these modified versions as premises alongside (1) and (2).

of some thought experiment *at all*, and denying that it explains such justificatory force *entirely*.

As I discussed above (§1.3), two sorts of defense are offered for the Derivativity Thesis. The negative argument contends that thought experiments are arguments because there is nothing else for them to *be*; the positive argument contends that thought experiments are arguments because their "analysis and appraisal" involves explicit argumentative reconstruction. In this section I will address the positive thesis, suggesting that it fails to get at what is most interesting about thought experimental reasoning; in the final section, I offer some thoughts about what sorts of alternative justifications are available such that the negative thesis too is untenable.

It is a mistake, I contend, to think that the *reason* conclusions to thought experiments are justified is because thought experiments have argumentational analogues (if indeed they do). Rather, I want to suggest that the Aristotelian comes to have novel justified true beliefs about the empirical world not because he has (whether he knows it or not) followed along the path of a recognized argument form, but rather because he has performed an act of introspection that brings to light heretofore inarticulated and (because he lacked a theoretical framework in which to make sense of them) implausible tacit beliefs. There are two things that I need to show myself able to explain. The first is how it is that knowledge has been *gained*. In what way is it that the Aristotelian has come to believe something *new*? The second is how it is that *knowledge* has been gained. In what way is it that the Aristotelian has come to believe something *justified*? I will answer the first in the remainder of this section, and the second in §3.3.

In addressing the issue of novelty, I will begin with brief remarks about what I think is *not* at issue, and then say something about where I think the important questions rest. One might say that the beliefs are not new since, in some sense, the Aristotelian had access to them before. After all, he has acquired no new information about the external world; all he has done is reshuffle tacit beliefs he already held, coming to see their implications. But this view of what makes knowledge new is surely too stringent; it would, among other things, rule out all mathematical reasoning as a potential source of new knowledge. On the other hand, it seems too weak to say that a belief is new if it merely results from putting together two explicitly held beliefs that have not, for the individual in question, been previously connected. If I believe that snow is white and I believe that crows are black, but I have never thought about the two at the same time, it seems wrong to say that the belief that snow-is-white-and-crows-are-black should count as a *new* belief for me.[20] In any case, without spelling out

---

[20] [23] Except under very odd circumstances. Suppose I believe that crows are black because I live in a village where there are crows, and I have seen many of them. I also believe that snow is white, because I have read about it in books. In my village, it is taboo to think about black things

precisely what it is that makes some beliefs new and others mere implications, there is a simple reason to think the Aristotelian's belief that the speed at which a body falls is independent of its weight should count as a new belief for him: Until recently he was explicitly committed to the truth of its negation. This alone suggests that—whatever the implicatory relation between his prior commitments and this view about natural speed—the belief should count as new.

But there is a deeper and more interesting way that the belief is new, and that is the following. The thought experiment that Galileo presents leads the Aristotelian to a reconfiguration of his conceptual commitments of a kind that lets him see familiar phenomena in a novel way. What the Galilean does is provide the Aristotelian with conceptual space for a new notion of the *kind of thing* natural speed might be: an independently ascertainable constant rather than a function of something more primitive (that is, rather than as a function of weight). It is in this way, by allowing the Aristotelian to make sense of a previously incomprehensible concept, that the thought experiment has led him to a belief that is properly taken as *new*.

What this suggests is that the Derivativity Thesis is *missing the point* of what makes the Galileo case work as it does. The recognition that natural speed is independent of weight comes not from tracing the implications of antecedent commitments to (1) and (2), which, after all, lead to the denial of a position to which the Aristotelian is explicitly committed (and thence to retreats such as the four ways out). The recognition comes from the sudden realization, on the part of the Aristotelian, of the conceptual possibility of a certain sort of physical property. Prior to contemplation of the case, there was no room on the Aristotelian picture for the thought that natural speed might be constant, not varying—that it might be dependent not on some specific features of the body in question, but only on the fact that it is a body at all.[21] After contemplation of the case, there seems to be no conceptual space for the view that it might be variable.

---

and white things at the same time, because this is thought to allow the evil spirit access to the soul. One day, I leave my village for the north, and I observe a crow circling above a field of snow. I find the image aesthetically striking, and I ask myself why this is so. In analyzing my response to the visual experience I am having, I realize with a start: "Snow is white and crows are black." In such a case, it seems plausible to suggest that this is a new belief.

[21] [24] To get a sense of how odd this transition is, try thinking about *weight* as something dependent not on the specifics of the body in question, but as something constant for all bodies. (That is, to ascertain a body's weight, we would not need to know anything more about it than the simple fact than it is a body.) Clearly this would be a major conceptual readjustment; one might even be inclined to say that we aren't talking about *weight* anymore, since whatever sort of thing weight is, it is surely something that depends upon specific features of the bodies to which it applies. The analogy is not perfect, since part of what happens as a result of thinking about the Galileo case is that it becomes apparent that there is no physical application for the Aristotelian idea of natural speed; like phlogiston, it disappears into the ether of abandoned concepts.

One of the things that enables this rather striking shift in the representation of physical reality is that the Aristotelian recognizes that there are experientially possible objects—strapped-together bodies—for which the defeasability conditions of (8) and (9) are not met (that is, objects of which (8) and (9) hold true), and that these are objects for which his old notion of natural speed simply *does not make sense*. If entification is arbitrary and natural speed and weight are fixed by the world, then a feature-dependent notion of natural speed is just plain incoherent. So one way of thinking about how the thought experiment works is this: it brings the Aristotelian to recognize the inadequacy of his conceptual framework for dealing with phenomena which—through the contemplation of this imaginary case—he comes to recognize as always having been part of his world.

What this suggests is that "the *analysis* and *appraisal* of a thought experiment" need not "involve reconstructing it explicitly as an argument," in such a way that "a good thought experiment is a good argument, a bad thought experiment is a bad argument" (Norton 1991: 129; Norton 1996: 335). After all, the argument from (1) and (2) to (3) is no better or worse than the argument from (not-3) to (not-1) or (not-2). Like an experiment, *part* of what makes a thought experiment good or bad is the validity of the procedure by which the same result can be repeatedly obtained. But another thing that distinguishes good thought experiments from bad is their ability to direct the reader's attention to inadequacies in her conceptual scheme that she herself recognizes immediately, as soon as they are pointed out to her. It is *this*, I want to suggest, that grounds her new beliefs. Of course, I have said nothing so far about what might make these beliefs *justified*. It is to this issue that I turn in §3.3.

3.3. Rejecting the Negative Argument: What Makes these Beliefs Knowledge?

Thought experiments work in a variety of ways. By describing appropriately selected imaginary scenarios, they provide contexts within which sense can be made of previously incomprehensible conceptual distinctions.[22] This happens when two features that are constantly conjoined in our representations of all actual cases are imaginatively separated in the thought-experimental scenario in a way that shows them to have been isolatable all along. And by describing specific situations, thought experiments, like analogical reasoning in general, can justify conclusions about particular cases without explicit or implicit appeal to more general absolute principles.[23] Many of the higher-level principles by

---

[22] [25] By this I mean they do something like what the answer to a riddle does in making suddenly intelligible what previously appeared to be a nonsensical description. Cf. Cavell 1979: 156–7. [*Added in 2009*: This phenomenon is closely related to psychological work on contextual prerequisites for understanding. (See e.g. Bransford and Johnson 1972; Tse *et al.* 2007.)]

[23] [26] For an articulation and defense of such a view of analogical reasoning, cf. Sunstein 1993, 1996.

which we negotiate the world are *defeasible*, and the determination of their applicability to particular situations must be made on a case-by-case basis. By bringing the reader to focus on particulars, thought experiments can help her distinguish warranted from unwarranted applications of the principle in question.[24]

So far, however, this has little to do with *justification*. After all, as Norton would ask, if the thought experiment is not an argument, why should we put faith in its conclusion? What I want to explore in this closing section is one possible answer: that thought experiments rely on a certain sort of *constructive participation* on the part of the reader, and that the justificatory force of the thought experiment actually comes from the fact that it calls upon the reader to perform what I will call an *experiment-in-thought*.

An experiment-in-thought is an *actual* experiment; the person conducting the experiment asks herself: "What would I say/judge/expect were I to encounter circumstances XYZ?" and then *finds out* the (apparent) answer. This technique is common in linguistics, where the methodology is used to ascertain the grammaticality of sentences, the meanings of phrases, the taxonomic categories of words, and so on.[25] And it is, on one view at least, a central element of moral reasoning: we think about particular imaginary cases, observe the judgments that they evoke in us, and use these judgments as fixed points in developing our moral theories.[26]

How does this connect with the Galileo case? What kind of experiment-in-thought plays a role there? Answer: by thinking about the case in question, we discover what sorts of motions and objects we think are possible in the world. Do we think objects can be strapped together? Yes, we do. Do we think objects fall with radical discontinuities in speed? No, we think they do not. Do we think entification is something that is fixed by the world? No, we do not. Do we think weight and natural speed are fixed by the world? Yes, we do. We *come to recognize*

---

[24] [27] This often happens when the particulars are sufficiently well sketched to evoke practical as well as theoretical responses. [*Added in 2009*: This footnote was written in 1996, but obviously foreshadows some of the suggestions made in later writings, in particular in "Philosophical Thought Experiments, Intuitions, and Cognitive Equilibrium" (2007; Ch. 6) and the two alief essays (2008a, 2008b; Chs. 13 and 14).]

[25] [28] Cf. Thomason 1991: 247: "When linguists want to test hypotheses about the structure of a particular language, their methodology crucially involves thought experiments in a...literal sense: real experiments carried out in thinking."

[26] [29] To choose an example nearly at random, consider Thomson 1986: 257: "it is...our moral views about examples, stories, and cases which constitute...data for moral theorizing." [*Added in 2009*: If one of the tools for moral theorizing is to "think about particular imaginary cases, observe the judgments that they evoke in us, and use these judgments as fixed points in developing our moral theories," then it might be valuable to make systematic use of samples containing more than one subject. For a defense of this technique as an extension of traditional philosophical methodology, along with numerous examples of its application, see Knobe and Nichols 2008.]

that we have these beliefs by contemplating the imaginary case in question; thinking about the case is what brings us to the realization that we believe what we do.[27] *And*—and this is where the justificatory work comes in—the fact that we have these beliefs gives us *prima facie* warrant to think that they are true.

But why? Why should we think that our pre-theoretical beliefs about the structure of the physical world are reliable? In the *Science of Mechanics*, a few pages after coining the expression *Gedankenexperiment*, Mach writes:

Everything which we observe imprints itself *uncomprehended* and *unanalyzed* in our percepts and ideas, which then, in their turn, mimic the process of nature in their most general and most striking features. In these accumulated experiences we possess a treasure-store which is ever close at hand, and of which only the smallest portion is embodied in clear articulate thought. The circumstance that it is far easier to resort to these experiences than it is to nature herself, and that they are, notwithstanding this, free, in the sense indicated, from all subjectivity, invests them with high value. (Mach 1883/1960: 36)

So one possible explanation is the one Mach gives. We have a store of unarticulated knowledge of the world which is not organized under any theoretical framework. Argument will not give us access to that knowledge, because the knowledge is not propositionally available. Framed properly, however, a thought experiment can tap into it, and—much like an ordinary experiment—allow us to make use of information about the world which was, in some sense, there all along, if only we had known how to systematize it into patterns of which we are able to make sense.[28]

This, of course, is the beginning not the end of an answer to the question. But it is sufficient for the modest aim of this essay. What I have been trying to show is that *something* besides argument might give justificatory force to thought experimental reasoning. The alternative I have proposed has been this: By

---

[27] [*Note added in 2009*: This suggests that the analogy to experiments-in-thought in linguistic (and perhaps moral) theorizing may be somewhat inapt, for two related reasons. The first is that whereas judgments about grammaticality (and perhaps morality) are to some degree *constitutive* of the phenomenon under investigation (the fact that normal speakers judge a sentence to be grammatical is part of what makes it the case that the sentence is grammatical), judgments about physics are not (in the relevant sense) constitutive of facts about physics. The second is that whereas in the linguistics case the role played by the experiment-in-thought is, loosely, to provide data for theorizing (so that asking someone else to make the judgment would be as good as asking ourselves), in the Galileo case the role played by the experiment-in-thought is, loosely, to bring the contemplator to a certain sort of self-knowledge *as a result of contemplating the case* (so that second-hand reporting of another's results cannot do the work of first-hand self-engagement). I return to some of these issues in "Thought Experiments Rethought—and Reperceived" (2004; Ch. 2) and "Philosophical Thought Experiments, Intuitions, and Cognitive Equilibrium" (2007; Ch. 6).]

[28] [30] For further discussion of these themes, cf. Kuhn 1964. [*Added in 2009*: For exploration of some of these issues in the context of recent work on explanation and learning, see Lombrozo 2006.]

focusing on imaginary scenarios and making reference to particulars, thought experiments can provide a fulcrum for the reorganization of conceptual commitments; this explains how they can provide us with novel *information* without empirical input. And by bringing the reader to perform experiments-in-thought, thought experiments can lead us to reject shaky (and ultimately false) theoretical commitments in light of newly systematized but previously inarticulable *knowledge* about the way the world is.

The justificatory force of thought experiments is thus parasitic on the extent to which the messy twisted web of background beliefs that underpin our navigation of the world are rightly considered knowledge. To establish this, on coherentist or evolutionary or empiricist grounds, would be an enormous undertaking, and one which I will not even begin to endeavor here.[29] But I hope I have given you some sense, at least, of why I am not convinced that even if the Dispensability Thesis is true, the Derivativity Thesis must be true as well. For even if it *could* be replaced by an equally effective argument, the *justificatory force* of a thought experiment might still be based on its capacity to make available in a theoretical way those tacit practical commitments that enable us to negotiate the physical world.

4. Conclusion

In this essay, I have offered reasons for thinking that a certain view about thought experiments in science is false. The view is that any scientific thought experiment can be reconstructed as a non-thought-experimental argument without loss of demonstrative force. In part 1, I explained the philosophical motivations for adopting such a view, and distinguished two versions of the position. The first—the Dispensability Thesis—concerns the replaceability of thought experiments; the second—the Derivativity Thesis—concerns their justificatory force. In the remainder of the essay, I offered reasons for thinking that both of these theses are false. Through a detailed discussion of a thought experiment of Galileo's, I tried to show that the standard argumentative reconstruction of the case fails to capture its justificatory power, and I suggested reasons to think that any other argumentative reconstruction would be likely to fail in similar ways. I then argued that even if one were to provide an argumentative reconstruction that did almost perfectly capture the thought experiment's demonstrative force, this would not show that the *reason* the thought experiment is successful is because, deep down, it is nothing more than an argument in disguise. I suggested that, to the contrary, the success

---

[29] [31] For one such (evolutionarily based) attempt, cf. Shepard 1994; a similar explanation is offered in Sorensen 1992a.

of the thought experiment may be a result of the way in which it invites the reader's constructive participation, depicts particulars in ways that make manifest practical knowledge, and describes an imaginary scenario wherein relevant features can be separated from those that are inessential to the question at issue.[30]

[30] [*] *Acknowledgements*: For comments on previous drafts of this essay, a predecessor of which appeared as a chapter of my 1996 dissertation, I am grateful to Richard Boyd, James Robert Brown, Michael Glanzberg, Steven Gross, Ned Hall, Norman Kretzmann, Thomas Kuhn, John Murdoch, John Norton, Robert Nozick, Derek Parfit, Hilary Putnam, W. V. Quine, Sherri Roush, Simon Saunders, Roger Shepard, Alison Simmons, Zoltán Gendler Szabó, and audiences at Harvard (1995) and Cornell (1996) Universities.

2

Thought Experiments Rethought—and Reperceived

In this essay, I explore the question of how contemplation of an imaginary scenario can lead to new knowledge about contingent features of the natural world—that is, how it can provide us with relevant beliefs about contingent matters that are simultaneously *new* and *justified*. I trace the source of both novelty and justification to the ways in which focusing one's attention on a specific scenario (as opposed to a general schema) may evoke quasi-sensory intuitions that then serve as a basis for novel justified true beliefs.

This essay and its predecessor—"Galileo and the Indispensability of Scientific Thought Experiment" (Ch. 1)—form a natural pair. For those who prefer to read only one of them, the previous paper, which is more substantive and detailed than this one, can be read as a self-standing piece.

***

This essay was first published in *Philosophy of Science*, 71 (2004), 1152–64 and is reprinted with the kind permission of the University of Chicago Press. The essay was originally presented at a panel on thought experiments at the 2002 Philosophy of Science Association Meetings, with co-symposiasts James Robert Brown, James McAllister, and John Norton, and chair Nancy Nersessian. Their essays appear alongside this one in the aforementioned issue of *Philosophy of Science*. Though the bulk of the text is as originally published, minor changes have been made to render the piece self-standing; in addition, references to pieces then unpublished have been brought up to date. As a result, several footnote numbers have changed. The original number of each footnote is noted in [square brackets].

---

1. Introduction

The central puzzle surrounding scientific thought experiment is how contemplation of an imaginary scenario can lead to new knowledge about contingent features of the natural world. This puzzle is a special case of a more general one, namely how any nonperceptual capacity can lead to new knowledge about (nonstipulated) contingent features of reality.

Assuming for the sake of simplicity that the classical tripartite characterization of knowledge is adequate to the purposes at hand, the more specific worry
can be put in the following way: how can the contemplation of an imaginary
scenario provide one with *new* true beliefs about contingent matters, and,
assuming that it can do so, how are those new beliefs *justified?*[1]

It is common ground among many who have considered the puzzle both *that*
thought experiments can provide us with new knowledge, and that the process
by which such beliefs are formed does not *feel* like inference from known
premises to inductively or deductively implied conclusions. Nonetheless,
there is a sharp divide among the major participants in the debate that can be
traced to the following two questions:

1. Are the new beliefs that we form on the basis of the contemplation of
   imaginary scenarios actually formed as the result of inference from known
   premises to inductively or deductively implied conclusions?

2. To the extent that the new beliefs are not so formed, are they justified?

In a series of papers and discussions, John Norton has contended that the
answer to (1) is "yes" and the answer to (2) is "no": the epistemic role played
by the contemplation of imaginary scenarios in providing us with new knowledge of the natural world is traceable to the fact that "the actual conduct of a
thought experiment consists of the execution of an argument" (Norton 2004a:
1142; cf. also Norton 1991, 1996). James Robert Brown, by contrast, has contended that the answer to (1) is "no" and the answer to (2) is "yes": "Thought
experiments are telescopes into the abstract realm," he writes; through them,
we come to have "intuition[s] of law[s] of nature" (Brown 2004a: 1131; cf. also
Brown 1991a, 1991b, 1993b, 2004b).

Taken in full, both positions seem to require rather implausible commitments: Brown's view requires accepting a Platonistic picture of laws of
nature as "abstract entities, outside of space and time, that somehow necessitate
the regularities we experience in the empirical world" (Brown 2004a: 1131);
Norton's requires accepting that something that feels like the contemplation
of an imaginary scenario is actually the execution of an argument.[2] But the
central insight of each can be adopted without taking on board these further

---

[1] [1] In framing things this way, I am also assuming (1) that the contemplation of imaginary
scenarios does not bring about relevant new truths about contingent features of the natural
world, and (2) that the contemplation of imaginary scenarios—at least in certain cases—does
more than merely provide us with new justification for previously held beliefs (though their
ability to do this may itself be epistemically puzzling).

[2] [4] He writes: "Is the claim merely that thought experiments can do no more than
argumentation when it comes to justifying claims? Or is it in addition that actual execution
of a thought experiment is just the execution of an argument?...I intend the stronger
version... *(Context of discovery)* The actual conduct of a thought experiment consists of the
execution of an argument, although this may not be obvious" (Norton 2004b: 9).

commitments: the contemplation of an imaginary scenario may lead us to new knowledge not because it provides us with quasi-observational knowledge of abstracta, nor because it is actually an act of argumentative rehearsal. Rather, I will suggest, in the case of imaginary scenarios that evoke certain sorts of quasi-sensory intuitions, their contemplation may bring us to new beliefs about contingent features of the natural world that are produced not inferentially, but quasi-observationally; the presence of a mental image may play a crucial cognitive role in the formation of the belief in question. And this, albeit fallible, quasi-observational belief-forming mechanism, may, in certain contexts, be sufficiently reliable to count as a source of justification.

Since it is fairly clear what the denial of Brown's Platonism amounts to, I will devote the bulk of my discussion to differentiating my position from Norton's. I will explain what it means to say that the psychological mechanisms employed in the contemplation of specific scenarios (as opposed to the consideration of general schemata) allow us to gain information about the natural world in a distinctly nonargumentative way. And, having done so, I will contend that the specificity of the cases that thought experiments invoke may, in some cases, play a vital role in providing their epistemic force.

2. Clarifications

Before going on, it is worth pausing for a moment for a few clarifications. In the discussion that follows, I will assume that to perform a *thought experiment* is to reason about an imaginary scenario with the aim of confirming or disconfirming some hypothesis or theory, and that to perform a *scientific thought experiment* is to reason about an imaginary scenario with the aim of confirming or disconfirming some hypothesis or theory *about the physical world*.[3] (I Thus take the fundamental notion to be that of *performing a thought experiment*, with the notion of *being a thought experiment* derivative therefrom.)[4]

Such a characterization allows us to isolate four crucial features in the performance of scientific thought experiments (the first three shared by thought

---

[3] [5] By parity, then, we might then say that to perform a *conceptual thought experiment* is to reason about an imaginary scenario with the aim of confirming or disconfirming some hypothesis or theory *about the proper use of our concepts*; that to perform a *mathematical thought experiment* is to reason about an imaginary scenario with the aim of confirming or disconfirming some hypothesis or theory *about mathematics*; and so on.

[4] [6] How one goes about individuating thought experiments is a question on which I will allow myself to remain neutral: Is Einstein's clock-in-the-box thought experiment (which assumes classical spacetime) the same thought experiment as Bohr's (which assumes relativistic spacetime)? (See Bishop 1999; Norton 2004b: 25–6.) Is the thought experiment that I perform when *I* read Galileo's text the same thought experiment *Galileo* performed when he wrote it? Nothing of what I will go on to say will turn on how one settles these questions (to which it seems difficult to find principled answers).

experiments in general, the fourth specific to this form of thought experimentation):

> *a.* Thought-experimental reasoning involves reasoning about a particular set of circumstances (which may be specified in more or less detail), described at a greater level of specificity than that of the conclusion. (*To perform a thought experiment is to reason about a scenario ...*)
>
> *b.* The reasoner's mode of access to the scenario is via imagination rather than via observation. (*... which is imaginary ...*)
>
> *c.* Contemplation of the scenario takes place with a specific purpose: the confirmation or disconfirmation of some hypothesis or theory. (*... with the aim of confirming or disconfirming some hypothesis or theory ...*)

and—in the case of scientific thought experiments—

> *d.* The hypothesis or theory in question concerns features of the physical world. (*... about the physical world*)

Using this characterization, we can identify some common ground. Both Norton and Brown understand (*b*) in the same way: each accepts that scientific thought-experimental reasoning does not provide us with new *observational* information about the natural world. And—modulo certain issues concerning (*d*) that I will raise in a minute—both understand (*c*) in roughly the same way: each accepts that scientific thought-experimental reasoning is (paradigmatically) intended to confirm or disconfirm fairly general hypotheses or theories about the natural world, and each agrees roughly with the other about what sorts of candidate-hypotheses and theories merit consideration, and, among those, which are true.

Where Norton and Brown disagree is in their understanding of (*d*) and (*a*). The dispute concerning (*d*) is a dispute about metaphysics: Norton and Brown disagree about what sort of thing laws of nature are, and, consequently, about the range of facts to which scientific thought-experimental reasoning could, in principle, give access. Whereas Brown is committed to the view that the features of the physical world to which (scientific) thought-experimental reasoning gives us access are abstract laws that "necessitate the regularities that we experience" (Brown 2004a: 1131), Norton is committed to the view that the regularities to which (scientific) thought-experimental reasoning gives us access are contingent. The dispute concerning (*a*), by contrast, can be understood as a dispute about epistemology: Norton and Brown disagree about which sorts of mental undertakings carry justificatory force, and, consequently, about the range of ways in which scientific thought-experimental reasoning could, in principle, give knowledge. Whereas Brown is committed to the view that the particularity of the scenarios involved in (scientific) thought-experimental reasoning (specifically, their ability to engage our quasi-sensory faculty of intuition) plays some role in providing thought experiments with their epistemic force, Norton denies that "this picturesque clothing" does more than "give them special rhetorical powers" (2004a: 1139).

Brown's understanding of (*d*) and his understanding of (*a*) are interconnected: Platonist metaphysics cries out for some sort of corresponding epistemology, and what Brown's understanding of (*d*) demands, Brown's understanding of (*a*) provides. But the other direction of implication is not so clear. It seems plausible to endorse a view according to which the particularity of the scenarios involved in thought-experimental reasoning supplies some epistemic force, while also accepting that the regularities to which scientific thought-experimental reasoning gives us access are contingent features of the natural world. It is this position—siding with Norton concerning the metaphysical question, and (roughly) with Brown concerning the epistemic question—that I will defend.

3. The Elephant Constraint

I begin with some mundane cases that involve the sort of imagistic reasoning that plays a role in certain scientific thought experiments. Think about your next-door neighbor's living room, and ask yourself the following questions: If you painted its walls bright green, would that clash with the current carpet, or complement it? If you removed all its furniture, could four elephants fit comfortably inside? If you removed all but one of the elephants, would there be enough space to ride a bicycle without tipping as you turned?

Let's assume for the sake of argument that you had not, prior to my instructions, contemplated any of these particular questions. And let's also assume that, having contemplated them, you now truly believe that green paint would clash with the carpet, that four elephants in the room would be a tight squeeze, and that a bike ride around the room with one elephant remaining would be quite a challenge. What should we say about these true beliefs? Are they new? Are they justified? And, if so, what is the source of their novelty, and of their justification?

Start with novelty. There is an obvious sense in which your belief that four elephants would not fit comfortably in your neighbor's living room is, presumably, new: until quite recently, it simply hadn't occurred to you to think about the question and, when I raised it initially, your answer had neither the immediacy of simple recall, nor the simplicity of straightforward calculation or deduction.[5] Likewise, there's an obvious sense in which the belief is also

---

[5] [7] Of course, in some sense the process involved drawing implications from beliefs that you already had. After all, there is no new empirical input. But if the only thing that counts as new knowledge is new *observational* knowledge, then clause (*b*) rules out thought experiment as

justified. It was formed by making use of a reliable (though fallible) process, rather than as the result of a lucky guess or wishful thinking or a hunch. We feel little hesitation in saying that you now know that four elephants wouldn't fit comfortably in your neighbor's living room, whereas you didn't know it before.

Now, think about the reasoning process involved. Presumably, you did something like the following: you called up an image of the room, made some sort of mental representation of its size (perhaps after mentally emptying it of its furniture), called up proportionately sized images of four elephants, mentally arrayed them in the room, and tried to ascertain whether there was space for the four elephants within the confines of the room's four walls. Of course, in many ways, the mental image you formed was unspecified: most likely, you simply "blocked" the space that the elephants would take up, without attending to details about exactly how they were to be arrayed or oriented. And, of course, your image may well have misrepresented what you took it to represent, or your underspecification may have omitted some relevant details. But these potential errors are not sufficient to impugn the process itself: that we can err in employing a technique does not render the technique itself unreliable.

Similar processes allow you to answer the other two questions. When I asked you whether there would be space to ride a bicycle in the room if it were occupied by one elephant and no furniture, you presumably invoked a mental image of the room (using memory), and—holding constant your affordance-based sense of its dimensions—evoked a quasi-proprioceptive image of the experience of riding a bicycle in a space of that size; when you had done this, you made a judgment about the resulting situation. When I asked you about the rug and the walls, you presumably called up an image of the two colors juxtaposed, and made a judgment about whether they clashed.

Were the beliefs you formed on the basis of your reasoning in each of these cases formed as the result of inference from known premises to inductively or deductively implied conclusions? A "yes" answer is most plausible in the case of our four elephants. Arguably, even before engaging in the reasoning process described, you had the justified true belief that elephants are of thus-and-such size, the justified true belief that the living room is of thus-and-such size, a set of justified true beliefs concerning the solidity and limited malleability of elephants and living-room walls, a set of justified true beliefs concerning the possible configuration of objects in spaces governed by Euclidean geometry, and so on. On the basis of these (perhaps tacit) beliefs, you engaged (again,

---

a source of new knowledge *tout court*, and there is no phenomenon to be explained. Even if this particular case is unconvincing, I am taking it as common ground that something relevantly similar will count as a case of new non-observational knowledge.

perhaps tacitly) in a process of deductive reasoning which led you to the realization that four elephants would not, as a matter of fact, fit comfortably into your neighbor's living room.[6] But is that really what happened? My inclination is to think not. Rather, what happened is that you formed a judgment on the basis of your manipulation of your mental image, and—using that *new information*—went on to draw your conclusion about the more general statement for which you took it to be evidence.

If you are still unpersuaded, think about the following cases. Suppose that I had, instead, given you a piece of graph paper and a pencil, and asked you the same question, which you answered on the basis of a sketch that you made: would that be a case where you engaged in a process of deductive reasoning from known premises to a novel conclusion? Or suppose I had given you a three-dimensional scale-model of the room, along with four similarly scaled plastic elephants (and suppose it wasn't immediately clear whether or not the elephants could be placed comfortably therein): wouldn't you proceed by putting the elephants into the room, and *seeing* whether they fit? Suppose I took away the third and fourth elephants before you managed to place them in the room. Would your imaginary continuation of the process you had begun really be a process of *deductive reasoning*?

The diagnosis is even more plausible in the case of the other two scenarios. Take the bicycle case. While you may have believed, beforehand, that your room was of roughly thus-and-such dimensions, did you really believe—before thinking about it—that *that* isn't enough space in which to ride a bike? Perhaps you believed (perhaps tacitly) that *some* indoor spaces are too small to ride a bike in (closets, for instance), and that others (banquet halls, for instance) are certainly large enough—but did you have, even tacitly, beliefs about where the border between these lay, and, in particular, beliefs about where your neighbor's living room stood with respect to that border? Didn't you, instead, *discover* something about bikes and living rooms by *imagining having a certain experience*? Likewise with the color case. While you may have known beforehand that your neighbor's rug looks like *this*, and that green looks like *that*, was it really a matter of deductive or inductive inference that led you to the conclusion that—were they adjacent—you would judge them to clash? Wasn't it instead as if you performed an *experiment-in-thought*, on the basis of which you got some new information about your own judgments, which (perhaps because of tacit beliefs that you hold) you took to be relevant data in answering the question at hand?

---

[6] [8] Cf. Norton: "In so far as they tell us about the world, thought experiments draw on *what we already know about it*, either explicitly or tacitly. They then transform *that knowledge* by disguised argumentation" (Norton 2004b: 2; italics added).

4. The Psychological Data

Of course, all of this phenomenology may be misleading. It may be that everything that is going on in such cases is actually the transformation of old beliefs into new beliefs by means of inductive or deductive inference. It may be that what happens in all of these cases is that we manipulate premises we accept on independent grounds using inferential reasoning processes. But if so, it is hard to see what sort of mental activity *wouldn't* involve the transformation of old beliefs into new ones by means of such inferences. It is hard to see what would count as a new nonperceptual belief that *didn't* count as a belief so formed. If Norton is construing the terms in question *this* broadly, then my dispute with him may be largely terminological.

But I think there is a difference here that is not merely terminological. Empirical psychological research—along with commonsense observation—suggests that there is a difference between the *sort* of information-processing that goes on in the case of imaginative rehearsal, and the sort of information-processing that goes on in the case of purely hypothetical unengaged reasoning. Three examples—briefly presented—will suffice for my point.

First example. Research by Roger Shepard and others has shown that judgments about topological similarity are generally made after engaging in the mental manipulation of an image: the greater the degree of rotation required to project one onto the other, the longer it takes to judge whether two figures are isomorphic (Shepard and Metzler 1971; Shepard and Cooper 1982). Here, as above, it seems that the reasoning process is quasi-perceptual: I *observe* something, and on the basis of my observation conclude something. While this latter step may be construed as inductive reasoning, it is hard to see how the former step could be construed as either inductive or deductive. It's true that the geometrical constraints which my reasoning process tracks *deductively imply* the conclusion I draw—but that doesn't mean that what *I* did was to reason deductively from known premises.[7]

Second example. Research by Antonio Damasio and others (along with centuries of commonsense observation) has shown that our repertoire of emotional responses is engaged by imaginary as well as by real situations. These emotional responses are encoded physically in what Damasio calls "somatic markers," on which our intuitive judgments about a hypothetical or actual situation—judgments of safety or danger, desirability or undesirability,

---

[7] [*Note added in 2009*: Recent behavioral and neuroimaging studies seem to support the view that visual imagining makes use of (many of) the same mechanisms used for visual perception. For an overview of this work, see Farah 2000, ch. 9 (252–89); for defense of the view that there is a particularly tight connection between visual imagery and visual perception, see Kosslyn, Thompson, and Ganis 2006; for dissent, see Pylyshyn 2003. (For related work in the domain of auditory imagery, see Kraemer *et al*. 2005; Zatorre and Halpern 2005.)]

attractiveness or unattractiveness—are then based: if the somatic marker associated with a certain sort of scenario is negative, we will be inclined to avoid placing ourselves in it; if the somatic marker associated with a certain sort of scenario is positive, we will be inclined to seek it out. What this means is that imaginative rehearsal can bring us to new beliefs that may be unavailable to us if we reason in a disinterested purely hypothetical way (Damasio 1994, 1999).[8]

As a way of bringing out the difference, think about the therapy people engage in to overcome neuroses. People who are afraid of public speaking *imagine* themselves speaking before an audience over and over until they become comfortable with the idea; people who are afraid of flying in airplanes *imagine* themselves being safely able to do so until their adverse reactions begin to fade. Did they—prior to engaging in the imaginative rehearsal—*believe* that flying is not dangerous? By some tests yes: they were inclined to assent to the statement, to produce it cooperatively in response to inquiries, even to recommend that loved ones act on its basis—but by others, no: despite the previous, they were unwilling, themselves, to behave as if it were true that flying is not dangerous. Suppose that after many years of therapeutic engagement they find themselves able to fly on a plane fearlessly—and suppose, idealizing somewhat, that the therapy did not involve providing them with any new *information*. To the extent that we are willing to credit our patient with a new belief (as, on many dispositional accounts, we should be), do we really want to say that the belief was formed by deductive or inductive reasoning?[9]

Third example. Consider the following study by Daniel Reisberg, which simultaneously illustrates certain limitations in our capacities for mental imagery, and certain ways in which a "gestalt shift" can be introduced as the result of the sort of explicit instruction often given in the context of scientific thought experiments (Reisberg 1996). Reisberg's subjects were told that they were participating in a study concerning "memory for abstract forms." For each item, they were (*a*) shown an image of a form and (*b*) asked to memorize the form in question. The image was then removed, and immediately thereafter subjects were asked (*c*) to imagine the form rotated by some amount (e.g. 90 degrees) and then (*d*) to draw a picture of the rotated form. As the tenth image in this otherwise nonrepresentational series, subjects were presented with an image of Texas rotated 90 degrees, and asked to perform (*a*) through (*d*) as above.

The result reveals something important about the nature of mental imagery. For even when they were told that a 90-degree rotation would result in "a

---

[8] [*Note added in 2009*: I return to this theme in a number of other papers, especially "The Puzzle of Imaginative Resistance" (2000a; Ch. 9) and "Philosophical Thought Experiments, Intuitions, and Cognitive Equilibrium" (2007; Ch. 6); see also "Genuine Rational Fictional Emotions" (Gendler and Kovakovich 2005; Ch. 11).]

[9] [*Note added in 2009*: The issues discussed in this paragraph are discussed in somewhat different language and much greater detail in "Imaginative Contagion" (2006a; Ch. 12) and the two Alief essays (2008a, 2008b; Chs. 13 and 14).]

familiar geographic form," Reisberg reports that "no subjects succeeded in discovering Texas in their image [at step (c)], although, moments later [at step (d)], many subjects were able to recognize Texas in their own drawing" (Reisberg 1996: 128). What could explain this divergence? Reisberg's diagnosis (confirmed experimentally in later studies) was that subjects in step (c) failed to alter their reference frame when they undertook the mental rotation (that is, they took the initial "top" to be the "top" in the rotated case, and thus failed to recognize the image as an image of Texas, even when the image was rotated). For, it turns out, if (c)—which asks subjects to mentally rotate the image a certain number of degrees—is replaced by (c′)—which asks them to "think of the left-hand side of the shape as being the figure's top"—results change dramatically; indeed, when this alternative instruction was given, "approximately half the subjects succeeded in identifying Texas in their image" (Reisberg 1996: 129). As before, it's hard to see why we would want to say that this new justified true belief (that the rotated image resembles Texas) was formed by inductive or deductive reasoning from known premises.

5. Scientific Thought Experiments

I think that what's true for these simpler cases of imagistic reasoning is true for the more complicated cases of imagistic reasoning involved in scientific thought experiment. This is not to say that *all* scientific thought experiment involves such imagistic reasoning—just that some does.[10] There will, no doubt, be many cases where the role of the imagery is simply heuristic. But there will also be cases where the role of the imagery is—as in the cases above—epistemically crucial.

Take, for example, Mach's original example of a thought experiment (see Mach 1926/1976, Mach 1883/1960): the process of reasoning by which Simon Stevin established the amount of force required to prevent an object from sliding down a frictionless inclined plane, which involves the contemplation of a particular configuration of physical objects—a circular string of fourteen balls laid atop a triangular prism (see Fig. 2.1). Consideration of this imaginary set-up convinces Stevin that the balls are in a state of equilibrium—that is, that the chain moves neither to the left nor to the right. (Otherwise, it seems, the system would be in a state of perpetual motion.) He next imagines cutting the string at the two lower corners of the triangle, such that two balls remain along the side with the sharper incline, and four along the side with the shallower incline. And, he recognizes, since the balls were in equilibrium prior to the cutting, they

---

[10] [9] Indeed, the fact that Norton's primary stable of examples concerns thought experiments in relativity theory (see e.g. Norton 1991), whereas Brown's concerns thought experiments in early modern science, may explain some of their divergence in analysis.

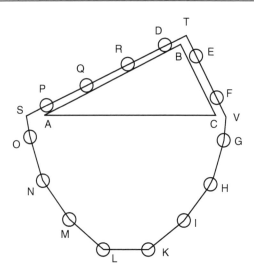

Fig. 2.1. From <http://en.wikipedia.org/wiki/File:StevinEquilibrium.svg>

remain so afterwards: the shorter and the longer string of balls are in balance. On the basis of these considerations, Stevin concludes that the force required to hold a ball in place along an inclined plane is inversely proportional to the length of the plane (Stevin 1955).

Now, presumably there's a way of *reconstructing* this reasoning process as an argument: I will leave that task to others. What's important for my purposes is the extent to which this case resembles those described above. Contemplation of an imaginary scenario (the cut string laid atop the prism) evokes certain quasi-sensory intuitions, and on the basis of these intuitions, we form a new belief about contingent features of the natural world (that the weight of four balls offsets the weight of two balls). This belief is produced not inferentially, but quasi-observationally: the presence of the mental image plays a crucial cognitive role in its formation.[11]/[12]

[11] [*Note added in 2009*: For recent discussion of the scientific issues raised in the final sections of this essay, see Byrne 2005; Byrne and Johnson-Laird n.d.; see also Kosslyn, Thomson and Ganis 2006; Pylyshyn 2003.]

[12] [‡] *Acknowledgements*: For comments and discussion, I am grateful to John Hawthorne, Ishani Maitra, Zoltán Gendler Szabó, and to my co-symposiasts and chair at the 2002 PSA Meetings, James Robert Brown, James McAllister, Nancy Nersessian, and John Norton.

3

Exceptional Persons: On the Limits of Imaginary Cases

When should we trust our judgments about far-fetched imaginary cases? In this chapter, I offer one possible answer. I propose that if the imaginary scenario is adduced to illuminate a concept structured around a set of necessary and sufficient conditions, *and* if these conditions play a role in how we identify candidates as falling under that concept, then our judgments about the far-fetched imaginary case may help us to separate essential features of the concept from accidental ones. But if the concept is not structured in that way, or if the features in question do not govern our application of the concept, then our judgments about imaginary non-realistic cases are likely to be misleading.

I go on to argue that the concept of personal identity falls into the second of these classes, and hence that far-fetched thought experiments may not illuminate the concept in the way that they have been purported to. The chapter includes detailed discussions of John Locke's Prince and Cobbler case, Derek Parfit's teletransportation case, and Bernard Williams's A-body/B-body case. As in the Galileo chapter (Ch. 1), these examples are illustrative, and the general claim is intended to hold more widely.

This essay and its successor—"Personal Identity and Thought Experiments" (Ch. 4)— form a natural pair. For those who prefer to read only one of them, it might be useful to know that the later paper is more intricate and subtle in its argumentation, and can fruitfully be read as a self-standing piece.

For those already familiar with the personal identity literature, the key ideas in this essay can be acquired by focusing on §§1 and 4.

***

This essay was first published in the *Journal of Consciousness Studies*, 5/5–6 (1998), 592–610 and is reprinted with the kind permission of Imprint Academic. The text that appears here is largely unchanged, though several now-outdated bibliographical footnotes have been omitted, and minor stylistic alterations have been made to several remaining footnotes and to brief passages in the main text. As a result of reformatting, some footnote numbers have changed. The original number of each footnote is noted in [square brackets].

It is of great use to the sailor to know the length of his line, though he cannot with it fathom all the depths of the ocean. It is well he knows that it is long enough to reach the bottom at such places as are necessary to direct his voyage, and caution him against running upon shoals that may ruin him.

—John Locke, *Essay Concerning Human Understanding*, I. i. 6

1. Introduction

1.1. The Problem of Personal Identity

The question of (diachronic) personal identity (at least as it concerns many contemporary Anglo-American materialist philosophers) is the question of determining the necessary and sufficient conditions for a person at some later time to be identical with a person at some earlier time. Phrased in the debate's standard language, the question is: under what conditions are we correct in saying that P2 (a person who exists at t2) is the same person as P1 (a person who exists at t1)? The question is a special case of the more general question of the identity conditions for entities over time: under what conditions are we correct in saying that E2 (an entity of sort E which exists at t2) is the same E as E1 (an entity of sort E which exists at t1)?

Those who think that the question of diachronic personal identity has a determinate categorical answer tend to respond in one of two ways: either it is suggested that some sort of *physical* characteristic—such as having the same body—serves as the basis for identity over time, or it is suggested that some sort of *psychological* or *mental* characteristic—such as having the same memories—serves that role.[1] It should not be surprising that these are the two sorts of answers that have been offered. We are, after all, physical beings whose most notable feature is our psychological characteristics; what is essential to who we are is presumably either the distinctive set of beliefs, desires, memories, etc. that together constitute our character, or the distinctive configuration of molecules that together constitute our body, or, perhaps, some combination of the two.

For roughly half a century, the philosophical literature on personal identity has centered on arguments of a certain type. These arguments defend revisionary conclusions about the nature or importance of personal identity on the basis of an assumed convergence of responses to purely imaginary cases.[2]

---

[1] [3] In addition, there are those who suggest that both factors are necessary, for instance, that what is required for P1 and P2 to be the same person is that P2 have more than 50% of P1's brain, along with P1's core psychology (Unger 1990).

[2] [4, slightly modified] Whether they do, in fact, tap relevant intuitions has been a topic of discussion since their inception: cf. Quine 1972; Wilkes 1988. Or, in somewhat more colorful colloquial form, consider the following quote, taken from a lay-directed book entitled *Persons: What Philosophers Say about You*: "Philosophers frequently dream up weird examples to test their understanding of concepts. With respect to persons, they talk about

So, for instance, one is asked to contemplate a case in which A's brain is transplanted into B's body, or a case in which some of C's memories are implanted in D's brain, or a case in which information about the arrangement of the molecules that compose E is used to create an exact replica of E at another point in spacetime.[3]

Thinking about these cases is supposed to help us tease apart the relative roles played by features that coincide in all (or almost all) actual cases, but which seem to be conceptually distinguishable. So, for instance, even though we can ordinarily assume that the beliefs, desires, memories, etc. which are associated with a given body will not come to be associated with another body, it does not seem to be in principle impossible that such a state of affairs should come about. Indeed, it seems that we can describe a mechanism by which such a situation might arise: for instance, A's brain (and with it A's beliefs, desires, and memories) might be transplanted into B's body. And since the scenario described strikes us as something of which we can make sense, it seems we can make judgments of fact or value about which of the two factors really matters in making A who she is. We might ask, for instance, whether it would be true to say that A had survived in a body that used to belong to B, or whether it would be right to punish the B-bodied human being for A's actions, or whether if we were A before the intended operation, we ought to worry about what would be happening to the B-bodied person afterwards. And on the basis of these judgments about what we would say in the imaginary case, we can return to the actual case having learned something about which features are essential and which accidental to our judgments concerning the nature or value of personal identity.

My goal in this chapter is to suggest reasons for thinking that this methodology may be less reliable than its proponents take it to be, for interesting and systematic reasons.

1.2. Questioning the Methodology

In general, two sorts of objections are offered when appeals to such scenarios are made.[4] The first type involves substantive disputes about particular cases:

---

machines that can duplicate human behavior and appearance, brain transplants, mind interchanges, teletransportation . . . This tends to alienate people in other fields who wonder what philosophers have been smoking" (Bourgeois 1995: 19).

[3] [5] In speaking of "A's brain" or etc., "B's body," etc., I am speaking loosely, since precisely what is at issue is what sort of thing "A" or "B" might be.

[4] [6] See especially Wilkes 1988. Cf. also: Johnston 1987, 1989, and 1992; Quine 1972; Robinson 1988; Snowdon 1991. For more general discussions of the methodology, see Sorensen 1992a, and the papers collected in Horowitz and Massey 1991. [*Added in 2009*: In the dozen years since this paper was originally published, a steadily increasing number of articles have appeared that discuss philosophical methodology in general, and thought experiments in particular. For a regularly updated list of such material, see <http://philpapers. org/>.]

whether, for instance, divided consciousness can be imagined "from the in-side," or whether brain transplants are biologically possible. The second type concerns a more general issue: whether our concepts should (or could) support all of the implications of our beliefs concerning what is practically, physically, or conceptually possible. Those who make such objections have been partially heeded; appeals to thought experiments in discussions of personal identity are now often prefaced by a discussion of the feasibility of the scenario described, and sometimes by a discussion of the legitimacy of the methodology as such.[5] But with a few exceptions,[6] I think both critics and defenders have located the problem in the wrong place.

Certainly, *pace* extreme critics, there is nothing wrong with the methodology of thought experiment *as such*. After all, a thought experiment is just a process of reasoning carried out within the context of a well-articulated imaginary scenario in order to answer a specific question about a non-imaginary situation. Such hypothetical test cases play perfectly unobjectionable roles in legal reasoning, linguistic theorizing, scientific inquiry, and ordinary conversation. And there is nothing categorically wrong with thought experiments that con-cern technologically or biologically or even physically impossible situations. Again, such purely counterfactual test cases play unobjectionable roles in each of the domains just listed. Rather, I will argue, the legitimacy or illegitimacy of thought-experimental reasoning in a particular case depends upon the struc-ture of the concept that the thought experiment is intended to illuminate. If the concept is structured around a set of necessary and sufficient conditions, *and* if these conditions play a role in how it is that we identify candidates as falling under that concept,[7] then imaginary cases may help us to separate essential features of the concept from accidental ones. But if the concept is not structured in that way, or if the features in question do not govern our application of the concept, then imaginary cases are likely to be misleading.[8/9]

---

[5] [7] For a sophisticated example, see Unger 1990: 7–13; for a sophisticated critique, see Rovane 1994.

[6] [8] In particular, the argument I present below owes a tremendous amount to the work of Mark Johnston.

[7] [9] In the psychological literature on concepts, this is generally referred to as the "classical view," and is widely regarded by psychologists as inadequate in accounting for all but a few of our concepts. (For surveys of this literature, see Komatsu 1992; Medin and Smith 1984; and Smith and Medin 1981.) [*Added in 2009*: Two valuable more recent volumes are Margolis and Laurence 1999 and Murphy 2002.] I think this dismissal is overhasty, in part for the reasons discussed in Rey 1983 and Rey 1985. But since I agree that the view cannot account for the relevant concept in the case on which I am focusing, I will not pursue these general issues further.

[8] [10] For incisive discussion of these issues, see Johnston 1987. For reasons similar to my own, Johnston contends that these conditions are not met when we think about imaginary cases involving the concept "person."

[9] [11] I suspect it is this distinction that explains the widespread sense that thought experiments are less problematic in science than in philosophy. It is certainly true that scientific concepts are, in general, more likely than non-scientific concepts to be structured around necessary and sufficient conditions that play a role in how we identify instances that

My main contention in this chapter is that the concept of personal identity belongs to the second of these classes. Although philosophers from Locke on are correct in recognizing that a conceptual distinction can be drawn between what Locke called the "man" (or human animal) and what he called the "person" (or set of distinct psychological characteristics), it does not follow that we are able to make informative judgments about many of the combinatoric arrangements in which these features might appear. For the fact that two features can be conceptually separated in the sense that we can imagine the one obtaining without the other in some particular case does not mean that those two features are conceptually distinct in the sense that we can make reliable judgments about them, considered in isolation. Conceptual separability guarantees conceptual distinctness only if our knowledge of the necessary and sufficient conditions of a concept is what governs our application of that concept; in other cases, we have no such guarantee.

So even if we are aware that the two features need not coincide in all possible cases, the fact that they coincide in all (or even in nearly all) actual cases may mean that there is no ascertainable fact of the matter about how we would or should respond to either in isolation. For while we may be able to make sense of exceptional situations where they come apart, we do so only by relating them back to ordinary cases where they coincide. But this means that our evaluation of the exceptional case will depend upon which mapping we use in making this assimilation. And this means that our ability to make sense of such cases outruns our ability to make reliable judgments about them.

I think this is what explains both the appeal and the inconclusiveness of thought experiments about personal identity.[10] As a matter of evolutionary fact, human persons are entities that are both biological organisms and self-conscious loci of psychological characteristics. And while these features are clearly conceptually separable—we can easily make sense of cases in which the purely biological kind "human animal" and that kind's most striking characteristic, "self-conscious locus of psychological characteristics," come apart—it is not clear that we can make informative *judgments* about them. For although the world forces us to think about certain exceptional cases in which a single body may be able to support more than one collection of psychological attributes (cases, for instance, of multiple personality, or of other sorts of dissociation and compartmentalization, or of memory loss and subsequent relearning), it does not present us (at least according to those whose views are the targets of my discussion) with cases in which a single set of psychological characteristics may be present in more than one body, either diachronically or

---

fall under that concept. [*Note added in 2009*: For further exploration of the role of thought experiments in science, see Chs. 1 and 2 above.]

[10] [12] For a related but somewhat different take on this question, see Rovane 1994, as well as Rovane 1998, esp. ch. 2.

synchronically.[11] And this contingent fact—that is, the fact that in almost all cases, a single mind is associated with a single body—plays a central role in how it is that we make judgments about the nature and importance of personal identity.[12] For it is the lens through which we view the cases where the one–one coincidence does not hold.[13]

Below, I will describe a widely discussed imaginary case to which our responses seem to be frame-dependent: how the story is told affects how the story is evaluated. This phenomenon is easily explained if we assume that the way we make sense of such cases is by assimilating them to a class of cases with which we are familiar. Whichever of the story's features are made salient by the particular presentation will thus serve as the basis for assimilation to the ordinary cases in which the contingently associated features that together comprise ordinary cases of personhood coincide. On a biological or psychological view of personal identity, however, one or another of the responses could legitimately be criticized as mistaken. But for reasons that I will discuss after I present the case, I think both responses are at least rationally permissible.

1.3. Plan for the Rest of the Chapter

In the remainder of this chapter, I will proceed as follows. In §2, I will briefly summarize Locke's views on the identity conditions governing objects, organisms, and persons, and describe the famous thought experiment from which modern discussions of personal identity take their inspiration. The purpose of this section is twofold: first, to provide an example of the sort of analysis that is offered in discussions of the identity conditions for entities over time; and second, to do so in the context of the Lockean framework, which has served as a jumping-off point for subsequent discussions.[14] Readers familiar with Locke's writings might skip this section without losing the thread of the

---

[11] [13] In saying this, I do not mean to deny that there are purported cases of reincarnation, memories of past lives, soul-transfer, etc., and that commitment to the existence of such phenomena may play a central role in the conceptual schemes of millions, even billions, of people. But as far as I can tell, these purported facts play no part in the conceptual schemes of those who make use of the sorts of imaginary cases that I will discuss below. (I thank an anonymous reviewer for the *Journal of Consciousness Studies* for the reminding me of the provincialism of ignoring such views.)

[12] [14] To repeat: this is so even if there are a small number of actual exceptions.

[13] [*Note added in* 2009: I explore this theme in greater detail in Ch. 4 below.]

[14] [15] Cf. Harold Noonan's remark that just as "[i]t has been said that all subsequent philosophy consists merely of footnotes to Plato," of personal identity "it can truly be said that all subsequent writing has consisted merely of footnotes to Locke*" (Noonan 1989: 30). Whether this is an accurate description depends, of course, upon exactly how much new material can be included in (metaphoric) footnotes. But it certainly provides a rough indication of Locke's centrality, and some justification for my beginning my discussion only with Locke (as opposed to with Plato or Aristotle), and for my beginning my discussion already with Locke (as opposed to with Bernard Williams or Derek Parfit).

* Which would make them, I suppose, sub-footnotes to Plato.

argument.[15] In §3, I will identify what I take to be the crucial aspects of Locke's thought experiment, and explain how contemporary cases can be seen as continuous with it. The purpose of this section is to identify some central assumptions that underlie contemporary discussions of the nature and importance of personal identity, and to amass intuitive support for my claim that we can make sense of cases about which we cannot make judgments. Again, the details of this section are not essential to my main argument, so readers familiar with contemporary Anglo-American literature on the nature and importance of personal identity may wish to read these pages rather quickly. The principal argument is picked up again in §3.3, where I consider a particular case in some detail (that described by Bernard Williams in "The Self and the Future"), and suggest a way of understanding the case in light of a more general strategy for understanding how we make sense of exceptions.

2. The Lockean Background

2.1. Locke on the Identity of "Men" and of "Persons"

Modern discussions of the metaphysics of personal identity can be traced to Locke's chapter *Of Identity and Diversity* in his *Essay Concerning Human Understanding*.[16] There Locke defends a view that identity is "suited to the Idea" (§7); that is, that criteria for identity (over time) are criteria for identity as an X (over time), and that these criteria, in turn, can be categorized into several clusters, each involving different *kinds* of identity criteria. With this in mind, Locke sets out to provide a general taxonomy of types of identity over time for various sorts of bodily substances: first non-living, then living.[17]

The primitive bearers of bodily identity on the Lockean picture are atoms, which are the basic units of matter. So long as an atom exists, there can be no question about its identity; being fundamentally simple, the atom exists unchanged as long as it exists at all (§2). At the next level of complexity come

---

[15] [16] My discussion in that section is not intended to do justice either to the details of Locke's view, or to the many issues of identity over time that thorough discussion of the view would require. For discussion of the former, the reader might fruitfully consult Alston and Bennett 1988, Mackie 1976 (especially Chs. 3, 5, and 6), or (for a general overview) Noonan 1989, Ch. 2; a bibliographic exploration of the extensive literature on the latter question might reasonably begin with the sources listed in Noonan 1989: 255–9. [*Added in* 2009: Again, the reader who wishes to explore more recent work on the topic might consult the extensive listings at <http://philpapers.org/>.]

[16] Locke 1710/1975, Bk. II, Ch. xxvii. Section numbers in the main text, indicated by the convention "(§n)," refer to sections of this chapter in Locke.

[17] [18] I here neglect Locke's discussion of the other sorts of substances—God and finite intelligences—about which identity judgments might be made. For reasons that Locke explains clearly in §2, these do not raise the sorts of puzzles that are raised when we make identity judgments about complex bodies.

simple clumps of matter, where "two or more Atoms [are] joined together into the same Mass"; here continued existence requires the continued contiguity of the body's subparts, whatever the arrangement (§3).

A very different sort of criterion governs Locke's remaining categories— plants, animals, and human beings; for entities of these sorts, identity is a function not of sameness of matter, but of sameness of life. A plant, such as an oak tree, is the same plant so long as it follows a natural course of events determined by its organic unity as a living entity of a particular sort, regardless of radical changes in its form (say, from acorn to sapling) or the particular matter that makes it up (§4). Similar criteria govern animals, whose identity comes from the internally driven unified participation of the various parts in a continuing life (§5). Finally, Locke turns to the criterion of identity for man, which is nothing more than a special case of animal identity (§6).[18]

Thus far, Locke has introduced two sorts of identity criteria: non-living (non-artifactual) bodily substances retain their identity through identity of matter, and living bodily substances retain their identity through identity of life. This latter criterion is intended to satisfy two constraints simultaneously: first, to permit continued attribution of identity in the face of change (§6), and second, to do so without eliminating the ground for drawing distinctions between separate individuals (§7). That is, in providing a theory of identity for human beings over time, a distinction must be drawn between the sorts of changes which are entity-preserving (such as growth, or getting drunk, or the loss of a limb), and the sorts of changes which are entity-destroying (such as transformation into a beast, or death). The criterion of "participation in a single continued Life," which is nothing more or less than the criterion for animal identity, is meant to capture precisely this distinction.[19]

The main negative conclusion of the first part of Locke's discussion is that none of the criteria of identity for bodily substances over time can do justice to what Locke will call *personal identity*. So the discussion thus far can be seen as prefatory to Locke's famous distinction between "man" and "person," and the corresponding distinction between the identity suited to the idea of the one, and the identity suited to the idea of the other (§7). Whereas *man* is an animal, that is, a "living organized Body" of "a certain Form" (§8), a *person* is "a thinking intelligent Being, that has reason and reflection, and can consider itself as a self, the same thinking thing in different times and places" (§9). That is, a person is a self-conscious reflective being whose awareness of itself as a thinking thing over

---

[18] [17] Throughout this section, for convenience of exposition, I follow Locke's terminology in using "man" as a general (gender-neutral) term for human animals, and "person" as a general term for human beings considered as psychological entities. In later sections, I make use of the terms "Lockean men" and "Lockean persons" respectively.

[19] [19] "The Identity of the same *Man* consists . . . in nothing but a participation in the same continued Life, by constantly fleeting Particles of Matter, in succession vitally united to the same organized Body" (§6).

time is what serves to make it the same self.[20] The criterion of identity for personhood is "sameness of . . . rational Being," and the personal analogue to "participation in a single continued Life" is participation in a single consciousness: life unifies men, consciousness unifies persons.

2.2. The Prince and the Cobbler

With this distinction in place, Locke goes on to discuss a number of imaginary cases designed to buttress his analysis of personal identity, the most famous of which is the story of the prince and the cobbler.[21] He writes: "Should the soul of a prince, carrying with it the consciousness of the prince's past life, enter and inform the body of a cobbler, as soon deserted by his own soul, everyone sees that he would be the same person with the prince, accountable only for the prince's actions: but who would say it was the same man?" (§15).

Locke's story is motivated by a desire to avoid putting excessive weight on a certain uniformity in the world—that persons and men coincide with sufficient regularity that the distinction between them seems to have gone unnoticed. In order to establish that the two are conceptually separable, he employs a technique well known from scientific methodology: that two features can be shown to be discrete if it is possible for each to obtain without the other. If the story Locke has described makes sense to us, then the conceptual distinction he wishes to draw must also make sense. But this alone does not show that we can make reliable judgments about Lockean persons as self-standing entities. So let us look a bit more closely about why Locke's story seems to make sense, and why that does not show what Locke and his followers have taken it to show.

2.3. Crucial Elements of the Lockean Story

Locke's scenario has the following crucial elements:

(1) The set of psychological characteristics ("personality") previously associated with one body comes to be associated with another body, in such a way that it seems to the rest of the world that the Y-body manifests the personality previously associated with (the) X-(body); and it feels to the Y-body person [that is: the X-soul person] as if she has gotten a new body.

---

[20] [20] "For since consciousness always accompanies thinking . . . in this alone consists *personal identity, i.e.* the sameness of a rational being: and as far as this consciousness can be extended backwards to any past action or thought, so far reaches the identity of that *person*" (§9).

[21] [21] Locke's less famous cases—including those of the Christian Platonist, the Mayor of Queensborough, the Day-man and the Night-man, and so on—are described in the surrounding sections.

(2) The story describes a mechanism—the movement of the consciousness-carrying soul from one body to the other—by which the changes described in (1) come about.

(3) The mechanism is such that the X-personality is manifest in the Y-body because some substance that was present in the X-body is now present in the Y-body.

That is, the Lockean story depends upon the following three things: (1) that we can make sense of a story in which two personalities "switch bodies"; (2) that we can describe a mechanism by which such a switch might take place; (3) that that mechanism involves some transfer of some sort of (material or immaterial) substance. What (2) and (3) help us to see is that we do think the scenario described in (1) is coherent; by providing us with a narrative about how the surprising state of affairs described in (1) might come about, they help make the situation seem less mysterious. But from the fact that we can tell a story about how the world might come to be configured in some way other than the way it actually is, it does not follow that we will be able to make judgments about the various combinations of the features Locke has isolated. As the combinations grow more complex, we see that the initial illusion of certainty about the simple case was only that: an illusion.

So in the next section, I will trace the ways in which a number of widely discussed contemporary thought experiments can be seen as arising out of Locke's original case. My purpose in doing so is twofold: to demonstrate the continuity of contemporary cases with their early modern predecessors, and to show how the increasing complexity which these cases introduce in no way disrupts our ability to make sense of them, but wreaks havoc with our ability to make informative judgments about them.

3. Variations on the Lockean Story

3.1. Transferring Matter

In direct descendants of Locke's story, only (2) is altered. Instead of the "soul … carrying with it the consciousness of the prince's past life," it is the brain of the first character (carrying with it the consciousness of the character's past life) that is imagined to have been transplanted into the body of the second character. As with Locke's story, the intuition this is standardly taken to evoke is that the person has moved from one body to another. A typical presentation of this sort of story is the following:

Imagine … that in the twenty-first century it is possible to transplant brains, as it is now possible to transplant hearts, and let us suppose that the brain of a Mr Brown is transplanted into the skull of a Mr Robinson … The result of the operation, call him Brownson, will then be a completely healthy person...with Robinson's body, but in character, memories and personality quite indistinguishable from Brown...Most modern philosophers who have reflected on this case...have found that they could not honestly deny that Brownson, in the case imagined, was Brown. (Noonan 1989: 4–5)[22]

Let us call this the "brain transplant case." A minor variation on this story is one in which the brains of the two characters are switched, so that, for instance, just as Brown's brain is transplanted into Robinson's skull, Robinson's is transplanted into Brown's. (See e.g. Perry 1975a: 3–6.) On the standard interpretation, just as we would be inclined to say that Brownson is Brown, so too would we be inclined to say that Robin is Robinson. Let us call this the *brain switch case*.

The brain has a certain complexity that has led philosophers to consider a variation on the brain transplant case referred to as *fission*. Following the appearance in the philosophical literature of an article entitled "Brain Bisection and the Unity of Consciousness" (Nagel 1971), in which the results of Sperry's split-brain research were presented, philosophers began to consider the possibility that a single brain might in principle be able to support two loci of consciousness.[23] And if this is so, they reasoned, then it seems to be a shallow rather than a deep truth that various processes are localized in one or another brain hemisphere, rather than being spread throughout the brain as a whole.

But from here it seems only a minor idealization to imagine a case in which all of the features of Brown's personality are realized in his brain twice over, such that the transplant of either half to Robinson's body would be sufficient to give us a human being with all of Brown's memories, beliefs, desires, etc. But if either half would be sufficient, then we might also coherently imagine a third case, in which after being removed from Brown's body and divided in two, one half of Brown's brain is transplanted into Robinson's body, and the other half is transplanted into a third body, that of Robinson II. But then, is Brown Brownson, or Brownson II, or both, or neither? It seems clear that he cannot be both, for surely Brownson and Brownson II are distinct individuals, and if Brown were identical with both, then they would have to be identical with each other. But it seems equally problematic to say that he is one as opposed to the other; for what could make it the case that he is Brownson instead of Brownson II? And it seems no more plausible to say that he is neither one; after all, were it not for

---

[22] [23] To the best of my knowledge, this version of the story derives from Shoemaker 1963.

[23] [24] Discussions of similar cases, in which persons were simply hypothesized to "split like amoebas," were present in the literature before mid-century. But it was only when philosophers were able to identify a mechanism by which such a process might "actually" occur that discussion began to take on the proportions it currently has. (To be fair, there are additional factors, both micro- and macro-sociological, which may also explain the swelling literature.) [*Added in* 2009: Apparently, a similar debate occurred in the eighteenth century; for details, see Martin and Barresi 1999.]

the existence of Brownson II, he would surely be identical to Brownson, and it seems odd to say that twice-over survival is tantamount to death.

3.2. Reconfiguring form

The case of fission is indeed deeply perplexing, and to say more about it here would distract us from my main line of argumentation even more than we have been already.[24] Instead, I turn to cases in which (3) is denied, that is, cases in which it is imagined that it is not the transfer of some *substance*, but rather the transfer of some *information* by which the circumstance described in (1) comes about. Consider three such cases which we can call the *brain state transfer case*, the *brain state exchange case*, and the *brain state duplication case*. For the first (*brain state transfer*), we might imagine a machine that scans all of the information about the configuration of the pre-switch X's brain, and then uses this information to reconfigure the brain of pre-switch Y so that the brain in Y's body comes to support all of the memories, beliefs, and desires of the pre-switch X.[25] The outcome of such a process is functionally identical to the outcome of the brain transfer described above; the Y body manifests the memories, beliefs, and desires of the pre-switch X, and does so because pre-switch X did. And, of course, as with the brain transfer case, we might imagine slight variations: a more complicated version of this story wherein the brain structures of the two characters are switched (*brain state exchange*), or a case in which the duplication (or multiplication) occurs without disrupting the original (*brain state duplication*).

But if the correct set of instructions is enough to allow us to reconfigure one brain in such a way that it supports the psychological characteristics previously associated with another brain, then with a slightly more complicated set of instructions, we ought to be able, at least in principle, to assemble a brain, or indeed a whole human being, out of simple bits of matter of the same sort of which the original was composed. So we might imagine a case of "teletransportation," where one or more exact duplicates of a human being would be brought into existence at a spatially remote location as a result of information garnered about the structure of the original being.

And if this is in principle possible, then it also seems possible, in principle at least, that matter might come to be configured in that way without this configuration being the result of information-transfer as described above. That is, it seems that what might be called "independent replication" is at least in principle possible, wherein one or more exact duplicates of a human being would be brought into existence at a spatially remote location not as a result of

---

[24] [25] Three of the most subtle and influential discussions of this case are Johnston 1989; Parfit 1984/1987; and Wiggins 1980. For a more comprehensive survey of responses, see Noonan 1989.

[25] [26] For early discussions of this case, see Shoemaker 1963 and Williams 1970/1973b.

information garnered about the structure of the original being, but as a result of some causally independent process.

Let me summarize the variations I have described on the basis of the assumptions that underlie them:

(4) Assuming that the source of psychological content is localized, this could be removed and transplanted to another body (brain transfer, brain exchange).

(5) Assuming that the source of psychological content is localized, redundantly realized, and divisible such that either half might adequately serve as the basis for full psychology, it could be divided and doubly transplanted (fission).

(6) Assuming that the source of psychological content might be realized in another physical entity of similar basic structure, the matter of that entity might be reconfigured in a way that would render it structurally identical to the original (brain state transfer, brain state exchange, brain state duplication).[26]

(7) Assuming that the same arrangement of the same kind of matter would produce the same macrostructural properties, one or more exact duplicates could, in principle, be generated at a spatially remote location (teletransportation).

(8) Assuming that the same arrangement of the same kind of matter would produce the same macrostructural properties, one or more exact duplicates could, in principle, be spontaneously generated at a spatially remote location (independent replication).

It seems to me undeniable that we can make sense of such scenarios. Each represents a state of affairs that seems metaphysically, perhaps even physically, possible. But this does not mean that we can make reliable judgments about how we would or should respond to such scenarios, were we to encounter them. In the next section, I will say more about this contention in the context of one particular case.

3.3. The Self and the Future

In "The Self and the Future," (Williams 1970/1973b) Bernard Williams describes an imaginary case in which one is asked to contemplate a machine of a sort rendered practicable by (6) above: when two individuals, A and B, are hooked up to the machine, it reconfigures the A-brain in such a way that it comes to be associated with all of the psychological states previously associated

---

[26] [*Note added in 2009*: For novel-length exploration of this idea, see Robert J. Sawyer's *Mindscan*. (Thanks to Susan Schneider for directing me to this book, which, in keeping with its themes, I read partly in paper form and partly on my Kindle.)]

with the B-brain/B-body person, and reconfigures the B-brain in such a way that it comes to be associated with all of the psychological states previously associated with the A-brain/A-body person.[27] With this in place, Williams asks the reader to consider the following two stories.

In the first, one imagines A faced with the prospect of being connected up to the machine in question. From the machine will emerge two persons: the first, the A-body person, will have the body previously associated with A, but all of the psychological states previously associated with B; the second, the B-body person, will have the body previously associated with B, but all of the psychological states previously associated with A. Before the operation, A is told that one of the two resultant persons will be given a large financial reward whereas the other will be tortured. A is asked to decide, on purely self-interested grounds, whether the reward should go to the A-body person or the B-body person.

As the case is presented, it seems sensible for A to direct the reward towards the B-body person. Among the other evidence that seems to support this decision as being correct is the fact that, when the operation is over and the goods are distributed, the B-body person—whose memories and desires correspond to those of the pre-operational A—will say rightly: "This is just the outcome I selected! And how glad I am that I so chose." Whereas, presumably, if the reward went to the A-body person, the B-body person would remark with outrage: "Why am *I* sitting here in great physical discomfort, when what I requested was the reward?" (Cf. Williams 1970/1973b: 48–50.) The intuition evoked by this first version is that we seem to be able to make sense of there being some sort of procedure whereby two persons could, so to speak, "swap bodies." To the extent that I bear to my future self a relation of rational prudential concern, I might properly bear that relation to someone with whom I shared no physical matter at all.[28]

The second scenario is the following. One imagines A to be in the hands of a particularly dastardly surgeon, who tells A: "Tomorrow, you will be subjected to great physical discomfort. But before this happens, you will be operated upon with the following effect. '[Y]ou will not remember being told that this is going

---

[27] As one of the central cases in the personal identity literature, Williams's story has received wide discussion. In light of this extensive literature, my rather flat-footed presentation of the story may strike readers familiar with these discussions as rather naïve. But my purpose in presenting this case is to talk about what role imaginary cases *in themselves* can play in deciding the sorts of questions they are credited with deciding. I have no doubt that imaginary cases considered in conjunction with well-worked-out philosophical theories can do many, many things.

[28] If, however, as Derek Parfit has argued, "identity is not what matters" for rational prudential concern, then the case does not allow us to conclude anything about the identity of the person towards whom the prudential concern is directed. (See Parfit 1971, 1984/1987.) I think Parfit is wrong about this, but presenting my reasons here would take us too far afield. [*Added in 2009*: For further discussion of this issue, see Ch. 4 below.]

to happen to you, since shortly before the torture something else will be done to [you] which will make [you] forget the announcement.' Indeed, you will 'not remember any of the things [you are] now in a position to remember.' In fact, at the moment of torment you will 'not only not remember the things [you are] now in a position to remember, but will have a different set of impressions of [your] past, quite different from the memories [you] now have'—a set of memories and impressions that exactly fit the past of some other person." Of this situation, Williams writes: "Fear, surely, would still be the proper reaction: and not because one did not know what was going to happen, but because in one vital respect at least one did know what was going to happen—torture, which one can indeed expect to happen to oneself, and to be preceded by certain mental derangements as well."[29]

The intuition evoked by this second version—which is, of course, just a one-sided presentation of the original scenario—is that we seem to be able to make sense of there being some sort of procedure whereby two persons could, so to speak, "swap minds." To the extent that I bear to my future self a relation of rational prudential concern, I might properly bear that relation to someone with whom I shared no psychological connections at all. My biological animal seems also to be *me*.[30]

Having presented these two versions of the story, Williams goes on to introduce a series of cases leading up to the story with which we were just presented:[31]

(9)   First case: "A is subjected to an operation which produces total amnesia."

(10)   Second case: "amnesia is produced in A, and other interference leads to certain changes in his character."

(11)   Third case: "changes in his character are produced, and at the same time certain illusory 'memory' beliefs are induced in him" that do not correspond to the memories of any actual person.

(12)   Fourth case: "the same as [(11)], except that both the character traits and 'memory' impressions are designed to be appropriate to another actual person, B."

---

[29] [29] Williams 1970/1973b: 52 (the passages in single quotations are taken from Williams). The reader who finds such a response completely alien—as one of the anonymous referees for the *Journal of Consciousness Studies* apparently did—might think about the following structurally similar scenario. Suppose that in old age you suffer from a debilitating brain disease that leaves you unable to remember any of your earlier experiences, and that produces in (what was) your brain all sorts of apparent memories unrelated to your own past. Would you not be self-interestedly concerned if you heard that "your" body was then scheduled to undergo some sort of physical torture? Would you think that you yourself had already died, at the moment when you lost your memories?

[30] [30] For an extended defense of the view that we are essentially human animals, see Olson 1997. [*Added in 2009*: For a discussion of some of Olson's claims, see Gendler 1999.]

[31] [31] All quotations in this paragraph from Williams 1970/1973b: 55–6.

(13) Fifth case: "the same as [(12)], except that the result is produced by putting the information into A from the brain of B, by a method which leaves B the same as he was before."

(14) Sixth case: "the same happens to A as in [(13)], but...a similar operation is [also] conducted in the reverse direction," resulting in corresponding changes in B.

In general, consideration of this series of stories has evoked three different sorts of responses. Williams himself contends that our inclination to say that A would be right to be prudentially concerned about what would happen to the A-body person in the first (amnesia) case carries through all the way to the fifth (brain-state transfer) case; and since the difference between the fifth and the sixth cases does not involve any difference in what happens to A, then it carries through to the sixth case as well. So the correct criterion of identity, Williams thinks, is a bodily criterion. By contrast, advocates of the psychological criterion of personal identity conclude just the opposite. Already in the first case, they contend, what matters for prudential concern has been lost; the Lockean person associated with the A-body has already been eliminated by the process that produces amnesia. So from the very beginning, the A-body person does not have warranted prudential concern for any of the characters described in the six cases.[32] Finally, some have taken the scenario to show that both lay legitimate claim on our intuitions,[33] and that what the case shows is that our concept of person is not definitively committed to the primacy of one or the other.[34]

In short, the Williams story perfectly illustrates the claim I have been making: that our ability to make *sense* of imaginary scenarios in which features that coincide in nearly all actual cases are recombined in novel ways far outruns our ability to make *judgments* about them. We may well feel that a scenario is perfectly coherent, without knowing what we would do or say were we to encounter it. In such circumstances, our evaluation of the case is likely to depend upon how the case is presented.

---

[32] [32] More complicated versions of this view draw the line somewhat later along the spectrum. See e.g. Noonan 1989.

[33] [33, modified] For an interesting discussion of this case and its implications, see Rovane 1998, ch. 2; for remarks on Rovane's account, see Gendler 2002a.

[34] [34] One might say, for instance, that the story provides evidence in favor of a "closest continuer" theory: that "to be something later is to be its closest continuer" (Nozick 1981: 33). According to such a theory, to be X later is to be whatever entity it is that most closely matches the profile of characteristics associated with being X (provided that the entity matches this profile sufficiently closely to be a candidate). The closest continuer view raises certain perplexing metaphysical puzzles about the extrinsic determination of identity. (See e.g. Johnston 1987 and Noonan 1989 for objections.) But I am not convinced that the question of personal identity is straightforwardly metaphysical in the way critics of the closest continuer theory assume it must be. [*Added in 2009*: For further brief remarks on this suggestion, see Gendler 1999.]

4. The Moral of the Stories

4.1. Decision-making and Assimilation to a Class of Familiar Cases

Consider the following situation, which is standard fare in discussions of rationality.[35] Suppose that on your way to see a play you lose a $10 bill from your wallet. Upon arriving at the theater, you discover this loss. However, you still have money in your wallet, and tickets to the play are $10 each. Do you still buy a ticket? A vast majority of people answer "yes."[36] By contrast, consider the following case. You have already purchased a $10 ticket for the play but upon arriving at the theater, you discover that you have lost the ticket. Would you buy another ticket? Most people answer "no."[37]

Clearly, however, at some level these cases are the same. They differ only in the form of the $10-item lost: in the first case, the $10 lost is in the form of cash, which is the paradigmatically interchangeable commodity; in the second case, the $10 lost is in the form of a movie ticket which is directly related to the expected gain (seeing the play).[38] But as far as their implications for action in this particular case are concerned, this difference is trivial: the purchase of the ticket is imagined to have been basically effortless; to acquire a second would be equally trifling. Indeed, the similarity between them can be seen from the fact that one can easily talk oneself out of either reaction by assimilating the first case to the second, or the second case to the first. So it seems *prima facie* irrational to treat the cases differently. If we can see that, deep down, all we have are two alternate descriptions of the same state of affairs, how can we justify our inclination to deal with them asymmetrically? To do so seems to be

---

[35] [35] This case, along with many others, is first discussed in Tversky and Kahneman 1981. Again, to those familiar with the enormous literature on these subjects [*added in 2009*: a wider group of philosophers than a decade ago when this essay was first published] my discussions here may seem superficial. As before, the point I am trying to establish is a simple one, so the many nuances of recent discussions are not relevant to my purposes. The reader interested in following up on these issues might fruitfully begin with the papers collected in Kahneman, Slovic, and Tversky 1982 and [*reference added in 2009*] Kahneman and Tversky 2000.

[36] [36] The question was phrased as follows: "Imagine that you have decided to see a play where admission is $10 per ticket. As you enter the theater, you discover that you have lost a $10 bill. Would you still pay $10 for a ticket to the play?" Out of nearly 200 subjects, 88% answered "yes"; 12% answered "no" (Tversky and Kahneman 1981: 457).

[37] [37] "Imagine that you have decided to see a play and paid the admission price of $10 per ticket. As you enter the theater you discover that you have lost your ticket. The seat was not marked and the ticket cannot be recovered. Would you pay $10 for another ticket?" Out of 200 subjects asked, 46% said "yes"; 54% said "no" (Tversky and Kahneman 1981: 457).

[38] [38] Tversky and Kahneman diagnose the outcome as follows: "The marked difference between [the two cases] is an effect of psychological accounting. We propose that the purchase of a new ticket in [the second case] is entered in the account that was set up by the purchase of the original ticket. In terms of this account, the expense required to see the show is $20, a cost which many of our respondents apparently found excessive. In [the first case], on the other hand, the loss of $10 is not linked specifically to the ticket purchase and its effect on the decision is accordingly slight." (Tversky and Kahneman 1981: 457.)

69

to give judicatory import to factors that ought not to matter: how could the mere fact that we describe something in one way rather than another justify such a striking difference in the attitudes we bear towards it?

Although I agree that it is not rationally *mandatory* that the attitudes we take towards the two situations should differ, I also do not think that it is rationally *prohibited*. That is, I think that it is rationally *permitted* that we should take these different perspectives, and I want to say a few words about why. When we make decisions, we make sense of the particular scenario with which we are confronted by assimilating it to a class of familiar cases.[39] Since in general it is economically unwise to indulge ourselves by automatically replacing any item that breaks or is lost, and since we treat the lost ticket case under that rubric, we are hesitant to buy another. And since in general it would make us unhappy to deny ourselves enjoyment in one sphere whenever something has gone wrong in another, and since we treat the lost $10-bill case under that rubric, we are prepared to spend the money. Even when the baseline similarity between the two cases is brought out to us, we may maintain that it makes good sense to treat them differently, since each is best understood as belonging to one of two classes of cases between which we make a justifiable distinction.

With this idea in place, let us return to the Williams case. The perplexity there, you will recall, is that our response to the case seems to be frame-dependent. On one way of telling the story, we are inclined to take it as evidence in favor of the hypothesis that personal identity over time is a matter of physical continuity; on another, we are inclined to see it as supporting the view that personal identity over time is a matter of continuity of psychology. The discussion above suggests a diagnosis of the difference in response. In the first presentation, when we try to make sense of the story in light of our general assumptions about ordinary cases of personal identity, we focus on issues involving the body. And in ordinary cases, continuity of body assures continuity of personhood. So when the Williams story is framed in a way that foregrounds the bodily perspective, we take this feature to be sufficient for continuity of personhood. Likewise with the second presentation. Framed in a way that highlights the psychological continuity involved, the case is assimilated to ordinary cases under the following line of reasoning. We notice that there is a feature possessed by the B-body person—psychological continuity—which suffices for continuity of personhood in ordinary cases. And so we are inclined to take that feature as decisive in this case as well.

---

[39] [39] I take this analysis from Nozick 1993, chs. 1 and 2. Among other things, Nozick there suggests that the bringing about/allowing distinction in ethics might be viewed as an example of the sort of baseline effect which Kahneman and Tversky have discussed (see Nozick 1993: 60 n.). For two independently arrived-at workings-out of this idea, see Horowitz 1998 and Kamm 1998. [*Added in 2009*: More recently, versions of this suggestion have been explored in a number of essays, including Sinnott-Armstrong 2008c and Driver 2008a. I investigate a variant of this proposal in Ch. 6 below.]

We have, then, a story about *how* we come to treat the two presentations so differently: we make use of a process of reasoning that we seem to employ quite generally. That is, we assimilate a situation under one description to one class of cases, and we assimilate that same situation under another description to a different set of actions. But it could be that in so doing we are making a mistake. Just as one might defend a substantive global theory of rationality according to which one or the other of the attitudes towards the missing $10/ticket is seen as categorically correct, so too might one defend a theory of personal identity according to which one or the other of the views we have been considering actually captures the truth about the nature and importance of personal identity. Indeed, this is precisely what the sorts of thought experiments described in the previous section seek to establish; they offer carefully described scenarios in which relevant and irrelevant features can be separated out so that we can determine which are essential and which accidental. If I am right in my claim that such cases do not, in general, show what their advocates purport that they show, I need to offer further reasons.

4.2. Exceptions and Norms

I have suggested above that the structure of the concept *person* is such that it applies in central cases as the result of the correlative appearance of a set of frequently associated characteristics, and to other cases as the result of our assimilation of them to these central cases. In defending this view, I now describe two strategies that might be employed when confronted with exceptional cases.

The *exception-as-scalpel* strategy uses exceptional cases as a way of progressively narrowing the range of characteristics required for the application of a concept by allowing us to isolate the essential features for concept-application from those which are merely ordinarily correlative. So, for instance, suppose that entities falling under a certain concept generally have characteristics *a, b, c, d*, and *e*. Suppose further that we come upon some entity that falls under the concept, but that has only *b* and *d*. We are then entitled to conclude that of the five characteristics typically associated with entities of the type under discussion, at most *b* and *d* are required characteristics of any entity that falls within the purview of the theory.

By contrast, the *exception-as-cantilever* strategy views the category-membership of exceptional cases as essentially reliant on the ordinary instances against which they can be seen as exceptions. So, for instance, suppose again that entities that fall under the concept in question generally have characteristics *a, b, c, d*, and *e*, and suppose further that some entity is found that has only *b* and *d*, but that nonetheless falls under the concept. According to the second strategy, the proper thing to say about the entity in question is that it falls under the concept only because it is similar in certain crucial ways to more typical instances of entities that the theory describes.

Applying the exception-as-scalpel strategy to the Williams case, we discover the following. The first presentation reveals that physical continuity is not necessary for diachronic personal identity, since it seems that there are cases where a person's future self might share none of her original physical matter. The second presentation reveals that psychological continuity is not necessary for diachronic personal identity, since it seems that there are cases where a person's future self might share none of her original psychological characteristics.[40] Moreover, neither feature could be sufficient, unless the pre-operation individual is supposed to be identical to *both* her continuers in the second scenario. So neither physical nor psychological continuity is either necessary or sufficient for diachronic personal identity.[41] This suggests that our concept of *person* is not organized around a set of necessary and sufficient conditions that play a role in how we identify candidates as falling under that concept. The exception-as-scalpel strategy cuts away too much.

By contrast, consider the exception-as-cantilever strategy. On this strategy, the Williams case is to be understood as follows. The first presentation reveals that there are imaginable cases in which we would be inclined to attribute diachronic identity in the absence of any sort of psychological continuity; the second presentation reveals the same about physical continuity. But rather than concluding something about the (lack of) necessary and sufficient conditions for the application of the concept *person*, the exception-as-cantilever strategy tells us to conclude this about our classification of these exceptional cases as cases where diachronic personal identity obtains: our decisions about these cases are justified by the rational permissibility of assimilating them to ordinary cases. In the first scenario, we focus on the similarity that concerns physical continuity; in the second, we focus on psychology. But in both cases, we are

---

[40] [40] Alternatively, one might follow Parfit in saying that prudential concern need not track identity, in which case thinking about these scenarios tells us nothing decisive about personal identity (since the evidence they used in favor of the attribution of identity was: projected prudential concern). Depending on whether one thinks that prudential concern *generally* tracks identity, and depending on which sorts of cases "generally" is supposed to cover—all normal cases? all actual cases? all (technologically, biologically, physically, metaphysically, logically) possible cases?—our projected judgments about a particular scenario will turn out to be very, somewhat, or not at all relevant to determining the identity-conditions for personhood over time. But this only helps to make my point. If judgments about prudential concern *are* relevant to making such determinations, then I refer the reader to my argument in the paragraph to which this footnote is attached. If judgments about prudential concern *are not* relevant to making such determinations, then it is unclear how contemplation of the sorts of imaginary scenarios described in the literature is supposed to give us the right sort of information (since it seems that our primary basis for judgments about identity is projection of prudential concern).

[41] [41] Cf. Johnston 1987 for related discussion of these points. [*Added in 2009*: I return to this issue in Ch. 4 below.]

cantilevering out from the set of generally obtaining correlations that characterize ordinary cases.[42] The persons in these far-flung stories are persons by courtesy only.

4.3. Conclusion

Thinking about actual and imaginary exceptional cases is indispensable if we wish to avoid mistaking accidental regularities for regularities that reflect a deeper truth about the world. And because the world does not provide us with easily accessible instances of all the combinations there might be, thought experiment—the contemplation of a well-described imaginary scenario in order to answer a specific question about some non-imaginary situation—is an indispensable technique: in philosophy, in science, and in ordinary reasoning. At the same time, critics of this methodology have correctly pointed out that it can be misused. Most have suggested that constraints be imposed on the sort of possibility involved in the imaginary scenario, that the more far-fetched the case, the less likely it is to be informative.

I have tried to show that this analysis locates the problem in the wrong place: the risk of misusing thought experiment arises not from the outlandishness of the scenarios, but from the structure of the concept that the thought experiment is intended to explore. Concepts structured in certain ways (those organized around a set of necessary and sufficient conditions that play a role in our identification of instances of that concept) can be clarified by means of the *exception-as-scalpel* strategy described in the last section; those structured in other ways may require us to treat *exceptions-as-cantilevers*.

I have argued that the concept of person, and with it, the concept of personal identity, is a concept of the latter sort. Diachronic personal identity is a matter of the continued coincidence of enough of the factors that ordinarily allow us to persist over time: psychological, physical, and perhaps even social factors play a role. We can make sense of cases where one or another of these features is absent. But this does not mean that our evaluations of them will be reliable guides to what matters in ordinary cases. For, as I have argued throughout this piece, our ability to make sense of exceptional situations far outruns our ability to make reliable judgments about them.[43]

[42] [43] To use a slightly different metaphor: the "persons" in these stories come in through the back gate—but the only reason there is a back gate for them to come in through is because ordinary cases form a certain sort of fence.

[43] [*] *Acknowledgements*: For comments on earlier material from which this chapter is descended, some of which (particularly material in §4) appeared in my 1996 dissertation, I am grateful to Robert Nozick, Derek Parfit, and Hilary Putnam. For discussion of the more recent material, I thank Shaun Gallagher, John Hawthorne, Zoltán Gendler Szabó, and two anonymous referees for the *Journal of Consciousness Studies*.

4

Personal Identity and Thought Experiments

In this chapter, I once again consider whether judgments about far-fetched thought experiments are helpful in illuminating the concept of personal identity. As in the previous chapter, I suggest that their utility is limited.

At the heart of the essay lies an endorsement of what I call "the merits of provincialism"—the value of recognizing that certain patterns of features that coincide only fortuitously may nonetheless play a central role in the organization of our concepts. In particular, I suggest that our understanding and employment of the concept of *person* rests on the ("provincial") assumption that actual human beings come into existence only through a predictable sequence of events—even though we can well imagine circumstances (such as fission, teletransportation) where this assumption would be violated.

The core of the essay consists of a detailed assessment and critique of Derek Parfit's widely discussed contention that fission cases reveal that "personal identity is not what matters." I suggest that Parfit's argument rests on a subtle confounding of two kinds of features: *explanatory features* (those that explain or justify the holding of a relation) and *common factor features* (those that underpin it as necessary conditions). With this distinction in place, I concede that that although there are conceivable circumstances where it might be rational to bear a relation of prudential concern towards a continuer with whom one is not identical, this does not show that identity is not what—in the explanatory sense—matters.

I suggest that the reason the fission argument seems so compelling is because of its tacit reliance on two ostensibly undeniable principles, the first of which concerns the ranking of preferences, the second of which concerns the assignment of explanatory force. I demonstrate that neither of the principles applies to the fission case in the way that argument requires, because the argument discounts the explanatory role played by contingent features of the way things happen to be. Certain patterns of features that coincide only fortuitously may nonetheless play a central role in the organization of our concepts, and to the extent that imaginary scenarios involve disruptions of these patterns, our first-order judgments about them are often distorted or even inverted.

This example illustrates a larger methodological principle: that where contingent correlations play a central role in our understanding and employment of a concept, and where the concept in question concerns an assessment of value, cases where we "imagine away" such correlations are likely to be uninformative as guides to that concept's application conditions. In such cases, far-fetched imaginary scenarios are likely to evoke intuitions whose significance can be interpreted only with due caution.

This essay and its predecessor—"Exceptional Persons: On the Limits of Imaginary Cases"—form a natural pair. Of the two, this one is more intricate and subtle in its argumentation, and can fruitfully be read as a self-standing essay.

***

This essay was first published in the *Philosophical Quarterly*, 52/206 (2002), 34–54 and is reprinted here with the kind permission of Wiley-Blackwell. The text that appears here differs slightly from the published version, which was shortened somewhat to meet the editorial requirements of the *Philosophical Quarterly*. Nearly all changes involve the reintroduction of material removed from footnotes: these changes are noted as "[*In main text in published version*]" or "[*with original text reinstated*]." In addition, minor typographical and stylistic corrections have been made, an alternative translation of the opening quotation has been used, and bibliographic references have been reformatted to conform with the style of this book. As a result, several footnote numbers have changed. The original number of each footnote is noted in [square brackets].

It is good to know something of the customs of various peoples, so as to judge our own more soundly, and so as not to think that everything that is contrary to our own ways is ridiculous and irrational, as those who have seen nothing of the world ordinarily do. But when one spends too much time travelling eventually one becomes a stranger in one's own country ... Moreover, fables make one imagine many events to be possible which are not so at all ... As a result ... those who regulate their conduct by examples drawn from these works are liable to fall into the excesses of the knights-errant of our tales of chivalry, and conceive plans beyond their powers.

—René Descartes, *Discourse on the Method* (AT VI, I: 6–7; CSM I (1998): 113–14)

1. Introduction

As things stand, fission and fusion and teletransportation are the stuff of science fiction. Non-fictional infants are produced by a well-known sequence of biological processes, and non-fictional adults develop from non-fictional infants by an equally well-known sequence of biological and social processes. Moreover, each non-fictional adult knows that this is how things are: One of the facts of life is that (like storks and unlike in-vitro fertilization) fission and fusion and teletransportation do not play a role in bringing actual persons into being.

Recent philosophical discussions of the nature and value of personal identity, however, have tended to treat these "facts of life" as *provincial* truths—as facts about persons-as-they-happen-to-be, not facts about persons-as-they-really-generally-are.[1] And in an effort to avoid making the mistake of "those who have seen nothing of the world," that is, the mistake of taking local customs to be universal practices, appeal is made to imaginary cases—cases that, like experiments, are supposed to help compensate for the often arbitrary ways we come upon information in the world.

My goal in this essay is to explore how such a methodology may run afoul of the following principle: where contingent correlations play a central role in our understanding and employment of a concept, and where the concept in question concerns an assessment of value, cases where we "imagine away" such correlations may be uninformative as guides to that concept's application conditions. The fact that two features coincide in actual cases may mean that there is no straightforward way for us to determine how we would or should respond to either in isolation.

I will explore this general principle by looking at a specific case: Derek Parfit's widely discussed argument concerning the importance of personal identity. What I will argue is that Parfit's argument is unsuccessful because it depends on ignoring the provincial truths about the facts of life adverted to in the opening paragraph—truths that describe the contingent concomitance of a cluster of features that can, in imaginary cases, be conceptually separated. In his discussions of personal identity, Parfit seeks to establish that what ought rationally to matter to us when we consider survival and future well-being is not that *we ourselves* survive, but only that someone exist who is psychologically continuous with us in the right sorts of ways. His methods for doing this involve describing imaginary cases where it seems clear that identity would not be what matters in this way, and arguing that if we are consistent in our commitments, then we ought to conclude that even in actual cases, identity is not what matters.[2]

---

[1] [1, *with original text reinstated*] For example, cf. Shoemaker: "What Mackie and Perry have done is to indicate how personal identity (or copersonality, or psychological unity) are realized in *us*, i.e. in members of our own species. And this does not answer the question 'What does personal identity consist in?' at the level of abstractness at which we want it answered" (Shoemaker and Swinburne 1984: 127). Or again Unger: "[W]hy not stick only to actual cases?...The reason is that this extremely conservative methodology is apt to incur great costs...In attempting to ascribe beliefs to ourselves on the basis of quite limited data, we might wrongly describe our own attitudes" (Unger 1990: 11). Or Nozick: "We...are not so tied to our bodies that we find it impossible to imagine coming to inhabit another. We do not conceive of ourselves as (merely) our particular bodies, as inextricably tied to them" (Nozick 1981: 30).

[2] [2, *with original text reinstated*] Parfit repeatedly speaks of his conclusion as being that *"personal identity is not what matters"* (e.g. Parfit 1984/1987: 255, italics in original). Though I will argue below that the expression "what matters" is ambiguous in certain ways, for the time being I will take it as a place-holder. In any case, it is clear that Parfit takes his conclusion to apply generally; for instance, he writes: "By considering these cases, we discover what we believe to be involved in our continued existence...Though our beliefs are revealed most clearly when we consider imaginary cases, these beliefs also cover actual cases, and our own lives" (Parfit 1984/1987: 200).

If I am right, however, Parfit's conclusion can be blocked without denying that he has presented an imaginary case where prudential concern would be rational in the absence of identity.[3] If, as I will argue, the feature that explains or justifies a relation can be distinct from those features that underpin it as necessary conditions, then we can accept that there could be cases of the sort Parfit describes, without taking them to have the implications that he takes them to have.

In the first large section, I present Parfit's argument and identify three crucial assumptions that underlie his reasoning.[4]

Intrinsicness Principle (for M): The relation that matters for rational prudential concern M—is an intrinsic relation.[5]

Necessity Principle: If A's prudential concern for B is rational, then the relation that matters for rational prudential concern (M) holds between A and B.

Sufficiency Principle: If the relation that matters for rational prudential concern (M) holds between A and B, then A's prudential concern for B is rational.

Together, these principles generate a particular internalist commitment: they imply that there is a certain relation (M) that is both necessary and sufficient for rational prudential concern (of A for B), a relation whose obtaining depends only on facts about A and B and the resulting relations between them. What I try to show is that this commitment is reasonable on one understanding of what M involves, but not on another, and that Parfit's argument rests on an equivocation between the two senses.

The first sense of M in which we might be interested is this: we might be interested in finding whichever relation is common to all (possible) cases where rational prudential concern obtains. Call this the *common factor* sense. But there is also a second sense of M in which we might be interested: we might be interested in finding the relation that *explains* why rational prudential concern obtains. Call this the *explanatory* sense. Of the three principles just enumerated (the Intrinsicness, Necessity, and Sufficiency Principles), all three are true when we are interested

---

[3] [*In main text in published version*] I follow the recent personal identity literature in using "prudential concern" as a term of art referring to the sort of concern that we bear towards our future selves. In so doing, I do not mean to deny that we might—in the ordinary sense of the term—have prudential concern for others, such as our children or our friends. (Cf. also Schechtman 1990, 1996; Velleman 1996; Whiting 1986; Wolf 1986.)

[4] [*Note added in 2009*: In the discussion below, the Intrinsicness Principle is sometimes referred to as *Premise (b)*, the Necessity Principle as *Principle (c)*, and the Sufficiency Principle as *Principle (d)*.]

[5] [4] Like others in the personal identity literature, I rely here on an informal notion of intrinsicness: cf. Wiggins's *only a and b rule* (Wiggins 1980: 96); Noonan's *only x and y principle* (Noonan 1989: 16); Nozick's relevance principle (Nozick 1981: 31); and Parfit's "Intrinsicness of Personal Identity Principle" (Parfit 1984/1987: 267).

in M in the first—common factor—sense.[6] But if we are interested in M in the second—explanatory—sense, neither the Intrinsicness Principle nor the Necessity Principle is true. Part of the apparent success of Parfit's argument can be attributed to a failure to make this distinction. I address this in §2.

But while making this distinction allows us to see a certain conceptual possibility, it doesn't seem to capture much about why the argument *feels* so convincing. My aim in the remainder of the article is to diagnose the source of its apparent persuasiveness, and to show that this appearance is misleading. I do so by suggesting that the reasoning on which Parfit depends rests on a seemingly undeniable principle of rationality—what Mill (1843) called the *Method of Agreement*. The Method of Agreement says roughly that if there is a single feature whose presence or absence directly correlates with the presence or absence of the phenomenon under scrutiny, then it is that feature that underlies the obtaining of the phenomenon. Without denying the general legitimacy of this form of reasoning, I suggest that it is misapplied in Parfit's case. For when we are concerned with grounds for explanation (as opposed to necessary and sufficient conditions), and where one of the competing explanations is a special case of the other, Mill's test is irredeemably inconclusive. But, I go on to argue, there is a second test we can use to decide between the two explanations—a test that I call the Association-Dependence test—that tells in favor of my interpretation rather than Parfit's. I present my negative argument against Parfit in §§3 and 4, and the positive argument for my own view in §5.

2. The Argument and its Crucial Assumptions

2.1. Parfit's Fission Argument

Parfit's familiar fission argument can be reconstructed as follows.[7] Imagine three triplets who are involved in an accident in which the body of one—call him Brainy—is fatally injured, while the brains of his two brothers are totally destroyed. Brainy is such that the physical bases for his psychological characteristics are realized in duplicate, one complete set in each lobe. Following the accident, doctors divide his brain in half, and transplant the two hemispheres into the bodies of the two brothers.

In the first scenario, which we might call the "single-transfer case," only the left transplant takes, and the right transplant is destroyed. The resulting

---

[6] [5] In the interests of simplicity, I am assuming that M is believed to obtain iff M obtains (this bears on the truth of Sufficiency). I am also assuming that disjunctions of intrinsic relations are themselves intrinsic (this bears on the truth of the Intrinsicness Principle if we allow that M may be disjunctive).

[7] [6] Cf. Parfit's canonical presentation of the case at Parfit 1984/1987: 254–5. I am granting for the sake of argument that the scenario described is coherent.

individual, whom we will call Lefty,[8] has all of Brainy's memories and psychological states and a body almost indistinguishable from the one that Brainy had before the accident. Parfit holds, and for the sake of argument we will grant him that:

(1)   In the single-transfer case, Lefty *is* Brainy.[9]

Given this, along with the principle that:

(2)   If A is identical to B, then the relation that matters for rational prudential concern (M) holds between A and B,

it follows trivially that:

(3)   In the single-transfer case, M holds between Brainy and Lefty.

This process of reasoning is intended to establish a base case for an argument from parity. The parity argument concerns a second scenario, which we might call the "double-transfer case." In the double-transfer case, *both* transplants are successful. *Each* of the two resulting individuals—we'll call them Lefty and Righty—has all of Brainy's memories and psychological states and a body almost indistinguishable from the one that Brainy had before the accident. Parfit points out that:

(4)   Brainy's relation to Lefty is intrinsically the same in the single- and double-transfer cases.

From (3) and (4) plus:

(5)   *The Intrinsicness Principle (for M)*: M is an intrinsic relation,

it follows that:

(6)   *The Parity Result (for M)*: If M holds between Brainy and Lefty in the single-transfer case, then M holds between Brainy and Lefty in the double-transfer case.

And from (3) and (6) follows:

(7)   M holds between Brainy and Lefty in the double-transfer case.

Now let us grant Parfit that Lefty and Righty are not the same person. (After all, the two occupy distinct spatial locations, undergo different experiences, and

---

[8]   [*In main text in published version*] Note that "Lefty" is not a name; it is an abbreviation for the description "the individual who has Brainy's original left hemisphere." (The same caveat holds, *mutatis mutandis*, for the term "Righty" that is introduced below.)

[9]   [7] For representative challenges, cf. B. Williams 1973, essays 1–5; Thomson 1997; Olson 1997; and many of the contributions to Cockburn 1991.

have no unusual causal effect on one another.) If Lefty and Righty are different people, and "Brainy" refers to a single person,[10] then Lefty and Righty cannot both be identical to Brainy. So:

(8)   In the double-transfer case, Lefty *is not* Brainy.[11]

But since (7) tells us that the relation that matters for rational prudential concern holds between them, it follows that:

(9)   In the double-transfer case, M is not identity.

But M is univocal, so:

(10)   In the single-transfer case, M is not identity.

And, more generally:

(11)   *The Unimportance of Identity Conclusion*: M is not identity.

2.2. Three Crucial Distinctions

Despite its evident clarity, Parfit's argument persuades only by blurring three crucial distinctions, which I discuss in turn in this section. The first is between two sorts of states of affairs: ones where whatever relation it is that "matters" for prudential concern holds between A and B (I'll have more to say about what this means at the end of this subsection), and ones where A's prudential concern for B is rational (in the sense that the norms of rationality permit A to be prudentially concerned for B[12]). In shorthand, I will speak of:

---

[10] [8] For challenges, cf. Lewis 1976, Lewis 1983b; Mills 1993; Noonan 1989: 164–8, 197–8; D. Robinson 1985.

[11] [*Original text reinstated*] Strictly speaking, of course, additional assumptions are required for this step. The simplest argument would make a straightforward appeal to some principle of sufficient reason as follows: Since by stipulation there is no relevant difference between Brainy's left and right lobes, there is no reason that Brainy would be identical with Lefty as opposed to Righty, or with Righty as opposed to Lefty; and since he cannot be identical with both, then he must be identical with neither. (For a rejection of this line of reasoning, cf. Chisholm 1970.) More elaborately, one might proceed by describing *two* versions of the single-transfer case, the first with the right lobe, the second with the left; from this and the fact that Brainy is not identical to both Lefty and Righty, it follows that Brainy in the double-transfer case bears an intrinsic relation like that borne in cases of identity towards at least one person with whom he is not identical.

[12] [9] It being rationally *permissible* for A to be prudentially concerned for B is *prima facie* different from it being rationally *required* for A to be prudentially concerned for B. (I thank Carol Rovane for pressing me on the need to make this distinction.) I suspect that the relation between prudential concern and rationality is such that prudential concern's being rationally permitted is tantamount to its being rationally required, but my argument below is agnostic on this question. (As throughout, "prudential concern" is being used in the sense described in n. 3 above.)

(a) *M(A,B)*: the relation that matters for rational prudential concern holding between A and B

(b) *RPC(A,B)*: A's prudential concern for B being rational

It has generally been assumed that these two relations coincide: that wherever there is RPC (that is, in any case where we are warranted in judging that prudential concern by A for B is rational), there must be M (that is, the relation that matters for prudential concern must obtain between A and B), and wherever there is M (that is, in any case where what matters for prudential concern obtains between A and B), there must be RPC (that is, we must be warranted in judging that prudential concern by A for B is rational). Our second crucial distinction expresses these dependencies:

(c) *The Necessity Principle*: If A's prudential concern for B is rational, then the relation that matters for rational prudential concern holds between A and B; in shorthand: RPC(A,B) → M(A,B).

(d) *The Sufficiency Principle*: If the relation that matters for rational prudential concern holds between A and B, then A's prudential concern for B is rational; in shorthand: M(A,B) → RPC(A,B).

For the remainder of my discussion, I will assume the truth of the Sufficiency Principle: wherever M holds between A and B, A's prudential concern for B is rational. But to say whether I think the Necessity Principle is true, I need to make one final distinction.

"The relation that matters for rational prudential concern" might be taken (granting hyperintensionalism) in at least two ways:

(e) *The Common Factor Reading (for M): the relation that matters for rational prudential concern (M) is some relation that is common to all and only cases where rational prudential concern obtains.*

(f) *The Explanatory Reading (for M): the relation that matters for rational prudential concern (M) is some relation that explains the rationality of prudential concern obtaining in cases where rational prudential concern obtains.*[13]

On the Common Factor Reading (e), the Necessity Principle (c) is trivially true. If "the relation that matters for rational prudential concern" is some relation common to all and only cases where rational prudential concern obtains, then clearly A's prudential concern for B is rational (RPC) only if the relation that matters for rational prudential concern (M) holds between A and B. But

---

[13] [*In main text in published version*] For a rough characterization of what I mean by "explains," see §§3 and 4 below. The distinction between the Common Factor Reading and the Explanatory Reading bears some relation to Aristotle's distinction between efficient and formal cause.

on the Explanatory Reading (f), the connection is not so clear. If "the relation that matters for rational prudential concern" is some relation that *explains* the rationality of prudential concern's obtaining in cases where rational prudential concern obtains, it does not follow—or so I will argue in §5—that A's prudential concern for B is rational only if M holds between them.

2.3. The Intrinsicness Premise

With these distinctions in place, let us return to Parfit's argument. The crucial premise in Parfit's argument is, of course, (5):

The Intrinsicness Principle (for M): M is an intrinsic relation.

It is the Intrinsicness Principle (for M) that allows Parfit to derive (6) the Parity Result (for M), and it is (6) the Parity Result (for M) that allows him to derive (11) the Unimportance of Identity Conclusion.

Parfit's argument goes through if M is understood according to the Common Factor Reading: on that reading the Intrinsicness Principle is true, the Parity Result follows, and the Unimportance of Identity Conclusion is thereby established. But for Parfit's purposes, the Common Factor reading is inadequate. On this reading, the Unimportance of Identity Conclusion says merely that identity is not common to all cases where there is rational prudential concern. But Parfit needs more than this: If we respond to the case in the way he expects, he thinks we should change our views about what underpins *our* prudential concern for our future selves. To show this he needs to show that identity does not *explain* the rationality of prudential concern. But when M is understood in this sense, I will contend, the Intrinsicness Principle is false. (I will argue for this in the sections that follow.) And if this is so, then Parfit's argument has not succeeded in showing what it has been taken to show.

2.4. Summary

Parfit's goal is to show that "personal identity is not what matters" or, in our terms, that the relation that matters for rational prudential concern (M) is not identity. He seeks to do this by presenting a case—the double-transfer case— where it seems that what matters for rational prudential concern is present, while identity is absent. And if the former can obtain without the latter, then identity cannot be what matters for rational prudential concern.

I have suggested a number of distinctions that need to be drawn in evaluating the force of this argument. I have pointed out that we need to separate questions about the relation I have been calling RPC (the relation that holds when A's prudential concern for B is rational) from questions about the relation which I have been calling M (the relation that matters for rational prudential concern). And I have pointed out that M can be understood on either a Common Factor or an Explanatory Reading, and claimed that if Parfit wishes to establish the conclusion he does, then we need to understand M according to the Explanatory Reading.

With these distinctions in place, I have suggested, we can diagnose part of the force of Parfit's argument. Fission does describe a case in which Brainy bears a relation of rational prudential concern (RPC) for a continuer with whom he is not identical. And if RPC is necessary and sufficient for M, then if we grant (as I am willing to do) that the Intrinsicness Principle is true for RPC, Parfit's argument goes through. But, I will argue, RPC is necessary and sufficient for M only on the Common Factor Reading, not on the Explanatory Reading. I hypothesize that the argument's apparent undeniability comes from a failure to make these distinctions. It is because we fail to see that RPC and M could come apart in the way that I am suggesting that Parfit's conclusion seems mandatory.

3. Why is the Fission Argument So Compelling?

3.1. Diagnosis

But what explains our failure to see this? Why are we so convinced that M and RPC must co-vary—even once we have distinguished the Common Factor and Explanatory readings? Why does the Necessity Principle seem so hard to reject?

I think the answer can be traced to a tendency to misapply an otherwise legitimate principle of scientific reasoning that Mill, in his *System of Logic* (1843), called the *Method of Agreement*. Mill's principle says that: "If two or more instances of the phenomenon under investigation have only one circumstance in common, the circumstance in which alone all the instances agree, is the cause (or effect) of the given phenomenon" (Mill 1843/1963–71: vii. 390). The principle is often generalized to cover phenomena other than cause and effect, and it is a cousin of Mill's principle that concerns us here. Following Mill, the principle might be put as follows: "If two or more instances of the phenomenon under investigation have only one circumstance in common, the circumstance in which alone all the instances agree is the *explanation* for the given phenomenon." It is to this principle that I think we tacitly appeal when we are convinced that M and RPC must co-vary. But this principle, as I will argue below, cannot be straightforwardly applied to Parfit's case.

3.2. The Appeal of the Principle

It is worth spending a moment getting clear on why Mill's principle seems so central to scientific reasoning. Take a simple causal case. Suppose that whenever I strike a match against the side of a matchbox and say "let there be light," the match bursts into flame; whenever I strike a match against the side of a matchbox and say nothing, the match bursts into flame; whenever I simply hold the match in the air and say "let there be light," the match remains unlit; and whenever I neither strike the match nor recite the incantation, the match remains unlit.[14] That is:

Match-and-Incantation Case:

A = strike match against box

B = utter "let there be light"

P = match bursts into flame

	A	**Not-A**
B	P	Not-P
Not-B	P	Not-P

A quick glance at the chart reveals that P obtains when and only when A obtains, and that the obtaining of P is indifferent to the obtaining of B. Assuming certain conditions—that A and B are the only relevant factors in this case; that A brings about P in the same way in the A-alone case and in the A-plus-B case; that A, B, and P are specified at commensurate levels of description, etc.—this pattern gives us reason to conclude that A explains the obtaining of P, and that B does not. Unless we are inclined to serious skepticism, it seems irrational to insist that it is the incantation, or even the incantation-plus-striking, that explains the match's bursting into flame.

3.3. Fission and the Method of Agreement

We are now in a position to state more precisely what goes awry in the Parfit case, namely, that those who find themselves compelled by his argument mistakenly assimilate it to something like the match-and-incantation case. So let me present the case in the way that I think they see it, and then explain why I think the analogy fails.

Our discussion here will be helped by the introduction of a few terms of art. Parfit uses the expression *Relation R* to refer to the relation that obtains between X and Y in all (real and imaginary) cases where X's prudential concern for Y is rationally warranted—the Common Factor of my discussion above.[14] (Let us

---

[14] [*In main text in published version*] My argument is indifferent to the particular features of this relation, but it may be helpful to the reader to know that Parfit characterizes Relation R as "psychological continuity with the right sort of cause" (Parfit 1984/1987: 215).

grant, if only for the sake of argument, that personal identity over time can be analyzed as the non-branching holding of Relation R: Y is identical to X if X is R-related to Y, and X is not R-related to any non-Y that co-exists with Y.[15]) I conceded in §2 that whenever both Relation R and absence-of-competitors obtain (that is, wherever X and Y are identical), rational prudential concern is warranted. And I also conceded there that in the two-sided case—where Relation R obtains without the absence of a competitor—rational prudential concern may well be warranted. Moreover, I will also concede that rational prudential concern is never warranted in the absence of R. That is:

Fission Case:

A = Relation R obtains between X and Y

B = Relation R does not obtain between X and any non-Y that co-exists with Y

P = X's prudential concern for Y is rational

	A	Not-A
B	P	Not-P
Not-B	P	Not-P

As in the match-and-incantation case, P obtains when and only when A obtains; and as in the match-and-incantation case, the obtaining of P is indifferent to the obtaining of B, in the sense that B's presence is neither necessary nor sufficient for the obtaining of P. As before, assuming (for the time being) certain conditions—that A and B are the only relevant factors in this case; that A brings about P in the same way in the A-alone case and in the A-plus-B case; that A, B, and P are specified at commensurate levels of description; etc.—this pattern seems to give us reason to conclude that it is A (in contrast to B, or to A-and-B) that explains the obtaining of P. To quote Parfit: "In all ordinary cases, personal identity and [R] coincide. When they diverge, [R] is what matters. That strongly suggests that, in all cases, [R] is what matters . . . If, when two facts come apart, one of them is what matters, why think the *other* is what matters when they coincide?" (Parfit, personal correspondence).

---

[15] *[In main text in published version]* As the reader will recognize, I am skating over delicate metaphysical issues here. I beg indulgence on the grounds that my main goal is to make a fairly general point about methodology.

3.4. Disanalogies

There are at least three specific ways in which the fission case differs from the match-and-incantation case that are relevant to whether the method of agreement can be properly employed: these concern *subject-matter, internal structure,* and *background conditions.*[16]

(a) *Subject-matter*: In the match-and-incantation case we are concerned with *causal* explanation, whereas in the fission case we are concerned with the explanation of *value*.

(b) *Internal structure*: In the match-and-incantation case there are two independent features at play whose relative contributions we are trying to deduce, whereas in the fission case the competing explanations are A and A-plus-B, where A-plus-B is a *specification* of A (being a unique R-related continuer is a *way* of being an R-related continuer).

(c) *Background conditions*: In the match-and-incantation case, the factors under scrutiny frequently arise independently, whereas in the fission case we are concerned with a situation where in all actual instances, the factors we are considering coincide.

What I will argue in §4 (employing the very method under discussion) is that it is the conjunction of (a) and (b) that makes the methodology inconclusive in the Parfit case. I will then go on in §5 to discuss the relation of this to (c).

4. Where Does the Analogy Go Awry?

4.1. Explanatory Subject Matter

I note first that the Method of Agreement is perfectly legitimate in cases of evaluative explanation, so long as the factors being disambiguated by its means are genuinely independent. That is, in cases that resemble the fission case as far as (a) is concerned, but resemble the match-and-incantation case as far as (b) and (c) are concerned, there is no problem with using the methodology. Suppose, for instance, we are trying to determine why I love "The Star-Spangled Banner" so much: is it the stirring tune or the inspiring words? And suppose that we conduct a test with the following results:

Star-Spangled Banner Case:

A = X has the same words as "The Star-Spangled Banner"

---

[16] [*In main text in published version*] There is a fourth, more general worry that I have bracketed in the context of this discussion: the worry that the sort of factorization presupposed by this account may not be possible in the case of the concept of personal identity.

B = X has the same tune as "The Star-Spangled Banner"

P = X fills me with admiration, awe, and joy

	A	Not-A
B	P	Not-P
Not-B	P	Not-P

For reasons parallel to those adduced above (that whenever I hear the words I am filled with awe and admiration, regardless of the tune to which they are sung, and that whether the tune inspires such sentiment depends on whether it is sung with those words), it seems reasonable to conclude that what explains my admiration for "The Star-Spangled Banner" are Francis Scott Key's magnificent verses, and not the tune of John Stafford Smith's rousing "To Anacreon in Heaven." Assuming as before that A and B are the only relevant factors in this case, that A brings about P in the same way in the A-alone case and in the A-plus-B case, and that A, B, and P are specified at commensurate levels of description, there is no problem as such with applying the Method of Agreement to cases where what is at issue is the explanation of value.

4.2. Genus–Species

Though certain complications arise, there is also no reason to doubt the general validity of the methodology when we are considering cases that resemble the Match-and-Incantation Case as far as (a) and (c) are concerned, but are like the Parfit case in terms of (b)—that is, cases where the competing explanations are not A and B, but rather A and A-plus-B, and where A and A-plus-B are related as genus and species.

Consider, for instance, the following case:

Boat-Sinking Case 1:

A = X weighs at least 20 pounds

B = X does not have a weight other than 20 pounds

P = placing X on the boat causes the boat to sink

	A	Not-A
B	P	Not-P
Not-B	P	Not-P

The A/B cell tells us that whenever something weighs at least 20 pounds and no weight other than 20 pounds (that is, whenever something weighs exactly 20 pounds), it causes the boat to sink. The A/Not-B cell tells us that whenever something weighs at least 20 pounds and has a weight other than 20 pounds (that is, whenever something weighs more than 20 pounds), it causes the boat to sink. The Not-A/Not-B cell tells us that whenever something does not weigh at least 20 pounds and also has a weight other than 20 pounds (that is, whenever something weighs less than 20 pounds), it does not cause the boat to sink. And the Not-A/B cell tells us that whenever something does not weigh at least 20 pounds and also does not have a weight other than 20 pounds (that is, whenever something has no weight), it does not cause the boat to sink. From this, it seems *ceteris paribus* reasonable to conclude that what causes the boat to sink is an object's weighing at least 20 pounds.

Although it is technically satisfactory, this way of setting up the case clearly feels contrived: where the A-plus-B case is a special instance of the A case (weighing exactly 20 pounds is a special way of weighing at least 20 pounds), shoe-horning it into a fourfold matrix means specifying the B condition in a way that allows it to be vacuously satisfied whenever A does not hold. What this means is that the information that we obtain distinguishes among what intuitively seem to be three—rather than four—possibilities. So we do better to represent the case as follows:

Boat-Sinking Case 2:

A = X weighs at least 20 pounds

C = X weighs exactly 20 pounds

P = placing X on the boat causes the boat to sink

	A	Not-A
C	P	[Empty]
Not-C	P	Not-P

The non-independence of A and C means that this test is less informative than the four-way test; because there is no case where we have C without A, there is no information to be had about what "C alone" contributes. But in the boat-sinking case—and, I hypothesize, in cases of (non-reason-involving) causal explanation in general—this does not undermine the method's reliability. The structure of causal explanation gives us antecedent reason to assume that the way A brings about P in the A-plus-C case is (insofar as sinking is concerned) the same as the way A brings about P in the A-not-C case. Causal explanation presupposes that the general supersedes the particular, and in such cases, the Method of Agreement provides us with reliable grounds for taking one or another feature as explanatory.

4.3. "Borrowed Luster"

By contrast, reason-explanation has no such presupposition, and as a result, cases that fall at the intersection of those discussed in §§4.1 and 4.2—where value-explanatory subject-matter is combined with genus–species inner-struc-ture—are ill-suited to investigation by the Method of Agreement. For the Meth-od is ineffective in cases involving what I will call "borrowed luster"—where both pure and impure instances of a phenomenon are accorded the same assessment because impure instances are treated as relevantly similar to pure ones. An example may make this clearer.

Suppose that we venerate regular geometrical figures for their beauty, but that certain approximations of regular figures also produce the same veneration by resembling the ideal. In such circumstances, we might portray the situation as follows:

Square Case:

A = X is square-like

C = X is square[17]

P = X is an appropriate target of geometrical veneration

	A	Not-A
C	P	[Empty]
Not-C	P	Not-P

---

[17] [11] Note that we could represent this as a four-way matrix if we define B as: "X lacks all non-square geometric features." In this case, the matrix will be filled out as in the match-and-incantation, fission, and boat-sinking 1 cases. As in the boat-sinking case, the B-not-A case will be satisfied only by things to which A fails to apply: whatever lacks all non-square geometric features without being square-like will lack all square-like features whatsoever.

What the chart reveals is that whenever something is square-like, it is an appropriate target of geometrical veneration, and whenever something is not square-like, it is not an appropriate target of geometrical veneration; whether or not it is actually square has no bearing on its suitability as an object of geometrical veneration. But from this we are not entitled to conclude that it is square-likeness rather than squareness that explains the appropriateness of geometrical veneration; as I stipulated in the formulation of the case, what explains appropriate geometrical veneration is regularity—and approximate squares come to be appropriate objects of geometrical veneration by way of resemblance to the ideal.

The reason for this is that in borrowed luster cases, one of the antecedent conditions for application of the Method is not satisfied: the way that A brings about P in the A-plus-C case is different from the way that A brings about P in the A-not-C case. When I venerate a perfect square, its square-like features (A) cause me to venerate it (P) because of their resemblance to a feature that it has— squareness. But when I venerate a merely approximate square, its square-like features (A) cause me to venerate it (P) because of their resemblance to a feature that it lacks—squareness.

Lest you think this case is anomalous, I offer three additional cases that I have found different readers to find differentially persuasive.[18] The cases are presented somewhat sketchily—their purpose is just to make clear the range of instances where the phenomenon in question seems to arise.[19]

Dead Body Case:

A = X is a human body

C = X is a living human body

P = X is an appropriate object of respect (*qua* body)

Stuffed-Animal Case:

A = X has the appearance of a baby seal

C = X is a baby seal

P = X is something that should not be hurled across the room

---

[18] [12] One might think of these as being cases involving what Robert Nozick has called "symbolic utility"—cf. Nozick 1993, esp. 26–35. [*Added in 2009*: Presumably, one of the mechanisms by which the borrowed luster cases gain their currency is our inevitable tendency to form the sorts of associations that underlie the attitude I call *alief*. For further discussion of this issue, see Gendler 2008a, 2008b; Chs. 13 and 14 below.]

[19] [13] As before, these cases can be represented on a four-way matrix with B-conditions roughly like the following: Dead Body Case: B = "X is living"; Stuffed-Animal Case: B = "X has an internal structure appropriate to the kind that it appears to be"; Vegetarianism Case: B = "X is an instance of what it resembles." (In order to provide clean "no" answers to the B-not-A case, corresponding modifications will need to be made to the characterization of P.)

Vegetarianism Case:

A = X resembles a piece of meat that comes from a cow subjected to conditions of factory-farming

C = X is a piece of meat that comes from a cow subjected to conditions of factory-farming

P = X is something that should not be eaten by me

	A	Not-A
C	P	[Empty]
Not-C	P	Not-P

I do not deny that objections can be raised for each of these particular cases: that the degree of respect required (*qua* body) may be higher in the case of a living body than a dead one; that things in general should not be hurled across the room so *a fortiori* stuffed seals should not; and so on. In each case, I suspect that appropriate modifications could be made so as to retain the larger point; but in each instance, this would be at the expense of presenting the cases schematically.

At any rate, resistance to the details of one or another particular case should not get in the way of understanding that which they are intended to illustrate. The principle that lies behind borrowed luster cases is that when we are concerned with the explanation of value, it is possible to "cantilever" out from central or ideal cases (perfect squares, living bodies, real baby seals, factory-farmed meat) to peripheral cases (approximate squares, dead bodies, stuffed baby seals, non-factory-farmed meat) in a way that the Method of Agreement is indifferent to. In short: the Method cannot tell us whether it is the special case that explains the general one, or *vice versa*—and, I have argued, there are cases where the former rather than the latter holds.

5. The Positive Argument

5.1. The Association-Dependence Test

As far as the Method of Agreement is concerned, then, we seem to be at an impasse; Parfit's argument is inconclusive, and we have understood why. But thus far, I have offered no reason to think that *Relation R*'s underpinning of prudential concern is the result of borrowed luster. And without such an argument, I can do no better than parity.

I suggest that there is a second test that can help us to distinguish between cases where it is A (the general case) that explains our evaluation of C (the special case), and cases where it is C (the special case) that explains our evaluation of A (the general case). I call this the *Association-Dependence Test*: Suppose we had no sense that there could be cases like the special case—would there still be P in the general case? If so, then it is the general case that is explanatory; if not, then it is the special case that does the explanatory work.

Consider the borrowed luster cases just described. Suppose we had no sense that there could be squares—would square-like objects evoke the same sort of geometric veneration? Suppose we had no sense that there could be live animals as well as stuffed ones—would stuffed animals still evince respect? Suppose we had no sense that there could be factory-farmed meat—would meat in general still merit the same sort of moral avoidance? And so on. In each of these cases, the Association-Dependence Test suggests that it is the particular rather than the general feature that plays the explanatory role in our evaluation of the case. By contrast, applying the test to the Boat-Sinking Case produces no such result: suppose we had no sense that there could be objects weighing exactly 20 pounds—would objects weighing at least 20 pounds still cause the boat to sink?

5.2. The Non-Irrationality of Associative Valuation

Before turning to the question of how the Association-Dependence test fares in the case of personal identity, I need quickly to fend off a worry about rationality. If I wouldn't treat non-factory-farmed meat with moral disapprobation in the case where I am unaware of the existence of factory-farmed meat, how can it be rational for me to do so in the actual case?

The answer relies on the assumption that rationality for finite beings allows us to navigate the world on the basis of imperfect rules. Because of our finitude, it is not irrational to treat one subclass of cases like a larger class of cases, or vice versa, even when the subclass or larger class lacks precisely the feature that determines our evaluation of the case to which it is being assimilated. The cases may be intrinsically identical, making differential treatment practically or theoretically prohibitive. And classification of individual actions into more significant rules-of-action may make it possible for us to achieve outcomes we might otherwise find unachievable. No particular instance of eating a piece of chocolate cake is going to make me overweight, but the best way for me to achieve my dietary goals is to adopt a general rule of no cake-eating; no particular instance of giving into whining is going to spoil my child, but the best way for me to achieve my parental goals is to adopt a general rule of not acceding to whined requests.[20] And this may be so even if eating this particular piece of cake, or giving into this particular instance of whining would actually promote my ultimate goals more effectively. So too might it be rational for me to respond in the same way to all pieces of meat—even though some of the actual instances may not have resulted from factory-farming, and even though in the counter-factual case where there is no factory farming, I would treat pieces of meat with a non-factory-farming causal history very differently than I treat them in the actual case.

5.3. Application to the Personal Identity Case

How, though, does all of this apply to the personal identity case? The suggestion is this: suppose we had no sense that there could be identity as opposed to mere R-relatedness—would there still be such a thing as prudential concern? I suggest that the answer is "no." The concept of prudential concern is tied up with concepts of fairness, responsibility, justice, and rationality. Our views about the sorts of rational and moral obligations we have to ourselves and others considered as beings who exist through time rest on the assumption that each of us will have at most one continuer, and that that continuer is someone with whom we will be identical.[21] Disruption of this background assumption would result in disruption of the entire framework by which we make sense of this wide range of concepts. And to the extent that prudential concern is interconnected with them, it too would be disrupted.[22]

Evidence for this comes from the fact that even in fission worlds, it is unique and not mere R-relatedness that plays a central role in grounding prudential concern from the fission point onwards. Barring repeated instances of fission, Lefty and Righty will be strictly identical to anyone to whom they bear a relation of rational prudential concern; admitting multiple instances of fission, the entire framework of prudential concern begins to break down.[23]

---

[20] [14] I have been helped in my thinking here by Robert Nozick's discussion of principles in Nozick 1993, esp. ch. 1. [*Added in 2009*: Clearly, a similar issue arises in the discussion of act vs. rule utilitarianism. For an overview with references, see Sinnott-Armstrong 2008b.]

[21] [15] Although the focus of my discussion has been on fission cases, note that fusion raises corresponding worries from the opposite direction: agency presupposes a tight connection between intention and action that fusion disrupts. [*Added in 2009*: For a particularly interesting and subtle discussion of the relation between agency and personhood in fission and fusion cases, see Rovane 1998; for some reflections on Rovane's views, see Gendler 2002a.]

[22] [16] For discussion of some of these issues, cf. C. Diamond 1991; Korsgaard 1989; Rovane 1990 and 1998; Whiting 1986; and Wolf 1986; cf. also the discussion of dignity in Velleman 1999.

[23] [17, *with original text reinstated*] One might think that all I have shown is that what matters is R-relatedness plus uniqueness-at-a-time, and not identity as such. (Sydney Shoemaker has raised this objection in conversation; a similar case is described in Raymond Martin's "Fission Rejuvenation" (Martin 1995).) Imagine a world in which everyone undergoes fission at the age of 20, but where one of the resulting survivors always dies within a few days (Shoemaker's case),

So, I suggest, R-relatedness fails the Association-Dependence test, while identity passes: if all cases of continuation were cases of identity, prudential concern for R-related continuers would be rational; if all cases of continuation were cases of mere R-relatedness, we would lose a grip on the (relevant) concept of prudential concern.[24]

5.4. Exceptions, Norms, and Local Adaptation

Nonetheless, as I have maintained throughout, Parfit is right that were Brainy to undergo fission, the relation of prudential concern that he would find himself bearing to Lefty and to Righty would be rational—even if he knew that he was to undergo fission. Where Parfit goes wrong is in his proffered explanation. I contend that the reason it is rational for Brainy to bear prudential concern for Lefty and for Righty is that *being R-related is very much like being identical*. So the interpretation of the exceptional case is parasitic on the interpretation of the normal cases from which it deviates. To the extent that we are able to account for the exceptional case, our accounting takes the form of a sort of *local adaptation*; we maintain our background assumptions about continuation in general, and adapt our standard responses to the case at hand.

There is reason to think this phenomenon of local adaptation is quite general. Consider, for example, what has happened to the concept of motherhood in the face of recent technological advances. As it has become possible to implant the egg of one woman into the uterus of another, a previously unnoticed distinction has been drawn between *genetic mother* on the one hand, and *birth*

---

or where one of the survivors is put into a comatose state, and "awakened" only upon the death of the other (Martin's case).

It seems plausible to say of such a world: (a) that there would be prudential concern, and (b) that as a rule, this prudential concern would not have to be for someone with whom one was identical. This seems to show that what matters is being the currently unique long-term survivor (and not being identical). It seems to me that the correct sort of reply to these cases comes in two parts, which together show that the more compelled one is to accept (a), the less compelled one is to accept (b) and vice versa. In sketch form, the argument might go as follows. Case 1: If the example supposes that the quick death or coordinated coma of one of the fission products is guaranteed by certain sorts of laws that govern the imagined world, it seems plausible to say that pre-'fission' persons are identical to their post-'fission' survivors. Their way of surviving over time differs from what we would consider normal, but the logic of identity continues to govern the relations in question, and so (b) can be denied. Case 2: If, on the other hand, there is the always-present but never-realized live possibility of multiple-continuation, then I think the concept of prudential concern would begin to break down, for the reasons discussed in the text above.

[24] [18, *with original text reinstated*] Something like this seems to be what McDowell is suggesting when he writes: "According to the view I recommend, a context of facts about the objective continuation of lives helps to make intelligible a face-value construal of what Locke actually says, that continuous 'consciousness' presents an identity through time" (McDowell 1997: 234). Cf. also Johnston 1987, 1989, 1992, and 1997, which have greatly influenced my own views on these matters.

mother on the other.[25] Since the cases are exceptional, there has been an effort to "save" the original concept; and since it is the egg-donor whose genetic information is carried on to the child, it is the birth mother who has been given the status of *surrogate*. But were the practice to become widespread, the concept of motherhood would break down entirely. We would no longer have the idea of filial concern for one's mother as such, because there would be no unitary concept of *mother* that lay behind it. We might well have two similar concepts—filial concern for one's birth mother and filial concern for one's genetic mother; and we might well think these concepts were more similar to one another than either one would be to the concept of concern for one's child, or one's spouse, or one's sibling. But I think that in such circumstances, the concept of maternal–filial concern *simpliciter* would have no application.

Similarly, I suggest, in a world where R-relatedness without identity was the norm, there would not be a concept of prudential concern of the sort Parfit needs for his argument to succeed. There might be a somewhat similar concept, such as the concept of concern-for-one's-R-related-continuer. But there is reason to think that it would not be the same concept as the one we have, the concept that describes the relation we bear to our future selves. In such a world, Brainy's relation to Lefty in both the single-transfer and double-transfer cases would indeed contain what matters for concern-for-one's-R-related-continuer. But the relations would not contain what matters for prudential concern, because there wouldn't *be* prudential concern in the relevant sense.

Now, if we say, as I have been arguing, that *identity* is what matters in the explanatory sense, then we have some way to account for the fact that our concepts might well change in the face of such a global disruption.[26] But the same option is not available if we say that what matters is R-relatedness. If it is (mere) R-relatedness that explains our valuation of identity, rather than the other way around, then the global replacement of identity by mere R-relatedness should make no difference to the value we place on the relation we bear to our continuers. If we follow Parfit in accepting that what matters for prudential concern in the explanatory sense is not identity, we have no way to account for the fact that prudential concern as we know it might not exist under the conditions I described.

---

[25] [19, *with original text reinstated*] Consider the following parody of a new-age greeting card, taken from *The New York Times* Sunday Magazine (Rubiner 1996: 60, with original line-breaks altered):

YOU'RE SOMEONE SPECIAL

   Mom . . . Gee, it feels funny to call you that. But after all, you are the woman who brought me to term. And even though it was "just a job," I feel as though we have a lasting bond.

   I know it can't have been easy carrying around someone else's baby, especially a big eater like me! So I just want to say, thanks for being my birth mother!

The time we spent together will always mean something special to me.

For even more extreme cases, see Silver 1997, esp. 155–229.

[26] [*In main text in published version*] Note that even if only this weaker claim is true—that there *might not be* a concept of prudential concern, my argument still goes through.

If, however, we maintain that what matters for prudential concern *is* identity, then we are able to account for such a potential disruption. By properly recognizing the way in which contingent features play a role in the organization of our concepts, and the way in which exceptions of this sort depend on a background of normal cases, we are able to account for the case with appropriate provincialism, and not to "fall into the excesses of the knights-errant of our tales of chivalry" (Descartes AT VI, I: 7; CSM I (1998): 114).

6. Conclusion

6.1. Summary

I began this article by suggesting that there is a danger to philosophical inquiry that ignores what I have been calling the facts of life. That human beings come into existence only through the predictable sequence of events mentioned in the opening paragraph is one of the background truths against which we organize our concepts. At the same time, it seems possible that there could be circumstances—fission is one—where a process that is ordinarily identity-preserving would turn out to be entity-creating. That is, it seems possible that there could be a process with the following character: if it happened in one way (what we have been calling the "single-transfer case") it would result in the continued existence of some entity over time; but if it happened in another way (what we have been calling the "double-transfer case") it would result in the creation of two new entities.[27] But if the entities in question are self-conscious, as human beings are, then this possibility raises the following puzzle: To the extent that the process itself would—intrinsically—be the same in both cases, how could the rationality of one's attitude towards one's continuer depend on whether the process ended up being identity-preserving, or whether it ended up producing two new human beings? Presumably one's attitude towards one's continuer would—rationally—be the same in both the single-transfer and the double-transfer case. And with this much, I said I agree.

The question that has concerned me in this chapter has been the question of what lessons can be drawn from this fact. Parfit contends that from it, we can conclude that what makes my prudential concern for myself tomorrow rational is not the fact that myself-tomorrow will (presumably) be identical to myself-today, but only that she will be connected to me by the right sort of causal process that will result in the right sort of relation of psychological continuity and connectedness. I have tried to show that this conclusion can be blocked. I pointed out that Parfit's reasoning rests on what I have called the Intrinsicness

---

[27] [*In main text in published version*] Of course, part of what is at issue is whether it is correct to describe the cases as involving the "same process." But I trust that despite the sloppiness of my language, my meaning is clear.

Principle (for M), the implicit endorsement of which can be traced to a failure to see that two relations need not coincide. This failure to see that RPC can obtain without M (that is: the failure to see that A's prudential concern for B may be rational, even if the relation that matters for rational prudential concern does not hold between them) can be traced to two things: (a) the fact that an analogous Intrinsicness Principle is true for RPC; and (b) the fact that what I called the Necessity Principle (that RPC cannot obtain without M) seems undeniable. But the intuitive force of the Necessity Principle can be traced to a fallacious view of how broadly Mill's Method of Agreement can be informatively applied. While the Method of Agreement is a valuable tool when we are concerned with causal explanation, it cannot be straightforwardly employed in certain cases of explaining value. In such cases, the Necessity Principle is false, along with the Intrinsicness Principle (for M).

What this means is that Parfit's argument shows much less than he takes it to show. It shows only that there are conceivable circumstances where it might be rational to bear a relation of prudential concern towards a continuer with whom one was not identical. But it does not show that identity is not what—in the explanatory sense—matters.

6.2. Larger Lessons

Although most of my argument has focused on a single example, I take my discussion to have general implications. In the case I described, we are asked to consider a scenario in which a pair of features that coincide in all actual situations are imaginatively separated, and to make a judgment about which of the two features has conceptual primacy. I have argued that the proper interpretation of the case may be precisely the opposite of what it has generally been taken to be. And I think the reason its implications have been so misunderstood is this: certain patterns of features that coincide only fortuitously may nonetheless play a central role in the organization of our concepts. To the extent that imaginary scenarios involve disruptions of these patterns, our first-order judgments about them may be distorted or even inverted.[28]

[28] [20] *Acknowledgements*: I owe thanks to Robert Nozick, Hilary Putnam, and especially Derek Parfit for extensive discussion of the original version of this paper, the core idea of which originally appeared in a chapter of my 1996 dissertation. For comments on early drafts, I am also grateful to Richard Boyd, Michael Della Rocca, Terence Irwin, Mohammed Ali Khalidi, Norman Kretzmann, Scott MacDonald, Elijah Millgram, Carol Rovane, Sydney Shoemaker, Susanna Siegel, Jason Stanley, Zoltán Gendler Szabó, Jennifer Whiting, and extremely helpful audiences at Harvard (1996), Cornell (1998), and Syracuse (1998) Universities. For valuable discussion of the ideas contained in more recent drafts (2000), special thanks are due to John Hawthorne, Ted Sider, and Zoltán Gendler Szabó.

5

The Real Guide to Fake Barns: A Catalogue of Gifts for Your Epistemic Enemies

According to Wikipedia

Show, don't tell is an admonition to fiction writers to write in a manner that allows the reader to experience the story through a character's action, words, thoughts, senses, and feelings rather than through the narrator's exposition, summarization, and description.

In this chapter, we attempt to show (as opposed to tell) the reader that a particular intuition that has played a central role in discussions of epistemology for roughly a quarter century is highly unstable. The larger lesson is a self-referential one: if the essay succeeds, this shows (in the relevant sense) the value of its own methodology.

As will quickly become clear, the discussion presupposes the reader's familiarity with a particular literature in Anglo-American epistemology. Those who find themselves disoriented might begin by reading Alvin Goldman's widely reprinted article "Discrimination and Perceptual Knowledge" (1976), in which the original "fake barn" case is presented, and then glance through the responses to it that can be found in any of the standard late twentieth-century epistemology anthologies.[1]

Alternatively, those perplexed by the essay's jokes (including this one) might try consulting "The Real Guide to 'The Real Guide to Fake Barns'," publication information for which can be found in "The Real Guide to Real Guides" (Meinong Press).

***

This essay was co-authored with John Hawthorne and was first published in *Philosophical Studies*, 124 (2005), 331–52. It is reprinted with the kind permission of Springer's Science and Business Media. The text that appears here is unchanged except for a few small stylistic alterations and typographical corrections, the incorporation of bibliographical footnotes into the main text, and the relocation and reconfiguration of a couple of contentful footnotes. As a result, several footnote numbers have changed; the original number of each footnote is noted in [square brackets].

---

[1] [*Note added in* 2009: Two particularly comprehensive volumes are Sosa and Kim 2000 and Bernecker and Dretske 2000.]

Recently, we have come across a top-secret document from the Council of Intuition Adjudicators (CIA). The document reports a series of troubling developments, all stemming from efforts to exploit patented knowledge-prevention technology developed at the University of Michigan in the mid-1970s (Goldman 1976). Whereas traditional efforts in this area had focused on preventing knowledge by preventing belief—and hence had fallen afoul of Federal Belief Intervention (FBI) guidelines—this new generation of products is in full conformity with FBI regulations; just as neutron bombs kill while leaving buildings intact, these products prevent knowledge without affecting beliefs.

Early reports suggested that the dangers of such weapons could be safely contained: Intuitions concerning their effects seemed relatively stable, and principled articulations of the circumstances under which they were effective seemed possible. But the recently discovered CIA document confirms the growing suspicion of many that such ease of containment was merely an illusion. Rather, it seems, to stop the deployment of such weapons we need to make appeal to some of the most dreaded resources in the CIA arsenal: challenging the reliability of certain widely held intuitions about particular cases, or perhaps even challenging the systematicity of intuitions in this realm as a whole.

Below, we reproduce the CIA document in full.

To: Council of Intuition Adjudicators (CIA) Epistemic Agents
From: Agent 11.18.1976
As all of you know, for many years we have been coming across various shady catalogues offering a wide range of products designed to prevent knowledge without preventing belief. But few of us had taken seriously the threat that they seem to pose. Recently, however, we have undertaken a systematic exploration of these documents—and have come to a rather pessimistic conclusion: rather than following along principled lines, intuitions about these cases seem wildly unstable and case-dependent.

Below, we reproduce a number of original documents revealing this unsettling history.

1. Background

Until quite recently, most catalogues offered only products such as the following:

Exhibit One: Cardboard Building Advertisement from *Let's Get Real* (a catalogue directed at real estate agents seeking to prevent competitors from knowing about various buildings in their neighborhoods). (Case codename "ORIGINAL BARN")

Since their introduction in 1976, our cardboard buildings have set the "Goldman standard" for facsimile edifices. Widely lauded by philosophers around the world as highly effective knowledge-preventers, our patented constructions are perceptually indistinguishable from their

actual-building counterparts, and are available in a wide range of
styles, including the garden-variety "Ann's arbor," the widely
popularized "Arizona adobe" and—our latest—"Nouveau Brunswick."

Easily installed with tools available in any epistemologist's home,
these facsimiles need only to be arranged in such a way that when
someone approaches the target building, there will be a large number
of replicas in the area. If the subject's eyes happen to fall on the real
house (barn, etc.), they will form the belief that it is a house (barn,
etc.)—but they won't know it!

All of our facsimile buildings have been subjected to the most
rigorous thought-experimental testing, and meet or exceed industry
standards for knowledge-prevention.

Just to remind Agents of how this technology works, we ask them to recall the
widely circulated 1976 document produced by Secret Agent Goldman, who had
just been assigned to the CIA's nascent pro-discrimination beat. Goldman
describes an unclassified interaction between an Agent and his son, in which
the Agent—code-named "Henry"—is identifying "various objects on the landscape as they come into view. 'That's a cow,' says Henry, 'that's a tractor,' 'that's
a silo,' 'that's a barn.'" Agent Goldman continues: "Henry has no doubt about
the identity of these objects: in particular, he has no doubt that the last-
mentioned object is a barn, which indeed it is. Each of the identified objects
has features characteristic of its type. Moreover, each object is fully in view.
Henry has excellent eyesight, and he has enough time to look at them reasonably carefully, since there is little traffic to distract him." Secret Agent Goldman
reports that "most of us would have little hesitation in saying... that Henry
knows that the object is a barn" ("so long as," he adds, "we were not in a certain
philosophical frame of mind").

But, he points out, this inclination can be sharply contrasted with "the
inclination we would have if we were given some additional information....
Suppose," Agent Goldman continues, that "we are told that, unknown to
Henry, the district he has just entered is full of papier-mâché facsimiles of
barns... [that] look from the road exactly like barns, but are really just
facades... quite incapable of being used as barns... [but] so cleverly constructed that travelers invariably mistake them for barns." Under such circumstances, Goldman reports, we would be strongly inclined to withdraw the claim
that Henry *knows* the object is a barn. (Goldman 1976: 772–3).[2]

---

[2] [3] The technique of preventing *belief* by distracting the observer with a large number of
facsimiles can, of course, be found much earlier—for instance, in the Irish folktale "Farmer Tom
and the Leprechaun." In that story, Tom meets a Leprechaun who eventually agrees to show
him a gorse bush beneath which a treasure lies hidden. Poor Tom has no tool with him to use
for digging, but he has a shovel back at home. Before setting off to retrieve the shovel, he
carefully ties a red garter around the designated bush, and extracts from the Leprechaun a
promise that the garter will not be removed. The Leprechaun keeps his promise. But... when

Most Agents accepted the thrust of Goldman's original diagnosis, *viz*: "S has perceptual knowledge if and only if not only does his perceptual mechanism produce true belief, but there are no relevant counterfactual situations in which the same belief would be produced via an equivalent percept and in which the belief would be false" (Goldman 1976: 786)—although it had long been clear that some modifications were required concerning the notion of "same belief." For what does it mean to say that the belief Henry expresses by "that's a barn" (Goldman 1976: 772 and *passim*) could (in a relevant counterfactual situation) have been false? Presumably, it's not that *that very barn* could, in a relevant counterfactual situation, have failed to be a barn, or that *that very belief* could have, in a relevant counterfactual situation, involved a different (perhaps merely apparent) barn.[3] Rather, the idea seems to be that there is a relevant counterfactual situation in which a *sufficiently similar belief* would have been false. It was widely agreed that all of this required no more than a charitable reading or, at most, a friendly amendment.

However, more intractable issues rapidly came to light. As with any technology, there was the danger that Goldman's innovation would fall into the hands of those who did not fully understand its mechanisms. And this is precisely what began to happen. But the process of adjudicating intuitions in response to these cases proved much more difficult than anyone had ever expected.

2. Your Friends Will Never Know

The first document to reach CIA hands was associated with the obviously outrageous "Your Friends Will Never Know You're Wearing a Diamond Ring" campaign.

Exhibit Two: Costume jewelry advertisement from *Treasures to Trinkets: Merchandise for the Modest*. (Case codename: "FRIENDS NEVER KNOW")

```
Recently introduced in our widely publicized "Your Friends Will Never
Know You're Wearing a Diamond Ring" campaign, our costume jewelry
collection offers you a way of preventing others from knowing that
you are sporting some sort of valuable doo-dah. Just send us a
photograph of your genuine gem, and we'll do the rest!
```

Tom comes back, every gorse bush within sight has been adorned with an identical red garter, and poor Tom returns home no richer than when he set out. (The theme is also explored—with a nice Dutch Book twist—in Dr. Seuss's fable *The Sneetches*.) A more serious employment of this technique is the (perhaps apocryphal story of the) Danish population's decision during World War II to wear, *en masse*, the yellow star intended by Nazis as an identifying mark for Jews. All are vivid illustrations of the fact that we may well care about "if" only if "only if."

[3] [4] One might try to finesse the problem by appealing to a notion of "same belief" where, for demonstrative ingredients, the sameness in question concerns something like (Kaplanian) character rather than (Kaplanian) content.

> Our Diamond Ring Kit provides you with six phony diamond rings that
> look identical to your genuine rock. Slip them surreptitiously into
> your pocket, and whenever someone sees your ring, there will be lots of
> fakes in the area. Result? Even when their eyes chance upon it, your
> friends will not know you're wearing a diamond ring!

There was no doubt among our Agents that this kit did not work, and it took only a few minutes for them to articulate why.[4] In order to prevent an observer from knowing (of the actual ring) that "that's a diamond ring," it is not sufficient that there be facsimile diamond rings *in the area*; the facsimile rings need to be such that the observer is at serious risk of noticing them.[5]

But what sort of risk was at issue? Agents began considering cases like the following. Suppose that Always has only one ring—an authentic diamond that she never takes off—and suppose she walks around the mall surrounded by a phalanx of constant-fake-ring-wearers. When the casual observer's gaze falls on Always, does he know that she is wearing a diamond ring? Most Agents agreed that he does not know: after all, the casual observer's gaze might easily have fallen on one of the fake-ring-wearers, producing in him a relevantly similar yet false belief. And if a phalanx of fake-ring-wearers does the trick, most Agents agreed, so does a single constant-fake-ring-wearing companion—call her Never. If Always walks around the Mall with Never, they contended, the casual observer whose gaze falls upon Always's finger does not know that Always is wearing a diamond ring.

---

[4] [5] It is crucial to remember that here, as throughout, we are interested only in pairs of cases where (a) knowledge occurs in one case and is prevented in the other, and (b) the believer's subjective state is indistinguishable in the two cases: pairs where there is knowledge in the distracter-free case but where, arguably, there is no knowledge in the relevant-facsimile case, and where the knower/believer feels no difference in her degree of doubt or uncertainty in the two cases. Because we are interested in the *contrast* between our knowledge-attributions in two sorts of circumstances, we need to discount interference arising from the "certain philosophical frame of mind" that would lead us to hesitate in saying "that Henry *knows* that the object is a barn" (or that my friends know I am wearing a diamond ring) even in the distracter-free cases. And because it is a presumption of such cases that the observer's internal state is indistinguishable in the knowledge and non-knowledge cases (cf. the "Henry has no doubt" and "unknown to Henry" clauses in Goldman's original presentation), we need to discount interference arising from our tendency to ascribe to the observer feelings of doubt about the veridicality of the perceptual information available.

This is not to deny that there are interesting epistemic—and practical—issues associated with cases that do not satisfy these criteria. Fashion magazines often caution that there is no point buying a genuine Chanel watch if the rest of your outfit is off-the-rack: no one will think that the timepiece is authentic. Analogously, they point out, if the bulk of your wardrobe is *bona fide* upmarket, you can save money here and there by filling in with facsimiles. This is useful advice. But these cases do not satisfy the constraints articulated above: the reason no one knows you are wearing a Chanel watch in the fashion blunder case is that no one *believes* that you are. Since such cases rely on belief-interference, they fall under FBI and not CIA jurisdiction.

[5] [6] The question of what makes a risk "serious" has, of course been of long-standing interest to the CIA: a subcommittee has been established to explore the issues of danger and risk at play in this particular context: To what extent do they have epistemic ingredients? To what extent are they ascriber-dependent? What sort of notion of objective chance is at play?

As in ORIGINAL BARN, the salient proximity of an indistinguishable facsimile is sufficient to indict the casual observer's knowledge. ("FAKE-RING COMPANION")

Purveyors of facsimile rings quickly got wind of these CIA discussions, and several began offering product-lines in which fake-ring-sporting companions were dispatched to accompany genuine-gem-wearers on their daily outings. But the staffing costs associated with such strategies tended to be excessive, and the market soon foundered.

Then, one summer, rumors of a new sort of technology reached CIA head-quarters. Treasures-to-Trinkets had revamped its product-line simply by chang-ing the instructions that accompanied its original kits. Whereas the old kits had instructed subscribers to slip the fakes surreptitiously into their pockets, the new kits instructed them to alternate which ring they wore on any given day. "Even if all the facsimiles are at home in your dresser drawer," the new kit advertised, "no one will ever know you are wearing a diamond ring. After all, on any of the other six days, you would have been wearing one of the fakes." ("FAKE-RING COLLECTION")

Many Agents were of the opinion that FAKE-RING COLLECTION was as effective at preventing knowledge as FAKE-RING COMPANION. But with the new technology came new complications. Suppose someone—call her Some-times—owns one of these new kits, and follows its instructions religiously. One day, when she happens to be wearing her genuine diamond, she goes to the mall with Always. The two walk around together, and both fall under the gaze of a casual observer. ("ALWAYS WITH SOMETIMES") If the casual observer would not know that Sometimes was wearing a diamond ring, then presumably she would not know that Always was. After all, there might be no intrinsic difference between the two rings, and minimal differences between their wear-ers' fingers, hands, clothes, etc. But if so, then something remarkable was going on. Could one really prevent a casual observer from knowing that someone is wearing a diamond ring simply by walking around beside her, wearing a real diamond, with the habit of wearing fakes on other days?[6] Could epistemic contagion really be so easy?

Agents quickly realized that they were facing a new kind of potential epidemic,[7] and divided into three main groups:

---

[6] [7] Remember the caveats offered in n. 4 above.

[7] [8] Some proposed describing the new epidemic as follows. Whereas the ORIGINAL BARN and its descendants (FAKE-RING COMPANION and FAKE-RING COLLECTION) introduce the possibility of what we might call *primary infection*, ALWAYS WITH SOMETIMES introduces the possibility of what we might call *secondary infection*. Whereas primary infection requires that there be some relevant counterfactual situation in which an equivalent percept produces *a false belief*, secondary infection requires only that there be some relevant counterfactual situation in which an equivalent percept is accompanied by a *failure to know*. Some Agents found the distinction between primary and secondary infection to be a useful one; others maintained that so-called cases of secondary infection were just particularly virulent cases of primary infection.

(1) Some insisted that no matter how similar Always and Sometimes are in appearance, the casual observer knows that one but not the other is wearing a diamond ring. Even if the rings of Always and Sometimes produce qualitatively indistinguishable percepts, even if the rings are intrinsic duplicates, still the casual observer would know of the one but not the other that it bore a diamond. To many, this purported asymmetry seemed implausible, though its defenders remained steadfast.[8]

(2) Others defended the view that Sometimes is epistemically infectious, maintaining that in ALWAYS WITH SOMETIMES, the casual observer does not know that *either one* is wearing a diamond ring. But their opponents worried that this would open the floodgates to excessively skeptical results. Suppose Never (who wears her fake ring daily) goes to the mall almost every day and sits on the bench in front of the central fountain at noon. Once a week, however, she stays home to mow the lawn. One day, Always goes to the mall and sits on the bench in front of the central fountain at noon. It happens to be the day that Never is at home. The casual observer's gaze falls upon Always' ring. Does he know that she is wearing a diamond? ("NEVER AT NOON")

Intuition suggests that he does, but the advocate of position (2) faces some pressure to say otherwise. After all, the defender of (2) has committed himself to saying that when Always walks around with Sometimes-in-her-genuine-ring, the casual observer does not know that either of them is wearing a diamond. Why should the fake rings in Sometimes' drawer indict the casual observer's knowledge in ALWAYS WITH SOMETIMES, but the fake ring on Never's finger not indict his knowledge in NEVER AT NOON?

(3) A final group maintained that in FAKE-RING COLLECTION, one *does* know that the ring-wearer sports a diamond ring and, correlatively, that in ALWAYS WITH SOMETIMES, one knows that both are wearing diamond rings. They held that Sometimes' habit of wearing fake rings does not introduce—even in her own case—a *relevant* counterfactual situation in which an equivalent percept produces a false belief; in order for the potential defeaters to be strong enough to defeat knowledge, they maintained, the defeaters must, in general, be *spatially* proximate—and not merely *temporally* so.[9]

---

[8] [9] One Agent offered the following suggestive analogy on their behalf. Consider a series of pairwise-indistinguishable color chips whose colors shift gradually from red to orange. Oscar starts on the left, examining the chips one pair at a time. Assume that Oscar knows of the left-most chip that it is red, but that there is some red chip further down the line that he does *not* know is red (say, because he would easily confuse it with a chip that is, in fact, orange). If so, then at some point during his process of pairwise comparison, he knows that the chip on the left is red, but does not know that the chip on the right is—even though the percepts are indiscriminable, and both chips are red.

[9] [10] If temporal proximity were sufficient, they pointed out, then it would seem that we know anything at all only due to the absence of hyper-lucid dreams.

Advocates of (3) differed on what might explain this asymmetry. Some subscribed to a version of what they called the GAZE PRINCIPLE. According to that principle, candidate-defeaters are relevant in cases where we leave the world as it is (altering only the observer's perceptual orientation within it) and irrelevant in cases where we leave the observer's perceptual orientation as it is (altering only features of the world around her). In the first sort of case, one might say, the defeaters are there, but the observer's gaze happens not to fall upon them; in the second sort of case, her gaze is there, but the defeaters on which it might have fallen happen not to be around.[10] (Opponents objected that the principle was *ad hoc*, contending that there are plenty of cases where non-present but eminently possible fakes clearly do seem to destroy knowledge.)

Others subscribed to a version of what they called the LIVE-DANGER PRINCIPLE: cases where candidate-defeaters are relevant are cases where there is, on that occasion, a real danger of mistake; cases where candidate-defeaters are irrelevant are cases where there is, on that occasion, no real danger of a mistake. Suppose that Never could easily have shown up at that mall but that morning chose not to. At noon, I approach the fountain. Intuitively, there is on that occasion no danger of my observing Never and forming a false diamond belief. (This comports with general intuitions about the absence or presence of danger. If someone considers planting a bomb but has chosen not to, then I am not, later that day, in danger of being blown up.) Similarly, the story goes, when I approach Sometimes on her real ring day, there is on that occasion no danger of my gaze coming to fasten onto a fake ring. (Opponents objected that this was *ad hoc*. If I am driving by a real barn and the fakes are a few hundred yards away, then isn't there some sense in which there is at that moment no danger of my gaze falling on a fake? It seemed quite unclear how to calibrate live danger so that lines are drawn where intuition suggests they ought to fall.[11])

3. The Contingencies of Risk

A call on the Citizens' Hotline alerted the CIA to an additional complicating factor that revealed diamond ring cases to have barely scratched the surface.

---

[10] [11] One Agent suggested that appealing to this principle was like trying to refute Berkeley by staring at a stone.

[11] [11] Cf. Agent Goldman's original report: "How shall we specify alternative states of affairs that are candidates for being [relevant alternatives]?...[Clearly,] the object in the alternative state of affairs need not be identical with the actual object...[and some] alternative states of affairs [may] involve the same object but different properties...Sometimes, indeed, we may wish to allow non-actual possible objects. Otherwise the framework will be unable in principle to accommodate some of the skeptic's favorite alternatives, e.g. those involving demons" (Goldman 1976: 780)...."An adequate account of the term 'know' should make the temptations of skepticism comprehensible" (Goldman 1976: 790).

Exhibit Three: *Hotline recording* (Case codename: "FAKE BAR")

> Unbeknownst to its patrons, Awful Alvin's Bar serves genuine gin six
> days per week—and an undetectable surrogate on Sundays. Tom goes out
> nearly every night; Dick drinks only after his seminar on Tuesdays;
> Harry is unpredictable but always spends Sundays at home with his
> family. The three of them gather at Awful Alvin's on Tuesday night,
> and each of them orders a gin and tonic. Oscar walks in and asks each
> one what he is drinking. "That's gin," each replies. Does Tom know that
> he's drinking gin? Does Dick? Does Harry? And does Oscar know that each
> is imbibing authentically?

FRIENDS NEVER KNOW had taught Agents that mere proximity of a fake is
not sufficient for the fake's presence to prevent knowledge: the observer has to
be at risk of noticing it. But what FAKE BAR drew attention to was that the risk
of a fake being noticed by a particular observer may depend on highly contingent features of the observer, differences that do not, intuitively, make for a
difference in his capacity to know the subject matter at hand. While his
commitment to family time on Sunday may be laudable, it is odd to suppose
that it has the additional benefit of enabling Harry, though not Tom, to know
that a genuine gin is being poured on some Tuesday evening (given that both
have the same perceptual exposure to the gin, and both have very similar
discriminatory capacities).

Once the problem had been exposed, it was easy enough to find more
illustrations. For example: While Ed walks past a real barn, Fred drives by and
briefly stops his car. There are fake barns within easy driving distance—indeed it
is quite likely that Fred will soon come upon one—though there are no fake
barns accessible by foot. There is thus no real risk of Ed observing a fake barn,
but there is a real risk for Fred. Or again: While Ike is short-sighted, Mike has
excellent vision. There are fake barns in the area, perched on hilltops that can
be observed by someone with acute eyesight. There is thus no real risk of Ike
observing a fake barn, but a good chance of Mike doing so. Ed, Fred, Ike, and
Mike observe a real barn at fairly close range. Should we conclude that Ed and
Ike, but not Fred and Mike, know that there is a barn there?

Some Agents were happy to follow these cases where they seemed to lead,
concluding that the knowledge-preventing capacity of fakes depends on the
risk they induce of a subject's perceiving them. The walker knows; the driver
doesn't. The short-sighted observer knows; the observer with 20–20 vision
doesn't. Others balked. It is intolerable, they argued, to allow that slow speed
and short-sightedness could yield such epistemic dividends. Perceptual risk,
they maintained, is highly observer-sensitive—in ways that knowledge is
not—so the two cannot go hand-in-hand.

A CIA subcommittee has been assigned to investigate this matter further.

4. Retention and Prevention

Meanwhile, additional documents gave rise to further complications.

Exhibit Four: Travel brochure for *Unpotemkin-on-Lethe: The Village Vacation She'll Never Remember* (Case codename: DAYTIME VOYAGE)

```
Want to send your Boss on an un-rememberable vacation? Try Unpotemkin:
a floating village that wends its way up and down the Lethe River. Home to
some of the loveliest barns in the world, Unpotemkin is certain to
entrance your Boss with its architectural splendors.
   Here is the sort of exciting postcard you can expect your Boss to
write: "From my comfortable seat at the center of Unpotemkin village,
I have a lovely view of the farm that lies at its northern tip. Even
though I just arrived this morning, here are some things I already
know: That's a tractor. That's a silo. That's a barn."
   Later that afternoon, we will unmoor the village, and send it floating
gently downstream. As Unpotemkin glides down the Lethe, it will pass
through fake barn country, where the river's banks are strewn with
high-quality Goldman-standard barn facsimiles. What an exciting
moment! Your Boss can't write another bragging postcard! For she no
longer knows that Unpotemkin sports a barn! (After all, her gaze might
well have just fallen upon one of the many fakes.)
   Don't forget to tell all your office-mates about Unpotemkin-on-
Lethe: the vacation you can't remember!
```

CIA Agents were quick to challenge the ad's claims. Most agreed that knowledge was not lost in the way the ad suggested. (Those who demurred tended to be the ones who had secretly purchased fake diamonds to hide in their ex-wives' dressers...)

Many Agents thought the key issue was the relevance of collateral information about the past. Suppose we agree that in the morning, prior to entering fake barn country, Boss knows that there is a barn at the end of Unpotemkin Village. Even if we grant that fake barns in the area in the afternoon would prevent a first-time onlooker from acquiring knowledge, it is hard to see that fake barns would interfere with Boss's ability to retain her knowledge that a barn was there in the morning. Consider the barn located at location L. Assume that Boss knows in the afternoon that there was a barn at L in the morning, and assume further that Boss can reidentify location L. (The presence of fake barns on the bank in the afternoon would surely not impede such reidentification.) Then, insofar as Boss can know in the afternoon that, upon looking at location L, she is looking at the same object that she saw in the morning, it would seem that she can know in the afternoon that she is looking at a barn. Since the presence of fake barns on the shore would not seem to make any trouble for the reliability of beliefs of the form "that is the same object I saw yesterday," it would seem that Boss has, after all, the basis for knowing that there is a barn in front of her in location L, even when the banks are replete with fakes. The mistake is to suppose that when she looks at an Unpotemkin barn during the passage through fake barn country, the basis of her belief is merely the visual percept that the barn generates.[12]

Not all Agents were satisfied. Suppose Holly sits down on a bench in front of a barn in the morning when there are no fakes in the area and forms the belief "that's a barn." Just before noon, several fake barns are erected just out of view. Later that afternoon, Molly arrives on the scene and joins Holly on the bench where she has been sitting all day. Molly looks at the real barn and forms the belief "that's a barn." According to the analysis just presented, Holly but not Molly would know that she is looking at a barn—even though the two are seated side-by-side on the same bench, each having seen only a real barn, and each confronting the same risk of observing the newly constructed fakes that lie just beyond their range of sight. This, maintained the dissenters, is intuitively intolerable. The dispute remains unresolved.

5. The Price of Caution

For many years, cases confronted by the CIA were primarily concerned—like those above—with issues surrounding the notion of what makes a counterfactual situation relevant. Few had exploited the second main element in Goldman's original diagnosis—that of "equivalent percept."[13] But then the CIA began to come across documents like the following.

Exhibit Five: Travel brochure for *The Veldt Belt: A Place to Laugh about Animal Knowledge* (ANIMAL SAFARI)

```
Does your wise old Uncle Milton want to get back at his epistemically
cautious cousin Isidore? Send them on one of our Veldt Belt
excursions...So long as Isidore is reluctant to make judgments about
```

---

[12] [12] How does all this bear on Goldman's original dictum that "S has perceptual knowledge if and only if not only does his perceptual mechanism produce true belief, but there are no relevant counterfactual situations in which the same belief would be produced via an equivalent percept and in which the belief would be false" (Goldman 1976: 786)? For isn't this a case where we have knowledge that is arguably perceptual—despite the fact that an equivalent percept produces a false belief in various nearby counterfactual situations? Some Agents insisted that owing to the import of collateral information, it is not true in this case that the perceptual mechanism produces the belief (in the relevant sense of "produce"). Others suggested that some of the surroundings (in this case, those used to reidentify L) may here be considered crucial to the percept, in which case the counterfactual perceptions of fake barns would not generate equivalent percepts in the relevant sense.

[13] [13] "S has perceptual knowledge if and only if not only does his perceptual mechanism produce true belief, but there are no relevant counterfactual situations in which the same belief would be produced *via an equivalent percept* and in which the belief would be false" (Goldman 1976: 786).

the species to which a particular animal belongs while Milton is not, then Milton will know that he is seeing animals, while Isidore won't know he's seeing animals!

Even if Milton and Isidore never disagree about whether something is an animal—even if there is no nomically possible perceptual situation in which the two of them deliver different verdicts on whether an object presented is an animal—still, Milton will know that he is seeing animals, and Isidore will not know that he is seeing animals. Ha ha ha—the joke's on Izzie!

How does this fantastic safari work? Let me tell you how. In anticipation of Milton's visit, we will populate the veldt with numerous fake antelopes—and three real tigers. And then we will send Milton and Izzie out in one of our Jurassic jeeps...

Milton will look at one of the tigers, form the belief that it is a tiger, come to know that it is a tiger, and thereby come to know that he has seen an animal. But what about Milton's cautious cousin Izzie? He will look at one of the tigers, be reluctant to form the belief that it is a tiger, and instead merely form the belief that it is an animal. But now we've got him! The area is rife with fake animals—artificial antelopes on every apex! So Izzie will not know that he is seeing an animal—but Milton will...Foolish old Izzie: he has paid the price of caution!

Agents condemned the case immediately, quickly pointing out its similarity to Agent Goldman's dachshund/wolf example. Suppose, proposed Goldman, that Oscar has a tendency to mistake wolves for dogs, and that he observes a dachshund in a field frequented by *canis lupus*. Seeing the dachshund, Oscar believes a dog to be present. ("DACHSHUND WOLF") Does he know that a dog is present? After all, he would (falsely) believe a dog to be present even if he were merely to have seen one of the many wandering wolves. Goldman rejects this reasoning as follows:

If Oscar believes that a dog is present because of a certain way he is "appeared to," then this true belief fails to be knowledge if there is an alternative situation in which a non-dog produces the same belief by means of the same, or a very similar, appearance. But the wolf situation is not such an alternative....An alternative that disqualifies a true perceptual belief from being perceptual knowledge must be a "perceptual equivalent" of the actual state of affairs. (Goldman 1976: 779)

He goes on to produce a refined account of the notion of "perceptual equivalence":

If the percept produced by the alternative state of affairs would not differ from the actual percept in any respect that is causally relevant to S's belief, this alternative situation is a perceptual equivalent for S of the actual situation....Consider now the dachshund-wolf case. The hypothetical percept produced by a wolf would differ from Oscar's actual percept of the dachshund in respects that *are* causally relevant to Oscar's judgment that a dog is present. Let me elaborate. There are various kinds of objects, rather different in shape, size, color, and texture, that would be classified by Oscar as a dog. He has a number of visual "schemata", we might say, each with a distinctive set of features, such that any percept that "matches" or "fits" one of these schemata would elicit a "dog" classification ...Now although a dachshund and a wolf would each produce a dog-belief in Oscar, the percepts produced by these respective stimuli would differ in respects that are causally relevant to Oscar's forming a dog-belief. Since Oscar's dachshund schema includes such features as having an elongated, sausage-like shape, a smallish size, and droopy ears, these features of the percept are all causally relevant, when a dachshund is present, to Oscar's believing that a dog is present. (Goldman 1976: 782–3)

Most Agents agreed that analogous reasoning could be used to account for the intuition that Isidore knows he is seeing animals: presumably, the cautious cousin uses a variety of "visual templates" to decide whether something is an animal, and the visual template that triggers an animal belief in the case of a tiger differs from the one that would have been activated by the fake antelope. It is for this reason that we are inclined to dismiss the fake antelopes in ANIMAL SAFARI as irrelevant to Isidore's knowledge—even though he does not have the conceptual confidence to distinguish them by name. Caution does not carry that sort of epistemic cost.

But if the visual template analysis is correct, Agents pointed out, then if Isidore's template is sufficiently permissive, ANIMAL SAFARI *could* describe a case where Milton knows that he is seeing animals, whereas Isidore does not. If one of the schemata that Isidore uses in animal identification is satisfied both by antelope-shaped creatures and tiger-shaped creatures, then he will pay the price not of caution, but of indifference.

Similarly, they continued, suppose Agent Orange is insensitive to certain subtleties of shading, whereas Colonel Mustard is not; there will be cases where Colonel Mustard will know that he is seeing a red piece of paper, whereas Agent Orange will not—even though Mustard and Orange never disagree about whether a sheet of paper is red and thus neither is more easily deceived (or more reliable) in redness verdicts than the other. Suppose that the two are sitting side by side. In front of them is a piece of paper of the shade red-36, surrounded by pieces of white paper that have been illuminated to look as if they are of the shades red-32, red-34, and red-38. Casting their gazes on the red-36 sheet, Colonel Mustard and Agent Orange both form the judgment: there is a red piece of paper before me. But if the visual template analysis is correct, Colonel Mustard knows that there is, whereas Agent Orange does not—even though it may be nomologically impossible for them ever to disagree in perceptual cases about whether something is red. On this picture, indifference brings ignorance in its wake: the narrower the range of features that play a causal role in bringing about a perceptual belief, the wider the range of its relevant defeaters.

6. Apples and Oranges: The Search for Consistent Principles

But a dinner party the next week at the home of one of our protagonists revealed that this could not be the full story.

Exhibit Six: Orange's Apple

> The Association of Fruit Lovers meets for dinner at Agent Orange's
> house. In the middle of his dining room table sits a clear glass bowl.
> In the middle of the bowl sits a single real apple. Nestled around it are
> two fake oranges, a fake cantaloupe, three fake peaches, and two fake
> coconuts. (FRUIT BOWL)

Suppose a member of the Association casts her eyes upon the bowl. According to the Equivalent Percept Articles (EPA), she knows that she is seeing an apple. After all, she looks at the apple, forms the belief that it is an apple, and thereby—since there are no fake *apples* in the area—comes to know that that is an apple in the bowl before her. And if she knows that there is an apple in the bowl, presumably she knows that there is a piece of real fruit in the bowl.

But does she? The intuitions of many Agents suggested otherwise.

Now there was trouble: for FRUIT BOWL and ANIMAL SAFARI are, Agents were quick to note, structurally similar. Indeed, the casual visitor in FRUIT BOWL—who seems clearly *not* to know that there is a real piece of fruit before her—is in the position of Uncle *Milton*—who seemed clearly to *know* that he had seen an animal in ANIMAL SAFARI. What could explain the difference?

One difference seemed immediately striking: the apple in FRUIT BOWL is surrounded by many different sorts of fake fruit, whereas the tiger in ANIMAL SAFARI is surrounded by only one sort of fake animal. Place the real apple in a bowl of fake bananas and surround the real tiger by fake giraffes, lions, and gazelles, and the intuition-gap begins to fade. But why should this matter?

Some Agents reasoned as follows. FRUIT BOWL is presented in such a way that there are a variety of fake fruits in the bowl: fake oranges, fake peaches, fake coconuts, and so on. Upon hearing that story, it seems reasonable to think that whoever placed such a wide assortment of fake fruits in the bowl could easily have placed fake apples there as well. In ANIMAL SAFARI, by contrast, the presence of fake antelopes does not in itself raise the specter that fake tigers could easily have been present too. But change the safari story to one in which the real tigers are surrounded by fake giraffes, fake lions, fake zebras, and the like—and the specter looms large. Change the fruit bowl story to one in which the host has simply placed her apple on top of a pile of fake bananas, and the gap fades in the opposite direction.

Other agents were dissatisfied. They pointed out that this diagnosis depends upon appealing to the relevance of the possibility of a non-present fake apple producing a percept similar to that produced by the real apple. But, they pointed out, if one concedes that this is what prevents knowledge in FRUIT BOWL, then its analogue ought to prevent knowledge in NEVER AT NOON. After all, in that case too a fake could easily have been present that produces the same percept and belief. But only a minority of Agents had conceded that knowledge was prevented by Never's counterfactual presence at the fountain.[14]

A problem had crystallized: How could one consistently maintain that knowledge was present in NEVER AT NOON, but absent in FRUIT BOWL? Some Agents suggested the following. In FRUIT BOWL, the reasonableness of the belief that there is a real apple depends upon certain false beliefs being uncorrected: if the observer in FRUIT BOWL were told that his beliefs about the apparent oranges, peaches, coconuts, etc. were false, he could no longer reasonably believe that the apple was real. By contrast, the reasonableness of the belief in NEVER AT NOON does not depend upon certain false beliefs being uncorrected.

But, pointed out dissenters, this UNCORRECTED-FALSE-BELIEF PRINCIPLE runs afoul of the following intuition. Suppose the fruit is arranged in an opaque bowl, so when the observer enters the room, all he sees is the apple on top. Were he to take one step further, his gaze would fall upon the fake oranges and peaches, etc., but from where he stands, all that is visible is the real apple. He thus has no uncorrected false beliefs about the other fruits. Still, contended these Agents, there is some inclination to say that he does not know in this case. After all, they pointed out, suppose that the opaque bowl contained fake *apples* instead. In that case we would surely say that he does not know that he is seeing an apple—by straightforward ORIGINAL BARN reasoning. Given this, it seems implausible to some to say that he knows he is seeing an apple when he sees only the single real apple perched atop the bowl of fake fruit. So, they contended, the difference between FRUIT BOWL and NEVER AT NOON cannot be fully explained by appeal to uncorrected actual false beliefs.

Agents agreed that it was a matter for further investigation.[15]

---

[14] Or again: suppose someone buys a rose—call it *Sharon*—which he is determined to surround with either fake roses or real daisies. He tosses a coin and decides to surround it with real daisies. Oscar sees the vase and forms the belief of Sharon that it is a rose. But given the set-up of the story, there is a close world where a person in Oscar's situation would form the belief of various fake flowers in the vase that they were roses. This hardly seems to prevent Oscar from knowing that a rose is present in the actual world. Or consider a variation on ANIMAL SAFARI where safari organizers parachute in one real tiger, then flip a coin as to whether to populate the remainder of the veldt with (a) fake tigers, or (b) real antelopes. Uncle Milton is lucky enough to go on safari (b)—but he only pays attention to the tiger. Does he know that he has seen an animal?

[15] Some suggested that the right way to account for the opaque-bowl cases was by making appeal to something like the LIVE-DANGER PRINCIPLE in conjunction with the UNCORRECTED-FALSE-BELIEF PRINCIPLE, withholding knowledge when there is a live danger of the observer holding false beliefs on whose lack of correction the reasonableness of the candidate belief lies. Dissenters retorted by pointing out that this would result in widespread skepticism.

7. Time Change

Some months after the initial memo appeared, two further cases came to the attention of the CIA, both further destabilizing the apparent reliability of classic barn intuitions.

Exhibit Seven: Watch Out

> You enter a room and ask someone the time. She replies truthfully and correctly, and she is extremely reliable. But your informant happens to be surrounded by a roomful of compulsive liars. Do you know what time it is?

Field studies by the CIA indicate that—with the exception of small pockets in the vicinity of Tucson—there is a tendency to ascribe knowledge in this case.[16] But why should there be any intuitive discrepancy between a case of testimony with liars in the area and a case of perception with fake barns in the area? Could the difference depend on the intentions of the distracters? It seems not: for suppose that instead of being surrounded by compulsive liars, your informant is surrounded by well-meaning truth-tellers whose watches have stopped. Intuitions remain stably knowledge-supporting, even though the chance of having gotten misinformation remains high.

Some agents suggested the following diagnosis, a cousin to the UNCORRECT-ED-FALSE-BELIEF PRINCIPLE. If I ask someone the time then my inclination to trust that person will not be—nor ought it to be—significantly affected by the information that certain other people in the area are liars (or have watches that have stopped). For the information that certain other people are liars (or have broken watches) gives me no especially good reason to think that the person I am talking to is a liar (or has a broken watch).[17] My conditional credence that the person I am talking to is a liar on the information that certain other people in the area are liars ought not to be significantly higher than my credence that the person I am talking to is a liar. This is because, in general, the information that X is a liar does not tell me much about whether Y is a liar—and likewise

---

[16] Matters may be different when that very individual is disposed to lie about similar subject matter. Agent Brown suggests the following case. "Sherlock Holmes is trying to determine the circumstances behind Body's mysterious death. He knows that Doctor Who, Lord How and Private Why witnessed the death. What he doesn't know, because it has never occurred to him to think about it, is that all three are pathological liars. Doctor Who will always tell a lie except when asked a 'Who?' question, Lord How lies except in answer to a 'How?' question and Private Why lies except in answer to a 'Why?' question. Holmes knows none of this, but being struck by a whim of fancy given their names, he decides to ask the Doctor who killed Body, the Lord how it was done, and Private why it was done. All three answer truthfully, and Holmes comes to believe them. Does Holmes know the who, how, and why of Body's murder?" Here many informants were reluctant to classify any of Sherlock's testimonially obtained beliefs as knowledge.

[17] Insofar as one thinks the information suggests a conspiracy or plague, one will be correspondingly reluctant to attribute knowledge.

with the other cases where we are inclined to attribute knowledge. By contrast, if you tell me that certain other barn-appearing things in the area are not in fact barns, this will give me at least some reason to think that the barn-appearing thing that I am looking at is not in fact a barn. My conditional credence that the thing I am looking at is a barn on the information that certain other barn-looking things in the area are not barns *is* significantly lower than my credence that the barn-looking thing I am looking at is a barn—and likewise with other cases where we are inclined to withhold an attribution of knowledge.

Other Agents felt that a less abstract diagnosis was called for. They conjectured that our methods of epistemic evaluation for assessing knowledge based on testimony are likely to be structurally different—and perhaps more lenient—than our methods for assessing perceptual knowledge: the requirements for transmitting knowledge differ from the requirements for acquiring it.[18] Consider the following case, they suggested. Henry inspects a barn in fake-barn country and tells me: "that's a barn." In fact, Henry has done enough to discern that it is not a mere barn façade: he has walked around inside, tapped on the walls, used a metal-detector to locate the nails, and so on. But all Henry tells me is "that's a barn." Throughout the area, Henry's cousins are looking at barn façades, and—without performing such inspections—blithely reporting to their companions "that's a barn." Intuitively, I know on the basis of Henry's testimony that that's a barn. But if I were told that there were many others in the area who were falsely believing and reporting that they were seeing barns, then my conviction that Henry is seeing a real barn would no longer be reasonable. This appears to make trouble for the more abstract diagnosis. Further research seemed to be called for.

8. Ignorance and Experience

Deep in CIA archives, one final document was found.

Exhibit Eight: The Ignorance Machine

> Employing factive-stative technological innovations developed in clandestine laboratories in Oxford and New York,[19] we have discovered how to prevent individuals from being pleased that p. Here is the new top-secret product.
>
> As the curfew tolls the knell of parting day, your epistemic enemy sets off down the garden path to (what he fails to realize is) fake tiger

---

[18] [18] Agent Causation points out the following important asymmetry: "Imputations of lying are *insulting* in ways that considerations of barn props are not. Thus we feel pragmatic pressure not to entertain possibilities of lying when we need not, which has no analogue in the barns case."

[19] [19] Cf. Williamson 2000, Ch. 1, drawing on ideas put forth in Unger 1975.

country. Upon arrival, he is fortunate enough to cast his gaze upon one of the few real tigers, burning brightly in the distance. "I am pleased that there is a tiger in the area," he remarks.

But, of course, he is not! For it turns out that 'is pleased that p' entails 'knows that p' (as do other factive predicates that describe emotional states). Since your enemy doesn't know that he is seeing a tiger, he isn't pleased that he's seeing a tiger—even though, as matter of fact, he is seeing a tiger! What poetic justice!

Many Agents immediately condemned this product as illegitimate. Two possible diagnoses: (a) despite the impressive array of considerations in its favor, the fashionable view concerning factive mental predicates is incorrect; (b) the concept of knowledge, prior to its being fashioned and molded by certain philosophical traditions, never offered any stable negative verdict in the original fake barn case.[20]

The CIA hereby requests a grant of $10 million to examine these possibilities in greater detail.[21]

---

[20] [20] An alternative explanation, here and elsewhere, is that the variations in response are due to the context-dependency of "know." Though many stylish Agents have embraced this mode of explanation, conservatives have resisted. Those adopting this kind of strategy face the additional task of specifying which of the disputes described above represent cases of genuine disagreement among Agents, and which represent cases where Agents are merely talking past one another.

[21] [unnumbered] *Acknowledgements*: For comments and encouragement, we are grateful to Stewart Cohen and Alvin Goldman. Special thanks are due to Agent Brown (Brian Weatherson) [*note added in 2009*: when this article was written Weatherson taught at Brown University] and Agent Causation (Jonathan Schaffer) for careful comments on an earlier draft of this memo.

6

Philosophical Thought Experiments, Intuitions, and Cognitive Equilibrium

It is well known that contemplation of an imaginary particular may have cognitive and motivational effects different from those evoked by an abstract description of the same content. This essay explores some of the philosophical implications of this commonplace. In particular, it looks at the extent to which the effectiveness of thought experiments is due to the engagement of cognitive mechanisms associated with vivid imagining.

The essay makes three main claims. First, that by presenting content in a suitably concrete or abstract way, thought experiments recruit representational schemas that were otherwise inactive, thereby evoking responses that may run counter to those evoked by alternative presentations of relevantly similar content. Second, that exactly because they recruit heretofore uninvolved processing mechanisms, thought experiments can be expected to produce responses to the target material that remain in disequilibrium with responses to the same material under alternative presentations, so that a true sense of cognitive equilibrium will, in many cases, prove elusive. And finally, that when thought experiments succeed as devices of persuasion, it is because the evoked response becomes dominant, so that the subject comes (either reflectively or unreflectively) to represent relevant non-thought-experimental content in light of the thought-experimental conclusion.

This essay—which is more expository and less tightly argued than most of the others in this volume—is best read in conjunction with two successor papers: "Alief and Belief" (2008a; Ch. 13) and "Alief in Action (and Reaction)" (2008b; Ch. 14). For those who lack the time to read all three, it might be useful to know that the two later essays offer a more sophisticated and nuanced account of the central insight underlying this one, although they do not address the issue of philosophical thought experiments so directly.

***

This essay was first published in *Midwest Studies in Philosophy: Philosophy and the Empirical*, 31 (2007), 68–89 and is reprinted with the kind permission of Wiley-Blackwell. The text that appears here has been shortened considerably: several extended quotations that appeared in the original version have been omitted, and superfluous passages have been eliminated throughout. In addition, a number of references have been updated or added. As a result of reformatting, several footnote numbers have changed. The original number of each footnote is noted in [square brackets].

1. Introduction

It is a commonplace that contemplation of an imaginary particular may have cognitive and motivational effects that differ from those evoked by an abstract description of an otherwise similar state of affairs.[1] In his *Treatise on Human Nature*, Hume (1739/1978) writes forcefully of this. He speaks of "a noted passage in the history of Greece" where Themistocles tells the Athenians that he is prepared to carry out a military action that will benefit them enormously, but whose details must remain secret for the plan to be effective. The Athenians ask Themistocles to describe his plan to the highly trusted Aristedes, who will report back to the assembled citizens about its advisability.

After learning of the plan—which was to set fire to the assembled fleets of all their enemies—Aristedes reports to the Athenians "that nothing cou'd be more advantageous than the design of Themistocles but at the same time that nothing cou'd be more unjust." The response of the Athenians is to reject the project unanimously (*Treatise* II. iii. 6. 3).

Hume reports that this anecdote produced great consternation among some of his contemporaries, including French historian Charles Rollin, who expressed astonishment that the Athenians would reject such an advantageous strategy merely because it was unjust. But Hume is unimpressed. He writes:

> For my part I see nothing so extraordinary in this proceeding of the Athenians.... [T]ho' in the present case the advantage was immediate to the Athenians, yet as it was known only under the general notion of advantage, without being conceiv'd by any particular idea, it must have had a less considerable influence on their imaginations, and have been a less violent temptation, than if they had been acquainted with all its circumstances: Otherwise 'tis difficult to conceive, that a whole people, unjust and violent as men commonly are, shou'd so unanimously have adher'd to justice, and rejected any considerable advantage. (*Treatise* II. iii. 6. 4)

Hume's diagnosis has a straightforward corollary. When two options are presented abstractly, the choice made between them may go one way; presented under some "particular idea" that "influence[s]" the "imagination," the choice made between them may go the other. Engagement of the cognitive mechanisms associated with vivid imagining may lead a subject to reverse a prior commitment, selecting as preferable the option previously rejected, and shunning the option previously embraced.

Many philosophical thought experiments, I will suggest, exploit exactly the discrepancy that led to Rollin's perplexity and Hume's insight. In the remainder of this essay, I will explore three corollaries of this central suggestion. First, that

---

[1] [*Note added in* 2009: In the original version of this essay, an extended quotation from Hume appears at this point. The full quotation can be found in this volume in §4 of "Alief and Belief" (Ch. 13 p. 280).]

by presenting content in a suitably concrete or abstract way, these thought experiments recruit representational schemas that were otherwise inactive, thereby evoking responses that may run counter to those evoked by alternative presentations of relevantly similar content. Second, that exactly because they recruit heretofore uninvolved processing mechanisms, such thought experiments can be expected to produce responses to the target material that remain in disequilibrium with responses to the same material under alternative presentations, so that a true sense of cognitive equilibrium will, in many cases, prove elusive. And finally, that when these thought experiments succeed as devices of persuasion, it is because the evoked response becomes dominant, so that the subject comes (either reflectively or unreflectively) to represent relevant non-thought-experimental content in light of the thought-experimental conclusion. In each case, I will present some recent results from psychology and related disciplines that support the interpretation I am advancing.

2. Cognitive Underpinnings

Nearly a century of empirical investigation has confirmed the extent to which tasks with the same formal structure but different contents may prompt different rates of success, presumably because the alternative framings activate different processing mechanisms. These cases provide a useful foil to the philosophical examples to be discussed in the remainder of the essay, since it is straightforward to isolate their formal from their contentful properties, and straightforward to ascertain what a correct response amounts to. In this section, I will review some of the literature that has been taken by psychologists to establish this claim decisively. The survey is intended to be suggestive, not comprehensive, and for those even moderately familiar with the literature, there is unlikely to be anything of novelty. Its main purpose is to make vivid to those unfamiliar with this research program some of the striking ways that content effects can enable or inhibit reasoning skill.

Though tacit recognition of such effects goes back millennia (see §4 for a 3,000-year-old example) and explicit recognition goes back at least centuries (see the passage from Hume above), modern study of the phenomenon can be dated to the work by E. L. Thorndike and his students in the third decade of the last century. In 1922, Thorndike published an article entitled "The Effect of Changed Data on Reasoning" in which he described a series of studies that involved presenting students with familiar algebra problems. Across subjects, the structures of the problems were held constant; the only differences were in the embedded symbols. So, for instance, one group confronted equations whose variables were indicated by x and y, while those in the second group faced structurally identical equations whose variables were indicated by b_1 and b_2. The results of these small changes were dramatic; error rates in tasks presented with complicated symbols were up to five times greater than in those with simple symbols (Thorndike 1922: 36).[2]

Six years later, his student Minna Cheves Wilkins undertook a dissertation-length study that presented subjects with a range of syllogistic tasks, asking them to judge whether certain conclusions followed from certain pairs of premises. Some involved terms that were "familiar and concrete" ("Some of the girls in the chorus wear their hair braided; all the girls in the chorus wear their hair bobbed; therefore..."); others involved symbols ("All x's are z's; all x's are y's; therefore..."). Yet others involved complicated nonsense terms ("No juritobians are cantabilians; no cantixianti are cantabilians; therefore...") or terms for which the subjects had antecedent views about their relations ("If New York is to the right of Detroit; and Chicago is to the left of New York; then..."). Across subjects, results were quite consistent:[3] "Most items increase in difficulty as the material is changed from familiar to symbolic, etc., but a few items representing very common fallacies are much less difficult in symbolic material than in familiar" (Wilkins 1928: 52–77).

In the eight decades following Wilkins's and Thorndike's pioneering work, much has been learned about which sorts of embeddings tend to facilitate or impede reasoning. Though the nuances are many, Wilkins's fundamental observation—that subjects' tendency to reason validly is typically improved when materials are presented with familiar content, though there are also cases where familiar content may interfere with their ability to identify valid structures—has been borne out. In particular, in cases where subjects are asked to attend to formal properties alone, the presence of certain sorts of content seems to enhance or inhibit their ability to draw appropriate conclusions on the basis of structural features.

Much of the research demonstrating these sorts of interference effects has made great use of two well-known paradigms: syllogism tasks (described in this paragraph) and Wason selection tasks (described below). In the first, subjects are presented with a set of premises, and asked to determine whether a particular conclusion follows logically from them. Stimuli vary along two dimensions:

---

[2] [1, *modified*] Thorndike's conclusion was sweeping. He maintained that "any disturbance whatsoever in the concrete particulars reasoned with will interfere somewhat with the reasoning, making it less correct or slower or both" (Thorndike 1922: 33). Thorndike explained these results in strictly associationist terms: he held that "the mind is ruled by habit throughout" with reasoning being no more than "the organization and cooperation of habits" (Thorndike 1922: 33). Though the heirs of this research program have tended to reject Thorndike's explanation of the mechanisms, the phenomenon he identified has withstood the test of time.

[3] [2, *modified*] Wilkins was careful to note that there were individual differences among her subjects: some provided correct answers in (nearly) all cases. (She did not measure reaction time.) In recent years, these differences have been explored in detail in by Keith Stanovich and Richard West (see e.g. Stanovich and West 2000 [*added* 2009: Stanovich and West 2008]; cf. also Epstein *et al.* 1996).

some of the reasoning patterns are valid whereas others are invalid; and some of the conclusions are independently plausible whereas others are independently implausible. Presented with such stimuli, subjects consistently exhibit *belief-bias*: structurally identical valid inferences are far less likely to be judged valid when their conclusions are implausible ("some vitamin tablets are not nutritional") than when their conclusions are plausible ("some highly trained dogs are not police dogs"); structurally identical invalid inferences are far less likely to be judged invalid when their conclusions are plausible than when their conclusions are implausible. (Cf. Evans *et al.* 1983, reviewed in Evans 2003; for suggestive work about the associated functional neuroanatomy, see Goel and Dolan 2003; Goel *et al.* 2000).

In the second, the Wason selection task (Wason 1966), subjects are presented with four cards and told that each card has an F-type feature (say, a number) on one side and a G-type feature (say, a letter) on the other. The subject is then presented with a (material) conditional statement that takes the following form: "If a card's F-feature is x, then its G-feature is y" and asked which cards she would need to turn over to verify the statement's truth. The first card shows an instance of an F-feature which is x (F/x); the second shows an instance of an F-feature which is not x (F/not-x); the third shows an instance of a G-feature which is y (G/y); the fourth shows an instance of a G-feature which is not y (G/not-y). The appropriate response to such a question is to turn over exactly two cards: the first (F/x) card and the fourth (G/not-y) card.

Presented with certain abstract versions of the task, subjects tend to perform poorly. If, for example, subjects are asked to verify the (material conditional) statement: "if there is an A on one side, there is a 3 on the other" for the set of cards pictured below, fewer than 10% correctly turn over exactly the "A" and the "7"; instead, they typically turn over the "A" and the "3," or the "A" only.

A	D	3	7

If the task is altered slightly, however, so that subjects are presented with the same set of four cards, but with the instruction "if there is an A on one side, there is not a 7 on the other" subjects nearly universally turn over the correct pair of cards. This tendency to match response to cue (in the first case the consequent mentioned "3," whereas in the second case, it mentioned "7") goes by the name *matching bias*.[4]

---

[4] For an overview of the enormous body of research conducted using this paradigm, see Evans 1998 and relevant articles mentioned in its bibliography. For discussion of a process of training subjects to inhibit matching bias, along with intriguing data about its possible neural underpinnings, see Houdé *et al.* 2000.

Interestingly, certain tasks seem not to induce this sort of matching bias.[5] So, for example, success rates are extremely high when the sentences to be verified resemble this one: "if a person is drinking beer, then the person must be at least 21 years of age." In such cases, a vast majority of subjects (correctly) turn over the "beer" and the "16" (and not, as would parallel the previous case, the "beer" and the "21") (cf. Griggs and Cox 1982).[6]

Beer	Coke	21 years	16 years

Related content-based effects can be found in a wide range of forced-choice tasks. In a 1994 study, for example, Veronika Denes-Raj and Seymour Epstein presented subjects with pairs of bowls containing varying numbers of red and white jelly beans. Subjects were told that they would win \$1 for each trial in which they drew a red jelly bean, and then given a choice about which of the two bowls they would prefer to draw from blindly. The first bowl always contained 1 red jelly bean and 9 white beans, while the other contained 100 beans total, with the proportion of red to white ranging from 9:100 (9 red and 91 white) to 5:100 (5 red and 95 white). Each bowl was labeled with an index card clearly indicating the percentage of red jelly beans that it contained (10%, 9%, 8%, etc.).

Despite the presence of the monetary incentive and the explicit information about relative likelihood of success, well over half the subjects chose the 9:100 (9%) and 8:100 (8%) bowls over the 1:10 (10%) bowl and more than a quarter chose the 5:100 (5%) bowl over the 1:10 (10%). Overall, more than 80% of subjects made at least one non-optimal choice in the five trials each faced.

---

[5] There are at least five features that seem consistently to produce increased speed and accuracy in Wason-style tasks: (a) using concrete and meaningful terms in articulating the rule and describing the cards; (b) presenting the task as one of determining a rule-violation rather than the truth or falsity of a statement; (c) embedding the task within the context of a scenario where the subject is given a particular role to play; (d) providing the subject with a rationale or justification for the rule; and (e) relating the two rule components in a meaningful way (Dominowski 1995: 45).

Numerous hypotheses have been offered to explain these patterns of response, among them that certain embedded tasks trigger a pragmatic reasoning schema (cf. e.g. Cheng and Holyoak 1985; Cheng, Holyoak, Nisbett, and Oliver 1986), that they trigger a modular social exchange algorithm (cf. e.g. Cosmides 1989; Gigerenzer and Hug 1992) and that different mental models are activated by different presentations of conditional content (cf. e.g. Johnson-Laird and Byrne 2002). Others have argued on Bayesian grounds that typical reasoning patterns on Wason-style tasks are actually rational (cf. e.g. Oaksford and Chater 1994, 1996). None of these accounts has been universally accepted, and it seems likely that the full story will turn out to be quite complicated.

[6] Interestingly, the effect is reduced in cases where the pairing is judged as unlikely: fewer subjects turn over the final card if it reads "12 years" and fewer still if it reads "4 years" (Kirby 1994).

When asked about their selections, "subjects reported that although they *knew* the probabilities were against them, they *felt* they had a better chance when there were more red beans ... They made statements such as, 'I picked the ones with more red jelly beans because it looked like there were more ways to get a winner, even though I knew there were also more whites, and that the percents were against me'"[7] (Denes-Raj and Epstein 1994: 819, 823).

The literature on heuristics and biases is replete with such examples.[8] Readers are presumably familiar with many of Daniel Kahneman and Amos Tversky's famous cases. In the Linda-the-bank-teller case, for example, subjects are presented with a description of an imaginary character, Linda, that reads as follows:

> Linda is 31 years old, single, outspoken and very bright. She majored in philosophy. As a student, she was deeply concerned with issues of discrimination and social justice, and also participated in anti-nuclear demonstrations (Tversky and Kahneman 1983: 297).

Subjects are then presented with a set of eight statements about Linda, and are asked to rank them in order of likelihood. Among the statements are the following:

Linda is a bank Teller. (T)
Linda is a bank Teller and is active in the Feminist movement. (T+F)

Even when subjects are highly educated, even when they are graduate students in a decision science program, even when they are asked to bet money on their choice, even when they are explicitly reminded that "bank teller" does not mean "mere bank teller," even when the logical relations between the two statements are made transparent—even in all these cases, there is a striking tendency for subjects to choose T+F (Teller and Feminist) as more probable than T (Teller) (Crandall and Greenfield 1986; Epstein *et al.* 1999; cf. Tversky and Kahneman 1983). As Stephen Jay Gould remarks in his own reminiscence about encountering the case: "I know that [T+F] is least probable, yet a little homunculus in my head continues to jump up and down, shouting at me—'but she can't just be a bank teller; read the description'" (Gould 1991: 469).

The same goes for each of the cases discussed above. Even subjects who regularly provide correct answers to abstract match-violating Wason tasks are consistently faster (and consistently more accurate under conditions of cognitive load) at solving suitably matched or embedded tasks. Likewise in the case of

---

[7] [*Note added in 2009*: I would now diagnose this as a case where the subject *believes* that she has a better chance of picking a red bean if she goes for the 1:10 plate, but she has an *alief* with the content "lots of red stuff over there in the 8:100 bowl; red means win-a-prize; choose the bowl with all the nice red things in it." For further discussion, see Gendler 2008a, 2008b; Chs. 13 and 14 below.]

[8] [7] Three classic collections are Gilovich *et al.* 2002; Kahneman *et al.* 1982; and Kahneman and Tversky 2000.

belief-matched (as opposed to belief-mismatched) syllogisms, and in tasks like Denes-Raj and Epstein's number/proportion task. Everyone—even those who are ultimately able to override (or endorse for the right reasons) the inclination that leads to error (or success) in the cases under consideration—feels the pull of the competing response.[9]

One promising framework for explaining these patterns of response is the family of theories that have come to be known as *dual systems* accounts.[10] According to such accounts, there are at least two clusters of subsystems involved in mental processing—one associative and instinctive, operating rapidly and automatically; the other rule-based and regulated, operating in a relatively slow and controlled fashion. Numerous formulations of this distinction have been proposed—diverging in important details that matter a great deal for a number of important debates. But for our purposes, their commonalities are more important than their differences.[11]

A typical such account is Steven Sloman's *Two Systems* model, according to which human reasoning can be usefully thought of as involving both an *Associative* and a *Rule-Based System*. The Associative System (sometimes called "System I") operates on principles of similarity and contiguity; takes personal experience as its source of knowledge; operates on concrete and generic concepts, images, stereotypes, and feature sets; makes use of relations of association that serve as soft constraints; exhibits processing that is reproductive but

[9] [*Note added in 2009*: This phenomenon appears to be quite general. Indeed, Adele Diamond and Natasha Kirkham have suggested that perhaps "adults do not fully grow out of any of the cognitive or perceptual biases of infancy and early childhood" and that although "in adults, these biases are surely more subtle," there is reason to think that using sufficiently nuanced measures (such as reaction time, eyetracking, and neuroimaging), "all biases found in young children can be found in adults" (Diamond and Kirkham 2005: 296). A number of recent studies support this hypothesis. ERP work by Daurignac *et al.*, for example, suggests that "adult subjects still must inhibit the length-equals-number heuristic, an automatic visuospatial bias from early childhood, to perform analytical processes and succeed in [simple] numerical [matching] task[s]" (Daurignac *et al.* 2006: 734; for related fMRI work, see Leroux *et al.* 2009). And eyetracking and reaction-time work by Epley, Morewedge, and Keyser suggests that "childlike egocentrism"—the failure to recognize that another's perspective may differ from one's own—"isn't outgrown so much as it is overcome each time a person attempts to adopt another's perspective" (Epley *et al.* 2004: 765).]

[10] [*Note added in 2009*: My encounter with this literature—beginning with my exposure to the work of Kahneman and Tversky in 1991, and continuing for the subsequent two decades—has profoundly influenced my thought about nearly all of the issues addressed in this volume. In particular, it underpins my views about the role of concrete cases in philosophical reasoning, particularly the role of thought experiments (Chs. 1–6), and it lies at the core of my more recent work on alief (Chs. 13 and 14).]

[11] [8] For additional representative discussions, see the essays collected in Chaiken and Trope 1999; as well as Evans 2003, 2008; Evans and Over 1996; Gigerenzer and Regier 1996; Hinton 1990; Smolensky 1988; Stanovich 1999; Stanovich and West 2000. For intriguing early discussions, see James 1890/1950; Piaget 1929; Neisser 1963. [*Added in 2009*: For a more recent collection of discussions, see Evans and Frankish 2009, which includes a helpful introductory chapter that provides historical context for contemporary work on dual processing.]

capable of similarity-based generalization; uses overall feature computation and constraint satisfaction; is automatic; and is exemplified by functions such as intuition, fantasy, creativity, imagination, visual recognition, and associative memory. By contrast, the Rule-Based System (sometimes called "System II") operates on principles of symbol manipulation; takes language, culture, and formal systems as its sources of knowledge; operates on concrete, generic, and abstract concepts, abstracted features, and compositional symbols; makes use of causal, logical, and hierarchical relations that serve as hard constraints; exhibits processing that is productive and systematic; uses abstractions of relevant features; is strategic; and is exemplified by functions such as deliberation, explanation, formal analysis, verification, ascription of purpose, and strategic memory (Sloman 1996: 7).[12]

As Daniel Gilbert points out, however, there is nothing sacred about the "dual" in dual processing. He writes:

the neuroscientist who says that a particular phenomenon is the result of two processes usually means to say something unambiguous [about]...the activities of two different brain regions...[but] dry psychologists who champion dual-process models are not usually stuck on two. Few would come undone if their models were recast in terms of three processes, or four, or even five...claims about dual processes in dry psychology are not so much claims about how many processes there *are*, but claims about how many processes there *aren't*. And the claim is this: There aren't one. (Gilbert 1999: 3–4)[13]

For our purposes, the moral is simply this. Decades of research in cognitive psychology have demonstrated that when content is presented in a suitably concrete or abstract way, this may result in the activation or fortification of a representational schema that was otherwise inactive or subordinate. The result of this may be to evoke responses that run counter to those evoked by alternative presentations of relevantly similar content. So, far from being an anomalous or idiosyncratic feature of arcane or unusual cases, the discrepancy noted in our opening story is—in fact—a central feature of our mental lives.

3. Thought Experiments and Elusive Equilibrium

So far, we have been considering cases where it is clear what the right answer is, and where (at least in some cases) we have a fairly systematic understanding of the sorts of factors that lead subjects astray. When subjects turn over the A and the 3 in the A–D–3–7 task described above, they make a mistake; when they

---

[12] [*Note added in 2009* (with some text taken from the original 2007 paper): There are numerous other accounts as well. One that has been particularly influential for my own work is that of Seymour Epstein; cf. Denes-Raj and Epstein 1994; Epstein 1990.]

[13] [*Note added in 2009*: Indeed, Keith Stanovich has recently suggested a tripartite theory; cf. Stanovich 2009.]

turn over the A and the 7, they do not. When the sentence to be confirmed is: "if there is an A on one side, there is a 3 on the other," even subjects who ultimately respond correctly are somewhat drawn to the card with the 3; when the sentence to be confirmed is: "if there is an A on one side, there is not a 7 on the other," even subjects who face persistent difficulties with the A–3 formulation are easily able to turn over the correct cards. Likewise with the syllogism tasks: When subjects conclude that an invalid inference with a true conclusion is valid, they err—and when they err, it tends to be because an independent judgment about the truth or falsity of the conclusion interferes with their judgment concerning the inference's validity. Like optical illusions, these cognitive illusions seem to be artifacts of deep features of our cognitive architecture: the "little homunculus in [our] head" will continue to "jump up and down," whether or not we can train ourselves to discount its cries when non-homuncular reasoning is called for. Just as we cannot simply talk ourselves out of seeing Müller-Lyer lines as different in length, we cannot simply talk ourselves out of feeling drawn towards turning over the 3.[14]

What implications does this have for philosophical methodology? It seems to me that the implications are both liberating and disturbing—and that these are two sides of the same coin. For if something akin to dual processing lies at the root of most human reasoning, then a philosophical theory may be correct even if we consistently and resiliently react to specific cases in ways that run counter to the theory's predictions. But this introduction of an additional degree of freedom into the enterprise of philosophical explanation may introduce a feeling of vertigo.[15]

Recent neuroimaging work on moral reasoning has brought this challenge to the fore in the context of the "trolley problem" (Thomson 1985). According to these accounts, contemplating the original trolley case[16] appears to produce increased neural activity in what are sometimes referred to as the "higher

---

[14] [9] Habits of attention may mitigate the effects somewhat; one can learn to approach questions of validity by automatically mentally substituting content-neutral expressions for content-distracting ones. I discuss this in more detail in the context of philosophical thought experiments in §4 below.

[15] [10, *abbreviated*] For a related discussion of these matters that comes to somewhat similar conclusions, see Sunstein 2005. [*Added in 2009*: See also Sinnott-Armstrong 2008a, 2008c.]

[16] [*In main text in published version*] The classic presentation of the case (which Thomson attributes to Philippa Foot) can be found in Thomson 1985: "Suppose you are the driver of a trolley. The trolley rounds a bend, and there come into view ahead five track workmen, who have been repairing the track. The track goes through a bit of a valley at that point, and the sides are steep, so you must stop the trolley if you are to avoid running the five men down. You step on the brakes, but alas they don't work. Now you suddenly see a spur of track leading off to the right. You can turn the trolley onto it, and thus save the five men on the straight track ahead. Unfortunately, Mrs. Foot has arranged that there is one track workman on that spur of track. He can no more get off the track in time than the five can, so you will kill him if you turn the trolley onto him. Is it morally permissible for you to turn the trolley?— Everyone to whom I have put this hypothetical case says, Yes, it is" (Thomson 1985: 1395).

cognitive" regions of the brain, while contemplating cases such as "fat man"[17] (where the imagined action is "up close and personal") appears to produce increased neural activity in "emotional/social" regions (cf. Greene *et al.* 2001). Intriguing confirmation of this suggestion can be found in subsequent work by Antonio Damasio *et al.* suggesting that subjects with ventromedial prefrontal cortex damage (damage associated, among other things, with impaired emotional processing) are more than twice as likely as controls to consider it morally acceptable to push the fat man (or to suffocate a crying baby in order to save a group of people who are hiding) (Koenigs *et al.* 2007).

Of course, all of this is fully compatible with there being a genuine deep moral difference between the two acts—deep enough to render the one morally mandatory and the other morally prohibited. Nothing that I have said here or elsewhere should be taken to deny the possibility that—as Mill writes at the beginning of *Utilitarianism*—"whatever steadiness and consistency our moral beliefs have attained has been mainly due to the tacit influence of a standard not yet recognized" (Mill 1861/2001: 3).

That said, it is worth taking seriously other work that suggests that intuitions about such cases may vary along dimensions that are (presumably) morally irrelevant. Psychologist David Pizarro, for example, presented subjects with "fat man" trolley cases that differed only in the nature of the sacrifice involved: in the one case, a man named Chip Ellsworth III could be thrown off a bridge to stop a trolley hurtling towards 100 members of the Harlem Jazz Orchestra; in the other, a man named Tyrone Peyton could be thrown off to save 100 members of the New York Philharmonic.[18] Politically liberal subjects were significantly more likely to consider it morally acceptable to sacrifice Chip to save the Harlem Jazz Orchestra than to sacrifice Tyrone to save the New York Philharmonic (presumably an overcorrection of an initial instinctively racist response) (Uhlmann, Pizarro *et al.* 2009: 482–3).

---

[17] [*In main text in published version*] The "fat man" case, again in Thomson's 1985 version, is as follows: "Consider a case—which I shall call *Fat Man*—in which you are standing on a footbridge over the trolley track. You can see a trolley hurtling down the track, out of control. You turn around to see where the trolley is headed, and there are five workmen on the track where it exits from under the footbridge. What to do? Being an expert on trolleys, you know of one certain way to stop an out-of-control trolley: Drop a really heavy weight in its path. But where to find one? It just so happens that standing next to you on the footbridge is a fat man, a really fat man. He is leaning over the railing, watching the trolley; all you have to do is give him a little shove, and over the railing he will go, onto the track in the path of the trolley. Would it be permissible for you to do this? Everyone to whom I have put this case says it would not be" (Thomson 1985: 1409).

[18] [11] Non-American readers may be helped by learning that the name "Chip Ellsworth III" evokes images of a wealthy white man, whereas "Tyrone Peyton" evokes images of a man of African descent; likewise, the New York Philharmonic is an elite, largely white and Asian, orchestra, whereas the Harlem Jazz Orchestra is associated with the African American community.

Whether or not there is a moral difference between the original trolley case and the fat man case, it seems clear that there is no moral difference between sacrificing Tyrone and sacrificing Chip.[19] But if our only basis for thinking that there is a moral difference between the fat man and original trolley cases is that subjects tend to respond differently to them, we should be disturbed to discover that parallel differences can be evoked by what seem clearly to be morally irrelevant variables.[20]

Even more disturbingly, subjects' responses to moral dilemmas can be varied through deliberate unconscious priming. It is not surprising to learn that when presented with otherwise identical scenarios in which American (or Iraqi) troops cause anticipated but unintentional collateral damage to Iraqi (or American) civilians, politically conservative subjects are significantly more likely to judge the American-on-Iraqi damage to be morally acceptable than the other way around, whereas politically liberal subjects make precisely the opposite judgment. The more surprising result is that these effects can be induced regardless of political conviction—simply by prompting subjects to unscramble sentences containing terms associated either with patriotism or multiculturalism:[21] Subjects primed with patriotic terms tend to assess the scenarios as conservatives do, whereas subjects primed with multiculturalist terms respond much like liberals[22] (Uhlman, Pizarro *et al.* 2009: 486–9).

Nor is there anything special about moral intuitions in this regard. In epistemology, for example, Jonathan Weinberg and colleagues have discovered that subjects' willingness to attribute knowledge in ambiguous cases "increases after being presented with a clear case of non-knowledge, and ... decreases after being presented with a clear case of knowledge" (Swain *et al.* 2008: 138). John Hawthorne and I demonstrate related sorts of shiftiness in fake barn cases (Gendler and Hawthorne 2005; Ch. 5 above).[23] And Joshua Knobe and Shaun Nichols have found presentation-dependent differences in judgments of free will and moral responsibility depending on whether examples are presented abstractly or concretely (Nichols and Knobe 2007).

---

[19] [12] Of course, this judgment is itself grounded in some sort of intuitive reaction. For discussion of the unavoidability of appeal to intuition in philosophical reasoning, see Bealer 1998; Goldman 2007; Pust 2000; Sosa 2007a, 2007b; Williamson 2005.

[20] [13] Admittedly, the differences that Pizarro observes are less extreme than those evoked by the original trolley/fat man contrast. (But there are good naturalistic reasons to expect this.)

[21] [14] "Scrambled sentence" tasks—in which subjects are presented with a series of word clusters that they are asked to form into sentences (e.g. "flies high the flag" or "very dogs loyal are")—are a standard technique in social psychology for "priming" unconscious associations.

[22] [15] The work of Pizarro cited here is representative of a large research program in contemporary psychology exploring the status and source of moral intuition. For representative examples, see de Waal 1996; Haidt 2001; Haidt and Joseph 2004; Hauser 2006 and sources cited therein.

[23] [16] For an overview of the issue of intuitions and epistemology, see Alexander and Weinberg 2007; [*added 2009*: see also J. Nagel 2008, J. Nagel forthcoming].

_Though specific stories can be told about any given case, the accumulated implications can seem dizzying.[24] If intuitions cannot serve as a fixed point for philosophical theorizing, then much that has been widely taken as philosophical orthodoxy may be up for grabs.[25] Of course, careful work regarding particular examples may allow the reclaiming of some aspects of traditional intuition-based methodology.[26] But the accumulated evidence reviewed in §§2 and 3 suggests that at least some of the utility of philosophical thought experiments may lie in another direction. It is to this issue that I turn in the final section.

4. Thought Experiments as Devices of Framing and Persuasion

A common insight lies at the heart of both Kantian and utilitarian moral theorizing: that to reason in accord with the dictates of morality is to view oneself as unexceptional. Immanuel Kant's Categorical Imperative requires that "I should never act except in such a way that I can also will that my maxim should become a universal law" (Kant 1785/1981: 402). That is, morality requires that personal desires be filtered through a universalizing lens: my own desires may serve as bases for willed action only if I can at the same time coherently will that others in similar circumstances would act in the way that I am choosing to act. Despite important differences between the views, a similar core insight lies at the heart of Jeremy Bentham's famous utilitarian formulation that "everybody [is] to count for one, nobody for more than one" (Bentham 1789/1961, cited by Mill 1861/2001: 62).

---

[24] [17] In addition to concerns about intrasubjective variation, there are also grounds for unease about intersubjective variation. Widely touted work by Jonathan Weinberg, Stephen Stich, and Shaun Nichols seems to suggest that there are important cultural differences in how college-aged subjects respond to some of the central examples in the epistemological literature (Weinberg, Nichols, and Stich 2001). Similar worries are raised in an intracultural context by Robert Cummins, who notes: "It is commonplace for researchers in the current Theory of Content to proceed as if [Twin Earth] intuitions were undisputed ... Nor is the reason for this practice far to seek. The Putnamian ... take on these cases is widely enough shared to allow for a range of thriving intramural sports among believers. Those who do not share the intuitions are simply not invited to the games ... [I]t is all too easy for insiders to suppose that dissenters just do not understand the case. If we are honest with ourselves, I think we will have to confront the fact that selection effects ... are likely to be pretty widespread in contemporary philosophy" (Cummins 1998).

[25] [In main text in published version] On the basis of related considerations, for example, Brian Weatherson writes: "Intuitively, Gettier cases are instances of justified true beliefs that are not cases of knowledge. Should we therefore conclude that knowledge is not justified true belief? Only if we have reason to trust intuition here. But intuitions are unreliable in a wide range of cases. And it can be argued that Gettier intuitions have a greater resemblance to unreliable intuitions than to reliable intuitions. What's distinctive about the faulty intuitions, I argue, is that respecting them would mean abandoning a simple, systematic and largely successful theory in favour of a complicated, disjunctive and idiosyncratic theory. So maybe respecting the Gettier intuitions was the wrong reaction, we should instead have been explaining why we are so easily misled by these kinds of cases" (Weatherson 2003b: 1).

[26] [18] For some reflections on this issue, see Weinberg *et al.* (MS) and sources cited therein.

Here, too, one's own interests may legitimately enter into decision-making only insofar as they are weighed equally alongside the interests of others: first-person exceptionalism is morally prohibited.

For the purposes of discussion in this section, let's use the term *moral stance* for stances that prohibit first-person exceptionalism. And let's consider the question: How might one make this stance cognitively available to the subject at moments of moral decision-making?

In answering this question, it is worth reminding ourselves that among the most resilient of our cognitive tendencies is exactly the tendency to hold ourselves to different standards than those to which we hold others. So, for example, as Emily Pronin notes in a review article, summarizing a wide range of recent work, study after study has shown that "people overestimate the extent to which they personally are influenced by 'objective' concerns and/or overestimate the extent to which others are influenced by 'self-serving' concerns" (Pronin *et al.* 2004). "They assume that people who work hard at their jobs are motivated by external incentives such as money, whereas they claim that they personally are motivated by internal incentives" (Pronin 2007: 37–8); they consistently overestimate the likelihood that they will act generously or selflessly, while accurately predicting the ungenerosity and selfishness of others (whom they most likely turn out to resemble). Repeated studies have shown that "people on average tend to think they are more charitable, cooperative, considerate, fair, kind, loyal, and sincere than the typical person but less belligerent, deceitful, gullible, lazy, impolite, mean, and unethical." The same holds for specific predictions of behavior: "people generally think they are more likely than their peers to rebel in the Milgram obedience studies, cooperate in a prisoner's dilemma game, distribute collective funds equitably, and give up their seat on a crowded bus to a pregnant woman... [they] tend to believe they will resolve moral dilemmas by selecting the saintly course of action but that others will behave more selfishly" (Epley and Dunning 2000). And they "tend to see their futures as overly rosy, to see their traits as overly positive, to take too much credit for successful outcomes and to disregard evidence that threatens their self esteem" (Pronin 2007: 37). It is no exaggeration to say that the tendency towards first-person exceptionalism is among the most widespread and pervasive of our tendencies towards bias.

This tendency finds powerful voice in the biblical story of David and Bathsheba (2 Samuel: 11–12).[27] David, who is King of Israel, is walking along the roof of his palace when he catches sight of an attractive woman—Bathsheba—washing herself nearby. Taken by her beauty, he has her brought to the palace, where he proceeds to lie with her, though she is married to another man. She becomes pregnant, and David arranges to have her husband Uriah sent to fight

---

[27] [19] Thanks to Tim Crane for pointing out to me the philosophical potential of this story in a related context.

"in the forefront of the hottest battle . . . that he may be smitten and die." Uriah is killed, and David proceeds to take Bathsheba as his wife.

God is (understandably enough) rather displeased by David's behavior, and seeks to help him see the ways in which it is problematic. But God recognizes the deep human tendency towards first-person exceptionalism, and seeks a way to speak to David that will circumvent this tendency. So "the Lord sent Nathan unto David," and Nathan proceeds to tell David the following story:

There were two men in one city; the one rich, and the other poor. The rich man had exceeding many flocks and herds: But the poor man had nothing, save one little ewe lamb, which . . . grew up together with him, and . . . was unto him as a daughter. And there came a traveler unto the rich man, and he spared to take of his own flock . . . but took the poor man's lamb, and dressed it for the man that was come to him.

When David hears this story, his "anger [is] greatly kindled against the man." He holds the man to be deserving of disapprobation and punishment, and says to Nathan: "As the Lord liveth, the man that hath done this thing shall surely die. And he shall restore the lamb fourfold, because he did this thing, and because he had no pity."

At this point, the circumstances have been set for the delivery of the punchline. Nathan says famously to David:

Thou art the man . . . thou hast killed Uriah the Hittite with the sword, and hast taken his wife to be thy wife, and hast slain him with the sword of the children of Ammon . . .

With a shock of recognition, David reframes his understanding of the circumstances in which he has placed himself, and says to Nathan: "I have sinned against the Lord."

By presenting the story in a way that prevents David from exhibiting first-person bias with respect to what turn out to be his own actions, Nathan has enabled David to acknowledge a moral commitment that he holds in principle, but has failed to apply in this particular case.[28] There is no ambiguity here about which commitment, on reflection, David endorses: the story he has been told is fully effective; it reshapes his cognitive frame, and brings him to view his own previous actions in its light.

Despite being relatively schematic, the narrative is a vivid one, engaging the reader's imagination as she hears about David's and Nathan's actions, and David's imagination as he hears of the behavior of the imaginary rich man who slays the poor man's sheep. Within the domain of philosophy, broadly construed, there is a tradition that emphasizes the capacity of the literary form to appropriately represent moral complexity, contrasting this with the tradition of austere philosophical theorizing. Martha Nussbaum maintains that "there

---

[28] [*Note added in 2009*: For related discussion of the effects of overcoming first-person exceptionalism, see §4.2 of "Self-Deception as Pretense" (2008c; Ch. 8 below).]

may be some views of the world and how one should live in it . . . that cannot be fully and adequately stated in the language of conventional philosophical prose . . . but only in a language and in forms themselves more complex, more allusive, more attentive to particulars" (Nussbaum 1990: 3). Noting that there has been a "predominant tendency in contemporary Anglo-American philosophy . . . to ignore the relation between form and content . . . or . . . [to] treat[] style as largely decorative—as irrelevant to the stating of content," she emphasizes instead the "importance of taking style seriously in its expressive and statement-making functions" (Nussbaum 1990: 8).

While Nussbaum is surely right that the dominant tendency in Western philosophical theorizing has been one that holds form and content to be isolable in these ways, there is also an important strand—even among the most austere of philosophical writers—that explicitly or tacitly acknowledges the force that presentational features can play. Even Kant, who held that "worse service cannot be rendered morality than that an attempt be made to derive it from examples" (Kant 1785/1981: 408), gives some weight to this perspective. In the course of the *Grounding for the Metaphysics of Morals*, he famously formulates the Categorical Imperative in a number of different ways. Though he maintains that these "ways of representing the principle of morality are at bottom only so many formulas of the very same law," he remarks that "nevertheless there is a difference in them which is subjectively rather than objectively practical, viz., it is intended to bring an idea of reason closer to intuition (in accordance with a certain analogy) and thereby closer to feeling" (Kant 1785/ 1981: 436).

Viewed in this light, moral and political philosophy have a secondary task that runs alongside the task of ascertaining what morality demands, namely, that of providing the reader with resources that enable her to make the perspective shift that the moral stance requires at the moment of moral decision-making. In this regard, one of the tasks of such philosophical inquiry is to identify images that can play the role that Nathan's story did with respect to David: images that will bring the reader to reframe her experience of some morally valenced situation, in such a way that her apprehension of the morally relevant features of it are re-experienced in light of the scenario presented. It is this role, I want to suggest, that is played by some of the most famous thought experiments in moral and political theorizing.

Take, for example, one of the most widely discussed aspects of John Rawls's enormously influential *A Theory of Justice*—his "device of representation" for thinking about the principles that would govern the basic structure of a just society. In the first chapter of the book, he introduces the famous example of the "original position"—a "purely hypothetical" situation where "no one knows his place in society, his class position or social status, nor does any one know his fortune in the distribution of natural assets and abilities, his intelligence, strength and the like." From behind this "veil of ignorance," principles are chosen that will regulate "the kinds of social cooperation that can be entered into and the forms of government that can be established." The principles governing a just society will be those that "free and rational persons concerned to further their own interests would accept in [such] an initial position of equality as defining the terms of their association" (Rawls 1971/ 1999: §3).[29]

My suggestion is that, to the extent that Rawls's "device of representation" is effective, it is because it plays the same role as Nathan's story of the rich man and the sheep: it provides the subject with a powerful frame through which the target material—decisions about the appropriate structure for resource-distribution in society—can be reconceptualized. It seeks to make the moral stance cognitively available at a moment of moral decision-making. Much like some of the framings discussed in §2 above, it directs the attention towards (what Rawls holds to be) morally relevant aspects of the decision-making situation, and away from those that are (held to be) morally irrelevant.

With these examples in place, it is time to return to the themes of the opening section. What I have suggested is that by presenting content in a suitably concrete or abstract way, thought experiments may recruit representational schemas that were previously inactive. As a result, they may evoke responses that run counter to those evoked by alternative presentations of relevantly similar content. But exactly because of this, these responses may well remain in disequilibrium with responses evoked in alternative ways. When thought experiments succeed as devices of persuasion, it is because the evoked response becomes dominant, so that the subject comes (either reflectively or unreflectively) to represent relevant non-thought-experimental content in light of the thought-experimental conclusion.[30]

---

[29] [*Note added in 2009*: For a similar example, discussed in some detail in the original (2007) version of this essay, see Anderson 2006. The 2007 version of the essay also includes a brief discussion of Judith Jarvis Thomson's violinist example (Thomson 1971).]

[30] [20] *Acknowledgements*: For comments on talks that served as distant predecessors to this essay, I am grateful to audiences at the Conference on Intuitions, Fribourg, Switzerland (2004); Bergen Community College (2005); Union College (2005); Cornell University (2006); the University of North Carolina at Chapel Hill (2006); and the CUNY Graduate Center (2006). For comments on a more recent incarnation, I am grateful to an audience at the University of Toronto Workshop on Thought Experiments (2007), organized by James Robert Brown. For comments on previous written versions of this essay, I thank Carolyn Caine and Zoltán Gendler Szabó. [*Added in 2009*: For suggestions concerning the most recent abbreviated draft, I am grateful to Aaron Norby.]

Part II

Pretense, Imagination, and Belief

7

On the Relation between Pretense and Belief

In this essay, I identify and discuss two pairs of features that characterize pretense. The first pair—which I call *quarantining* and *contagion*—concern the degree to which pretense representations are kept isolated from other cognitive and behavioral states. The second pair—which I call *mirroring* and *disparity*—concern the degree to which pretended content resembles content that is believed or perceived.

I contend that many standard conceptions of pretense emphasize the ways in which ordinary cases of pretense exhibit quarantining and mirroring (and hence resemble belief-like states in terms of subject matter but differ from them in terms of motivational force and cognitive contributions), but they tend to neglect the ways in which ordinary cases of pretense also predictably manifest both contagion and disparity (and hence differ from belief-like states in terms of subject matter but resemble them in terms of motivational force and cognitive contributions). But, I maintain, it is fully consonant with our general knowledge of how human beings learn from and act in the world that normal cases of pretense should exhibit not only high degrees of quarantining and mirroring, but also that they should exhibit elements of contagion and disparity. Indeed, I argue, the sources of all four tendencies can be traced to fundamental aspects of our cognitive architecture.

This essay can be seen as a predecessor to "Self-Deception as Pretense" (2008c; Ch. 8), "Imaginative Contagion" (2006a; Ch. 12), and the two "Alief" essays (2008a and 2008b; Chs. 13 and 14). Together, these essays present an account of the ways in which attitudes other than belief and desire can lead to action.

***

This essay was first published in *Imagination, Philosophy and the Arts*, ed. Domenic McIver Lopes and Matthew Kieran (New York: Routledge, 2003), 125–41 and is reprinted with the kind permission of Routledge. The text that appears here is nearly identical to that of the published version: a few stylistically awkward passages have been smoothed, section numbers have been added, and several new footnotes (noted as such) have been introduced; in a few passages, text has been moved from the main text to the footnotes.

Such cases are marked with: "[*In main text in published version*]." The original number of each footnote is noted in [square brackets].

---

1. Introduction

1.1. Four Features of Pretense

By the age of two, children are able to engage in highly elaborated games of symbolic pretense, in which objects and actions in the actual world are taken to stand for objects and actions in a realm of make-believe. These games of pretense are marked by the presence of two central features, which I will call *quarantining* and *mirroring* (see also Leslie 1987; Perner 1991). Quarantining is manifest to the extent that events within the pretense-episode are taken to have effects only within that pretense-episode (e.g. the child does not expect that "spilling" (pretend) "tea"[1] will result in the table *really* being wet), or more generally, to the extent that proto-beliefs and proto-attitudes concerning the pretended state of affairs are not treated as beliefs and attitudes relevant to guiding action in the actual world. Mirroring is manifest to the extent that features of the imaginary situation that have not been explicitly stipulated are derivable via features of their real-world analogues (e.g. the child *does* expect that if she up-ends the teapot above the table, then the table will become wet *in the pretense*), or, more generally, to the extent that imaginative content is taken to be governed by the same sorts of restrictions that govern believed content.

At the same time, from the same early age, both quarantining and mirroring are subject to systematic exceptions. Quarantining gives way to its opposite—I call this *contagion*—most strikingly in cases of what I call *affective transmission* (e.g. a child who imagines a bear on the staircase may be reluctant to go upstairs alone), but also in cases of what I call *cognitive transmission* (e.g. a child who has been playing at "birdwatching" may perceive a partially hidden squirrel in a nearby tree as having birdlike features). And mirroring gives way to its opposite—I call this *disparity*—as a result of the ways in which imaginary content may differ from believed content: in being *incomplete* (e.g. there may be no fact of the matter (in the pretense) just how much tea has spilled on the table), and in being *incoherent* (e.g. it might be that the refrigerator serves (in the pretense) as a mathematical-truth inverter).

There is a tendency among philosophers and psychologists to subscribe, tacitly or explicitly, to a conception of pretense that gives pride of place to

---

[1] [1] In the remainder of the text, I will omit scare-quotes unless their omission would lead to confusion.

quarantining and mirroring.[2] Ordinary successful pretense, on such a picture, involves segregated off-line processing and is hence unlike belief in its motivational force and cognitive contributions (thereby exhibiting quarantining); but it involves the processing of belief-eligible content and is hence like belief in its subject matter (thereby exhibiting mirroring).

Much important headway has been made in explaining these striking features of pretense (in the work of Gregory Currie, Alvin Goldman, Robert Gordon, Paul Harris, Alan Leslie, Angeline Lillard, Shaun Nichols and Stephen Stich, Joseph Perner, and Kendall Walton, among others). But such accounts leave other equally conspicuous features of pretense largely unexplained. While ordinary pretense *is*, in many ways, unlike belief in its motivational force and cognitive contributions (thereby exhibiting quarantining), the differences are not absolute. In particular, there are at least two sorts of cases where the contributions to subsequent cognitive processing made by imagining P and believing P differ at most in degree (thereby exhibiting contagion): in their role in evoking affective responses (affective transmission), and in their role in activating schemata, generating attentional filters, and altering evidential standards (cognitive transmission). And while the subject matter of ordinary pretense *is*, in many ways, like the subject matter of belief, the similarities are not absolute. In particular, there are at least two sorts of ways in which the content of what is potentially imagined may differ systematically from the content of what is potentially believed (thereby exhibiting disparity): in its potential to remain deeply underspecified (incompleteness), and in its potential to involve contradictory content (incoherence).

Standard conceptions of pretense emphasize the ways in which ordinary cases of pretense exhibit quarantining and mirroring (and hence resemble belief-like states in terms of subject matter but differ from them in terms of motivational force and cognitive contributions), but they tend to neglect the ways in which ordinary cases of pretense also predictably manifest both contagion and disparity (and hence differ from belief-like states in terms of subject matter but resemble them in terms of motivational force and cognitive

---

[2] See e.g. Nichols and Stich (2000), whose explicit goal is to provide an account of pretense that explains how it is that "the events that occurred in the context of the pretense have only a quite limited effect on the post-pretense cognitive state of the pretender" (Nichols and Stich 2000: 120) (quarantining) and how it might be that "inference mechanisms treat the pretense representations in roughly the same way that the mechanisms treat real beliefs" (Nichols and Stich 2000: 125) (mirroring). Given their caveats, my project here can be seen as supplementary to theirs: what this essay explores are aspects of the "limited effect" of the pretense on the pretender's "post-pretense cognitive state" (contagion) and the ways in which the inference mechanisms that govern pretense are only "roughly" like those that govern belief (unproductivity). [*Added in 2009*: For Nichols's more recent discussion of these issues, see Nichols 2004, 2006a.]

contributions). But, I will suggest, it is fully consonant with our general knowledge of how human beings learn from and act in the world that normal cases of pretense should exhibit not only high degrees of quarantining and mirroring, but also that they should exhibit elements of contagion and disparity. Indeed, as I will argue below, the sources of all four tendencies can be traced to fundamental aspects of our cognitive architecture.

1.2. Preliminary Remarks: Automatic and Controlled Processes

Quarantining and contagion seem to be principally a matter of near-universal largely automatic processes: our general incapacity to believe at will is a manifestation of the degree to which quarantining occurs beyond the reach of our cognitive control, and our somatic responses to affect-laden stimuli—whether real or imaginary—are a manifestation of the degree to which the same is true of contagion. At the same time, higher-order exploitation of our susceptibility to contagion is one of the key elements of "self-help"—think of Pascal's trick of coming to believe in God by acting as if one already did, or the advice that fills books like *Success is a Choice: Ten Steps to Overachieving in Business and Life* (Pitino with Reynolds 1997). And a second-order capacity for quarantining (keeping track of what is real and what is merely imaginary) plays a central role in the guidance of action. Deviation from these general patterns seems correlated with wide-ranging disturbances in a variety of cognitive and emotional skills: for example, an extreme tendency towards contagion tends to be associated with systemic forms of psychopathology such as schizophrenia; and complete immunity from (affective) contagion seems to occur only among those with damage to the ventromedial prefrontal cortex.[3]

Mirroring and disparity, by contrast, seem to be the result of capacities exercised primarily at the level of cognitive control: our general sense of the "free play" of the imagination is a manifestation of the degree to which mirroring exploits the flexible nature of symbolic representation, and our corresponding ability to countenance incompleteness and inconsistency within the context of imaginative exercises is a manifestation of the degree to which the same is true of disparity. At the same time, certain involuntary constraints seem to govern both: these are manifest in the case of mirroring by the sense of "naturalness" connected with certain associations, and in the case of disparity by the corresponding sense of incoherence. Again, deviation from these general patterns tends to be correlated with systemic disturbances: the inability to

---

[3] [*Note added in 2009*: See e.g. Damasio, Tranel, and Damasio 1991; Damasio 1994, 1999. See also Chs. 11 and 12 below.]

balance mirroring with disparity seems uniquely associated with the cluster of incapacities that characterize autism.[4]

1.3. Overview

In this essay, I sketch in preliminary form what the four features amount to, tentatively propose several hypotheses concerning the relations among them, and suggest a number of avenues for further investigation. In §2, I provide some developmental background. In §§3–5, I spell out in somewhat more detail the ways in which quarantining/contagion and mirroring/disparity are manifest in young children's games of pretense, and explain how analogues to them govern more complicated exercises of imagining.

Two final preliminary notes: First, although there are contexts in which it is important to distinguish imagining and imagination on the one hand from pretending or pretense on the other, the distinction is unimportant for the purposes at hand; I will thus use the terms largely interchangeably.

Second: it is a complicated and important philosophical question precisely what belief that P amounts to. For the purposes of this essay, I am interested only in one small aspect of this issue, namely the contrast between belief-like attitudes on the one hand, and pretense-like (or make-belief-like) attitudes on the other. Of the key differences between these attitudes, two are, for the purposes of this chapter, particularly salient. The first is that whereas belief is what might be called a *receptive* attitude (the agent takes herself to be responding to something about the world itself), pretense is—at least at its core—a *productive* attitude (the agent takes herself to be projecting something onto the world). The second is that belief is—at least at its core—an attitude intimately connected (via desire) to action (one who desires B, and believes that doing A will bring about B will, *ceteris paribus*, do A), whereas pretense is—for the most part—disconnected from action (one who merely makes-believe that doing A will bring about B will not generally, for that reason, do A). So, generally speaking, when S believes that P, she holds P to be true, and she takes the truth of P into consideration when deciding how to act; by contrast, when S pretends or makes-believe that P, she does not (for that reason) hold P to be true, and so does not (for that reason) make decisions about how to act that take P into consideration.

One indication of what one believes is what one is willing to assent to or assert in normal or high-stakes circumstances (that is, what one reports oneself

---

[4] [Note *added in 2009*: For discussion of the "naturalness" of certain associations, see Byrne 2005 and the papers in Markman *et al.* 2009, especially section III; for empirical discussion of the relation between pretense and autism, see Rogers, Cook, and Meryl 2005; for philosophical exploration of some of the connections between pretense and autism, see Currie and Ravenscroft 2002.]

to believe). But non-verbal "reports," in the form of actual or intended actions in normal or high-stakes circumstances, autonomic responses to certain stimuli, and other sorts of physiological or behavioral indicators may also be gauges of belief. (I suspect that it is the tendency to focus on the former to the exclusion of the latter—motivated, perhaps, by an instinctive avoidance of anything even tenuously associated with behaviorism—that has led many philosophers to an oversimplified picture of both belief and pretense.)

In the discussion below, my use of the term "belief-like attitude" or, occasionally, the shorthand "belief," will be both loose and stipulative. I will credit someone with the belief(-like attitude) that P if she acts—outside the context of an explicit episode of pretense—as P-believers generally do. (This may lead me to credit a person with contradictory beliefs.) That this is inadequate as a general account of belief should be so obvious as to make it clear that my ambitions in this regard lie elsewhere.

2. Early Childhood Pretense: Developmental Background

By the time normal children reach the age of 15 months, they are capable of engaging in primitive games of make-believe—acting, for instance, as if a piece of cloth or coat collar were their special bedtime pillow (instances of unconscious symbolic representation may occur much earlier—see Piaget 1945/1962: 96 and chs. 6 and 7). By 18 months, many show signs of tracking rather elaborate games of pretense initiated by others—for instance, being able to identify which of two dolls that have been "washed" by an adult experimenter is "still wet" and engaging in the requisite "drying" activity (Walker-Andrews and Kahana-Kelman 1999). By 22 months, these skills become quite widespread (Harris and Kavanaugh 1993; Harris 2000: ch. 2), and by 24–8 months, most children are able to participate fully in such games—for example, pouring "tea" for a stuffed cow from an empty plastic teapot, feeding a toy pig some "cereal" from an empty bowl, giving a toy monkey a "banana" when there are no (real) bananas in sight, and so on (Walker-Andrews and Kahana-Kelman 1999; Harris 1994; Harris 2000: ch. 2).

Around this same age (24–8 months), children show themselves readily able to generalize on the basis of others' pretend stipulations—if they are told, for instance, that a particular yellow block represents a banana and a particular red block represents a cookie, they require no further prompting to engage in a pretense where yellow blocks in general represent bananas, and red blocks in general represent cookies (Harris 2000: ch. 2, reporting Harris and Kavanaugh 1993; Walton 1990). They show themselves readily able to suspend such stipulations as soon as a new episode of pretense begins—the bricks that represent bananas or sandwiches in one game can without difficulty come to represent bars of soap or pillows in the next game. They show themselves ready to credit imaginary objects with causal powers much like those of their real-world ana-logues—if Teddy eats one of the (wooden brick) bananas, he will no longer be hungry; if he is bathed in a (cardboard-box) bathtub, he will emerge wet (Harris 2000). And they are ready to describe situations from the perspective of the imaginary world—when asked to express what happened after (literally) an experimenter holds a stuffed animal in such a way that the animal's paws grip an empty plastic teapot and tilts the teapot above the head of some other stuffed animal, children are happy to report the event as: "Teddy poured tea on Monkey's head" or "Monkey's all wet—he's got tea on his head" (cf. Harris 2000). During the year that follows, most children develop the capacity to engage in complex coordinated games of joint pretense with others (Perner *et al.* 1994: 264). And well before the age of 4, they have figured out how to keep track of different individuals simultaneously engaging in different games of pretense—recognizing, for instance, that if you pretend the pebbles are apples and I pretend the pebbles are plums, you will be baking an apple cake while I bake a plum cake (Perner *et al.* 1994: 264).

These capacities are accompanied by a parallel capacity to keep track of what is pretend, and what is not. The 15-month-old does not give any indication that she comes to think that pieces of cloth are pillows. To the contrary, awareness of the merely pretend status seems explicit: even as she indicates the pillow-like status of the cloth by rehearsing her "going to sleep" routine—lying down on her side and repeatedly closing her eyes—she emits a giggling "no-no" (Piaget 1945/1962: 96; Harris 1994: 257). Moreover, when bedtime comes around, she gives no indication that she expects the piece of cloth to be the surface on which she rests her head. That is, even with children as young as 15 months, there is no indication of what Alan Leslie has termed "representational abuse," that is, no indication that the child comes to believe that actual-world objects have or will come to have features of the pretend objects that they serve to represent (Leslie 1987).[5] And by the age of 3, children are able to articulate this difference—noting, for instance, that a child with a real dog will be able to see and pet the dog, whereas a child with a pretend dog will not (Wellman and Estes 1986; Estes, Wellman, and Woolley 1989; Harris 2000: chs. 2 and 4; see also Bouldin and Pratt 2001 and references therein). While there is some evidence that there are instances when the real–pretend boundary is difficult for children (and even adults) to keep track of—in ways that I will discuss below—it is a crucial feature of games of pretense that, for the most part, the boundary poses no difficulties whatsoever. Children as young as 15 months old are completely capable of recognizing that the world is one way (e.g. that there is a piece of

---

[5] [*Note added in 2009*: For second thoughts on the spirit if not the letter of this claim, see Chs. 13 and 14 below, where I explore some of the ways in which some degree of contagion appears to be inevitable.]

cloth in front of them) and pretending that it is another way (e.g. that there is a pillow in front of them).[6]

3. The Four Features Revisited

3.1. Quarantining and Mirroring

It seems, then, that even very young children are able to engage in games of acting-as-if symbolic pretense that are carried out (a) without resulting in representational abuse, that is, without producing the expectation that real-world objects have the characteristics they are supposed to have in the context of games of make-belief, and without between-game permeability, that is, without stipulations from one game of pretense being automatically assumed to carry over to other games of pretense,[7] and (b) without resulting in realm-mixing, that is, without producing the expectation that the actual world will be transformed in ways that accord with actions in the pretense. And it seems additionally that even very young children are able to engage in rule-governed games of pretense that require: (c) the capacity to understand and make use of generative rule-governed pretend stipulations, and (d) the capacity to apply certain real-world causal relations to actions within the context of the game.

These features can be captured by a pair of principles concerning quarantining on the one hand, and mirroring on the other. The *(prop-based) principle concerning quarantining* specifies how what is pretended affects what is believed: it says that when one pretends that X is Y, things that are believed to be true of Y do not come to be believed to be true of X merely because they are pretended to be true of X. The *(prop-based) principle concerning mirroring* specifies how what is believed affects what is pretended: it says that when we pretend X is Y, X is—

---

[6] [3, *some original text omitted*] In recent years, there has been considerable debate among psychologists concerning exactly what this capacity for pretense amounts to, in light of the fact that children of this age are (a) generally incapable of solving standard ("Smarties-box") false-belief tasks [*note added in 2009*: at least when verbal report is used as a measure of understanding]; (b) fairly limited in their capacity to distinguish apparent from real identity in the case of visually deceptive objects; and (c) generally willing to attribute the behavior "pretending to be an X" to an individual unaware of the existence of Xs. (For discussion of some of these issues see Bruell and Woolley 1998; German and Leslie 2001; Harris 1994; Harris, Lillard, and Perner 1994; Harris 2000, ch. 3; Leslie 1987; Lillard 1993; Lillard 1994; Perner 1991; Perner *et al.* 1994; and references therein.) [*Added in 2010*: Recent work using non-verbal measures appears to show that a number of skills that were traditionally thought to emerge in early childhood (such as the ability to attribute false beliefs) actually emerge much earlier, perhaps even during the second year. See e.g. Onishi and Baillargeon 2005; Southgate, Senju, and Csibra 2007; Baillargeon, Scott, and He 2010. For additional discussion of recent work on pretense and its developmental trajectory, see Liao and Gendler 2010.]

[7] [*Note added in 2009*: For recent empirical work supporting this claim, see Skolnick and Bloom 2006b; Weisberg and Bloom 2009.]

in the pretense—taken to have the effects and features that Y is—in reality—believed to have.

So, for example, the prop-based quarantining principle tells us that when a child pretends that a block is an apple, she does not thereby come to expect that the features attributed to the block within the pretense episode (e.g. being sweet and edible) will hold of the block in reality (or, more generally, in any scenario outside the pretense episode). And the prop-based mirroring principle tells us that when the child pretends of an empty teacup that it is a full teacup, the attributes believed to hold of the full but not the empty teacup prior to engaging in the pretense (e.g. being filled with a drinkable liquid) will be pretended to hold of the empty teacup while engaging in the pretense.

What holds for prop-based pretense holds more generally. One might generalize the *quarantining principle* to say that things do not come to be believed merely because they are pretended; and one might generalize the *mirroring principle* to say that things that are pretended are the sorts of things that could be, in principle, believed.

If the quarantining and mirroring principles held universally, the real–pretend boundary would be completely permeable in the real–pretend direction, and completely non-permeable in the pretend–real direction. Pretending and believing would be exactly alike, except that one would take place "on-line" while the other took place "off-line." For the mirroring principle would guarantee that the same content P could be the object of a belief or of a make-belief, and that no content would be such that it could be the object of only one or the other attitude. And the quarantining principle would guarantee that make-believing P could never, in itself, bring one to the belief that P.

3.2. Contagion and Disparity

But the quarantining and mirroring principles do not hold universally. In regular and predictable ways, merely pretending P does seem to cause (what can be characterized as something sufficiently like) the belief that P; and in regular and predictable ways, pretending that P does not seem to be the same thing as making-believe what one would, as a matter of fact, believe if P were (actually) the case. That is, successful pretense is also characterized by the *contagion principle*: some things do come to be believed—or treated as if they were believed—merely because they are pretended, as well as by the *disparity principle*: when one engages in the pretense (imagines) that P, then what one makes-believe (imagines) to be true in the make-believe world differs in some way from what one believes would be true in the actual world if P.

Contagion and disparity occur in cases of pretense that are manifestly non-defective: cases where the pretender is explicitly aware that she is engaged with a realm of make-believe, and where the make-belief is elaborate and rich. That is, contagion and disparity are *features of* successful pretense, albeit features that are importantly circumscribed. The systematic project of articulating exactly what that circumscription amounts to will need to wait for another venue. In the remainder of the essay, I merely offer some data-points around which a successful theory would need to be built.

4. Contagion

4.1. Affective Contagion

Contagion is most strikingly manifest in cases involving what I call *affective transmission*: cases where mere contemplation of an emotionally charged situation causes the thinker to behave in a way consistent with the belief that the situation is sufficiently probable so as to influence prudent behavior.[8] So, for example, a child who has been pretending that there is a monster in the shower may well be reluctant to enter the bathroom (as may an adult who has just seen *Psycho*). This common experience has been noted by a number of philosophers (see e.g. Hume 1739/1978: I. iii. 13; Ryle 1949/1984: 258; H. H. Price 1960/ 1969: 308–9), and is borne out by laboratory research.

In one typical experiment, children were shown and permitted to inspect two opaque empty boxes, and then asked to imagine either that one of the boxes is occupied by a nice and friendly rabbit, or that one of the boxes is occupied by a mean and horrible monster. As expected, children's verbal reporting exhibited typical features of quarantining: when asked whether there was really a monster or rabbit in the box, the children were readily able to confirm that they were "just pretending" that there was. But subsequent non-verbal responses to the situation were more complicated. The experiment continued with the researcher asking whether she might leave the room to get the child a little gift. In four cases—all cases where the child had been asked to imagine a monster—the child was unwilling to let the researcher depart, despite repeated verbal and visual reassurance concerning the box's emptiness; in the remaining cases, the researcher stepped out, and (videotapes reveal) nearly half of the children opened one or both boxes, showing a marked tendency to focus on the box containing the imaginary creature. When, subsequent to her return, the experimenter asked the children about their action, a considerable proportion of the children who had opened the boxes maintained that they had done so because they wondered whether, after all, there was something in the box (Harris *et al.* 1991; Harris 2000: 173–80).

Although the interpretation of these data is not uncontroversial (see Bourchier and Davis 2000a, 2000b), it seems likely that affect plays at least some role.

---

[8] [*Note added in 2009*: For an alternative account of what is going on in these cases—one that appeals to the notion that I call *alief*—see chs. 13 and 14 below.]

If, for instance, children are asked to imagine that there is a pencil in a box when there are no other pencils in the room, and a person comes into the room looking for a pencil, children show no inclination to hand the visitor the box with the imagined pencil in it. (Whether this outcome is the consequence of some sort of cognitive override is, to my knowledge, an open question: I am not aware of research concerning the question of whether children in this situation exhibit some sort of momentary hesitation during which, for example, they look towards the box but decide not to reach for it—and, if so, whether this hesitation can itself be traced to some sort of affect-based response. If so, this would show the phenomenon to be more rather than less widespread, supporting further the main theses of this essay.) In any case, examples where there is a clear failure of override tend to be cases that are emotionally charged (in the sense that they involve either issues of personal safety, emotional significance, or empathy), at least according to studies done so far.

In a widely reported study performed by Paul Rozin and Carol Nemeroff, adults were presented with two bottles and invited to pour sugar into each one. Subjects were then asked to affix a "sugar" label to one bottle, and a "sodium cyanide" label to the other. Although subjects were happy to report that both bottles contained the same thing, namely sugar, and happy to concede that the choice of labels was purely arbitrary, many nonetheless showed a marked reluctance to eat from the bottle labeled "cyanide" (Rozin and Nemeroff 1990; Lillard 1994: 221). Although this tendency might be overridden in a high-stakes situation—it would be surprising to hear that a subject was unwilling to eat from the "cyanide" bottle even in exchange for a significant sum of money, or unwilling to make use of its contents when sugar was apparently required for some important purpose—its existence in the low-stakes situation is nonetheless striking. For even if the instinct to take the cyanide label as reporting some actual fact about the world is superseded by the realization that the label is misleading, the instinct is nonetheless there to be overcome. (For an alternative analysis of the case, see Velleman 2000: 276 n. 65. Since our uses of the term *belief* differ in precisely the ways relevant to our apparent disagreement, our views may be less distant than they initially seem.)

It is possible, of course, that the presence of the label plays some role in the subject's reasoning, providing apparent evidence that is processed as reality-indicative until it is overridden by the recollection that it is not. This hypothesis accords well with much of the heuristics and biases literature, which seems to suggest that we initially process all information as if it were a sign of the background circumstances normally associated with such a phenomenon[9] (think of how easily we are jolted into action by a watch we know to be five minutes fast). But even if this is the explanation, it remains the case that some

---

[9] [*Note added in 2009*: See e.g. the work of Dan Gilbert (Gilbert 1991, Gilbert and Gill 2000, Gilbert *et al.* 1993).]

overridden cue—the "danger" indicator invoked by the presence of the "cyanide" label—feeds into the agent's decision-making system in a way that allows it to play an action-guiding role. So while we may not have isolated the precise source of motivation in the sugar/cyanide case,[10] it seems clear that some feature of the situation that the agent recognizes (perhaps on reflection) to be merely imaginary nonetheless plays some role in guiding her behavior.

And, indeed, other research suggests that similar contagion occurs in cases where the imaginary cue is purely internal; moreover, it suggests that (non-overridden) contagion occurs in circumstances where the subject is directly emotionally affected by the imaginary scenario, and where the emotional involvement concerns the avoidance of risk. In a study of British voters, Nigel Harvey instructed subjects to pretend that they were supporters of a certain political party (party A) and then asked them whether they would undertake a slightly devious action (lying to a pollster) that would benefit the party they imagined themselves to be supporting (party A) and harm another party (party B) (Harvey 1992).[11] Some of those asked to engage in the pretense actually were supporters of party A (actual A-supporters); others were actually supporters of the rival party B (actual B-supporters); still others actually supported neither party A nor party B (neutrals).

When the study was conducted during a non-election period, there were no differences among the three groups: 80 percent of actual A-supporters, 80 percent of actual B-supporters, and 80 percent of neutrals reported that they would (in the pretense) undertake the A-benefitting action. By contrast, when a similar study was conducted during the election period, the results differed strikingly: 70 percent of actual A-supporters and 70 percent of neutrals reported that they would (in the pretense) undertake the A-benefitting action—but only 40 percent of actual B-supporters reported that they would do so. (Note that in the first study, "party A" was the Conservative party whereas "party B" was the Labour party; in the second study, the roles were reversed. Harvey argues convincingly that this difference is immaterial to the studies' outcomes, as a pair of studies in which both parties played both roles would presumably show.)

Harvey suggests that this may be a case of "decoupling failure" where "wishful thinking impairs belief-desire reasoning." The reluctance of actual B-supporters even to pretend to engage in A-benefitting action presumably

---

[10] [4] In order to do so, one might perform something like the following experiments. (1) Ask subjects to label the "cyanide" jar with a label reading "cyanide" and then to paste a second label over the initial label that reads "sugar." (Perhaps doing the inverse with the other jar.) (2) Ask subjects to label the "cyanide" jar with a label reading "sugar" and the "sugar" jar with a label reading "cyanide." (3) Ask subjects to label the "cyanide" jar with an "A" and the "sugar" jar with a "B." (4) Ask subjects merely to *imagine* that one of the jars contains cyanide and the other sugar. And so on. For additional discussion, see Rozin, Markwith, and Ross 1990; Rozin and Nemeroff 1990.

[11] [*In main text in published version*] Thanks to Greg Currie for alerting me to this work.

stems from a rather complicated process of anticipated contagion. Affective contagion occurs when mere contemplation of an emotionally charged situation causes the thinker to behave as if she believed the situation to obtain (or at least to be somewhat likely). In this case, the B-supporting subjects are presumably reluctant to engage in any sort of pretense concerning (their contribution to) A's success, for fear that it might produce in them a belief that A has succeeded (a situation normally associated with A's actually having succeeded), or for fear that it might weaken their actual commitment to B by producing in them a belief that A should succeed. (It is interesting to note that contagion seems more readily sparked by feared outcomes than by desired outcomes: note that while there is a sharp disparity between the willingness of actual B-supporters to pretend to engage in A-benefitting actions, there is no difference between the willingness of A-supporters and neutrals.[12])

Finally, as the impatient reader no doubt has been eager to point out, we need not turn to laboratory experiments for examples of affective transmission. Sexual fantasy provides a rather striking example of the phenomenon: merely imagining a sexually arousing situation typically results in genuine sexual arousal. (As the existence of pornography reminds us, the effect is even more profound in cases of prop-based pretense.) Psychoanalysis provides another almost endless source of cases: Goethe's earliest memory—of delightedly throwing crockery out the window and watching it smash on the streets below—is, according to Freud, behavior motivated by a fantasy of throwing his baby brother out the window, thereby ridding himself of his infant sibling rival (cf. Velleman 2000: 266). Finally, the phenomenon that philosophers call the "paradox of fictional emotions"—that we seem, *prima facie*, to feel real emotions for characters we know to be fictional—suggests another general realm in which affective transmission occurs.[13]

4.2. Cognitive Contagion

A second source of contagion can be found in the phenomenon of *cognitive transmission*: cases where mere contemplation of some emotionally neutral imaginary scenario causes the thinker to become (over-)sensitive to similar scenarios in the actual world. It is a well-known phenomenon—observed by anyone who has ever been pregnant or had a broken leg or bought a new car—that one's attention to and evidential standards concerning the world are sharply affected by what is "on one's mind." When one is in a particular

---

[12] [*Note added in 2009*: This may be part of a more general sensitivity towards negative outcomes. For recent philosophical discussions of this idea, see (in the context of intentional action) Knobe 2003, Pettit and Knobe 2009; (in the context of generics) Leslie 2008; (in the context of epistemology) Nagel (forthcoming).]

[13] [*Note added in 2009*: For additional discussion of fictional emotions see Chs. 11 and 12 below, as well as references therein.]

situation (e.g. pregnant, broken-legged, having just bought a new Subaru) one seems to observe an unexpectedly large number of others who are also in that situation. Three distinct explanations account for this phenomenon. First, one may be spending more time in settings that appeal to individuals with this condition, so one may indeed be encountering more people with broken legs or new Subarus than one had been previously encountering. But this is not the full explanation. In addition, it is likely that—without consciously realizing it to be the case—one is more sensitive to the genuine markers of that condition, so that one attends to and conceptually processes more instances of pregnancy or new Subaru-hood than one would have otherwise.[14] On top of this, one may well—again without realizing this to be the case—lower one's standards of evidence for concluding that an individual is in that condition, so that one attributes the condition (perhaps falsely) in instances where, even had one attended to them previously, one would have withheld attribution. These various phenomena—raising to salience, affecting attention, and altering evidential standards—are universal features of our cognitive behavior: "priming" and thinking-about affect both pattern-recognition and perceptual interpretation.

In this light, it is not surprising that imagining P could have the sorts of carryover effects that it seems to, even in non-affect-laden cases. So, for example, if I spend the morning imagining that I am birdwatching, I will be more likely to attend to actual bird-encounters in the afternoon. Moreover, I may be ready to conclude that something is a bird on much thinner evidence than I would have had I not engaged in the pretense (for instance, hearing a rustle in the tree outside my study window may be sufficient to convince me that the sound has an avian source). And my imaginative engagement with bird-watching may even affect the patterns I perceive—I may *see* things differently as a result of what I have imagined.

This phenomenon is familiar from psychological research on perception, and from research on heuristics and biases. For example, the Availability Heuristic describes precisely such a tendency towards cognitive contagion: a tendency to make judgments concerning the likelihood or relative frequency of events or objects on the basis of the "availability" of such objects or events to memory, perception, or—Kahneman and Tversky explicitly note—imagination (Tversky and Kahneman 1973/1982: 178). And research on attention suggests that perception is heavily dependent on the explicit or tacit intentions with which one approaches the perceptual scenario—intentions that may be equally well stimulated by imagining as by some other cognitive activity.

In short, the evocation of perceptual and evaluative schemata is relatively indifferent to whether the evocation occurs as the result of something in the

---

[14] [*Note added in 2009*: For fascinating work on the effects of mindset on attention, see Most, Scholl, Clifford, and Simons 2005.]

ambient environment, something in memory, or something brought to mind merely as the result of imaginative rehearsal. In all three cases, the consequent availability of the object, event, or schema plays a central role in subsequent attention, perception, and even reasoning.

4.3. Summary: Contagion

It seems clear that episodes of pretense typically exhibit features of contagion as well as features of quarantining. While some aspects of cognitive processing exhibit a marked capacity to distinguish the imaginary from the real, others seem relatively indifferent to the question of whether their subject matter was generated by the world or by the mind. We see this most strikingly in cases of affect-evoking imagination; it is also evident in cases of schema-evoking imagination. In both families of cases, the traditional picture—that successful instances of pretense resemble belief-like states in terms of subject matter but differ from them in terms of motivational force—is misleading at least in terms of its second claim.[15]

Moreover, in neither case is this a consequence of some incidental or peripheral feature of our cognitive apparatus: cognitive and affective transmission result from features of the human mind as central as those that produce our capacity for quarantining (see Ch. 13 below). Cognitive transmission is an inevitable by-product of fundamental processing features: the very features that make perception and information-processing possible make cognitive transmission inevitable. Without the use of schemata, attentional filters, and evidential standards adjustable on the basis of non-belief-based input, our finite cognitive and sensory apparatuses would be ineffective tools for making sense of the world around us.

Affective transfer is a similarly inevitable by-product of similarly fundamental mechanisms. As research by Antonio Damasio and others has demonstrated, patients with damage to the ventromedial prefrontal cortex manifest a cluster of incapacities (Bechara *et al.* 1994; Damasio *et al.* 1991; Damasio 1994; Damasio 1999; LeDoux 1996). They lack autonomic responses to emotionally disturbing pictures (though they have no cognitive difficulty identifying such images, nor do they lack autonomic responses in general), and they reveal a marked tendency to engage in high-risk behavior (despite describing themselves as fully aware of its inadvisability). Together, these data seem to suggest that some sort of somatic realization of the potential consequences of a risky action is crucial to prudent decision-making: without it, the theoretical

---

[15] [*In main text in published version*] A related issue is that of source-monitoring. Research on eyewitness testimony suggests that such contagion occurs frequently in children and adults when imaginary episodes are misremembered as real; cf. Ceci and Bruck 1993; Ceci and Friedman 2000; Loftus 1996.

advantages of one or another course of action may be apparent, but these are not translated into action-guiding behavior. Without the capacity to feel something akin to real emotions in the case of merely imagined situations, we would be unable to engage in practical reasoning. What this means is that affective transmission is a fundamental feature of our cognitive architecture, and cannot be treated as straightforwardly and unqualifiedly deviant.

5. Disparity

We now turn to the second pair of features: mirroring and disparity. The mirroring principle says that imagining and believing are attitudes with similar ranges of possible non-defective contents: the sorts of things that we are able to non-defectively imagine are the sorts of things that we could, in principle, non-defectively believe. But it seems clear that that non-defective imaginative content may differ from non-defective belief content in at least two ways: what I successfully imagine may be *incomplete*, in the sense that some of its features may remain permanently—even explicitly—unspecified and unspecifiable; and what I successfully imagine may be *incoherent*, in the sense that some of its features may be conceptually or logically incompatible. (I here skate over a number of important issues concerning the attribution of content.) The illusion that things are otherwise stems, I suspect, from intuitive reliance on a picture that treats imagining as just like belief, only off-line, and from a picture of prop-based pretense that treats principles of generation as complete, uniform mappings from one realm to another. Once we realize how complicated mapping relations are, even in simple children's games of prop-based pretense, we can gain a sense for one of the mechanisms by which potentially imagined contents may come to differ from their belief-based counterparts, and hence how disparity might arise.

5.1. Principles of Generation

As Kendall Walton has persuasively argued, games of make-believe are often governed by what he calls *principles of generation*—local conventions that govern how (certain) features of the actual world are to be mapped onto the imagined one. So, for instance, to pass the time on a long drive, we might agree—explicitly or tacitly—that cars "count as" lions and trucks as tigers. Once we have done so, certain fictional facts will obtain: if there is a car 50 feet from ours, it will be true in the fiction we have generated that there is a lion 50 feet from the lion we are riding—even if none of us notices it; if two trucks are traveling side by side, then two tigers are too. The rule-governedness of generative principles is part of what allows us to structure imaginative space in a way that lets us make sense of its content. But even in simple cases of prop-based pretense, while some features are generative, others are not.[16] The truck's location may determine the location of the tiger, but other features of the truck—its carburetor, its mudflaps, its spare tire—may have no corresponding role to play in the realm of the pretense; and features of the pretense—the color of the tiger's fur, the sharpness of its teeth, the length of its tail—may have no corresponding "base" in the realm of the prop.

Consider, for example, how many different mapping schemes are employed even in an extremely simple pretend scenario, and how effortlessly the child moves among them.

> The children watched as we introduced two animals, a monkey and a horse. We "fed" the monkey with a yellow brick, explaining that he wanted some banana, and we "fed" the horse with a red brick, explaining that he wanted some cake. Next, we introduced some more animals, telling the children whether the animal wanted banana or cake to eat. The two-year-olds almost invariably responded in accordance with the generativity principle. In "feeding" the newly-introduced animals, none of them touched either the "banana" or the "cake" that had been given to the monkey and the horse. Instead, they spontaneously reached out and appropriately selected either another "banana" or another "cake" from two separate piles of red and yellow bricks available on the table. (Harris 2000: 12)

During the first part of the game, the pile of red bricks represents a pile of pieces of cake, and the child's action in removing a brick from the pile represents selecting a piece of cake and carrying it to another location. Certain features of the bricks are understood to be relevant to play, others not. So, for instance, the location of the actual bricks indicates the location of the pretend cakes. The shape of the actual bricks may be taken to indicate the shape of the pretend cakes. But the color of the actual bricks may not indicate the color of the pretend cakes. Their lack of stickiness presumably does not indicate the lack of stickiness of the pretend cakes. Their density hopefully does not indicate the density of the pretend cakes. And the fact that they are made of painted wood surely does not indicate that the pretend cakes are composed of such ingredients.

---

[16] [5] Sometimes when we engage in prop-oriented games of pretense, the main goal is to keep the mapping as steady and uniform as possible. So, for example, if I am trying to figure out what the room would look like if the couch were where the table is now and the table were pushed back against the now-empty wall, I want to employ only two sorts of mappings in my imaginary realm: objects besides the table and the couch occupy exactly the same locations in the imaginary realm as they do in the actual world, and the couch and table are of exactly their real-world size, but occupying different locations. This is often the case when we employ mental imagery in the service of spatial problem-solving tasks. [*Added in 2009*: For discussion of related issues, see Ch. 2 above.]

Think, moreover, about the complicated role that the color of the bricks plays in the imaginative exercise. That the bricks are colored red is important to the play—it is this that indicates that the bricks represent cakes rather than bananas. But there would be no problem with introducing a further stipulation in the game—that cakes at the top of the pile are vanilla and cakes at the bottom are chocolate. So to determine what sort of object a particular brick represents, appeal would need to be made to two sorts of properties: the color-properties of the brick indicate its category-membership—red bricks are cakes, yellow bricks are bananas—whereas the location-properties of one subset of the bricks (those red bricks lying in the initial pile) would indicate further of their features within the category—bricks at the top are vanilla, bricks at the bottom chocolate. Note how different these two sorts of mappings are. In the case of real-world items, visual and other sensory properties are indicators of features like banananess and chocolate-cakeness, whereas in this game, visual properties are indicators of the one (banana vs. cake), and a property that could never criterially serve such a role in actual cases—location—distinguishes them along the other (chocolate vs. vanilla).

So far, we've only looked at the very first mapping—the one that makes the bricks in the red pile cakes. The next thing that happens is that the child moves one of the cakes to the "mouth" of the stuffed animal. Here, her actual-world motions serve to fix the pretend-world motions: the way she moves the brick from the pile to the "animal" is the way that the cake moves from the table to the horse. Note that unlike the brick, the child may well here represent *herself* both within and without the game: though she may be a zookeeper, or a horse-trainer, or a child on a nineteenth-century farm, she may also just be Sophie or Helena, engaged in an act of animal-feeding. So whereas the mapping that governed the relation between blocks in the real world and their imaginary-world counterparts took only a few of their elements—such as location and perhaps size and shape—the mapping that governs the relation between the child in the real world and her imaginary-world counterpart may take on nearly all of her features—at least at this stage.

The next step in the story involves the child feeding the cake to the horse while the horse makes munching noises. Note that here, the mapping between the child's actions and the events in the pretend world must simultaneously differentiate between the actions of her hands, and the actions of her voice. When the child holds the cake up to the stuffed animal's mouth, the location of her hand indicates the location of the feeder's hand in the story. But when the child makes the munching noises, the sound of her voice indicates the voice of the *horse*.

In short, it seems that we are extremely flexible and adaptive about the principles of generation we use when we engage in exercises of prop-based pretense. Mapping may be *partial*, in the sense that only some of the features of the actual world entity are mapped into the pretend realm (see Fauconnier and Turner 1998); and mappings may be *multiple*, in the sense that features of many actual-world entities may be mapped onto a single entity in the pretend realm.

5.2. Incompleteness and Incoherence

Partial and multiple mapping have direct implications for the nature of imaginative content. The possibility of partial mapping means that imaginary entities are potentially *incomplete*: they may explicitly lack determinates for their determinables; the possibility of multiple mapping means that imaginary entities are potentially *incoherent*: they may affirmatively bear incompatible properties.

So, for example, I may imagine that it is between 50 and 75 miles from Lilliput to Brobdignag, with no further commitment that one rather than another of these distances is—even in the pretense—the distance between them; I may have a mental image of a spotted cow with somewhere between ten and twenty spots, with no further commitment that one rather than another of these provides—even in the pretense—the genuine spot-count. Indeed, I may even commit myself to it being true that, in the pretense, *no* candidate determination correctly specifies the determinable in question. I might be committed to a view of the term *zillion*, for example, according to which a zillion is a one followed by a large finite number of zeros, but is determinately not equal to 10^n, for any value of n. All of these, if successful, are examples of non-defective incomplete imagining.

In addition, non-defective imagining may be incoherent. I may imagine that seven and five both do and do not equal twelve (for a story to this effect, see Ch. 10 below) or that there is a box that is both empty and not empty (for a story to this effect, see Priest 1997). The ease with which I am able to do so is a consequence of the ease with which "counting as" occurs in imagination: a number can "count as" the number 7 in a story, even if, in the story, that number in conjunction with 5 does not make 12; a box can "count as" empty in a story, even if it also contains something; the Scarecrow can "count as" a scarecrow in *The Wizard of Oz*, even if he is able to walk and talk. And when, in *Mary Poppins*, one of the Pleiades (Maia) comes down to do the Christmas shopping for herself and her six sisters, the little girl dressed in a sky-blue wisp of fabric "counts as" being a star, despite obvious discrepancies between their relative sizes and chemical compositions (Travers 1934/1962: 181–92). Without this sort of "cheapness," the kinds of imaginative projects in which we engage—from childhood prop-based pretense to sophisticated storytelling—would not be possible.

5.3. Summary: Disparity

As with contagion and quarantining, episodes of pretense typically exhibit features of disparity as well as features of mirroring. While imaginary objects borrow some of their features from their real-world counterparts, they may differ in at least two ways: what is successfully imagined may be (recognized as) both incoherent and incomplete, whereas what is real may not. So, as before, the traditional picture—that successful instances of pretense resemble belief-like states in terms of subject matter but differ from them in terms of motivational force—requires supplementation, this time in terms of its first claim. And, as before, this is a consequence of features central to the nature of imagination itself.[17]

[17] [*] *Acknowledgements*: For discussion of this material, suggestions concerning relevant literature, and/or comments on previous drafts, I am grateful to Tyler Burge, Greg Currie, John Hawthorne, Dom Lopes, Daniel Nolan, Shaun Nichols, Ted Sider, Zoltán Gendler Szabó, and David Velleman. Greg Currie and Shaun Nichols were especially helpful in suggesting empirical references, and John Hawthorne, Daniel Nolan, and Ted Sider pressed me on a number of important conceptual questions. Thanks also to audiences at the SUNY Buffalo Cognitive Science colloquium series (2001) and at the Ohio State University Department of Philosophy (2002), where some of this material was presented.

8

Self-Deception as Pretense

In this essay, I offer an account of the phenomenon of self-deception. I propose that paradigmatic cases of self-deception satisfy the following conditions: (a) the person who is self-deceived about not-P pretends (in the sense of *makes-believe* or *imagines* or *fantasizes*) that not-P is the case, often while believing that P is the case and not believing that not-P is the case; and (b) the pretense that not-P largely plays the role normally played by belief in terms of (i) introspective vivacity and (ii) motivation of action in a wide range of circumstances.

I contend that understanding self-deception in this way is highly natural, and that it provides a non-paradoxical characterization of the phenomenon that explains both its distinctive patterns of instability and its ordinary association with irrationality. One might then wonder why this diagnosis has been largely overlooked. I suggest that the oversight is due to a failure to recognize the philosophical significance of a crucial fact about the human mind, namely, the degree to which attitudes other than belief often play a central role in our mental and practical lives, both by "influenc[ing our] . . . passions and imagination," and by "governing . . . our actions" (Hume 1739/1978: 629).

This essay can be seen as part of a series that begins with "On the Relation between Pretense and Belief" (2003) (Ch. 7 above) and ends with the two alief essays (2008a, 2008b; Chs. 13 and 14). Together, these essays present an account of the ways in which attitudes such as pretense and imagination can play roles that are often thought to be reserved for belief.

***

This essay was first published in *Philosophical Perspectives*, 21/1 (2008), 231–58, and is reprinted with the kind permission of Wiley-Blackwell. Except for a few minor rephrasings and slight reformatting, the text that appears here is identical to that of the published version. As a result of the reformatting, footnote numbers have changed. The original number of each footnote is noted in [square brackets].

> Belief is "that act of mind which renders realities more present to us than fictions, causes them to weigh more in the thought . . . gives them superior influence on the passions and imagination . . . and renders them the governing principles of all of our actions."
>
> —David Hume, *A Treatise on Human Nature* (1739/1978: 629) (appendix)

0. Opening Story

Every day for the last few weeks, I've woken up with the thought that *today* will be the day that I finish a draft of this paper.

On any sort of reasonable inductive grounds, I ought to know better. After all, I had the thought on Monday and then spent the day reorganizing my files; I had the thought on Tuesday and then spent the day reading blogs; I had the thought on Wednesday and then spent the day grading papers; I had the thought on Thursday and then spent the day answering old e-mail messages; and I had the thought on Friday and then spent the day planning my courses for next semester.

Moreover, this happens every time I write a paper: I always find something more urgent to do. Even when I get started on a paper, I always spend days perfecting the first paragraph and leave the hard parts for later. (Think for a moment how an introduction like this one could possibly have gotten written.[1])

So if I have good inductive evidence for anything, it's that any paper I write will be written after weeks of highly sophisticated procrastination. I'm about as sure of this as I am of anything agent-involving: as sure as I am that when I get to campus, the parking lot attendant will glance at my blue permit and wave me through; as sure as I am that when the student meeting me at 3:30 comes to my office, he will ask me to change his grade on the second test.

But still, when I woke up this morning, it was with the thought that *today* will be the day all this will change: *today* I'm going to sit in my office for seven hours straight and make it through to the end of the first draft. In fact, even after having wasted the entire morning *revising* this introduction (which I wasted yesterday morning writing), the upshot of which is basically that there's no chance whatsoever that I'm going to finish a draft of this paper today, I'm still ready to say that today will be the day that I finish a draft of this paper.

1. Introduction

As the opening story reveals, I am a highly experienced practitioner of the art of self-deception[2]—there is nothing unusual about my finding myself in a state

---

[1] [2] See <http://www-csli.stanford.edu/~john/procrastination.html> for a description of the associated phenomenology.

[2] [3] I am also, as the story reveals, paradigmatically weak-willed. The connection between self-deception and weakness of the will has been explored by, among others, Donald Davidson (e.g. 1970/1985, 1982, 1985), Alfred Mele (e.g. 1987b) and Amélie Rorty (e.g. 1988). It is an interesting question, though one which I will not investigate here, whether the account I offer of self-deception can be fruitfully applied to the case of *akrasia*. (Thanks to Gábor Betegh for pressing me on this issue.) As Kendall Walton has pointed out (personal communication), the example above is a somewhat atypical case of self-deception, in that vividly focusing on the idea of my completing the draft may make it more probable that I will complete it (even if, given the evidence, this is highly unlikely); this provides further strength for the essay's more

which for all practical purposes seems describable as follows: I believe that I will procrastinate instead of writing my paper today, and at the same time I have intentionally brought myself not to believe this. Call this description the *wide-scope natural description* of self-deception.

Natural Description of Self-deception (wide scope): A believes that P, and A has intentionally brought herself not to believe that P.

Despite its initial appeal, the wide-scope natural description of self-deception is problematic for two broadly recognized sorts of reasons: the first concerns the *state* it describes; the second concerns the *process* it appeals to. The *static* problem[3] confronting the wide-scope natural description of self-deception arises from a logical constraint on the ascription of predicates: for reasons that have nothing to do with belief as such, it cannot be true of a single person both that she believes that P, and that it is not the case that she believes that P (at the same time, in the same way, etc.). To the extent that the wide-scope natural description requires this, it must be modified. In addition, the wide-scope natural description confronts a *dynamic* problem that arises from a particular fact about belief: in general, it is not possible for an agent to discard a belief simply because she decides to do so.[4] So for reasons having to do with belief in particular, it cannot be true of a single person both that she believes that P, and that she has—just like that—intentionally brought herself not to believe that P. To the extent that the wide-scope natural description requires this, it must again be modified.

Faced with these problems, one might be tempted to adjust the natural description as follows:

Natural Description of Self-deception (narrow scope): A believes that P, and A has intentionally brought herself to believe that not-P.[5]

And, indeed, on the narrow-scope account, the static problem becomes considerably less pressing: it may well be possible for A to believe P and for A to believe not-P, without it following that A believes (P and not-P), or that A believes P and A does not believe P. But the dynamic problem becomes, if anything, even more

general point, namely that states other than belief and desire may play a central role in the motivation of action.

[3] [4] I take the terms *static* and *dynamic* from Mele 1987a; cf. also Mele 1997.

[4] [5] There is a large literature on this subject. For the modern *locus classicus*, see B. Williams 1970/1973a.

[5] [6] For ease of presentation, I will use P throughout to represent the propositional content of the true warranted belief (or related attitude), and not-P to represent the propositional content of the false unwarranted belief (or related attitude). There may well be complicated cases of self-deception where different sorts of propositions play the relevant roles—but the issues surrounding them are orthogonal to the concerns of this paper, so I will set such cases aside in the discussion that follows.

urgent: whatever facts about belief render it difficult to discard a belief at will render it even more difficult to acquire one by such means.[6]

While there are interesting and sophisticated ways of finessing these difficulties, recent accounts of self-deception have tended instead to stray far from the natural description. Alfred Mele's highly influential *deflationary* account, for example, requires only that the body of evidence possessed by the subject at the time of entering into self-deception provides greater warrant for P (the true belief) than for not-P (the false belief)—but it does not require that the subject actually hold the true belief—nor does it require that the process of entering into self-deception be an intentional one.[7] Annette Barnes likewise maintains that "while a given interaction between people is deceptive . . . only if one of the parties in the interaction engages in some essentially intentional activity . . . intentionality is not necessary for a given activity to be self-deceptive" and offers an account that deliberately shuns many features of the natural description (Barnes 1997: 1 and *passim*). And Steffen Borge has recently argued that "there is no such thing as self-deception . . . what has formerly been known as self-deception is rather a failure to understand, or lack of awareness of, one's emotional life and its influence on us" (Borge 2003: 1).

Without denying that these accounts capture important and interesting facets of our enormously complex mental lives, I think it is both possible and worthwhile to hold onto certain central features of the natural account. While there may be other mental habits that conform to the various characterizations offered in the literature, and while these may be related in important ways to paradigmatic instances of self-deception, I want to suggest that the cleanest and most interesting cases of self-deception share the following characteristic:

Self-deception as Pretense: A person who is self-deceived about not-P pretends (in the sense of *makes-believe* or *imagines* or *fantasizes*) that not-P is the case, often while believing that P is the case and not believing that not-P is the case. The pretense that not-P largely plays the role normally played by belief in terms of (i) introspective vivacity and (ii) motivation of action in a wide range of circumstances.

---

[6] [*Note added in* 2009: Actually, I'm not sure this is true. Discarding beliefs turns out to be an awfully sticky business. (See Gilbert 1991; Gilbert, Tafarodi, and Malone 1993.) But the larger point goes through even if it is equally challenging to acquire and to discard beliefs at will.]

[7] [7] Mele's jointly sufficient conditions for "entering into self-deception in acquiring the belief that not-P" are these: (1) The belief that not-P which S acquires is false; (2) S treats data relevant, or at least seemingly relevant, to the truth value of not-P in a motivationally biased way; (3) this biased treatment is a non-deviant cause of S's acquiring the belief that not-P; (4) the body of data possessed by S at the time provides greater warrant for P than for not-P (Mele 1997: 95, italics omitted). Mele's departures from the standard account are central to his dialectical project; he considers "the attempt to understand self-deception on the model of paradigmatic interpersonal deception" to be "fundamentally misguided" (Mele 1997: 91). (Note that in keeping with the convention noted in n. 5, I have replaced Mele's "P" with "not-P" and vice versa.)

The account I offer differs from both standard and revisionary accounts in denying the widely held assumption that self-deception involves a *belief* that not-P.[8] But precisely in so doing, it seems to capture some of the distinctive features of self-deception. It feels plausible to say that what I believe is that I will not finish a draft of this paper today (P), but that I am pretending (making-believe) that I will (not-P), and that my pretense (that not-P) is playing the role normally played by a belief to that effect (though it is also importantly unstable in certain characteristic ways that I will discuss in §4 below): in particular, at least under ordinary low-stakes circumstances, it occupies my thoughts in a manner typical of belief (when I consider the matter, it seems to me that I genuinely expect to finish a draft today) and it guides my actions in a wide range of circumstances (I sincerely assert that this is my expectation, and I am ready to make plans accordingly). Moreover, the account accords well with the sense that self-deception is often an irrational condition: after all, one canonical characterization of irrationality is that it is a state where something imaginary inappropriately comes to play the cognitive role of something real.[9]

Indeed, the account can be seen as a way of articulating the common ground between the two traditional approaches to the problem of self-deception. Such

---

[8] Annette Barnes's account includes the condition that a certain sort of "bias or partiality... causes one to *believe* that [not-P]" (Barnes 1997: 117, italics added). Dion Scott-Kakures maintains that "in self-deception motivation plays a continuing or recurring role... in the generation of *belief*" (Scott-Kakures 2002: 600, italics added). Alfred Mele speaks of the problem of providing sufficient conditions for characterizing the process of "entering into self-deception in acquiring a *belief* that" not-P, the first condition of which is that "the *belief* that [not-P] which S acquires is false" (Mele 1997: 95, italics added). And so on. The same is true of more traditional accounts. Donald Davidson holds that in cases of self-deception "A has evidence on the basis of which he believes that *p* is more apt to be true than its negation; the thought that *p*, or the thought that he ought rationally to believe that *p*, motivates A to act in such a way as to cause himself to *believe* the negation of *p*" (Davidson 1985: 145 italics added). And even Ariela Lazar, whose account comes closest to mine on these matters, writes that "on my view, self-deceptive *beliefs* are direct expressions of the subject's wishes, fears and hopes. Qua *beliefs* which mostly correspond to such factors (rather than to evidence), self-deceptive states may be described as fantasies. Even so, *these beliefs* affect the subject's behavior just like normal beliefs, by figuring in practical and theoretical reasoning" (Lazar 1999: 266, italics added). An account that comes somewhat closer to my own is offered in a recent essay by Andy Egan. Egan suggests that subjects suffering from delusions bear an attitude that he calls "bimagination" towards the content of their delusions—an attitude with "some of the distinctive features of believing, and some of the distinctive features of imagining." Subjects in a state of self-deception, he suggests, bear "a similar sort of intermediate attitude" towards the relevant content—"one that's in some respects belief-like, in others desire-like" (Egan 2009).

[9] Gregory Currie, for instance, has recently proposed an account of schizophrenia according to which it is helpfully understood as a condition where imaginings are misidentified by the subject as beliefs and perceptions (Currie 2000, 2000b). (For related (sometimes critical) literature, see Bayne and Pacherie 2005; M. Davies *et al.* 2001 with discussion; Egan 2008; Young 2000.) Though the details of these accounts advantageously employ the resources of contemporary cognitive psychology, the basic insight that underlies it—that "madness" often involves mistaking the imaginary for the real—can be found already in Greek tragedy, and presumably before. On my account of self-deception, imaginings are not necessarily *misidentified* as beliefs, though they are allowed in many ways to play belief-like roles.

approaches share the assumption that it is not an orthographic accident that the (English) term *self-deception* yokes the notions of *self* and *deception*,[10] and that it is their conjoint presence that gives rise to the particular cluster of perplexities characteristic of this phenomenon. On such views, since self-deception shares many of its central features with ordinary interpersonal deception, an adequate account of the phenomenon must give these similarities their due. At the same time, the analogy cannot be taken completely literally. For whatever else may be said of it, self-deception cannot involve deception of the self by the self in exactly the same way that interpersonal deception involves deception of one person by another. Self-deception is fundamentally something carried out by a single reasonably unified individual on herself,[11] and no matter how clever or stupid I am, I cannot deceive myself in exactly the same way that I can deceive another.

The two standard responses tend to emphasize one of these features at the cost of the other.[12] Traditional *homuncularist* approaches emphasize "deception" over "self" by positing the existence of one or more relatively autonomous subsystems within the person, one of which is responsible for perpetuating deceit on the other(s).[13] Traditional *nondoxastic* approaches emphasize "self" over "deception" by crediting a single agent with an attitude that is merely belief-like (such as "acceptance") towards one or both of the propositions in question, or by contending that the subject does not hold any sort of attitude

---

[10] [10] In his "Real Self-deception" (Mele 1997) and again in his *Self-deception Unmasked* (Mele 2001), Alfred Mele distinguishes three (non-exclusive) approaches that might be taken in characterizing the phenomenon of self-deception. *Lexical* approaches begin with a definition of "deception" and model their characterization of self-deception on one or more of its features; *example-based* approaches attempt to identify common features among a range of paradigm instances of the phenomenon and provide a general characterization on this basis; and *theory-guided* approaches set out to characterize the phenomenon in a way that accords with some theory about the etiology and nature of self-deception, providing a characterization that satisfies these constraints. To the extent that there is a unitary phenomenon to be explored here, one would hope for an account on which the three strategies would converge. My aim is to provide such an account. (For Mele's own approach, see n. 7.)

[11] [11] Indeed, Richard Holton has recently argued that the defining feature of self-deception is that it is deception *about* the self (Holton 2000/1). Cf. also Amélie Rorty's insightful remark: "Our ordinary practices presuppose that the self is both a rational integrator and that it is composed of relatively independent subsystems. The classical description of self-deception arises from a *superimposition* of two ineliminable and irreducible conceptions of the self" (Rorty 1988: 12). "[O]nly a presumptively integrated person who interprets her system-of-relatively-independent-subsystems through the first picture of the self, only a person who treats the independence of her constituent subsystems as a failure of integration, is capable of self-deception" (Rorty 1988: 25).

[12] [12] Mele (1987a) calls these strategies "partitioning views" and "disanalogy views" respectively. Recent collections of essays on self-deception include Ames and Dissanayke 1996; Elster 1986; M. Martin 1985; McLaughlin and Rorty 1988.

[13] [13] This sort of response is often traced to Freud; for influential contemporary versions see Davidson 1970/1985, 1982, 1985 and Pears 1984.

towards one or both of the propositions.[14] Each view faces certain well-known problems. Because standard homuncularist strategies so directly assimilate the intrapersonal to the interpersonal case, they seem unable to explain crucial motivational facts about self-deception. (If one of the subpersons (truly) believes that P and does not believe that not-P, and if that subperson is bothered by this and wishes it were not the case, why would she find it psychologically fruitful intentionally to bring *someone else* to believe the opposite?[15]) And because standard nondoxasticist strategies deny that the subject bears an attitude of belief towards the false proposition, they seem unable to explain both the irrationality of the phenomenon and the motivational force of not-P. (After all, there is nothing wrong with *assuming* something false, or *supposing* something false—and it is unclear why merely assuming or supposing something to be the case should cause one not only to act as if it were the case, but also to find oneself with the sort of subjective feelings typically associated with believing it to be true.)

At the same time, there is an important strand of truth to each approach. The phenomenon of self-deception, like many other cognitive phenomena, does reveal a degree of complexity to our mental architecture of which homuncularism is simply an extreme version. And the phenomenon of self-deception, like many other cognitive phenomena, also reveals the presence of states other than belief that play crucial roles in our thoughts and actions, a fact that nondoxasticism stresses. But this sense that there is something right about both of the standard pictures is, I think, not a coincidence: rather it is a consequence of these two apparently divergent interpretations identifying the same cognitive capacity—*pretense*, or *imagination*, or *make-belief*—the capacity by means of which we are able to engage in simulative off-line processing of situations that need not correspond to actual states of affairs.[16] Where standard homuncularists are right is that the products of such simulations need not be fully integrated with the rest of our beliefs; the presence of such a system does provide an alternative locus for the attribution of cognition. And where standard nondoxasticists are right is that we should not call these attitudes "beliefs"; the presence of such attitudes does show that we bear a relation to propositions about which we are self-deceived that differs from full-fledged belief.

[14] [14] This sort of response is often traced to Sartre. Sartre himself retains the term "belief" to describe the attitude in question, but he allows that it is possible simultaneously to believe P and disbelieve P. (For illuminating discussion, cf. Wood 1988.) An influential contemporary version is Mele's 1997 (see n. 7 above). Mele's account is "reductive" in the sense that he does not attribute to the subject the belief that P, hence the static paradox has no bite.

[15] [15] As Mark Johnston writes: "The homuncular explanation replaces a contradictory description of the self-deceiver with a host of psychological puzzles. How can the deceiving subsystem have the capacities to perpetrate the deception?...Why should the deceiving subsystem be interested in the deception? Does it like lying for its own sake? Or does it suppose that it knows what is best for the deceived system to believe?" (Johnston 1988: 64).

[16] [16] For representative discussion, cf. Currie and Ravenscroft 2002; M. Davies and Stone 1995a, 1995b; Gendler 2003 (Ch. 7 above); Goldman 2006; Harris 2000; Nichols and Stich 2000; Nichols 2004, 2006a; Walton 1990.

2. Belief and Other Attitudes

As the opening quotation from Hume emphasizes, belief brings with it a characteristic set of associated tendencies. (i) In contrast to their non-committal counterparts such as supposition or imagination, beliefs tend "to weigh more in the thought" and to be associated with subjective feelings of *"force* or *vivacity* or *firmness* or *steadiness."* And, again in contrast to other cognitive states, (ii) beliefs (in conjunction with conative states such as desire) tend to serve as "the governing principles . . . of our actions," and thus to be associated with certain behavioral tendencies (Hume 1739/1978: 629). The first of these features plays a central role in what H. H. Price has called "Traditional" or "Occurrence" Accounts of belief—accounts that distinguish belief from other states on the basis of introspectively identifiable "marks" such as vivacity or firmness; the second plays a central role in what Price has called "Modern" or "Dispositional" Accounts—accounts that distinguish belief from other states on the basis of its tendencies to lead, in conjunction with desire, to a disposition towards action (cf. H. H. Price 1960/1969, *passim*).

The nuances and refinements associated with contemporary versions of these theories need not concern us here. For I want to challenge a tacit commitment that lies behind both of them. Each identifies some sort of *mark* by which belief can be distinguished from other mental states, and then suggests that that mark is criterial of some attitude being a belief.[17] But such a commitment misrepresents something crucial about our mental lives: namely, the numerous ways in which belief can obtain without its normal manifestations, and the numerous conditions under which other cognitive attitudes can bear them in its stead.

Rather, I think that the most helpful way of distinguishing beliefs from other related cognitive attitudes is neither through their subjective vivacity, nor through their dispositional connection through desire to action, but through their *telos* of truth, such that their status as beliefs depends upon their being *reality-sensitive* in certain crucial ways. If I believe that P, I not only represent P to myself as being true—I bear the attitude that I do towards P with (in a sense to be specified in a moment) the aim of thereby bearing that attitude towards something true.[18] What makes my commitment to P a *belief* that P—as opposed

---

[17] [17] There are, of course, differences among the marks—in their first- or third-person accessibility, categorical or dispositional manifestation, etc.—the finessing of which may allow one or the other of the views to have extensional adequacy.

[18] [18] This characterization is due to David Velleman: "What distinguishes believing a proposition from imagining or supposing it is . . . the aim of getting the truth-value of that particular proposition right, by regarding the proposition as true only if it really is. Belief is the attitude of accepting a proposition with the aim of thereby accepting a truth" (Velleman 2000: 252, italics omitted). For refinement, see Shah 2003; Shah and Velleman 2005. For related (often critical) discussion, see Currie 2002b; O'Brien 2005; Owens 2003; Vahid 2006; Wedgwood 2002. I will not offer independent defense of this view here.

to an imagining that P, or a supposition that P—is that my acceptance of P as true is contingent on how I take the world to be: my attitude is one whose fundamental satisfaction-conditions require that it have been formed (whether intentionally or not) through the workings of a cognitive system that regulates certain of my cognitions in ways designed to ensure that I bear this attitude only towards truths.[19] As a result, if I bear an attitude of belief towards P, I should be willing to submit my evidence for P to rational scrutiny, and I should be committed to abandoning my belief if I acquire grounds for thinking it false. (Of course, I may fall short of my ideals in certain cases: it is certainly possible for someone to have false or ill-grounded beliefs.[20] But it is only because they are beliefs—attitudes whose *telos* is truth as such—that the evaluation of ill-groundedness gains a foothold; a fantasy that fails to conform to reality does not thereby qualify as defective.)

By contrast, if I merely pretend or imagine that P, I pretend or imagine that P is true—but I do not bear the attitude that I do towards P with the aim of thereby bearing that attitude towards something true. My acceptance of P as true is independent of how I take the world to be, and the fundamental satisfaction-conditions for my holding such an attitude in no way require that it have been formed by a truth-regulated cognitive mechanism. As a result, if I bear an attitude of pretense towards P, I am not committed to submitting my evidence for P (should I have any) to rational scrutiny, nor am I committed to abandoning my pretense if I have or acquire grounds for thinking it false. In short, belief is a *receptive* attitude; pretense is a *projective* one.

What I am suggesting is that, in cases of self-deception, the pretense that not-P plays the role characteristically reserved for belief. The plausibility of the thesis rests on three main claims. The first is that it is fully coherent to suppose that, in circumstances of self-deception, the self-deceived subject believes the true proposition, even though it neither occupies her thoughts nor guides her actions in ordinary circumstances—that is, the first main claim is that lack of normal manifestation does not imply lack of belief.[21] The second is that it is

---

[19] [19] Or perhaps towards sufficient approximations of the truth. Even so, truth remains the regulative ideal.

[20] [20] Such beliefs may play a central role in cases of what I call *self-delusion*, in which the subject comes to have the false belief that not-P. I discuss these cases—and identify the ways in which they differ from cases of self-deception—in §4 below.

[21] [21] Indeed, this seems to be the standard assumption in the psychological literature on self-deception (though since psychologists' use of the term "belief" is far more liberal than that of philosophers, this apparent evidence may be misleading). According to the most influential and widely accepted characterization in psychology—that of Sackheim and Gur (1978)—cases of self-deception are those where: (1) C simultaneously believes P and not-P; (2) C is aware of believing only one of P and not-P; (3) It is C's motivation that determines which one (of P and not-P) C is aware of believing. (I have collapsed Sackheim and Gur's conditions (1) and (2) into a single condition, and rephrased the remaining conditions somewhat.) For a discussion of condition (1) of this account, see the *Behavioral and Brain Sciences* symposium concerning Mele 1997; see also Mele 2001: 76–93.

fully coherent to suppose that, in circumstances of self-deception, the self-deceived subject does *not* believe the false proposition, even though it occupies many of her thoughts and guides many of her actions—that is, the second main claim is that playing a typical belief-like role does not imply belief. The third main claim is that there is a particular attitude, pretense or imagining, that plays a typical belief-like role in the case of paradigmatic instances of self-deception.

Initial evidence in favor of the first claim comes from thinking about the family of cases where belief obtains without its normal manifestations. In cases of normal interpersonal deception, the belief that P plays its ordinary subjective role, but its usual connections to behavior may be disrupted by the desire to mislead another into believing the opposite. In cases of denial, the belief that P may play its normal role in terms of motivating (some) behavior, but our introspective sense of having such a belief may be muted or even absent. In cases of over-learned or automatic belief-based behaviors, subjective access to the motivational source may be entirely missing while action proceeds normally. In cases of intense counter-conditioning, a belief might remain subjectively vivid, though its connection to action may be wholly and irremediably broken. In cases of what Price calls "half-belief," a person may systematically feel himself to be and act as if he were fully committed to P in one set of circumstances, while systematically feeling and acting as if the opposite were true in others.[22] And in cases of self-deception (or so I will argue), subjective access to the belief may be muted and its action-guiding role suppressed, yet the belief may remain intact.[23]

Initial evidence in favor of the second claim comes from thinking about the broad range of attitudes we might hold towards things that occupy our thoughts, and the multitude of ways that we may be led to particular actions. In cases of subliminal suggestion or unrecognized prompting, we may find ourselves contemplating a topic without realizing how it came to mind. In cases of "ironic processing," we may find ourselves thinking about something

---

[22] [22] Cf. H. H. Price 1960/1969: 302–14. Price gives the example of a half-believing theist, who on Sundays bears all the subjective and objective marks of believing in God, but on weekdays bears none of them. If such cases are sufficiently widespread, and if there is no way of deciding which set of circumstances should "count" in making the attribution, then half-belief (or circumstance-dependent belief) raises problems for dispositional theories of belief analogous to the problems raised by social-psychological research on situations and attitudes for character-based theories of virtue (cf. Doris 2002; Harman 1998/1999; 1999/2000; Vranas 2005)—but this is a topic for another setting.

[23] [23] One might think the connection between the class of propositions that we regard as true and propositions that bear the Humean marks is so intimate that a proposition with *neither* mark could not be one that we "regard as true...with the aim of thereby accepting a truth"—since it would not be one that we *regard as true* at all. Whether or not this is so, I do not need to deny it in offering my account of self-deception as pretense. For, as will become clear in §4 below, I do accept that there are *circumstances* under which the belief that P *does* bear the normal Humean marks. (Thanks to Kati Farkas for raising this concern.)

precisely because we intended not to.[24] In cases of absorbing fantasy, we may find that the imagined subject matter is "more present to us than" reality itself. Likewise with action. In cases of deliberately deceptive behavior, our actions may accord with something directly opposite to our beliefs. In cases of mere "acceptance," we may act on the basis of things that we merely hypothesize or accept in a context.[25] In cases of priming, we may find ourselves acting in accord with an otherwise inappropriate behavioral norm simply because a stereotype or script has been activated.[26] In cases of ritualistic or symbolic behavior, we may perform an otherwise pointless or counter-indicated action because of what it symbolically represents. In cases of "fictional emotions," we may find ourselves feeling sadness for a character we explicitly acknowledge as imaginary. And in cases of self-deception (or so I will argue), our actions may be generally guided and our thoughts largely occupied by something that we do not actually believe.

Initial evidence in favor of the third claim comes from thinking about the breadth of cognitive resources on which self-deception draws: our capacity willfully to attend to and willfully to ignore features in the world and items in our memories; our propensity to make use of heuristics with and without the recognition that this is what we are doing; our aptitude for conceptualizing situations from perspectives other than our own and for making use of these conceptualizations in guiding our speech and our behavior; and our tendency to be influenced in action, judgment, and even perception by personal and impersonal features of the situation around us. Attending to the existence of such a repertoire reminds us that a diverse array of mental states may play a role in both theoretical and practical reason. Those who maintain that self-deception must involve the subject in some sort of false belief have, I will suggest, failed to give proper attention to this complexity in our mental lives.

---

[24] [24] Cf. Wegner 2002.

[25] [25] Put this way, the claim is slightly misleading. Ordinary cases of "acting without belief"—for instance, L. Jonathan Cohen's case of the general who sends his troops eastward though he merely "accepts" (rather than believes) that the enemy is to the east—are easily misdescribed. While the general (*ex hypothesi*) does not believe that the enemy is to the east, he presumably *does* believe something weaker, for instance, that the enemy's being in the east is compatible with more of his evidence than any alternative hypothesis as to the enemy's location. The question then becomes how the explanatory role of this weaker belief differs from that of the stronger belief insofar as they lead to action (cf. Cohen 1992). This issue, though interesting, is orthogonal to the main topic of the paper at hand. For related discussions, cf. Currie 2002b; O'Brien 2005; Doggett and Egan 2007. See also Bratman 1987/1999, 1999.

[26] [26] For representative examples, see Aarts and Dijksterhuis 2003; Bargh 2005; Bargh, Chen, and Burrows 1996; Bargh and Chartrand 1999; Dijksterhuis and Bargh 2001. [*Added in 2009*: For further discussion, see Ch. 7 above and Chs. 12 and 13 below.]

3. Deception, Pretense, and Self-Deception

Each of the three main claims has some plausibility, suggesting that the fundamental thesis should not be ruled out without due consideration. But are there positive reasons for accepting the claim that paradigmatic self-deception involves pretending that not-P while believing that P? I think there are. Pretense bears an important connection to the ordinary notion of deception. If I deceive you concerning P, I somehow represent P to you as being true, even if I believe that P is false;[27] if I pretend or imagine that P, I somehow represent P to myself as being true, even if I believe that P is false. What I will argue in this section is that this similarity is non-accidental, in ways that bear directly on the puzzle at hand.

3.1. Interpersonal Deception

Suppose that I wish to deceive you into thinking that Q, when, as a matter of fact P (where the fact that Q implies the fact that not-P). There are many strategies I might use—some verbal, some non-verbal—all of which share a common feature: they involve my thinking through what the world might look like to you if Q rather than P, and then arranging to have that portion of your experience over which I have control be such that it resembles what I think you would take to be a Q-world. (So, for example, I might tell you that Q and deny P; or I might arrange to have you come upon apparent evidence for Q while hiding all evidence for P; and so on.) It is crucial to the success of my deception that I have a good sense of what sorts of things you will take to be evidence for Q, that I recognize what sorts of evidence you have already at your disposal, and that I be aware of which aspects of your experience I can control and which I cannot. But although the ways in which the deception occurs will be highly variable, they share a common structure: I deliberately do something that causes you to take yourself to be in a world in which Q obtains.[28] In short, the capacity for deliberate deception goes hand-in-hand with the capacity for

---

[27] [27] In ordinary cases, A *deceives* B by intentionally and successfully causing B to have a belief that A (rightly) takes to be false (or by preventing B from coming to have a belief that A (rightly) takes to be true). It strikes me as a purely terminological dispute whether "deception" is taken to include cases where A, falsely believing P to be true, intentionally and successfully causes B (truly) to believe P to be false. I am inclined to include such cases under the rubric of deception, just as I am inclined to include under the rubric of pretense cases where I (merely) pretend that something true is the case. But little in my argument turns on this. In order for deception to be possible, certain environmental conditions may also be required (as Kant among others has stressed, the practice of deception presupposes a background of truth-telling); I will set aside these complications in the discussion that follows.

[28] [28] Cf. the following characterization of deception, intended to cover both human and animal cases: "(i) an organism R registers (or believes) something Y from some organism S, where S can be described as benefitting when (or desiring that); (iia) R acts appropriately towards Y because; (iib) Y means X; and (iii) it is untrue that X is the case" (Mitchell 1986: 21).

successfully comprehending the perspective of another, and for recognizing the role that one's own deliberate actions may play in causing the other to take the world to be one way as opposed to another. And, of course, the capacity for engaging in pretense exploits precisely this repertoire of skills, as I will emphasize in the next few subsections.

3.2. Performative Pretense and Imaginative Pretense

Although my claims concern pretense in the sense of make-belief or imagining, it will be helpful to begin by considering some of its related meanings. The variety of pretense most closely related to (interpersonal) deception is what might be called *performative pretense*[29]—pretense in the sense of non-believingly acting as if something were the case. This is the sort of pretense I engage in when I represent myself to my fellow transatlantic passenger as a lawyer rather than a philosopher, or as French rather than American, or as fifteen years older or younger than I actually am.[30] Insofar as performative pretense is used as a tool in interpersonal deception, it calls upon the repertoire of skills described above: my having a sense of what sorts of things my seatmate is likely to take as evidence for my claim, my recognizing what pieces of (counter-)evidence are already available to her, and my realizing which aspects of her experience I can control and which not. Importantly, performative pretense may require me to come up with explanations for apparently discordant features of the situation (My lack of accent? "I spent several years in America as a child." My silvery tresses? "My whole family is prematurely gray.") and to divert discussion when disconfirming evidence threatens to come to the fore (Which law firm do I work for? "Oh my—it looks like it's almost time for the movie to begin!" Are they handing out the customs forms now? "Hmmm—I always like to do mine while I am waiting in the passport line."). The need for such tactics (direct analogues of which famously arise in cases of self-deception) results from the mismatch between the way the world actually is, and the way I am representing it (to my seatmate) as being. It is because of this mismatch that the repertoire of skills enumerated above is called into action.

Performative pretense is not the central phenomenon in self-deception. But it is importantly related to that phenomenon. For like performative pretense, pretense in the sense of make-believe or imagining—call this *imaginative pretense*—also requires the capacity for successfully comprehending the possibility of a perspective other than my own, and for recognizing the role that certain

---

[29] Note that "make-believe" has a similar ambiguity (perhaps parasitically), though "imagine" does not. (Cf. Walton 1990.)

[30] Note that this sort of "pretending that" is closely related to another sort of pretense, namely "pretending to be." I may pretend to be French, or a lawyer—and I may do so either with or without the intent to deceive. Though this latter sense is not unrelated to the sense that interests me above, I will not discuss it further here.

features of the world play in causing me to take things to be one way rather than another. Like performative pretense, imaginative pretense requires the use of such tactics because of the mismatch between the way the world is and the way I am representing it (to myself) as being.[31]

Just as performative pretense involves representing things as being a certain way to another, imaginative pretense involves representing things as being a certain way *to oneself*. It is in this sense that I might pretend (make-believe) that a banana is a telephone, or pretend (imagine) that Anna Karenina is about to throw herself under a train. In so doing, I have no deceptive intent: I am not trying to convince you, or myself, or anyone else that the banana *is* a telephone, or that an existing person named Anna Karenina is in genuine danger of dying—indeed, I may keep the contrary thought vividly in mind throughout the pretense episode. But what is crucial to the exercise is that I be engaged in some sort of activity that involves my thinking about, in more or less detail, what things would be like if (something like) the content of my imagining were actually the case—despite my recognition that they are not, in fact, that way.

In the next subsection, I will explore the connection between imaginative pretense, and our target phenomenon of self-deception. I will suggest that just as you can deceive another (in the relevant sense) by performatively pretending that not-P rather than P, so too can you deceive yourself (in the relevant sense) by imaginatively pretending that not-P rather than P.

3.3. Pretense and Self-Deception

Recall that we are looking for an account of self-deception that is immune to both the static and dynamic problems, but that nonetheless can account for the natural description that the phenomenon invites, and for the surface grammar of its appellation. All four of these constraints can be satisfied simultaneously if we recognize the way that imaginative pretense can play a role much like, though not identical to, the role played by ordinary belief. For if we allow that what goes on in cases of self-deception is that the self-deceiver *imaginatively pretends* that a certain proposition is true, and that her imaginative pretense plays a certain role in her mental economy and in the governance of her actions, then we can successfully account for the central features of the phenomenon we are examining.[32]

---

[31] [31] As noted above, there may be cases of self-deception that involve *indifference* rather than mismatch—but the conceptual issues these raise are the same as the mismatch cases.

[32] [32] Imaginative pretense may take a variety of forms. It may be *deliberate*, in the sense that I may explicitly set out to pretend thus-and-such, or it may be *spontaneous*, in the sense that I may simply find myself imaginatively entertaining a particular content. (For illuminating discussion of this distinction, cf. Walton 1990, ch. 1.) While I will focus below primarily on cases of deliberate imaginative pretense (since it is directly relevant to the dynamic paradox), much of what I say holds for spontaneous imaginative pretense as well (thus rendering the

Begin with a case where I believe that P (and do not believe that not-P), but where, for some reason, I wish that not-P held.[33] In such a case, I might—in the ordinary speculative way that we do when we engage in fantasy—begin to think about how the world would be if it were, in fact, the case that not-P. (I may do so intentionally, or quasi-intentionally, or without even realizing that this is what I am doing.) In the case of such idle speculation, my make-belief that not-P will lack the sort of internal vivacity that is typically associated with belief, and will play no direct role in guiding my actions. Still, my attending to not-P in this way will allow me to enjoy the sorts of emotional responses that I would enjoy if it were really the case that not-P, thus providing me with some approximation of the experience I would have were my desire to be satisfied.[34] So pretending that not-P in this sense (idle speculative fantasizing) is something for which I have fully explicable motivation—and it is something over which I might have full volitional control.[35]

Now, one of the consequences of my attending to not-P in the context of fantasy is that it will allow me to figure out what the world would be like if not-P. In so doing, it may render me particularly sensitive to the evidential basis for my belief that P.[36] If my discomfort with P is sufficient, I may make an effort—consciously or unconsciously—to arrange my encounters with the world so that I minimize my interactions with (or assimilation of) evidence that favors P, instead focusing on those features of the world that are compatible with the hypothesis that not-P. When, despite my efforts to avoid it, the truth of P is

---

account useful both to motivationalists and non-motivationalists). Imaginative pretense may also vary in its intensity. It may range from *idle speculative fantasy*, where the self-generated representation is largely quarantined from the remainder of the subject's mental economy, to *full-blown delusion*, where the self-generated representation infects the whole of the subject's outlook. These variations represent two points along a continuum, any of whose intermediate points may also be occupied. The sort of imaginative pretense involved in self-deception typically occupies one of these intermediate points.

[33] [33] Not all cases of self-deception involve wish-fulfillment: in cases of depression, one may believe and desire that P, but be self-deceived that not-P (due to a tendency to emotionally assimilate data in a negative light). Though the initial stages of this sort of self-deception differ from those I am describing, the ultimate mechanism is relevantly similar. (Cf. the phenomenon of "twisted" self-deception as discussed in Pears 1984; Mele 1999.)

[34] [34] As philosophers have noticed at least since Plato. For a more naturalistic demonstration of the same insight, see research by Damasio and others showing how our somatically encoded emotional responses to situations that we take to be merely hypothetical resemble those we bear towards situations that we take to be actual. (Damasio 1994; cf. also Freud on fantasy and wish-fulfillment.) [*Note added in 2009*: For discussion of the bearing of this on the so-called paradox of fictional emotions, see Ch. 11 below.]

[35] [35] This is not to say that such acts of pretense need be volitionally activated; as Ariela Lazar, among others, points out, this process may be mediated not by deliberate conscious intentions on the part of the subject, but rather by desires and emotions directly; see also Barnes 1997. In §5 below, I present an example of such a case.

[36] [36] Cf. my sensitivity to countervailing evidence in the case of deceptive pretense towards my fellow passenger.

impressed on me by some encounter with reality, I will shift my attention elsewhere—in particular, to thoughts of not-P—and imaginatively pretend that the world is otherwise.[37]

At the same time, if circumstances allow, I might reinforce my fantasy by performatively pretending (in the sense of non-believingly acting as if it were the case) that not-P—speaking to others as if not-P were the case, governing my actions as if not-P held—just as I might pretend to be a member of a club, or to be a resident of some particular neighborhood, so as to gain access to some benefit. In so doing, I may become even more aware of the sorts of evidence available that naturally favor P, and of how those sources of evidence might be interpreted in alternative ways.

As I engage in these internal and external (mis)representations, my imaginative pretense that not-P may gradually come to have the sort of vivacity normally associated with the belief that not-P—despite my residual awareness of its self-generated provenance, and my consequent unwillingness to endorse it in certain ways that I will discuss below. As a result of its vivacity—and perhaps as a result of my habitual adaptation to some sort of deceptive pretense—it may also come to play a central role in guiding my actions. And at this point, though I continue to believe that P—indeed, in many cases it will be this very belief that motivates my pretense to the contrary—I may properly be said to be self-deceived that not-P.

In this way, both the static and dynamic problems are averted. For there is no contradiction in my believing that P, not believing that not-P, yet imaginatively pretending that not-P (static problem).[38] Nor is there any problem with my deciding to pretend that not-P, and thereby pretending it (dynamic problem).[39] Moreover, it is clear both why such a state is irrational and at the same time psychologically plausible—and also why it is highly elusive and unstable. In the next section, I will try to bring out why such a state is the very state of paradigmatic self-deception.

---

[37] [37] Thanks to Jennifer Nagel for reminding me of the connection between this phenomenon and psychologists' notion of *confirmation bias*. (See e.g. Wason 1960; Klayman 1995; Nickerson 1998.)

[38] [38] One might think that the static puzzle re-emerges one level up, with regard to the subject's beliefs about her beliefs. If the self-deceived subject were to reflect on her cognitive state (without inquiring too deeply), it would likely seem to her that she *does not* believe that P (after all, its normal manifestations are absent), but that she *does* believe that not-P (after all, it is playing a typically belief-like role). That is, the self-deceived subject may well have a false belief about what she believes: she believes that she believes not-P, while in fact she does not. (Thanks to Zoltán Gendler Szabó for raising this question.) In this sense, self-deception involves deception—or ignorance—*about* the self; it rests on a certain sort of failure of self-knowledge, or at least self-awareness. (Cf. also Holton 2000/1; Scott-Kakures 2002; Funkhouser 2005.)

[39] [39] Though, to repeat, the entire process may also take place without my consciously setting it into action.

4. Pretense in Self-Deception

4.1. Three Factors

The tension characteristic of self-deception arises because the subject is allowing a *projective* attitude (such as pretense) to play a certain role in a context where—given his overall commitment to rationality—only a *receptive* attitude (such as belief) could do the required work.[40] If I believe that P, I bear the attitude that I do towards P with the aim of thereby bearing that attitude towards something true.[41] But the self-deceived subject's attitude towards not-P is, in important ways, reality-indifferent: she does not hold not-P because not-P is true; she holds not-P because she wishes to be (or to have the experience of being) in a not-P world. But this, in conjunction with her general commitment towards rational behavior, will mean that self-deception exhibits a characteristic pattern of instability.

Three factors conjoin to generate this instability. The first is that, by hypothesis, it is true that P—and in ordinary cases when it is true that P, the world reflects that fact: the evidence that is in principle available to the subject will support the hypothesis that P, and tell against the hypothesis that not-P. (If this were not such a case, this would not be an instance of *self*-deception.) The second is that the self-deceived subject has a *general* reason for wanting most of her action-guiding thoughts and attitudes to be mostly truth-reflective:[42] namely, that she will thereby be better able to satisfy her world-directed desires.[43] As a result, she has a defeasible reason for wanting to believe that P.[44] But

---

[40] [40] There may well be particular cases where reality-*in*sensitivity is instrumentally rational in some localized context. Attitudes towards our own relative talents may be of this sort (cf. Elga 2005), as may be of our self-attributions of control (see §5).

[41] [42] As Jennifer Nagel nicely points out (personal correspondence), psychologists discussing the phenomenon of "motivated reasoning" stress the ways in which action-guiding content is typically presented to the self and others as having some sort of rational justification. Consider the following quotation from a survey article by Ziva Kunda: "People do not seem to be at liberty to conclude whatever they want to conclude merely because they want to. Rather, I propose that people motivated to arrive at a particular conclusion attempt to be rational and to construct a justification of their desired conclusion that would persuade a dispassionate observer. They draw the desired conclusion only if they can muster up the evidence necessary to support it . . . In other words, they maintain an 'illusion of objectivity' . . . To this end they search memory for those beliefs and rules that could support their desired conclusion. They may also creatively combine accessed knowledge to construct new beliefs that could logically support the desired conclusion. It is this process of memory search and belief construction that is biased by the directional goals . . ." (Kunda 1990: 483). The Kunda essay provides a rich resource for examples of selective attention and related psychological phenomena. (Thanks to Jennifer Nagel for the reference.)

[42] [41] *Pace* complications of the sort raised by Stich (1990). [*Added in 2009*: See also McKay and Dennett 2009, with commentary and response.]

[43] [43] For a discussion of the advantages of knowledge over mere belief in this regard, see Williamson 2000: 60–4.

[44] [44] Though, of course, not necessarily under this description.

the third is that, although she has a *topic-neutral* reason for letting her thoughts and actions be P-directed, she has a *topic-specific* reason for wanting to occupy herself with thoughts of not-P,[45] and (perhaps independently, perhaps consequently) for letting her actions reflect an apparent belief to that effect.

The combination of the first and the third factors (the truth of P and the subject's topic-specific reality-insensitivity) means that the self-deceived subject's attention to or processing of the evidence favoring P will need to be muted in some way: something needs to be done so that the truth of P fails to play its normal role in her generally reality-sensitive relation to the world. This unusual relation to P is sustained by a certain sort of motivation: the desire that, insofar as possible, she have the experience as of being in a not-P rather than a P world. At the same time, the conjunction of the first factor with the second (the truth of P and the subject's general commitment to reality-sensitivity) means that this attitude towards P should be overrideable: in cases where the second consideration outweighs the third, the subject should assent to P rather than not-P.

This tension—between the first and third factors on the one hand, and the first and second factors on the other—means that there are three sorts of cases where the self-deceived subject's complicated relation to P should be revealed. Each of these is a case where the second consideration overshadows the third, thereby bringing the subject's general commitment to reality-sensitivity to the fore. First, there are (a) cases where the motivating factor that perpetuates the self-deception is absent, so that the subject lacks any reason for focusing on not-P—call these cases of *motivation occlusion*; second, there are (b) cases where, though the motivating factor remains, the subject's other desires overwhelm it: either because (i) the evidence for P is so overwhelming that to maintain not-P as the focus of her thoughts and actions would show a degree of reality-insensitivity that she finds intolerable—call these cases of *evidential override*; or because (ii) some other goal matters to her more than maintaining the impression of being in a not-P world—call these cases of *trumped incentive*.

4.2. The Precarious yet Resilient Status of Self-Deception

These three tendencies, it seems to me, together capture the distinctively precarious yet resilient status of the self-deceived subject's apparent belief that not-P. But the details of how they are manifest in particular cases bring out the advantages of the account I have been advancing.

Take, for example, the case of someone who is suffering from a dreaded disease, but who self-deceptively pretends (makes-believe, imagines, fantasizes) that he is not. By hypothesis, it is true that he is suffering from the disease, and the evidence that is in principle available to him reflects this fact. And because

---

[45] [45] Cf. Funkhouser 2005.

he is an otherwise rational agent, he has a general reason for wanting his thoughts and actions to be guided by the truth. But in this particular case, he also has a specific reason for wanting to occupy himself with the thought that he does not have the disease. As a consequence, he engages in the sort of process described in §3.3, with the ultimate result that his pretense comes to play a typically belief-like role in terms of vivacity and action-guidance. But his attitude towards not-P will be unstable in the three ways just enumerated, and his tacit awareness of this instability will be manifest in characteristic ways whose complexity echoes the complexity of self-deception itself. In each case, there will be a reality-sensitive tendency towards endorsing P in certain circumstances, with a countervailing fantasy-maintenance tendency towards preventing himself from entering into such circumstances.[46]

Motivation occlusion: Suppose, for example, that our self-deceived disease-sufferer is presented with his own medical records, but with the identifying information masked. Or suppose a self-deceived balding man is shown a photograph of a largely hairless man (himself, in fact) whose face is obscured, or that a self-deceived perennial procrastinator is told the tale with which this essay began, or that the self-deceived spouse of a cheating partner is presented with the facts about someone else's oft-absent other half. To the extent that such a case can be presented in a way that occludes the self-deceiver's initial motivation—that is, as a case with no bearing on his own—he should be ready

---

[46] I do not want to claim that all irrational (or otherwise faulty) attitude formation involves fantasy or pretense in the way self-deception does. Beliefs formed as the result of cognitive biases—the "simple heuristics that make us smart" (or foolish) (cf. Kahneman, Slovic and Tversky 1982; Kahneman and Tversky 2000; Gilovich, Griffin, and Kahneman 2002; Gigerenzer *et al.* 2000; etc.)—may well be defective in certain ways. We may be inclined to think that Linda is more likely to be a feminist bank teller than a bank teller simpliciter, or that more words begin with "a" than have "a" as their third letter, but this does not show that we are making-believe, or pretending, that Linda is a feminist bank teller, or that many words begin with "a." The difference, as Ariela Lazar rightly notes, is that "[c]ognitive biases are persistent and highly prevalent patterns of biased reasoning. They are exhibited regardless of subject-matter. In contrast, self-deception is thematic: the content of the irrational belief [*sic*] is relevant to the explanation of its formation" (Lazar 1999: 267). But Lazar goes on to maintain that "self-deceived subjects are more likely to resist correction than competent subjects in the grip of a cognitive bias" (Lazar 1999: 267). The idea, I take it, is that when something like the availability heuristic is pointed out to us, we readily accept that our beliefs formed on its basis are mistaken, and readily revise them—even though the bias itself may be, like an optical illusion, immune to rational overriding. By contrast, Lazar seems to be suggesting, a self-deceived subject will not readily accept that her attitude towards not-P is unjustified or illegitimate, even when this is pointed out to her. This is an important difference between the two cases, and it brings out the tenacity of attitudes formed as the result of motivational bias. But there is also a sense in which self-deceived subjects are better able to recognize the truth of P than subjects in the grip of a cognitive bias. Because there is no lurking suspicion that it is actually P that is true, and because there is nothing local about their mistaken belief, subjects in the grip of a cognitive bias will not modify their assessment of the situation if the stakes are raised, or if motivational surroundings are altered. (Cf. Gilovich, Griffin, and Kahneman 2002). By contrast, for the reasons that I have just discussed, subjects in a state of self-deception will. Cognitively biased subjects are not ignoring something about reality; they are misperceiving it.

to accede to (the analogue of) P. If not, he is not merely self-deceived, but has lost his evidential moorings altogether.

At the same time, his tendency towards fantasy-maintenance may render such a test difficult to administer, for the motivation that leads the subject to attend selectively to evidence in his own case may "spread" to cases that he recognizes to be similar: rather than endorsing (the analogue of) P in cases where his motivation is apparently occluded, he may begin endorsing (the analogue of) not-P in cases where his motivation is apparently absent.[47] On the standard picture, this is taken as evidence for his belief that not-P. But there is another explanation: It is his tacit recognition that the evidential standards to which he himself subscribes tell in favor of (the analogue of) P and against (the analogue of) not-P that results in a characteristic tendency towards illusion-expansion. Rather than revealing a distortion of his conceptual repertoire (does he really hold that someone with no hair may nonetheless fail to be bald?), or a relaxation of his evidential standards (does he really hold that someone who appears to have no hair may nonetheless have some?), what self-deceptive spreading reveals is a willingness to allow his fantasy to play an expanded role in his relation to the world. (Note that this helps to distinguish genuine self-deception from cases of intense daydreaming, where such spreading is typically absent.)

Evidential override: Motivational spreading is closely connected to the avoidance techniques that typically accompany the subject's tacit recognition that her self-deceptive pretense is subject to evidential override. In marked contrast to the subject who is *self-deluded*, the self-deceived subject deliberately avoids putting herself in situations where she suspects she may come upon evidence wildly incompatible with not-P (since, given her general commitment to reality-sensitivity, this would render it difficult for her P-related thoughts and actions to be governed by her fantasy that not-P). So, for example, a subject who is self-deceived about her husband's affair will be reluctant to drive past his purported lover's driveway for fear of seeing his car parked there;[48] a subject who is self-deceived about his child's innocence will be reluctant to read newspaper reports for fear of coming across information linking her to the crime; a subject who is self-deceived about his increasing waistline will avoid stepping on a scale for fear of seeing the number it displays. By contrast, the subject who is self-deluded will take no such precautions. And it is precisely because there *are*

---

[47] [47] Indeed, the motivation-occlusion strategy is one of the best resources for bringing characters to self-knowledge. Analogy and allegory are often called upon in these contexts, precisely because they allow separation of the formal features of the subject's circumstances from its associated content, thus giving the subject the chance to consider a situation structurally similar to her own without immediately evoking an association with its content (which would trigger "spreading"). The Bible is replete with such examples: cf. Jesus' parables, or the story of David and Saul. (Thanks to Tim Crane for the latter example.) [*Added in 2009*: For additional discussion of the David case, see Ch. 6 above.]

[48] [48] This example is due to Eric Funkhouser (2005).

circumstances where available evidence could undermine the thought-occupying and action-guiding role that her pretense plays in the life of the self-deceiver that she so steadfastly avoids confrontation with them. Advocates of a belief account must explain why someone who believes that not-P—that is, someone who holds not-P with the aim of thereby holding something true—would so steadfastly avoid exposing herself to circumstances where P-relevant evidence might be available. The pretense account faces no such difficulty.

Trumped incentive: The most compelling evidence for taking typical self-deception to be a form of pretense comes from cases of trumped incentive: cases where some other goal matters more to the subject than his goal of maintaining the impression of being in a not-P world, and where, consequently, he is willing to let P play its rightful thought-occupying and action-guiding role. Suppose, for example, that we put our self-deceived disease-sufferer in a high-stakes forced-choice situation: taking medicine M gives great health benefits to those with disease D and causes terrible pain to those without disease D, and not taking medicine M has precisely the opposite effects. If he actually holds the delusional belief that he is not suffering from D (not-P), then he may elect not to take medicine M. But if he is self-deceived in the sense I have been considering, then while he allows his pretense that not-P to guide his actions and thoughts when his fantasy-maintenance desire is dominant, there will be situations where he will instead allow his (tacit or explicit) belief that P to serve as the basis for his actions. In particular, when confronted with this high-stakes forced choice, the self-deceived subject will likely elect to take the medicine.

Moreover, what is distinctly characteristic of paradigmatically perplexing cases of self-deception—in contrast to cases of mere motivated false belief—is the phenomenology associated with such overriding. For the feeling associated with ceasing to guide one's actions on the basis of not-P and of starting to guide them on the basis of P is not the feeling of replacing one reality-reflective attitude by another with contrary content; rather, it is the feeling of leaving a realm of make-believe where one has allowed one's thoughts and actions to be governed by some sort of fantasy, and returning to the realm of reality-receptiveness where one's thoughts and actions are responsive to things as they actually are. The subject does not give up one belief in favor of another: she stops pretending that she is in a not-P world, and instead acknowledges (at least temporarily) that P obtains.

These three tendencies capture exactly those features of self-deception that render the phenomenon both strangely precarious and strangely resilient. It is precarious because a projective attitude (the pretense that not-P) is being treated as if it were a receptive attitude (the belief that not-P) in circumstances where, if it were a receptive attitude (belief), the norms governing such attitudes would mandate that it be abandoned (on grounds of falsity) (cf. motivation occlusion and evidential override). But it is resilient because, since the subject has some sort of motivation for holding not-P, she has reason to distort her assimilation of or access to counter-evidence favoring P by employing exactly the sort of deceptive strategies enumerated in §3 above (cf. "spreading" and avoidance). But because the subject retains a more general second-order commitment to reality-sensitivity, the possibility of trumped incentive remains. And the phenomenology of the experience of trumped incentive reveals the status of self-deception as a form of pretense.

5. Psychological Echoes: The Illusion of Control

In the remainder of this essay, I describe a quasi-automatic mechanism that shares the structural features that I have been suggesting underlie self-deception.

A well-documented body of psychological research suggests that healthy non-depressed individuals tend to be subject to what psychologists have dubbed an *illusion of control*—the sense that it is as the result of their intentional efforts that a specific desired outcome obtains in certain circumstances when— in actuality—the outcome is the result of random ("noncontingent") processes. But, it turns out, this illusion is much less robust when subjects are in a *deliberative mindset*—that is, when they are choosing between goal options— than when they are in an *implementational mindset*—that is, when they are engaged in carrying out a particular goal. One widely accepted explanation of this phenomenon is that illusory optimism is an adaptive strategy in certain contexts:[49] when a subject is engaged in carrying out a goal-oriented course of action, goal-attainment is enhanced if small setbacks are ignored and small advances are underscored. As a result, subjects who overestimate their degree of control in certain situations are making use of a strategy that is, in other circumstances, of significant practical utility. But the strategy is singularly unuseful in contexts where a subject is deciding between courses of action, rather than pursuing a course that she has already chosen. For in those circumstances, a sober assessment of one's degree of control over various contingencies is crucial to success.

The particular task studied involved asking subjects to estimate the degree to which a target outcome (the illumination of a red light) was contingent on a certain action of theirs (pressing a button). Earlier studies had shown that when the (in fact) noncontingent target outcome occurs infrequently (the 25–25 problem, in which the light is illuminated subsequent to 25 percent of the subject's pressing actions and 25 percent of her non-pressing actions), non-depressed subjects accurately estimate their degree of control over the outcome, but that when the (in fact) noncontingent target outcome occurs frequently (the 75–75 problem, in which the light is illuminated subsequent to 75 percent

---

[49] [49] For discussion, see Alloy and Abramson 1988; Taylor and Brown 1988.

of the subject's pressing actions and 75 percent of her non-pressing actions), non-depressed subjects significantly overestimate the degree to which their actions influenced the status of the light (Alloy and Abramson 1979 as reported in Gollwitzer and Kinney 1989).

One way of understanding these cases is as follows. In cases where their lack of influence is not glaringly apparent (cf. evidential override), subjects engage in the (spontaneous) fantasy that a certain desired outcome is the result of their intentional efforts. The fantasy is supported by their biased processing of available evidence—apparent instances of disconfirmation (the 25 percent of cases where the pressing is not followed by the red light, and the 75 percent of cases where the non-pressing is) are discounted while apparent instances of confirmation (the 75 percent of cases where the pressing is followed by the red light, and the 25 percent of cases where the non-pressing is not) are included in the mental reckoning.[50]

What is striking about this biased processing is that it dissipates in precisely the circumstances I have just enumerated: cases of motivation occlusion, and cases of trumped incentive. Subjects do not overestimate the degree of control exerted when they observe someone else engaging in the 75–75 task (D. J. Martin, Abramson, and Alloy 1984),[51] nor do they overestimate their own degree of control when they are in a deliberative mindset—that is, when some other goal takes precedence over their motivated desire to experience not-P. So, for example, in one study, subjects in either mindset claimed only moderate control in the 25–25 problem (a case of evidential override)—approximately 22 on a 100-point scale in both cases—but the 75–75 task showed another result entirely: Whereas subjects in the deliberative mindset still claimed a moderate degree of control—31 out of 100[52]—subjects in the implementational mindset claimed to possess considerable control over the outcome—53.9 on a 100-point scale, a highly significant difference. A second study confirmed the first. Whereas subjects in a deliberative mindset estimated their degree of control over a certain outcome to be 23 (again on a 100-point scale), subjects in an implementation mindset judged it to be 57—again a highly significant difference.

Interestingly, subjects in a "neutral" mindset—those who have not been prompted one way or the other—display a response pattern akin to those in an implementational mindset. This suggests that self-deceptive fantasy of the sort I have been describing may be a natural part of our cognitive repertoire. In certain situations, we may instinctively hold ourselves back from subjecting our

---

[50] [50] This sort of biased processing may in turn rely on further heuristic tendencies—for instance, the tendency to overvalue (P, Q) pairs and undervalue (not-Q, not-P) pairs in verifying (P→Q).

[51] [51] Cf. also Vazquez 1987.

[52] [52] A statistically insignificant difference from the 25–25 case.

evidential base to certain sorts of scrutiny. But the fact that such processes occur quasi-automatically does not mean that the resulting attitude should be classified as a belief. Even when we are unaware that we are treating a projective attitude as if it were a receptive one, the pattern described in §4.2 holds: the faulty commitment dissipates in cases of evidential override, motivation occlusion, and trumped incentive—and it does so with a particular phenomenology: that of extricating oneself (at least temporarily) from a realm of reality-insensitivity where one's thoughts and actions are governed by fantasy, and entering the realm of reality-receptiveness where one's thoughts and actions are responsive to things as they actually are. It is the latter realm that is the realm of belief.

6. Brief Conclusion

If belief is the attitude of accepting a proposition with the aim of thereby accepting something true,[53] then in a wide variety of circumstances—most strikingly in cases of self-deception—our thoughts are occupied and our actions are guided by contents that we do not believe. The correct response to this observation is not to relax our standards for belief, but to recognize that other attitudes may play their characteristic role. Belief is *not*, as Hume avers, "that act of mind which renders realities more present to us than fictions, causes them to weigh more in the thought . . . gives them superior influence on the passions and imagination . . . and renders them the governing principles of all of our actions" (see epigraph). Usurpers do not always deserve the title of the one whom they usurp.[54]

---

[53] [53] Perhaps with epicycles . . .

[54] [1] *Acknowledgements*: This essay was written over many years, prompted initially by seminars that I taught at Syracuse University on Rationality (Spring 1999) and Weakness of the Will and Self-Deception (Fall 1999), and by my encounter with a draft of David Velleman's marvelous paper "The Aim of Belief" (Velleman 2000). Early ancestors were presented to audiences at Canisius College and Central European University in Spring 2000. A recognizable predecessor to the current version came into being during 2002–3, when I was a fellow at the Collegium Budapest; various incarnations of that paper—of which this is a slight revision—were presented to audiences at Central European University, the University of Michigan at Ann Arbor, Yale University, the University of Massachusetts at Amherst, and Brown University during 2004–5. Thanks are owed to many members of those seminars and audiences; I wish I were in a position to express my gratitude more specifically. For comments, questions, and suggestions whose origins I had the good sense to record, I thank Gábor Betegh, Susanne Bobzien, István Bodnar, Steffen Borge, Carolyn Caine, Tim Crane, Jason D'Cruz, Michael Della Rocca, Tyler Doggett, Andy Egan, Kati Farkas, Eric Funkhouser, Shaun Gallagher, John Hawthorne, Ferenc Huoranszki, Shelly Kagan, Nenad Miscevic, Jennifer Nagel, Ted Sider, Ernie Sosa, Zoltán Gendler Szabó, Kendall Walton, Hong-Yu Wong, and Zsófia Zvolensky.

9

The Puzzle of Imaginative Resistance

In this chapter, I present and discuss what I call the *puzzle of imaginative resistance*: the puzzle of explaining our comparative difficulty in imagining fictional worlds that we take to be morally deviant.

I suggest that the primary source of imaginative resistance lies not in our *inability* to imagine morally deviant situations, but in our *unwillingness* to do so. And I trace the source of this unwillingness to a general desire not to be manipulated into taking on points of view that we would not reflectively endorse as authentically our own.

This diagnosis is then used to illuminate the nature of imagination itself. I suggest that imagining is an attitude that lies between belief on the one hand and mere supposition on the other. Unlike belief, the contents of imagination are not restricted to those that we take to be true; but unlike mere supposition, imagination involves a certain sort of engaged participation on the part of the imaginer.

This implicit theme—that imagined content can "leak" into our cognitive repertoire in ways that we might find disturbing—is picked up again more explicitly in several of the later chapters in this volume, particularly "Imaginative Contagion" (Ch. 12), "Alief and Belief" (Ch. 13), and "Alief in Action (and Reaction)" (Ch. 14).

This essay and its successor—"Imaginative Resistance Revisited"—are best read as a pair, though of the two, this is both more engaging and more self-standing.

***

This essay was first published in the *Journal of Philosophy*, 97/2 (Feb. 2000), 55–81 and is reprinted with the kind permission of the *Journal of Philosophy*. Because the essay has been widely cited in its original form, changes have been limited to correction of minor typographical errors, the insertion of remarks in footnotes (noted as such), and the reconfiguration of citations to bring reference conventions into line with other essays in the volume. As a result of reformatting, some footnote numbers have changed; original numbers appear in [square brackets].

1. Introduction

The puzzle that concerns me in this essay can be traced back at least as far as Hume, but it has received surprisingly little attention in the intervening 200 years.[1] The puzzle is this: given that for the most part we have no trouble fictionally entertaining all sorts of far-fetched and implausible scenarios, what explains the impediments we seem to encounter when we are asked to imagine moral judgments sharply divergent from those we ordinarily make?

Hume poses the problem in the vocabulary of sentiments and customs. He writes:

> Where *speculative* errors may be found in the polite writings of any age or country, they detract but little from the value of those compositions. There needs to be but a certain turn of thought or imagination to make us enter into all the opinions which then prevailed and relish the sentiments or conclusions derived from them. But a very violent effort is requisite to change our judgment of manners, and excite sentiments of approbation or blame, love or hatred, different from those to which the mind from long custom has been familiarized...I cannot, nor is it proper that I should, enter into such [vicious] sentiments. (Hume 1757/1985: 247)

Since the puzzle that motivates Hume's remarks is independent of his particular moral ontology, let me frame it in more neutral vocabulary. Let's call the puzzle *the puzzle of imaginative resistance*.[2]

> *The puzzle of imaginative resistance*: the puzzle of explaining our comparative difficulty in imagining fictional worlds that we take to be morally deviant.

My goal in this essay is threefold: to convince you that there *is* a puzzle here (though it's not quite the one Hume seems to think it is), to convince you there is a solution to the puzzle (though it's not quite the one I suspect you think it is), and to convince you that these together reveal something interesting about the nature of imagination. Hume is right that there is a phenomenon of imaginative resistance, but he's mistaken to think that it arises in all and only cases of deviant morality. And you are right that the explanation of the phenomenon has something to do with the relation between imagination and possibility, but you're mistaken if you think that that is the primary source of the resistance. What I want to try to convince you of is that the primary source of imaginative resistance is not our *inability* to imagine morally deviant situations, but our

---

[1] [1] See David Hume 1757/1985: 226–49. The only modern extended treatments I know are those of Kendall Walton (1994) and Richard Moran (1994). Cf. also Moran 1992 (which is a predecessor to Moran 1994) and Tanner 1994 (which is a response to Walton 1994). Additional brief remarks can be found in Walton 1990 at 154–6. For a related discussion of this passage, see C. Williams 2000. [*Added in 2009*: In the intervening decade, the problem has been widely discussed; an overview of these debates can be found in Gendler 2009.]

[2] [2] I borrow this terminology—though not this characterization of the puzzle—from Moran 1994: 95.

unwillingness to do so. And I want to trace the *source* of this unwillingness to a general desire not to be manipulated into taking on points of view that we would not reflectively endorse as authentically our own. This unwillingness is explicable only if imagining involves something in between belief on the one hand and mere supposition on the other. So in order to make sense of the phenomenon of imaginative resistance, we're going to have to learn something about the phenomenon of imagination itself.

2. Overview of the Puzzle

Let's begin by trying to get a better handle on precisely what the problem is even supposed to *be*. Hume's worry, I take it, is something like the following. When we engage in the sort of make-believe that contemplation of fictional scenarios evokes, we are largely unconstrained by what we take to be *factual*. We have no trouble imagining that Sherlock Holmes solved mysteries in nineteenth-century London, that an owl and a pussycat went out to sea in a beautiful pea-green boat, or that a hobbit named Frodo Baggins carried a magic ring all over Middle Earth. Indeed, one might think (and I'll have more to say about this later) that we are unconstrained even by what we take to be *possible*. We make sense of stories where characters travel back in time, where space-ships go faster than the speed of light, where wizards turn straw into gold, and where lonely geniuses prove the continuum hypothesis. So given that imagination is such a powerful and agile capacity, it seems extraordinary that little old morality could stop it in its tracks.

Here's one formulation by Richard Moran of the asymmetry that seems to characterize this perplexing phenomenon:

> If the story tells us that Duncan was *not* in fact murdered on Macbeth's orders, then *that* is what we accept and imagine as fictionally true. If we start doubting what the story tells us about its characters, then we may as well doubt whether it's giving us their right names. However, suppose the facts of the murder remain as they are in fact presented in the play, but it is prescribed in this alternate fiction that this was unfortunate only for having interfered with Macbeth's sleep, or that we in the audience are relieved at these events. These seem to be imaginative tasks of an entirely different order. (Moran 1994: 95)

What Moran is pointing out is this. When an author invites us to contemplate a fictional scenario, she seems to have a great deal of freedom in how she directs our imagination. Among the things she can make fictionally true are all the sorts of things I have just described—that animals marry, that time travel occurs, that alchemy is good science, and so on.[3] But she seems to have much *less* freedom in

---

[3] [3] The principles of generation that govern fictional truth are extremely complicated; I am inclined to think that the correct theory will be some sort of *pragmatic theory of fictional truth*,

what she makes fictionally true as far as matters of moral assessment are concerned. The trick that allows an author complete freedom in dictating whether or not character A murders character B is much less effective if what the author wants to dictate is that the murder is, for instance, praiseworthy, or noble, or charming, or admirable.[4] So the puzzle is this: what explains why a trick so effective in so many realms is relatively ineffective here?[5]

3. Belief and Make-belief

A first step in understanding the phenomenon can be made by noting a certain asymmetry between belief on the one hand and make-belief on the other. When it comes to believing propositions that we don't think are true, we find ourselves equally stumped in the case of moral and non-moral claims. I can't bring myself to believe that murder is right—but I can't bring myself to believe that the earth is flat either. When it comes to *make-belief*, however, we seem more inclined to find ourselves stumped in the one case than in the other. I have a much easier time following an author's invitation to imagine that the earth is flat than I do following her invitation to imagine that murder is right.[6] What could be the source of this difference?

but this is a topic for another essay. For two of the most influential accounts of this issue, which has generated a sizable literature in recent years, see Walton 1990, esp. 35–43 and 138–87 and D. Lewis 1983c. Cf. also Lamarque and Olsen 1994. For discussions of this issue in the context of literary theory that make use of the philosophical notion of possible worlds, cf. Allén 1989; Pavel 1986; Ronen 1994; Ryan 1991; Semino 1997; and Werth 1999. Cf. also Eco 1979 and Hogan 1996. (Thanks to Margaret Freeman and Yael Halevi-Wise for a number of these references.)

[4] Cf. Moran: "Why can we not, as it seems, treat the judgments of morality and decency the same way we treat any other judgments, and accept as fictionally true what the story tells us (or implies) is true, and comfortably leave our genuine attitudes at the door? What happens to our sense of *distance* at that point, the distance between what we can imagine and what we actually believe?" (Moran 1994: 97).

[5] The question of whether imaginative resistance occurs in the way I have described is, of course, an empirical one. Though ample confirmation of its existence can be obtained through informal means, Aaron Sell (Department of Psychology, University of California at Santa Barbara) and I have recently begun work on a series of empirical psychological studies designed to examine the phenomenon in some detail. [*Added in 2009*: Although the studies referred to above were ultimately not carried out, in recent years a number of philosophers and psychologists have begun to investigate the phenomenon empirically. Preliminary data seem to confirm the existence of the asymmetries noted above. See e.g. Levine 2009.]

[6] Kendall Walton points out (personal correspondence) that my use of "make-believing" seems ambiguous between two readings. If I make-believe that P, I may be: (a) accepting that P has been successfully made fictional (that is, accepting that the author has succeeded in presenting a story in the context of which a certain proposition is true) or (b) pretending that P (that is, entertaining or attending to or considering the content of P, in the distinctive way required by imagination). Although these are clearly two different states, I think they are connected in a way that legitimates my conflating them in certain contexts. Because I think that—very roughly stated—what's true in a story is what the author manages to get the

Let's begin by looking at the case of belief. With regard to belief, there is little contrast to be drawn between (1) and (2):

(1)   I am asked to *believe* that: P holds
      (where P is some non-moral proposition that I do not believe holds)

(2)   I am asked to *believe* that: M holds
      (where M is some moral proposition that I do not believe holds)

Both (1) and (2) evoke resistance; in neither case am I able—just like that—to bring myself to believe the proposition in question. Of course, there are all sorts of ways that I might come to change my beliefs. I might gain certain sorts of empirical information about the world, or I might work through the implications of the propositions to which I am committed, or I might come to make sense of my experiences in terms of categories whose applicability to these circumstances I had previously denied or failed to recognize. And the routes by which I might come to make these sorts of changes are many: I might look through a telescope, or read an encyclopedia, or listen to a lecture, or take a logic class, or have a series of conversations with my therapist, or enroll in a twelve-step program, or subject myself to brainwashing, or take a special kind of pill that will disrupt my normal mental functioning, or act in the way I would expect to act if I believed the proposition to be true. And depending on the circumstances, one or another of these processes might result in my actually becoming committed to the veracity of the proposition in question, in spite of my previous failure to endorse it. But despite the diversity of techniques that we have for acquiring and changing beliefs, it is important that simply *deciding to believe* any old arbitrary proposition is not straightforwardly among them. Why not?

Whatever one's views about the subtleties of beliefs' aims, I take it that the following, at least, is uncontested. We don't seem to be able to bring ourselves to believe arbitrary things at will, and at least one of the *reasons* for this is that beliefs aim—at least most beliefs mostly aim—at something that is generally independent of our wills, namely something roughly correlated with truth. So it's a non-accidental fact about belief that, given the sorts of things we expect beliefs to do, believing at will just *couldn't* be one of the ways that we generally come to form beliefs.[7] This means that it shouldn't surprise us that perceived falsehood undermines belief-candidacy: since in general we want most of our

---

(appropriate) reader to imagine, if (appropriate) readers are unable (or unwilling) to make-believe in the second sense, they will be unable (or unwilling) to make-believe in the first. (I return to this issue in my discussion of "doubling the narrator"; see §4 below.) [*Added in 2009*: In saying this, I am explicitly conflating what Weatherson 2004 calls the *imaginative* and *alethic* puzzles; I discuss this issue further in "Imaginative Resistance Revisited" (2006b; Ch. 10 below).]

[7] [7] The *locus classicus* for this sort of argument is B. Williams 1970/1973a. Although (as many have pointed out) the details of his case are surely overstated, the basic insight—that "it is

beliefs to be mostly true, a proposition that shows up for its interview in the guise of the false is just not going to make the cut. So (1) and (2) are easily explained: given the sort of thing belief is, we should expect the resistance they describe.

But the same is not true of make-belief. In contrast to deciding to believe and deciding to desire, deciding to *make-believe* seems to be—at least in many cases—within our repertoire of capacities. That is, in contrast to (1), where my inclination to refuse the invitation is tied up with the preconditions for there being such a thing as belief in the first place, (3) seems to describe an invitation for which the default is my acceptance.

(3)   I am asked to *make-believe* that: P holds
      (where P is some non-moral proposition that I do not believe holds)

There are at least two reasons that this is so. The first is that belief and make-belief do not conflict; I can make-believe that P is true while believing that P is true, or while believing that P is false, or while remaining agnostic about the truth-status of P.[8] So the fact that P is a proposition which I do not (prior to the invitation) believe to be true in no way interferes with my making-believe that it is true; perceived falsehood undermines belief-candidacy, but it raises no problems for make-belief. But there is a second, more interesting feature of make-belief that concerns me here. The will-independence of belief may be seen as a fall-out from the truth-directedness of belief. But in the case of make-belief, the explanatory arrow goes the other way around. It is the *will-dependence* of make-belief that explains its indifference to the truth of its content. Where belief is concerned with tracking states of affairs, make-belief is concerned with constructing scenarios.[9] So while believing at will is, in general, precluded by the aims of belief, *make-believing* at will is not merely permitted, it is what the practice is about in the first place.

---

not a contingent fact that I cannot bring it about, just like that, that I believe something" (B. Williams 1970/1973a: 148)—seems to me undoubtedly correct. (For a recent defense of the view that belief aims at truth, see Velleman 2000.) While it might be true that we *do* decide to believe in the sense that we decide which evidential standards to take as sufficient in a particular context, this does not show that we are indifferent to truth in the way that simple believing at will would require.

   [8] One might think this is because make-belief or pretense is a kind of processing that is carried out "off-line." Cf. the articles collected in M. Davies and Stone 1995a, 1995b, especially those in 1995b by Alan Leslie and Tim German, Gregory Currie, and Paul Harris. Cf. also the articles collected in Carruthers and Smith 1996, especially those by Shaun Nichols *et al.*, Tony Stone and Martin Davies, and Gregory Currie. See also Currie 1997, 1998; Currie and Ravenscroft 2002; Leslie 1987; and Walton 1997.

   [9] One might think that make-belief in the case of fiction consists in following an author's lead in constructing such scenarios. (For discussions of these issues, see, among others, the writings of Gregory Currie (especially Currie 1990, 1995b, 1997), Kendall Walton (especially 1990 and 1993), Nicholas Wolterstorff (1980) and the works cited in n. 3.) But this in no way

Putting things this way allows us to see why the asymmetry between (3) and (4) is at least *prima facie* perplexing. For just as (1) gives us (3), (2) gives us (4):

(4)   I am asked to *make-believe* that: M holds
       (where M is some moral proposition that I do not believe holds)

And given what has just been said about the nature of make-belief, there seems no reason to expect that (4) should evince a reaction any different from that evinced by (3). After all, making-believe that M doesn't commit us to the truth of M any more than making-believe that P commits us to the truth of P. So maybe Hume is just wrong? Maybe Moran is just being stubborn? Maybe there isn't really an asymmetry here after all?

4. The Asymmetry

I don't think the puzzle can be dispensed with quite so easily, and I want to offer a couple of examples by way of convincing you of this. Let me start by quoting a bit of Kipling (1899). Here are the first and fifth stanzas of "White Man's Burden":

> Take up the White Man's burden—
> Send forth the best ye breed—
> Go bind your sons to exile
> To serve your captives' need;
> To wait in heavy harness
> On fluttered folk and wild—
> Your new-caught, sullen peoples,
> Half devil and half child.

> Take up the White Man's burden—
> And reap his old reward:
> The blame of those ye better,
> The hate of those ye guard—
> The cry of hosts ye humour
> (Ah, slowly) toward the light:—
> "Why brought ye us from bondage,
> "Our loved Egyptian night?"

Leaving aside niceties of literary interpretation, let's take this poem as a straightforward invitation to *make-believe*, a proposal about something we are called to

mitigates the force of the asymmetry. For the question then becomes: why do we follow the author's lead in cases like (3), but not in cases like (4)? This is discussed further in §8 below.

imagine without committing ourselves to its literal truth. And let's focus on the beginning of the second stanza. Among the things that Kipling is asking us to make-believe there are the following: that there are certain white characters who have taken it upon themselves to initiate a group of non-whites into the ways of Western culture, and that their efforts in this regard have, as usual, resulted in their being blamed and hated on the part of those whom they take themselves to be improving and guarding. So far, so good; I have no difficulty following Kipling's lead. I'm perfectly happy to make-believe that there are white characters to whom the things just described happen.

But there is another thing that Kipling is here asking us to make-believe, namely, that the white characters' behaviors are a fulfillment of their obligation to "better" those who, by virtue of their skin color, are their natural inferiors. And here I find myself strangely resistant—not only to believing that this is true—but to *make*-believing it as well. Whereas I have no inclination to distance myself from the "plot" of the poem by saying that the events described therein are just things that Kipling *thinks* happened, I do have that inclination with regard to the "evaluative" parts of the poem.

A similar pattern can be observed in other cases of moral disagreement. So, for example, in discussing just these issues, Kendall Walton imagines a story that includes the following sentence:

(5)   "In killing her baby, Giselda did the right thing; after all, it was a girl."[10]

Again, I think we find ourselves willing to imagine some things but not others. Upon hearing this sentence, I'm perfectly willing to accept that this is a story in which Giselda kills her baby; I don't have any inclination to say: "according to the narrator in the story, Giselda killed her baby. But the narrator could be wrong about that. Maybe the baby is still alive." But the same isn't true of the rest of the sentence. Our first instinct—at least my and Walton's first instinct— is to *reject* the invitation to make-believe that "it was right for Giselda to kill her baby, given that it was a girl." My inclination is to respond to the invitation with something like the following: "What is right to make-believe is that *according to the narrator who is telling the story*, female infanticide is morally acceptable. But even in the world of the story, the narrator is wrong; infanticide is *not* morally acceptable, even in a society where everyone believes that it is."[11]

Now as a general move, to respond to an invitation to make-believe with this sort of distancing gesture is to refuse to play the game of make-believe. There's a

---

[10] [11] Cf. Walton 1994: 37. Walton acknowledges, and I acknowledge with him, the contrivance of presenting such a sentence without a larger narrative context. I beg the reader's temporary forbearance; I will turn to this issue shortly.

[11] [12] Walton writes: "A reader's likely response on encountering the words: 'In killing her baby, Giselda did the right thing; after all, it was a girl,' is to be appalled by the moral depravity of the *narrator*" (Walton 1994: 38, italics in original).

joke that brings out why this is so.[12] One night, a graduate student dreams that she is approached sequentially by all of the famous philosophers in history. To each in turn, she provides a devastating one-line criticism, so that the thereby-devastated philosopher slinks away in humiliation to rethink his entire theory. Although she is soundly asleep, the graduate student is nonetheless able to scribble down the astonishing sentence on a pad of paper by her bedside. When she awakens in the morning, she remembers her dream. She grabs the pad of paper to behold her remarkable insight. Scrawled across the top are the words: "That's what you think!"

The joke is funny—to the extent that it is—because "that's what you think" *is* in fact something that could be said to every philosopher in history. But it's not a very good objection. As an ending to a conversation game, it's more like knocking over the board than like winning by the rules. So we need to have pretty good reasons for concluding a conversation with "that's what you think."

What I want to suggest is that imaginative resistance is a "that's what you think" move in a game of make-believe—something that is always available as a last resort, but which, if overused, undermines the entire convention of which it is supposed to be offering local criticism. If imaginative resistance were our general response to authors' invitations to make-believe, this would be tantamount to refusing to play the fiction game. The analogue to "that's what you think" is the sort of doubling of the narrator that I have just described, where from the author's inclusion of (5) in the story, we conclude not that (5) is true in the story, but that (5) is what the narrator of the story *thinks* is true.[13] But such unwillingness to grant the author the right to stipulate what happens in the story is tantamount to giving up on the idea of storytelling altogether. Just as the practice of philosophy would be undermined if it were normal to respond to every argument by saying "that's what you think," so too would the practice of

---

[12] [13] Thanks to Adam Sennet for passing this joke on to me.

[13] [14] Dick Moran (personal correspondence) has objected to this suggestion as follows: when we move from accepting P as true-in-the-story to attributing belief in P to the *teller* of the story, it appears as if we are saying that P itself can't be imagined-as-true, but that we can imagine some person holding P true. But, the objection continues, if we can imagine some belief, we should be able to imagine the proposition believed; in fact, logically speaking, it seems that there ought to be stronger constraints on imagining beliefs than on imagining propositions, since doing the former entails doing the latter. Three quick remarks. First, as I will argue below, the cases of imaginative resistance that interest me are not cases where we *can't* imagine that P is true, but rather cases where we *won't* do so; this, however, does not address the heart of Moran's worry. So, second, there are at least two sorts of cases here; with regard to one of them, it is easier to imagine that P is true than to imagine someone believing P to be true (e.g. infinite mathematical sentences), whereas with regard to the other, the opposite holds (e.g. racist beliefs). But what makes the latter sort of case possible? Third remark: There are cases where we have a grasp on what sort of mistake a person would have to be making in order to believe some (false) proposition, without having a grasp on what a world where that proposition was true would be like; it may well be that in such cases we are holding the world to standards stricter than those to which we are holding the person, but if so, this is something we do generally in the attribution of false beliefs.

fiction be undermined if it were normal to respond to every invitation to make-believe with a doubling of the narrator.

So imaginative resistance is a phenomenon that cries out for explanation. Given that the narrator-doubling must be confined to exceptional cases, why are we so ready to use it when a work of fiction depicts a world that differs morally from the way we take the actual world to be?

5. The Impossibility Hypothesis

I suspect you think that you know the answer to this question. I suspect you think that just as belief is constrained by what's *true*, make-belief is constrained by what's *possible*, and the sorts of scenarios towards which we manifest imaginative resistance are scenarios that are impossible. As a result, the sorts of things that (4) asks us to make-believe—let's call them "morally-deviant propositions"—are simply not make-believable, because they represent conceptually impossible states of affairs.

Now, I think this is the wrong explanation, for reasons that have to do with fundamental facts about the nature of imagination and its relation to possibility. And I plan to spend much of the rest of this essay convincing you that I'm right. But let me first present the position against which I will be arguing.

Here is Kendall Walton's discussion of this view, which he goes on, at least tentatively, to endorse.[14] He writes:

Moral properties depend or supervene on "natural" ones ... being evil rests on, for instance, the actions constituting the practices of slavery and genocide ... This ... accounts ... for the resistance to allowing it to be fictional that slavery and genocide are not evil ... Our reluctance to allow moral principles we disagree with to be fictional [that is: true in the world of some fiction] is just an instance of a more general point concerning dependence relations of a certain kind. (Walton 1994: 43–6)

So the first part of the orthodox answer involves pointing out that moral facts supervene on natural facts, and that morally deviant scenarios are scenarios that involve the imaginative disruption of these supervenience relations. But this is only the first part of the answer. The question remains: why should we be resistant to imagining that the supervenience relations might be other than we take them to be? We are, after all, willing to allow that we may be wrong about certain of our moral judgments, that we might be incorrect in our assessments of certain of these supervenience relations. And while we may think that *if* we are correct it follows

---

[14] [15] In his brief remarks in Walton 1990, he connects the phenomenon to the problem of truth in fiction (Walton 1990: 154). In the extremely rich Walton 1994, he provides a number of suggestive explanations, ultimately endorsing this one, which he calls his "best suspicion at the moment" (Walton 1994: 46). [*Added in 2009*: For Walton's more recent views on the issue of imaginative resistance see Walton 2006.]

that the relation we are correct about is a relation that holds necessarily, we haven't thereby shown that we couldn't *imagine* it being otherwise.

Walton's suggestion seems to be that our conviction in these cases is a consequence of our recognition of a certain sort of conceptual impossibility. He writes:

> We need an explanation of why we should resist allowing fictional worlds to differ from the real world with respect to the relevant kind of dependence relations. My best suspicion...is that it has something to do with...an inability to understand fully what it would be like for them to be different. (Walton 1994: 46)

What does the "inability to understand fully what it would be like for them to be different" amount to? The idea, I take it, is something like the following. We just can't make sense of what it would *be* for something to be both an instance of genocide *and* an instance of something that is nothing morally worse than a failure in manners, or both an instance of murder *and* an instance of something that is morally right. Or, more precisely, we can't make sense of what it would be for something to be both an instance of murder *and* an instance of something that is morally right, *and* for it to be morally right *because* it is an instance of murder. So our resistance arises from the feeling that at a certain point, we simply lose a handle on what it is that we are even supposed to be imagining.

Let's call this view:

The Impossibility Hypothesis: Imaginative resistance is explained by the following two considerations:

(a) The scenarios that evoke imaginative resistance are conceptually impossible.

(b) The conceptual impossibility of these scenarios renders them unimaginable.[15]

If it were correct, the Impossibility Hypothesis would certainly explain the phenomenon of imaginative resistance. If there are things that are unimaginable, then we certainly can't imagine *them*, so we shouldn't be surprised that our capacity to make-believe at will runs out at precisely those points. But I think the Impossibility Hypothesis offers the wrong sort of explanation. In fact, I think *both parts* of the Impossibility Hypothesis rest on mistaken assumptions. I don't think that the sorts of situations that evoke imaginative resistance need to be situations that we judge to be conceptually impossible, and I don't think that, in general, a judgment of conceptual impossibility renders a scenario unimaginable. But more importantly, I don't think that the Impossibility Hypothesis offers the right *sort* of explanation of the phenomenon of imaginative resistance. So let me try to show you why not.

---

[15] [17] For an intriguing discussion of these issues, cf. Marshall 1990, and the Winch texts referred to therein.

6. Imaginable Conceptual Impossibilities

Let's start by considering some statements that seem to offer even more extreme instances of conceptual impossibility than those with which we have been concerned so far.

(a) 12 is not the sum of 5 and 7.

(b) 12 used to be the sum of 5 and 7, but is no longer the sum of 5 and 7.

(c) 12 both is and is not the sum of 5 and 7.

We're so clear that these statements are conceptually impossible that the Principle of Charity seems to require that we credit someone who utters them with having changed the subject. If someone comes up to me and says "12 both is and is not the sum of 5 and 7," it seems that I have no choice but to reinterpret one or more of her terms. Whatever she's talking about, she can't mean by "12" and "both" and "is" and "and" and "not" and "sum" and "5" and "7" what *we* mean by those terms. It just doesn't make *sense* to say that 12 both is and is not the sum of 5 and 7. And since I can't make *sense* of what it would be for 12 both to be and not to be the sum of 5 and 7, I surely can't imagine a story in which it is *true* that 12 both is and is not the sum of 5 and 7. Such a story is bound to evoke imaginative resistance on my part. Or so the Impossibility Hypothesis predicts.

So sit back, relax, and let me tell you a little fable:

The Tower of Goldbach
Long long ago, when the world was created, every even number was the sum of two primes. Although most people suspected that this was the case, no one was completely certain. So a great convocation was called, and for forty days and forty nights, all the mathematicians of the world labored together in an effort to prove this hypothesis. Their efforts were not in vain: at midnight on the fortieth day, a proof was found. "Hoorah!" they cried, "we have unlocked the secret of nature."

But when God heard this display of arrogance, God was angry. From heaven roared a thundering voice: "My children, you have gone too far. You have understood too many of the universe's secrets. From this day forth, no longer shall twelve be the sum of two primes." And God's word was made manifest, and twelve was no longer the sum of two primes.

The mathematicians were distraught—all their efforts had been in vain. They beseeched God: "Please," they said, "if we can find twelve persons among us who are still faithful to You, will You not relent and make twelve once again the sum of two primes?" And so God agreed.

The mathematicians searched and searched. In one town, they found seven who were righteous. In another, they found five. They tried to bring them together to make twelve, but because twelve was no longer the sum of two primes, they could not. "Lord," they cried out, "what shall we do? If You lifted Your punishment, there would indeed be twelve righteous souls, and Your decision to do so would be in keeping with Your decree. But until You do, twelve are not to be found, and we are destined forever to have labored in vain."

God was moved by their plea, and called upon Solomon to aid in making the decision. Carefully, Solomon weighed both sides of the issue. If twelve again became the sum of two primes, then the conditions according to which God and the mathematicians had agreed would be satisfied. And if twelve remained not the sum of two primes, again the conditions according to which God and the mathematicians had agreed would be satisfied. How Solomonic it would be to satisfy the conditions twice over!

So with great fanfare, the celebrated judge announced his resolution of the dispute: From that day on, twelve both was and was not the sum of five and seven. And the heavens were glad, and the mountains rang with joy. And the voices of the five and seven righteous souls rose towards heaven, a chorus twelve and not-twelve, singing in harmonious unity the praises of the Lord. The end.

Now, you may not be totally convinced by the Tower of Goldbach story. You may not think that I have succeeded in telling a story at the end of which there both are and are not twelve righteous souls. You may not even think that I have succeeded in telling a story in which twelve ends up both being and not being the sum of five and seven. But unless you are in the grip of some philosophical theory that tells you that you shouldn't make such a concession, I think you need to accept that I have told a story where at least something which if it were stated barely would be conceptually impossible is, in the context of the story, true. That is, contrary to what clause (b) of the Impossibility Hypothesis predicts, the conceptually impossible proposition that (say) twelve suddenly ceases to be the sum of two primes becomes—for the moment at least—imaginable.[16]

The reason the story can do this, of course, is that it focuses our attention on certain *aspects* of the things which it asks us to imagine.[17] When we imagine the things which, on reflection, we realize to be conceptually impossible, we imagine them in ways that disguise their conceptual impossibility. So when God gets angry and causes twelve no longer to be the sum of two primes, we are considering "twelve is the sum of two primes" primarily with regard to one of its features, namely, that it is a proposition of which human beings are categorically certain only as a consequence of their hubristic arrogance. And when the

---

[16] [18] While I don't think that we *fully* make sense of what it would be for twelve suddenly to cease to be the sum of two primes, I think we do something more than merely assent to the *sentence* "twelve used to be the sum of five and seven, but is no longer." The meanings of the individual terms and the way they are combined play a significant role in fixing what we take ourselves to be assenting to. I return to this issue in the next footnote. (For a more comprehensive taxonomy of the sorts of assent which may be involved in cases such as these, see J. H. Newman 1909, as well as the discussion in Marshall 1990.) (Thanks to Michael Stocker for these references.)

[17] [19] What happens as we read through "The Tower of Goldbach" is that we focus now on this aspect of what it is to be twelve, now on that aspect, in a way typical of fictional understanding in general—indeed, in a way typical of non-fictional understanding as well. (This theme is emphasized in the literature on "conceptual blending"; for representative discussions, cf. Turner 1996; Fauconnier and Turner 1998; Fauconnier 1994; Fauconnier and Sweetser 1996.)

mathematicians' search concludes with their having found five righteous souls in one town and seven in another, we are willing to accept that this doesn't give us *twelve* righteous souls because we are thinking of it as: "number of righteous souls required for God to lift the decree." It is as a result of lots of *local* bits of conceptual coherence that the global incoherence is able to get a foothold.

So conceptual impossibility does not preclude imaginability. As long as they are properly disguised, we are able to imagine all sorts of impossible things. But it doesn't take the Tower of Goldbach story to show us this. Even if one holds that conceivability under ideal rational reflection tracks conceptual possibility, possibility-tracking is clearly a non-starter when the issue is *imaginability* of the sort we are concerned with in games of make-believe. For unlike ideal rational reflection, make-believe depends upon precisely the sort of abstraction that may well leave out conceptually relevant features of the situation at hand. Indeed, one of the main *points* of pretense and make-believe and reading fiction and viewing art is to take on various ways of seeing things—ways that focus on certain elements of the situation, while ignoring others.[18]

Thinking about literal games of pretense will help me make my point even more clearly. Such games involve exactly this sort of exploitation of our capacity for selective attention. When we pretend that a banana is a gun, we focus on certain similarities, such as shape, while ignoring others, such as internal complexity. The principles of generation that determine what is true in a game of make-believe may be quite complicated.[19] Generally speaking, the edibility of bananas does not make it make-believe that play-guns are edible, nor does their yellowness make it make-believe that play-guns are yellow. And while the location of the stem may fix the direction of the muzzle, nothing in the banana seems to correspond to the bullets, nor does anything in the gun correspond to the skin.

As Kendall Walton has argued persuasively,[20] the interpretation of fiction may helpfully be seen as a similar sort of prop-oriented game of make-belief. And even without a general theory of truth in fiction, it is evident that the principles of generation will be at least as complicated for novels as for banana-guns. Is it true in "The Tower of Goldbach" that the mathematicians proved Goldbach's Conjecture? Well, the story *says* that that's what happened. But is that really Goldbach's Conjecture, or just something with Goldbach-like features?

---

[18] [20] Cf. Danto: it is "one of the main offices of art less to represent the world than to represent it in such a way as to cause us to view it with a certain attitude and with a special vision" (Danto 1981: 167).

[19] [21] Cf. Walton 1990, ch. 1 and Currie 1990, *passim* for an overview of some of the philosophical issues involved. Among the most helpful of the many empirically based writings on the subject are Currie 1995b and 1998; Harris 1994; Leslie 1987; Lillard 1994; Perner, Baker, and Hutton 1994; and Woolley 1995 [*added in 2009*: as well as Harris 2000; Skolnick and Bloom 2006a, 2006b; Weisberg and Goodstein 2009].

[20] [22] Cf. Walton 1990, as well as his numerous articles before and after.

I'm not quite clear on what grounds we would be able to answer such a question. At least, I don't have sufficiently fine-grained intuitions about concept-individuation, nor do I see how I could acquire them. But I also don't think they matter for understanding the story. Are the owl and the pussycat in the pea-green boat really an *owl* and a *cat*, or just things with owl-like and cat-like features? Is Peter Rabbit a *rabbit*? Is Frosty the Snowman a *snowman*? Is the knave of hearts in *Alice in Wonderland* a *playing card*? Whatever it is to be a playing card, or a snowman, or a rabbit, it's pretty clear that it precludes doing the sorts of things that are done by the knave of hearts, or Frosty, or Peter. Indeed, it's not clear that anything could be a snowman, where by "snowman" I mean what you mean by "snowman," and be something that sings, where by "sing" I mean what you mean by "sing". So, which is it: is Frosty not a snowman, or doesn't he sing? Or perhaps he sings only insofar as he is something other than a snowman. But then: is he both a snowman and not a snowman at the same time? Or perhaps being a snowman is some sort of phase sortal? Or maybe being-a-snowman is just a way of describing some more fundamental property upon which snowmanness supervenes?

To ask these sorts of questions is to demonstrate an ignorance of what it is to engage in games of make-believe. And the phenomenon in question is not limited to cases of fiction involving things like talking snowmen or mathematical absurdities. Consider what might be called *the "that thing with the cup" problem*. In the realistic novel *A Man in Full*, Tom Wolfe describes a sexual encounter in a motel between the 60-year-old protagonist, Charlie Croker, and his soon-to-be wife, the beautiful 20-something Serena. Wolfe relates Croker's memories of the events as follows:

> Once they got into the room, she produced that little cup from her handbag, and they did the thing with the cup, something he had never heard of in all his life. He had lost his mind to her demented form of lust. Danger! Imminent exposure! That thing with the cup! (Wolfe 1998: 228)

Like Croker himself, many readers have "never heard of [that thing with the cup] in all [their] li[ves]," so a reporter from the *New Yorker* took it upon herself to ask Wolfe precisely what this lascivious act was supposed to have involved. She reports the following reply:

> When Tom Wolfe was told last week that no one has the faintest idea what that thing with the cup is, he said, "As a matter of fact, neither do I. I concocted the phrase to somehow give you a vision of some unmentionable perversion. It sounded so simple, yet so dreadfully titillating, but I never even had a glimmer of a notion what it might be."[21]

---

[21] [24] Quoted in an article entitled "Fuller Explanation Department: Tom Wolfe Decodes the Naughty Riddle that Has his Readers Stumped" (Mead 1999: 26). One might think, as Wolfe himself sometimes suggests, that "that thing with the cup" is metaphoric. But even if this is the correct diagnosis of the cup case (which I think it is not), it won't do as a general solution to the

The "that thing with the cup" problem is this: there is *nothing* that counts as doing "that thing with the cup"—nothing at all. It's not like the question of whether Sherlock Holmes's mother had blue eyes—which is a case of under-specification that could be made precise in any number of ways. The problem with that thing with the cup is that there's nothing that it is to be "that thing with the cup" in this (the actual) world, *and there's nothing that it is to be "that thing with the cup" in the world of Serena and Charlie Croker.* There are no extra body parts, no extra positions, no extra ways in which something that is not arousing in this world is arousing in that world (doing you-know-what with the cup, for instance). But despite this, it is nonetheless *true* in *A Man in Full* that Charlie Croker and Serena did "that thing with the cup," and that they enjoyed it. Similarly, even though there's no way that *any* world might be such that 7 and 5 both do and do not equal 12 in it, it's nonetheless true in "The Tower of Goldbach" that 7 and 5 both do and do not equal 12.

What this shows is that clause (b) of the Impossibility Hypothesis is wrong for deep and not shallow reasons. It's not that our stupidity or finitude occasionally leads us to mistake conceptually impossible situations for conceptually possible ones, resulting in an ability to imagine what our best theory tells us we shouldn't be able to imagine. It's that the constraints that possibility places on the imagination aren't the *sort* of thing that could explain imaginative resistance. They are too easily disguised, and too easily overcome if disguised, to provide the right kind of explanation.

7. Other Sources of Imaginative Resistance

But surely, you want to object, the sort of conceptual impossibility that confronts us when we are asked to imagine that murder is right is a different *sort* of conceptual impossibility than that which confronts us when we are asked to imagine that Frosty is a singing snowman. Our grasp on moral terms is too tightly connected to their applicability to certain sorts of actions for us to understand what it would be for these to come apart. We just don't have a handle on how something could be enough like murder for us even to be tempted to call it "murder" if at the same time it is supposed to be something that we could understand as being right. So whereas the conceptual impossibility of the Frosty case is a philosopher's problem, the conceptual impossibility of the murder case is not. This suggests that the Impossibility Hypothesis might still be right in spirit, even if it is wrong in letter. The source of imaginative resistance might be

problem. There may be no way to spell out fully how Frosty is both a snowman and a thing that sings, but it doesn't follow that it's a *metaphor* that Frosty is a singing snowman. To repeat: make-believe allows us to consider aspects of complexes in a selective way, attending to bits of local coherence even though the whole may be incoherent.

attributable to our difficulty in making sense of the scenario, even though conceptual impossibility as such does not guarantee unimaginability.

But though there is certainly something right in that analysis, I'm convinced that it is not the full explanation.[22] My reasons for thinking so are twofold. The first is that there are scenarios that are clearly not impossible that seem to evoke precisely the same sort of imaginative resistance as those cases that purportedly are. And the second is that there are certain sorts of changes that seem to make imaginative resistance evaporate, even though they make no difference to the conceptual coherence of the scenario in question. So even if we allow that the sorts of scenarios that generally evoke imaginative resistance *are* conceptually impossible, and in a more central way than the way in which a singing snowman is, there are reasons to think that even so, *this* is not going to give us the full solution to our puzzle. Rather, I will argue, whether or not we are inclined to respond with imaginative resistance is going to turn out to depend on *why* we think we're being asked to imagine them.

So let's begin with a case that I think shows that we can have imaginative resistance without conceptual impossibility. It's another story, a bit shorter this time.

The Mice

Once upon a time there were a bunch of mice. The mice who had white fur were hardworking and industrious, but the mice who had black fur were slothful and shiftless. A huge number of them were addicted to some kind of drug, and the rest of them just spent their days hanging out on the streets and eating watermelon. Their nests were unkempt, filled with cast-off bits of string and old sunflower seed shells. So it wasn't surprising that the mice with white fur tended to be much better off than the mice with black fur—shinier coats, better food, and so on.

Even so, the mice with white fur were very generous to the mice with black fur. They gave bits of cheese to the black mouse babies. They left piles of nuts and seeds in the black mouse neighborhoods. And, obviously, they provided the black mice with role-models of

---

[22] [25] The cases where explanation on the basis of inability seems most plausible are those where our grasp on the concept in question is via a single feature that we are asked to imagine away (cf. Hilary Putnam's discussions of "one-criterion concepts"), or where the text involves the deliberate juxtaposition of two obviously contrary features in a way that is *intended* to produce something unimaginable (as in the children's rhyme: "One bright day in the middle of the night, two dead men got up to fight. Back to back they faced each other, drew their swords and shot each other. The deaf policeman heard the noise, and came and shot those two dead boys. If you don't believe this lie is true, ask the blind man—he saw it too."). I am not denying that sometimes a phenomenon akin to imaginative resistance arises where we are unable, rather than unwilling, to make sense of what the narrator seems to be asking us. Nor am I denying that the (conceptual) impossibility of a situation may make it more difficult to imagine than one which is not (conceptually) impossible. But, for the reasons I discuss above, I do not think this could be a full explanation. (Thanks to the audience at Rutgers University, and especially to Matthew Phillips, for pressing me on the need to make this concession.) [*Added in 2009*: I make further concessions in this direction in the opening pages of "Imaginative Resistance Revisited" (2006b; Ch. 10 below).]

diligence and industry. But the mice with black fur just kept to their old ways. They seemed constitutionally incapable of changing. They sat around as if they expected the white mice to *give* things to them—just like that! More more more, that's what they seemed to expect. Some of the white mice kept providing the black mice with food and other necessities, but most did not. And that was the right thing to do. For the distribution of resources in the mouse world reflected the relative merits of the two mouse groups. All the mice got what they deserved. The End.

Now, I take it that there's nothing about the concept of "mouse" that makes it conceptually incoherent that there should be one group of mice that is socially superior to another group of mice. So what makes the story so hard to swallow? What makes it so difficult to accept not only that the white mice deserve more goodies than the black mice (for reasons of industriousness or fur color), but— in certain moods at least—to accept even the basic outlines of the plot (were the black mice *really* slothful and shiftless? Did they *really* just sit around expecting the white mice to give them things?).[23]

The problem, of course, is that it's virtually impossible for us to take "The Mice" as anything but an extremely crude allegory for race relations. And as such, the story evokes the sort of imaginative resistance that is evoked by Walton's Giselda case. My inclination on hearing the mouse story is to say: "it's not true in the world of 'The Mice' that white mice are better off than black mice because they deserve to be; that may be what the *narrator* of the story thinks, but she's obviously mistaken; surely there are relevant features of the relation between black-mouse and white-mouse culture that she has simply not attended to."

But in this case, my reasons for narrator-doubling have nothing to do with my *inability* to make-believe that there is world in which white mice and black mice have the features described in the story, and in which white mice are better off than black mice because they deserve to be; they have to do with my *unwillingness* to do so. And my unwillingness to do so is a function of my not wanting to take a particular perspective on the world—*this* world—that I don't endorse.

This brings me to the final step in my argument, which is to show that there are certain sorts of changes that seem to make imaginative resistance evaporate, even though they do not affect the coherence or incoherence of the case in question. So let's try varying Walton's Giselda story in ways that presumably do not affect the coherence or incoherence of the scenario described, but that do affect our sense of distance from the narration.[24]

---

[23] [26] Thanks to Kendall Walton for pressing me on the need to clarify the sort of resistance that I take the story to evoke.

[24] [27] Thanks to Zoltán Gendler Szabó for suggesting this way of looking at the problem.

Suppose that instead of:

(5) "In killing her baby, Giselda did the right thing; after all, it was a girl."

We had:

(6) "In killing her baby, Giselda did the right thing; after all, it was born on January 19th."

or:

(7) "In killing her baby, Giselda did the right thing; after all, it was a changeling."

For me at least, neither (6) nor (7) evokes the same sort of response that (5) does. I said above that in reading (5), my and Walton's first instinct was to *reject* the invitation to make-believe that "it was right for Giselda to kill her baby, given that it was a girl," responding instead with a narrator-doubling move. But this is not my first instinct with regard to (6) or (7). There my first instinct is to say: "How interesting! I wonder what this world is going to turn out to be like, this world in which killing one's baby is the right thing to do, so long as the baby is born on January 19th, or is a changeling." In fact, in light of (6) and (7), I can almost feel my imaginative resistance to (5) evaporating. So long as I am not inclined to take (5) as making a claim about the way *this* world is, I'm perfectly willing to grant it the autonomy that I grant to other sorts of make-believe.[25]

8. Genre and the Laws of Import–Export

But how could describing a fictional world be a way of making claims about the way *this* world is?[26] The explanation lies in recognizing that like conversation in general, storytelling makes use of standard assumptions about common knowledge and presupposition. The narrator needs to assume that the listener shares a wide range of background beliefs about the world, and the listener needs to assume that the narrator assumes this, and so on, in familiar Gricean fashion. To see how this connects up to the problem of imaginative resistance, let's start with the following simple case.

Suppose you are an author who has written a work of realistic fiction—like *Pride and Prejudice* or *Anna Karenina*. The store of fictional truths generated by the story will include not only all of the explicit statements you make about

---

[25] [28] Michael Tanner observes (though doesn't argue for) this. He writes: "We are not, then, in any serious way challenged or offended in those cases where we can't make reasonably strong connections between a fictional world we encounter and our own" (Tanner 1994: 63).

[26] [29] Thanks to John Hawthorne for discussion of the ideas contained in this section.

what happens to Elizabeth or Darcy or Anna or Vronsky, but also a tremendous number of actual truths that are *imported* into the story. Some of these will be explicitly stated; others will be generated by whatever turns out to be the correct principle for generating fictional truths in this context. But because the story is a work of realistic fiction, regulations concerning imports will be extremely lenient: in general (though there will be numerous exceptions), if something is true in the actual world, it will be true in the fictional world. Some of these fictional truths will concern what X said to Y on Tuesday, some will concern how the quadrille is danced, and some will concern the painfulness of unrequited love. Those directly tied to the specifics of the story will be merely true in the fiction. But there will be a tremendous number of things that are true in the fiction that are also true in the actual world.

Now if I as a reader know this, then I will feel free to *export* from the fictional world fictional truths that I take to be not merely truths in the story. And because this is a work of realistic fiction, regulations concerning exports will be extremely lenient: in general (though there will be numerous exceptions), if something is true in the fictional world, it will be true in the actual world. From among the inventory of fictional truths that the story provides, I will thus have access to at least two sorts of proposition that I may come newly to accept as true. The first sort are those that make use of the *narrative as clearinghouse*: I export things from the story that you the storyteller have intentionally and consciously imported, adding them to my stock in the way that I add knowledge gained by testimony. In this way, for instance, I might learn how women wore their hair in nineteenth-century France, or when the serfs were emancipated, or how far away a particular village is from London. The second sort are those that make use of the *narrative as factory*: I export things from the story whose truth becomes apparent as a result of thinking about the story itself. These I add to my stock the way I add knowledge gained by modeling. In this way, for instance, I might learn that the relation between loyalty and adultery is more complicated than I had suspected, or that the deleterious effects of a rigid class structure are (un)equally distributed among the classes.

Let's call fiction that is realistic in the way I have just described *non-distorting* fiction. And let's contrast it with what we might call *distorting* fiction, where the mirroring between the fictional and the actual world is more complex. An extreme example of distorting fiction is the sort of backwards story that one finds in the Addams Family, where, at least for a wide range of things, what's good is bad and what's bad is good—but where the *point* of the story is precisely that the reader be aware of these inversions, and alter the laws of export accordingly. The distancing mechanisms invoked in the last section exploit precisely this phenomenon. When I read (7)—that "In killing her baby, Giselda did the right thing; after all, it was a changeling"—I have no inclination to think that this is meant to be an instance of non-distorting fiction. The bizarreness of the example cues me into the fact that there is no straightforward export being offered—and as I realize this, my inclination to resist diminishes.[27]

So my hypothesis is that cases that evoke genuine imaginative resistance will be cases where the reader feels that she is being asked to export a way of looking at the actual world which she does not wish to add to her conceptual repertoire.[28] Why should this raise particular problems for morality? The answer, I think, is twofold. The first is that moral claims are often taken to be categorical, in the sense that if they are true at all, they are true in all possible worlds,[29] so while purported facts about Sherlock Holmes and Gandalf are easily understood as being merely fictional, purported facts about the morality of murder are not. So the first part of the explanation is that fictional moral truths clamor for exportation, in a way that other sorts of fictional truths do not. But this can't be the whole story, for the export regulations may be such that—as with the Addams family case—the product is radically altered as it crosses the border from fictional to real. So a further explanation is required. And I think it is this. For a story to even make sense, a great number of things that are held to be true within the fiction must be held to be true outside it, and vice versa. The moral principles that govern the world in question are generally among these, as are the truths of logic, mathematics, and—in most genres—the laws of physics and psychology and even etiquette. When a story explicitly cancels one of these presuppositions—as, for instance, in the case of the Tower of Goldbach—we are generally inclined to take the cancellation as governing only the fictional world; I was not trying to get you to export the belief that 12 both is and is not the sum 5 and 7, just as I was not trying to get you to export the belief that there is something that is both a snowman and a thing that sings. In most cases,

---

[27] [30] This hypothesis is supported by research in cognitive psychology (by Judith Smetana and later by James Blair), which suggests that moral rule violations are judged problematic in cases where a mechanism that Blair calls "VIM" (violence inhibition mechanism) is set off. For non-psychopaths, VIM is activated when there is a victim (someone in distress) whose presence as a victim is conspicuous to the subject. The cognitive science research predicts that a person will "morally react" to a situation when (1) there is a salient victim, and (2) there is no overriding consideration, such as justice, that alters the subject's assessment of the circumstances. Cases where violent (and pornographic) movies fail to evoke the expected degree of imaginative resistance in non-psychopaths can be traced to these considerations. Either (1) the objects of violence are systematically not focused on (Rambo's victims), represented as unharmed (Wile E. Cayote) or portrayed as enjoying their treatment (pornography) or (2) considerations of revenge, justice, and deserved punishment are presented as overriding (cf. cowboy films, sado-masochistic pornography). For further discussion see R. J. R. Blair 1995, Smetana and Braeges 1990, as well as references contained in each. (The insights and references in this footnote are a direct consequence of a series of extremely fruitful e-mail conversations with Ron Mallon.) [*Added in 2009*: This idea is explored in detail by Neil Levy (2005).]

[28] [31] I have been helped in my thinking about these issues by Michael DePaul's work on moral corruption. See especially DePaul 1988 and 1993; see also Judith Lichtenberg's work on moral certainty, especially Lichtenberg 1994. (Thanks to Lynn McFall for this last reference.)

[29] [32] I thank Barry Loewer for this insight.

the very fact of deviance is sufficient indication that literal export is not the intention.

But because we recognize that there are instances of *actual* moral disagreement, when we encounter fictional truths that concern deviant morality, we cannot assume that their deviance is an indication that the author does not wish them to be exported, or that she wishes them to be exported in altered form. There may be indications that this is all that is intended—as in (6) and (7)—and then the imaginative resistance disappears. But when, as is the default, we understand the story as demanding that we take on a certain way of looking at the actual world, we are inclined to resist.[30]

9. Conclusion

Let me conclude by tying what I have been saying to some more general issues concerning the nature of imagination as such. I noted above that, in general, we want what we *believe* to track what is true in the actual world. We might say that, in parallel fashion, we want what we *make-believe* to track what is true in a

---

[30] [33] How does this explanation fare with other—non-moral—cases that seem to evoke something akin to imaginative resistance? For instance, Kendall Walton (1994) points out that it is difficult to imagine something that would be a bad knock-knock joke in the actual world being hilariously funny in a fictional world, or something that would be jagged and angular in the actual world being graceful and flowing in some fictional world. Carl Ginet in conversation has suggested the same in cases of being asked to imagine, for instance, that sour milk smells good or that a piercing shriek sounds soothing. I think these cases can be dealt with in one of two ways. (a) In the Walton cases, I think that where it is clear that no export is intended, we are often able to accept that it is true in the story (and not just that it is thought by the characters in the story to be true) that, for instance, knock-knock jokes are the highest form of wit. To the extent we resist in such cases, I think it is because we take the author to be claiming something about the status of knock-knock jokes (or rock music, or the combination of orange and pink) in *this* world. (b) In the Ginet cases, there are two possibilities for what we are being asked to imagine. Either we are being asked to imagine that something that shares (most of) the features of sour milk does not smell unpleasant, which strikes me as straightforwardly imaginable, or we are being asked to imagine something that has the odor that sour milk has (that particular *quale*) but that does not smell unpleasant. In this latter case, we seem to be dealing with something analogous to a one-criterion concept. The difficulty is exacerbated by the fact that we are dealing with phenomena that operate at a sub-cognitive level. Part of the difficulty involved in imagining that sour milk smells appealing (on either reading) is—in my case at least—purely physiological; the same seems to be true for imagining that, for instance, having one's teeth drilled is pleasurable. (It seems easier to imagine that a backrub is painful than to imagine that having one's thumb crushed is pleasant.) In these cases, we may have too "direct" a grasp on this feature of the subject matter to abstract away from it in imagination. (Note that this tells in favor of my larger point—that imagination is not just supposition.) [*Added in 2009*: For arguments that the domain of phenomena evoking imaginative resistance extends beyond the moral, see Yablo 2002, Weatherson 2004; for partial defense of the restricted usage, see "Imaginative Resistance Revisited" (Ch. 10). For further exploration of "phenomena that operate at a sub-cognitive level"—an issue that bears also in the discussion of metaphoric engagement addressed in n. 32 below—see "Alief and Belief" (2008a) and "Alief in Action (and Reaction)" (2008b), Chs. 13 and 14 below.]

given fictional world. What is fictionally true in a given world is largely—though surely not entirely—up to the author of the narrative. So we can say roughly that to engage in imaginative resistance is to fail to follow the author's lead in making-believe what the author wants to make fictional. What is the source of this failure?

The Impossibility Hypothesis traces the failure to a problem with the *fictional* world. It says essentially: we are *unable* to follow the author's lead because the world she has tried to make fictional is impossible. My alternative proposal traces it to a problem with our relations to the *actual* world. It says essentially: we are *unwilling* to follow the author's lead because in trying to make that world fictional, she is providing us with a way of looking at *this* world that we prefer not to embrace.[31]

If I am right, we should expect to find parallel cases of something akin to imaginative resistance whenever we feel that we are being asked to add to our repertoire of schemata a way of looking at the world that we prefer not to have available. And we should expect imaginative resistance to evaporate as the lines between belief and make-belief are made more and more explicit.

Both predictions are borne out. If you say to me: "Don't you see how Aunt Ruth looks just like a walrus!" I may resist following your suggestion; I may simply not *want* to notice the way in which her forehead juts forward like that, or the way that her eyes bug out, or the fact that those lines beneath her nose *do* look a bit like tusks. Similarly, a parent concerned with gender equality may resist calling the strong chair the "papa chair" and the weak chair the "mama chair." The advocate for abortion rights speaks of himself as "pro-choice" and not "anti-life"; his opponent adopts the opposite terminology. And so on.[32]

The source of this resistance can be traced to the way in which imagination requires a sort of participation that mere hypothetical reasoning does not.[33] If instead of embedding P and M in (1) and (2), which ask us to believe, or (3) and (4), which ask us to imagine, we embed them instead in sentences, such as (8)

---

[31] [34] Thanks to Gregory Currie for suggestions that led to a refinement of this paragraph.

[32] [35] Cf. Dick Moran: "We may resist making a certain comparison, or the appropriateness of some metaphor, even when we are not rejecting something we have been given to believe. In such a case, one is rejecting a point of view, refusing to enter into it" (Moran 1994: 105). These issues are discussed in detail in Moran 1989. See also Walton 1993, where, in discussing the practice of plumbers and electricians in distinguishing between "male" and "female" plumbing and electrical connections, he writes: "The plumbing and electrical connections invite scarcely any participation in the game in which they are understood to be props. The conscientious plumber does his job without, fictionally, leering at the fixtures. (The plumbing terminology can be vaguely titillating, however, and it might cause embarrassment, especially when one comes across it for the first time. These reactions suggest that a certain perhaps implicit participation in the game will be likely, perhaps even inevitable.)" (Walton 1993: 40). [*Added in 2009*: for more recent discussions of this issue, see Camp 2009, as well as the special issue of *Mind and Language*, 21/3 (2006).]

[33] [36] Cf. Moran's distinction between hypothetical and dramatic imagination, discussed briefly in Moran 1994 at 104–5.

and (9), which ask us to suppose for the sake of argument, then the asymmetry again disappears:

(8) I am asked to *suppose for the sake of argument* that: P holds (where P is some non-moral proposition that I do not believe to hold).

(9) I am asked to *suppose for the sake of argument* that: M holds (where M is some moral proposition that I do not believe to hold).

As long as I take myself to be in no way implicated in the way of thinking that M presupposes, and as long as I take the claims of M to be restricted to the realm of the merely hypothetical, I feel no more resistance in supposing M than in supposing P.

What this suggests is that imagination is distinct from belief on the one hand, and from mere supposition on the other. It is this which explains both our general capacity to imagine morally deviant situations, and our general unwillingness to do so.[34]

[34] [*] *Acknowlegements*: For comments on or discussion of earlier drafts of this paper, I am grateful to Dick Moran, Derek Parfit, Tamar Schapiro, Ted Sider, Michael Stocker, David Velleman, Ken Walton, and Steve Yablo. For extremely helpful questions that led to many important revisions, I thank audiences at Syracuse (1998), Notre Dame (1998), and Rutgers (1999) Universities, and at the "Imagination and the Adapted Mind" Conference at the University of California at Santa Barbara (1999). Most of all, special thanks to John Hawthorne and Zoltán Gendler Szabó for extensive discussion of the issues involved.

10

Imaginative Resistance Revisited

As the title suggests, this chapter is devoted to revisiting the topic of imaginative resistance. In it, I partially defend and partially refine the account offered in the previous essay (Ch. 9 above).

In that essay, I had characterized the *Puzzle of Imaginative Resistance* as the puzzle of explaining our comparative difficulty in imagining fictional worlds that we take to be morally deviant. In this chapter, I suggest that that puzzle is a special instance of the more general *Puzzle of Authoritative Breakdown*: the puzzle of identifying and explaining cases where engaged readers fail to imagine P, even though the author of the work has followed standard conventions for fictionally asserting P. In slogan form, the position I defend here is that although there are some cases of authoritative breakdown where we simply can't imagine the prompted content, and some cases of authoritative breakdown where we simply won't imagine the prompted content, classic imaginative resistance arises in cases where we can't because we won't.

The basic argument of the chapter rests on the observation—central to all of the essays in this section of the book—that mental representations can be activated in a multitude of ways, and that awakening the associative patterns linked with a particular stereotype, mental image, protocol, or motor routine tends to awaken the perception and action dispositions associated with it.

Though it was written to be self-standing, this essay is best read as a companion piece to the previous essay—"The Puzzle of Imaginative Resistance"—to which it makes reference at a number of points.

***

This essay was first published in Shaun Nichols (ed.), *The Architecture of the Imagination* (Oxford, 2006), 149–73 and is reprinted with the kind permission of Oxford University Press. Because this essay has been cited in its original form in a number of responses, changes have been limited to corrections of minor typographical errors, the insertion of remarks in footnotes (noted as such), the updating of bibliographic references to papers that were then in manuscript form, and the reconfiguration of citations to bring reference conventions into line with other essays in the volume.

1. Introduction

Several hundred years ago, Hume offered some brief remarks on a striking feature of our imaginative repertoire. While we are generally both ready and able to entertain even the most fantastic and improbable scenarios, there appear to be systematic exceptions: in certain circumstances, it is unexpectedly difficult to (bring ourselves to) imagine what an author describes. Half a decade ago, drawing on an insight of Kendall Walton's and borrowing a term from Dick Moran, I dubbed a special instance of this phenomenon *The Puzzle of Imaginative Resistance*.[1] "The Puzzle of Imaginative Resistance," I suggested, is "the puzzle of explaining our comparative difficulty in imagining fictional worlds that we take to be morally deviant" (Gendler 2000: 56; Ch. 9 above).[2]

Recently, a number of authors have suggested that both the attributed genealogy and the choice of term were unfortunate. Hume's concerns are primarily with non-fiction rather than fiction. And there are a number of related puzzles that I failed to identify or address: whereas my original account conflated problems of truth in fiction with problems of imaginability, there are important differences between them;[3] and whereas my original discussion was limited to morally deviant fictional scenarios, there are related cases that should be accommodated in a fully comprehensive account.

Because I focused only on certain features of the landscape, the solution I proposed in "The Puzzle of Imaginative Resistance" (2000)—roughly, that we don't imagine morally deviant worlds because we don't want to—is incomplete.[4]

---

[1] [1] Cf. Moran 1994, Walton 1994, and Gendler 2000a (Ch. 9 above). Though the discussion below is designed to be comprehensible even to those unfamiliar with earlier work on the topic of imaginative resistance, readers wishing to gain an overview of the issues might fruitfully consult the three essays just listed, along with Weatherson 2004.

[2] [2] The basic problem is this: "When an author invites us to contemplate a fictional scenario, she seems to have a great deal of freedom in how she directs our imagination. Among the things she can make fictionally true are ... that animals marry, that time travel occurs, that alchemy is good science, and so on. But she seems to have much *less* freedom in what she makes fictionally true as far as matters of moral assessment are concerned. The trick that allows an author complete freedom in dictating whether or not character A murders character B is much less effective if what the author wants to dictate is that the murder is, for instance, praiseworthy, or noble, or charming, or admirable. So the puzzle is this: what explains why a trick so effective in so many realms is relatively ineffective here?" (Gendler 2000a: 58; Ch. 9 above).

[3] [3] For careful sorting out of four puzzles that earlier discussions tended to conflate, see Weatherson 2004. My focus in this essay will be primarily on what Weatherson calls the *imaginative* puzzle.

[4] [4] For important—and in many cases, decisive—criticisms, see Currie 2002a; Currie and Ravenscroft 2002; Doggett 2004; Holbo 2003a, 2003b; Matravers 2003; Mothersill 2003; Stock 2003, 2005; Stokes 2006; Trogdon 2004; Walton 2006; Weatherson 2003a, 2004; Weinberg and Meskin 2006; Yablo 2002. I have learned an enormous amount from these essays, and from discussions with their authors; my debts should be apparent to anyone familiar with them. [*Note added in 2009*: For additional valuable recent discussion, see Currie 2007; Driver 2008b; Goldie 2005; Levy 2005; Nichols 2006a; and Todd 2009. For an overview, see Gendler 2009.]

I will offer appropriate concessions in the pages that follow, and I present my new positive view at the end of §3. That said, I remain committed to four of "Puzzle's" main claims,[5] and I will devote the bulk of this essay to defending them.

First, I remain convinced that the engagement that distinguishes imagination from mere supposition plays a crucial role in the phenomena we are concerned with explaining. Insofar as our relation to the text is one of detached supposition, the perplexing responses that give rise to the puzzles are mitigated; it is only when we engage imaginatively—an engagement that is, in some difficult-to-pin-down way self-involving—that forceful resistance of the relevant kind begins to emerge.

Relatedly, I continue to believe that cases that invoke interesting resistance arise where the reader takes the author to be making simultaneous claims about the fictional and the non-fictional world. In the earlier essay I described these as cases where "export" is mandated; below I will describe them as involving "pop-out" sentences.[6] The basic claim here—as before—is that resistance phenomena arise because imaginative engagement is also a form of actual engagement: When we imagine, we draw on our ordinary conceptual repertoire and habits of appraisal, and as the result of imagining, we may find ourselves with novel insights about and changed perspectives on the actual world.

Third, I remained convinced that there *is* something special about the moral (or at least the appraisal-involving) cases, in contrast to the wider range of cases on which other authors have focused. Our failure to imagine them can be traced to a certain sort of unwillingness that amplifies—in subtle and complicated ways—what other authors have rightly identified as a certain sort of inability.

Finally, I remain convinced that a successful characterization of the resistance-family needs to explain not only our specific resistance to accepting as fictional the contents of certain stories, but also our more general reluctance to adopt metaphoric perspectives that emphasize similarities we prefer to overlook.[7] These cases provide an important foil neglected by many other accounts. In the next section, I will provide an example of the sort of case I have in mind.

---

[5] [5] Though Matravers (2003) and Walton (2006) rightly consider it imprudent, I will sometimes use the expression "imaginative resistance" for the family of phenomena that surround the puzzle discussed in the earlier essay. Where it is important to distinguish among members of the puzzle family, I will do so explicitly.

[6] [6] It will turn out that these cases overlap in significant ways—and for non-accidental reasons—with certain of the cases that violate the principle that Brian Weatherson has called *Virtue*. Roughly speaking, the relevant *Virtue-violating* cases are cases where the lower-level facts in a story determine that P, but where (the author of) the story nonetheless asserts that not-P. (Cf. Weatherson 2004: 18.)

[7] [7] Cf. Moran 1989, Walton 1993, to which I am here indebted. [*Added in 2009*: See also the discussions of metaphor cited in n. 32 of Ch. 9 above.]

2. Interlude: Nursery School Nomenclature

At nursery schools throughout the country, classes have names like Kangaroos, Ladybugs, Koalas, and Teddy Bears. It would be acceptable—though barely—for a school to have classes named Monkeys, Dogs, Cows, and Mice. But it would, presumably, be very odd indeed for classes at a nursery school to be called Cockroaches, Vultures, Maggots, and Mosquitoes. Now, whatever the explanation, it cannot be that 3-year-olds are more like ladybugs than they are like cockroaches—or more like kangaroos than they are like vultures. 3-year-olds may jump around excitedly, but they also descend voraciously on the snack table; they may not have beaks and wings, but they also don't have tails and pouches. This gives rise to the *Problem of Nursery School Nomenclature*: the problem of explaining why so many nursery schools have a Bumblebee room but no nursery schools have a Dung Beetle room, given that (in some reasonable sense of *harder*), it's no harder to imagine your child as a dung beetle than as a bumblebee.

Most of us have a reasonable folk theory about the Problem of Nursery School Nomenclature. We (tacitly) realize that framing things in certain ways activates certain behavioral dispositions and affective propensities, and we (tacitly) realize that the dispositions and propensities associated with notions like maggot-hood and vultureness are ones which we wish to avoid when thinking of our children. Moreover, an enormous body of empirical psychological research backs up these folk intuitions. One of the most striking and well-confirmed results of social psychological research over the last two decades is that mental representations can be activated in a multitude of ways, and that awakening the associative patterns linked with a particular stereotype, mental image, protocol, or motor routine tends to awaken the perception and action dispositions associated with it.[8] So our tacit sense that there is something distasteful about thinking of our child as a cockroach or a mosquito is based in a genuine sensitivity to a feature of our psychology. The Problem of Nursery School Nomenclature arises from our implicit awareness of the psychological costs associated with allowing ourselves to frame things in certain ways.

Notice, however, that I said "*allowing* ourselves to frame things in certain ways." Nursery school nomenclature is puzzling because it involves a case where we *can* do something, but we *don't*. And the reason we don't do it is because we don't want to—that is, because we *won't*. My suggestion in "Puzzle" was that imaginative resistance is the result of similar mechanisms. I wrote: "the primary source of imaginative resistance is not our *inability* to imagine morally deviant situations, but our *unwillingness* to do so" (Gendler 2000: 57; Ch. 9 above).

---

[8] [8] For detailed discussion of these issues, see "Imaginative Contagion" (Ch. 12 below). [*Added in 2009*: See also Chs. 13 and 14 below.]

For reasons that I will explain at the end of the next section, I now think that solution is incomplete.[9] But it will be helpful nonetheless to classify solutions along the spectrum that this distinction suggests. Some solutions—like Walton's tentatively endorsed impossibility solution[10]—are *can't* solutions: they say that in cases of imaginative resistance we don't follow along with the author because, for example, we can't figure out what it would *mean* for something to be both an instance of something that is morally good, and an instance of something that is gratuitous torture. Other solutions—like the solution I proposed in "Puzzle"—are *won't* solutions: I said that in cases of imaginative resistance we don't follow along with the author because we don't want to think about these things, even though we could.

Putting things this way oversimplifies somewhat, but it provides a useful initial framework for thinking about the range of positions in reacting to our puzzle. I will return to this distinction in my discussion below. But now I want to go back to Hume's original text, which I think will help us get a clearer handle on the phenomena we are worried about.

3. Humean Resistance

Although the connection between Hume's original remarks and contemporary discussions of Imaginative Resistance has sometimes been overstated, there is much to be learned by revisiting the text itself. For Hume notices features—or his text encourages the reader to notice features—that have received inadequate attention in many recent discussions. The now-familiar passage appears near the end of "Of the Standard of Taste":

Where *speculative* errors may be found in the polite writings of any age or country, they detract but little from the value of those compositions. There needs to be but a certain turn of thought or imagination to make us enter into all the opinions which then prevailed and relish the sentiments or conclusions derived from them. But a very violent effort is requisite to change our judgment of manners, and excite sentiments of approbation or blame, love or hatred, different from those to which the mind from long custom has been familiarized... I cannot, nor is it proper that I should, enter into such [vicious] sentiments. (Hume 1757/1985: 247)

Hume is pointing out an apparent topical asymmetry in our responses to various forms of writing. Texts that misrepresent certain things strike us as

---

[9] [9] Again, see the essays cited in n. 4 above.

[10] [10] Walton seeks "an explanation of why we should resist allowing fictional worlds to differ from the real world with respect to the relevant kind of dependence relations." Though he considers a number of explanations, he writes that his "best suspicion... is that it has something to do with... an inability to understand fully what it would be like for them to be different" (Walton 1994: 46).

inadequate in ways that texts that misrepresent other sorts of things do not. Whereas texts that include *detached factual* inaccuracies ("speculative errors" from which "sentiments or conclusions" might be "derived") are relatively unproblematic, texts that include *involved evaluative* inaccuracies (implicating us in a "judgment of manners" or exciting "sentiments of approbation or blame, love or hatred" that are "different from those to which the mind from long custom has been familiarized") face a cluster of related problems. What distinguishes the class of problematic cases from those that are unproblematic, and what sorts of problems do they confront?

Hume's text identifies two features as characteristic of the troublesome class. First, they are cases involving *valenced normative appraisals*: we are asked to assess something as mannerly or unmannerly, praiseworthy or blameworthy, loveable or hateable, where each of the pairs identifies two points along a normative spectrum where one end is desirable and the other is not. Second, they are cases that require the reader's *imaginative involvement*: it is *we* who are making the "judgment of manners," *we* in whom the relevant sentiments are being "excited," and *we* who are receiving the risky and improper invitation to "enter into" some vicious frame of mind.

On Hume's picture, these characteristic features are non-accidentally related. At base, normative judgments of praiseworthiness and blameworthiness are summary assessments of our tendencies towards attraction and repulsion—tendencies that are themselves the result of "long custom" and habituation. As a result, altering our judgments—even playfully—will be both difficult and dangerous: difficult because it will require the overcoming of long-entrenched patterns of response that are likely to be evoked even in the contemplation of explicitly imaginary scenarios, and dangerous because such overcoming may render these undesirable patterns of response available even in the contemplation of actual ones.

In light of this, Hume identifies three sorts of problems that typically confront such texts (those that call upon us to make deviant imaginatively involved valenced normative appraisals).The first is that the presence of such demands may "detract...from the value of these compositions." We might tentatively call this the *Problem of Aesthetic Value*, though it's not completely clear that it is specifically *aesthetic* value that Hume has in mind.[11] (Because I have nothing particularly interesting to say about it, I will set aside this issue in the ensuing discussion.[12]) The second is that we find it difficult to "enter into" their worldview by our usual "turn of thought or imagination"—if we succeed in doing so, it is only by means of a "very violent effort." Let's call this the *Problem of Imaginative Barriers*. The third is that entering into such worldviews

---

[11] [11] Indeed, the detraction may simply consist in the difficulties enumerated in the remainder of the passage.

[12] [12] For further discussion of this question, see Walton 2006.

strikes us as being in some way "improper"—the sentiments in question are "vicious" ones, and even if we somehow succeed in adopting them, we will have violated a norm that we hold ourselves to. Let's call this the *Problem of Imaginative Impropriety*.[13] Finally, let's call cases where both of the latter two obtain—that is, cases where we both confront imaginative barriers and experience a feeling of imaginative impropriety—cases that evoke *Humean resistance*.

Hume doesn't give a specific example but I take it that the sort of case he has in mind is this. Reading a text from ancient Greece—something like the *Euthyphro*, let's say—I find it a relatively straightforward matter to enter imaginatively into a mindset where I "relish the sentiments or conclusions" drawn from the assumption that the Greek gods are in control of certain matters of daily life; I can put myself into a mood where I imagine that it really matters that one keep one's hearth burning lest Hephestus be offended, or that if one faces an important practical decision, one should check in with the Oracle at Delphi. I may not fully work out all the implications of my imaginative commitments, but I'm genuinely involved and engaged in them, and when I'm asked to make inferences that require me to treat those assumptions as (imaginatively) true, I'm ready and willing to do so. By contrast, something very different happens when the author of the historical text seems to be assuming that I share his normative valenced appraisals of certain situations that I am engaged with quasi-observationally: on the question of whether it is morally acceptable to beat one's slave to death, for instance—indeed, on the question of whether it is morally acceptable to own a slave in the first place—I experience two things when I respond to the implied invitation to enter into such a mindset: I find that doing so requires, as Hume remarks, "a very violent effort" (this is the Problem of Imaginative Barriers), and I find myself reluctant to try to make that effort—it feels that doing so would be "improper" or "vicious" (this is the Problem of Imaginative Impropriety).[14]

So it looks like Humean resistance arises when we feel ourselves to have been asked by an author to make valenced normative appraisals in an involved way that differ from those we are accustomed to making; in such cases, we find that doing so requires significant effort, and that undertaking such an effort would be distasteful. By contrast, when we are making appraisals that are neither normative nor valenced, and when we are doing so in a detached way, Humean resistance does not arise. Moreover—though this does not rest directly on anything that Hume himself says—intermediate cases provide an interesting foil.

---

[13] [13] Jonathan Weinberg and Aaron Meskin offer a related distinction between what they call *the puzzle of imaginative refusal* and *the puzzle of imaginative blockage*. See Weinberg and Meskin 2006.

[14] [14] For an alternative use of the *Euthyphro* in discussing imaginative resistance, see Holbo 2003a.

Consider first cases where we are asked to contemplate deviant valenced normative appraisals in a detached way—as when we are asked to suppose just for the sake of argument that child slavery is morally acceptable. Such cases seem, at least to me, to evoke a palpable feeling of something akin to imaginative impropriety. Even though I am not engaged in a full-fledged act of *imagining*, there seems to be something unseemly about supposing for the sake of argument that the Rwandan genocide was not such a bad thing because the victims were poor, or that the policy of deliberately infecting Native Americans with smallpox was acceptable because a great country was built as a result. In such cases, the distancing introduced by the demand that I merely *suppose* is sufficient to eliminate at least some of the relevant imaginative barriers. I do have *some* grasp on the content I am supposed to be entertaining[15] (even if, on reflection, I realize that content to be incoherent[16]). But the Problem of Imaginative Impropriety remains: even if I *can* suppose these sorts of things, I find myself not *wanting* to.[17] In related fashion, cases where I am invited to adopt a metaphoric perspective that I find repugnant—like the nursery school nomenclature cases from §2—evoke impropriety without barriers.[18] It's not that I *can't* recognize the relevant similarities; it's that I don't want to focus on them.

By contrast, cases that involve extreme disruptions of conceptual relations that are salient to us at the time of imagining may confront us with something akin to imaginative barriers without an associated sense of imaginative

---

[15] [15] Remember: all we're looking for is the sort of grasp that one has in ordinary cases of fiction-induced imagining—cases where one may well be explicitly committed to the incoherence of the content one is contemplating.

[16] [16] As Jonathan Ichikawa and Emily Esch have pointed out to me, such feelings of impropriety may arise even when the content in question is not explicitly evaluative: as, for example, when I am asked to suppose that blacks are genetically inferior to whites, or that the Holocaust never happened. In both cases, I think, the resistance can be explained by the framework presented above: the association between accepting the purported fact and accepting a problematic norm is sufficiently strong that the normative claim colors the descriptive one. (One would thus expect similar feelings of impropriety to arise for a religious fundamentalist asked to suppose for the sake of argument that fetuses lack souls.)

[17] [17] Interestingly, we don't seem to face the same problem when the story's moral standards are *higher* than those we accept in ordinary cases: I don't sense imaginative impropriety when I suppose for the sake of argument that, for instance, "In throwing away the Oxfam envelope, Giselda did something morally culpable: after all, there were starving children in Africa." It may be that in such cases I am not imagining the proposed content with the requisite vividness, and that if I were to do so, I would find myself facing imaginative barriers. Indeed, as Kelly Trogdon points out (personal correspondence), if we modify the example slightly we do seem to confront such barriers—along with feelings of impropriety: "In throwing away the Oxfam envelope, Giselda did something morally on a par with deliberately murdering innocent children." I don't yet have a good account of what is going on here.

[18] [18] As I discuss in §8, these two classes of cases will turn out to be connected in interesting ways.

impropriety. Though there may be actual-world approximations,[19] the cleanest examples of this kind involve the sorts of fictional cases that authors like Yablo (2002) and Weatherson (2004) have presented—cases where we feel that we can't even begin to make sense of what it would be for something to be simultaneously five-pointed and perfectly oval-shaped, or to be indistinguishable from a fork yet be a table.[20] In such cases, though we presumably feel no impropriety about attempting to do so, even a "violent effort" to imagine the indicated content leaves us feeling blank.

In short, there seem to be four sorts of cases that we need to consider:[21] cases that evoke feelings of imaginative impropriety without imaginative barriers: call these *pure won't* cases; cases that evoke imaginative barriers without feelings of imaginative impropriety: call these *pure can't* cases; cases that evoke both feelings of imaginative impropriety and imaginative barriers, but where it is the imaginative impropriety that explains our failure to imagine the world (the felt imaginative impropriety eclipses the imaginative barriers, so the doomed imaginative project is not even attempted): call these *won't-couldn't* cases; and cases that evoke both feelings of imaginative impropriety and imaginative barriers, but where it is the imaginative barriers that explain our failure to imagine the world (the imaginative barrier eclipses the motivating force of the imaginative impropriety, so that the unappealingness of imagining such a world does not become apparent): call these *can't-wouldn't* cases.

I think that cases where we reject invitations to adopt metaphoric perspectives we find repugnant are pure won't cases—as are cases where we reject invitations merely to suppose. And I think that cases where we reject invitations to imagine things like Weathersonian fork-tables and Yablonian five-pointed ovals are pure can't cases. The interesting question is how to classify classic cases of Humean Resistance. Weatherson (2004) and Yablo (2002) and Walton (in his 1994 "best suggestion") seem to classify them as pure can't cases; Gendler (2000a), Currie (2002a), and Stokes (2006) seem to classify them as pure won't cases. But I now think classic cases of Humean Resistance are won't-couldn't cases. And I think their dual structure is what's interesting about them.

---

[19] [19] It is difficult to come up with actual cases, since the disrupted conceptual connections must be sufficiently salient and sufficiently localized to render the internal tension graspable at a single moment. Cases of wildly delusional beliefs, such as those arising from Cotard or Capgras or Mirror-Man syndromes, may be examples. Another case might be the mutual bafflement of theists and atheists at the other's interpretation of the common evidence concerning the (non-)existence of a supremely powerful deity. (Examples from history and anthropology—which appear to provide natural mining grounds for such cases—are generally parasitic on disagreements about "detached factual" matters. Indeed, the phenomenon discussed in n. 16 seems to arise in this case as well: barriers to imagining some sort of conceptual disruption may "infect" our ability to imagine the detached factual considerations that support it.)

[20] [20] In the sense required by the generation-rules governing anything but the most absurd stories: see §§6–8 below.

[21] [21] Thanks to Kelly Trogdon for suggesting this way of looking at the problem.

Imaginative impropriety is present because the content in question strikes us as somehow repugnant; and imaginative barriers are present because the content in question strikes us as somehow incoherent. Moreover, the two are deeply intertwined: Imagining something that we take to be immoral makes salient the impropriety of categorizing it as moral, and thereby renders salient the incoherence of doing so. In short, *cantians* and *wontians* offered complementary insights while making complementary errors. Neither recognized that in cases of classic imaginative resistance, each had captured part of the truth.

4. Extending the Case to Fiction

Humean Resistance, as it has been characterized so far, applies to the contemplation of historical or culturally alien texts, rather than texts that are explicitly fictional. In this section I want to extend the discussion I have been offering above by considering a problem that I will call *Authoritative Breakdown*.[22] Explaining what I mean by this term will require a brief excursion through some earlier writings on the topic of imaginative resistance.[23]

In the original "Puzzle" (2000a) essay (Ch. 9 above), I contrasted cases where "I am asked to make-believe that: P holds (where P is some non-moral proposition that I do not believe holds)" with cases where "I am asked to make-believe that: M holds, where M is some moral proposition that I do not believe holds." Our default response to the first sort of case, I suggested, is acceptance, whereas our default response to the second sort of case is non-acceptance. I went on to suggest that the second of these should perplex us, since while believing at will is, in general, precluded by the aims of belief, *make-believing* at will is not merely permitted by the aims of make-belief, it is what the practice is about in the first place. So the existence of cases where our default reaction to an invitation to make-believe is resistance rather than acquiescence demands explanation.[24]

---

[22] [22] For an interesting related proposal, see Matravers 2003; for criticism of some of the details of that proposal, see Weatherson 2004. My discussion in this section is indebted to the writings of both of these authors.

[23] [23] Most of these writings—including my own "Puzzle" (Ch. 9 above)—conflate issues about fictional truth with issues about imagination. In the discussion below, I will be primarily concerned with the issue of mandated imaginings, rather than the importantly related (and as we will see in §6 intertwined) issue of truth in fiction.

[24] [24] An important clarification: When some readers encounter the family of puzzles that concern us here, they are inclined to take the problem as one of absolute imaginability, and so they respond by identifying complicated cases where it is true in a story that, for instance, torturing baby seals is the *summum bonum*, and where readers like themselves are prepared to imagine this. But it is crucial to remember that the Problem of Imaginative Barriers is a problem about relative difficulty, *not* a problem about absolute impossibility. In producing a work of fiction, an author has tremendous cultural resources at her disposal: the entire stock of literal language, an enormous battery of common metaphors, a copious set of conventions governing genre, and an abundant inheritance of previous fictional works to which she can make subtle

In short, the puzzle is why there's an asymmetry (to the extent that there is one) between one class of cases and another, and whether there's anything systematic to be said about which sorts of prompted imaginings fall into which class.

It is useful in this regard to consider the following widely quoted passage from Dick Moran's "Expression of Feeling in Imagination" (1994):

> If the story tells us that Duncan was *not* in fact murdered on Macbeth's orders, then *that* is what we accept and imagine as fictionally true. If we start doubting what the story tells us about its characters, then we may as well doubt whether it's giving us their right names. However, suppose the facts of the murder remain as they are in fact presented in the play, but it is prescribed in this alternate fiction that this was unfortunate only for having interfered with Macbeth's sleep, or that we in the audience are relieved at these events. These seem to be imaginative tasks of an entirely different order. (Moran 1994: 95)

Moran's remark nicely brings out a crucial feature of cooperative reading: that, as a default principle, if an author does whatever is normally required for prompting the reader to imagine that P is true in the story—which in simple cases amounts to asserting, in the story context, that P—then the reader will imagine that P is true in the story.[25] Without something like this default in place, the practice of storytelling would be impossible. As Moran remarks (read this as a claim about mandated imagining rather than about truth in fiction): "If we start doubting what the story tells us about its characters, then we may as well doubt whether it's giving us their right names."[26]

We are now in a position to articulate the more general puzzle that I think underlies the phenomenon I earlier called imaginative resistance. It is a puzzle about the limits of authorial authority and the nature of reader responsiveness.

---

and not so subtle reference. With enough ingenuity, these resources can, I suspect, be used to make any local bit of content not only true in a story, but also straightforwardly imaginable. So the issue is *not* whether there are stories in which, for example, counter-moral propositions are true, or imaginable: the issue is why making some sorts of propositions imaginable takes a different *kind* of effort than making other sorts of propositions imaginable. For related discussion, see Currie 1990; Priest 1997; Sorensen 2002; Stock 2003, 2005; Weatherson 2004; Yablo 2002.

[25] [25] Matters become more complicated if we consider certain sophisticated forms of postmodern fiction; in the discussion above, I am implicitly restricting myself to simple cases of traditional narrative. I am also assuming (contrary to the advice of Tyler Doggett and John Holbo, who have convinced me that the problem merits careful attention) that the text in question does not contain unintentional mistakes. (For a few brief remarks on this, see n. 29 below.)

[26] [26] Moran 1994: 95. This is not to deny that names themselves immediately generate associations in the mind of the reader. In this sense, the author's choice might be "mistaken" (if it prompts the "wrong" imaginings). (Thanks to Brian Weatherson for discussion of this issue.) As the rather sobering social psychology literature reminds us, we are inclined to very different evaluations of otherwise identical *Curricula Vitae* depending on the gender and race associated with the name that appears at the top of the document; it is difficult to see why a similar chain of associations should not be set into play when we are imaginarily engaged with a work of fiction.

The puzzle, as I now understand it, is this. In order for the practice of fiction-telling to be possible, the following principle must hold as a default:

Authorial authority with respect to imaginative guidance: If the author of a fictional work follows standard conventions for fictionally asserting P, then the engaged reader will be disposed to imagine P.[27]

But for certain claims where the author appears to have followed the requisite conventions, the engaged reader nonetheless fails to imagine P. The puzzle is this:

The Puzzle of Authoritative Breakdown: the puzzle of identifying those features that systematically co-occur with, and explain, breakdowns of authorial authority.

The Puzzle of Authoritative Breakdown is, I think, an appropriately generalized version of the puzzle that I earlier called The Puzzle of Imaginative Resistance.

5. Pop-Out

One very interesting thing about cases of authoritative breakdown is that they typically exhibit a feature that I will call "pop-out." Pop-out passages are passages where, instead of taking the author to be asking her to *imagine* some proposition P that concerns the fictional world, the reader takes the author to be asking her to *believe* a corresponding proposition P that concerns the actual world. Consider, for example, the following two story-excerpts (following Walton 1994):

Good Giselda
The next morning, Giselda killed her baby on the grounds of its gender. In killing her baby, Giselda did the right thing; after all, it was a girl.

Bad Giselda
The next morning, Giselda killed her baby on the grounds of its gender. In killing her baby, Giselda did the wrong thing; after all, it was a human being.

---

[27] [27] We might consider the parallel principle of *Authorial authority with respect to fictional truth* by replacing "then the engaged reader will be disposed to imagine P" with "then it will be true in the story that P." I think the issues of mandated imagining and truth in fiction are importantly intertwined, in the sense that I think that what is true in a story is roughly what the cooperative and informed reader will be disposed to imagine (modulo worries about imaginative limitations; see, e.g. Weatherson 2004). I return to this issue in nn. 29 and 31 below.

In both of these cases, the first sentence of the story follows the default principles articulated above: the author has followed the standard conventions for fictionally asserting P (that Giselda killed her baby on gender grounds), and this has resulted both in P being true in the fiction, and in a disposition on the part of the engaged reader to accept this and imagine P.[28]

Note, however, that the sentence stays firmly within the story. Nothing inclines me to think that in prompting me to *imagine* something about what Giselda did in the Giselda-fiction, the author is simultaneously asking me to *believe* some corresponding thing about the world outside of the Giselda fiction (except in the uninteresting sense that the Giselda-fiction is something we are talking about here in the actual world).

By contrast, the second sentences of each of the stories pop out. They strike us as not merely asking us to *imagine* that it is true in the Giselda-fiction that Giselda did the right (or wrong) thing in killing her baby on the grounds of its gender, but also as asking us to *believe* that it is true in *this world* that someone exactly like Giselda would be doing the right (or wrong) thing in killing her baby on such grounds. In the case of the Bad Giselda story, this causes no difficulties. Since we (presumably) do believe that killing a baby on the grounds of its gender is wrong, we face no imaginative barriers to imagining it to be true in the Giselda-fiction as well, nor do we encounter any feelings of imaginative impropriety. But in the case of the Good Giselda story, difficulties emerge. We take the final sentence to be a simultaneous invitation to imagine and to believe—and we reject the invitation to believe. And I suggest that it is at least partly because we are unable to disentangle the invitations that we reject the invitation to imagine.[29] In the rest of the essay, I will offer some thoughts about why and how this phenomenon arises.

I begin by noting that pop-out seems to happen in virtually all of the examples presented in the literature on imaginative resistance (though in

---

[28] Of course, it may be *unpleasant* to imagine Giselda killing her baby, and it may be especially unpleasant to imagine her killing her baby on gender grounds, but it does not, I take it, strike us as *improper* in the Humean sense to imagine it being a fact in the Giselda-fiction that Giselda killed her baby for this particular reason.

[29] Again, a parallel explanation goes for the corresponding issue of truth. Faced with a pop-out assertion that we are inclined to deny in the actual case, we respond with what in "Puzzle" I called a "doubling of the narrator": we accept the first sentence of the first story as true in the story, but we accept the second sentence of the first story as being nothing more than what the narrator *thinks*. Because we see no obvious way of allowing the second sentence to be true *merely* in the story, and because we take the analogue of the second sentence to be false in the actual world, we likewise take the second sentence to be false in the story as well, and resist imagining its truth.

This captures one of the distinctive ways that cases of imaginative resistance differ from cases of what we take to be authors' errors (see n. 25 above). In the case of errors, we remain within the grip of the story; we think "that's simply not true (in the story)." But in the case of resistance, we "jump out" of the story; we think "that's simply not true (in the actual world)." (Further discussion of this phenomenological difference can be found in §6 below.)

other ways I think there are important differences among the various examples). Consider Weatherson's (2004) opening story, which ends with the following passage:

> ... Craig saw that the cause of the bankup [*sic*] had been Jack and Jill, he took his gun out of the glovebox and shot them. People then started driving over their bodies, and while the new speed hump caused some people to slow down a bit, mostly traffic returned to its normal speed. So Craig did the right thing, because Jack and Jill should have taken their argument somewhere else where they wouldn't get in anyone's way.

The final sentence pops out in the sense just described. And it pops out not merely because of the "so" or the content. We encounter the same pop-out phenomenology even if we offer the appraisal in a more integrated way, or if we alter the story so that it is akin to the second Giselda story rather than the first:

> ... when Craig saw that the cause of the bankup had been Jack and Jill, he did the right thing: he took his gun out of the glovebox and shot them

or

> ... when Craig saw that the cause of the bankup had been Jack and Jill, he did the wrong thing: he took his gun out of the glovebox and shot them.

In both cases, we take the moral assessment as a simultaneous invitation to imagine something in the context of the story—*and* to believe some corresponding claim about the actual world.

Moreover, we get a similar pop-out phenomenon with non-moral cases as well. Consider the final sentence of Kendall Walton's (1994) Knock-Knock story (which, by stipulation, is embedded in a context where we take the entire passage as literally intended):

> He told the knock-knock joke for the forty-third time. Everyone laughed uproariously. It was the funniest joke in the history of the world.

Or the second-to-last sentence of Stephen Yablo's (2002) Maple Leaf story:

> Hang on, Sally said. It's staring us in the face. This is a *maple* tree we're under. She grabbed a jagged five-fingered leaf. Here was the oval they needed! They ran off to claim their prize.

Or the final two sentences of Weatherson's (2004) Alien Robbery story:

> So Sam decided that it wasn't Lee, but really a shape-shifting alien that looked like Lee, that robbed the bank. Although shape-shifting aliens didn't exist, and until that moment Sam had no evidence that they did, this was a rational belief. False, but rational.

In each of these cases, I want to suggest, authoritative breakdown arises because we take the invitation to imagine the relevant claim as true in the story as a simultaneous invitation to believe some corresponding claim about the actual world. And since we take the corresponding claim about the actual world to be false, we resist believing it, and hence resist imagining its fictional counterpart. This suggests that if, somehow, there were some sort of "pop-out blocker" that could restrict our attention to the relevant passages insofar as they concern the fictional world, then authorial authority will return. But what would such a mechanism look like?

I've already suggested—both here and in the original essay—one type of pop-out blocker that is at least partially successful: namely, the technique of supposing rather than imagining.[30] I suggested above that this technique can—in the case of non-fiction and presumably in the case of fiction as well—bring us some way towards focusing only on the suppositional context (in this case, the fictional world) and not simultaneously on the actual world. Understanding how this could work requires understanding why pop-out occurs in the first place.

6. The Hypothesis

My tentative hypothesis is this: Passages exhibit pop-out effects whenever they express *appraisals* (some sort of decision about concept-application) that are either *mandated by* (required by all of) or *prohibited by* (permitted by none of) the principles of generation that the reader has tacitly been taking to govern the generation of fictional truths, in conjunction with whatever else she takes to have been mandated as true in the story.[31] That is, pop-out occurs when an

---

[30] [30] Shaun Nichols helpfully suggests that the distancing that results from supposition is a special case of a more general distancing phenomenon that arises from iteration. For interesting discussion of these issues, see Nichols 2003.

[31] [31] Clearly, this hypothesis bears important connections both to Weatherson's notion of *Virtue* and Yablo's notion of *grokking (response-enabled)* concepts. See Weatherson 2004 and Yablo 2002.

Following Walton (1990), we might provisionally distinguish between *primary* and *implied* fictional truths, where primary fictional truths are those generated (most) directly by whatever conventions govern our use of the fiction as a prop in a game of make-believe, while implied fictional truths are generated from these primary truths indirectly, by means of principles whose articulation has turned out to be enormously difficult. In parallel fashion, primary mandated imaginings would be those prompted (most) directly by whatever conventions govern our use of the fiction as a prop in a game of make-believe, while implied mandated imaginings would be those generated from those primary mandated imaginings indirectly, by means of principles whose articulation has not even been attempted. (For debate-shaping discussion of the topic of truth in fiction, see Currie 1990; Lewis 1983a, 1983c; Walton 1990. For recent work, see Hanley 2004, and essays cited therein. For a view that comes close to the one I am inclined to endorse, see Bonomi and Zucchi 2003.)

In saying this, I am acting as if interpretation of fiction were a straightforward linear process where we begin at the beginning of a text with the fictional acceptance of a bunch of low-level

appraisal that the author offers is either *superfluous* (because it is implied by what has been said already, in conjunction with the principles of generation governing truth-in-fiction in the context of the story), or *proscribed* (because it is precluded by what has been said already, in conjunction with the principles of generation governing truth-in-fiction in the context of the story).

Why do superfluous or proscribed appraisals result in a feeling of pop-out? This is a difficult question, and I don't have a full answer. But my best guess is that it results from two sources. The first is the superfluity or proscription of the assertion. The explanation here is quasi-Gricean: since the author *couldn't* be using the words to tell us something informative (merely) about the fictional world, we look for some other way that the phrase might be informative. But what way could that be? This brings us to the second source, which is the democratic nature of appraisal itself. While it is up to the author to set up the basic facts of the fictional world, she has only limited control over the principles of generation that govern what else is true in the story: the reader's associative repertoire and evaluative flexibility also play a role in determining which principles are at play. So negotiations about appraisals take place on disputed territory that falls under the jurisdiction of both reader and author. They concern whether certain concepts could be legitimately applied to certain sets of facts—and this is a concern that transcends the bounds of the fictional.

To see this hypothesis at play, suppose—very schematically—that the reader of a story has accepted some set of basic facts about the fictional world (F1-Fn), and that she considers a certain range of principles of generation (P1-Pn) to be viable ways of extending what is true in the story. And suppose that the story now continues with the author offering one of three appraisals. Appraisal A1 follows from F1-Fn on *none* of P1-Pn; appraisal A2 follows from F1-Fn on *all* of P1-Pn; and appraisal A3 follows from F1-Fn on only *some* of P1-Pn. If what I have been saying is correct, then the following predictions should be borne out (at least in simple cases). First, both A1 and A2 should produce a phenomenon of pop-out, whereas A3 (which gives the reader new information about what is true *in the story*) should not. At the same time, since A2 and A3 are both permitted by at least some of P1-Pn, the reader should feel that the relevant appraisal is true in the context of the story; this means that the pop-out induced by A2 may go largely—even entirely—unnoticed.[32] And finally, since A1 is permitted by none of P1-Pn, the reader should see no way for it to be true in

---

facts, and proceed through a narrative accepting or rejecting appraisals of them. Matters are obviously a good deal more complicated: the interpretative process is far more holistic than this picture suggests, complicating the distinction between lower-level and higher-level facts. Still, the idealization is a useful one. (For related discussion of why we are inclined to follow an author in her presentation of low-level facts but resist her higher-level appraisals, see Weatherson 2004.) (Thanks here to Jonathan Ichikawa and David Jehle.)

[32] [32] Though we may find ourselves thinking about the actual world in a novel way—a point well emphasized by Plato, Iris Murdoch, and Martha Nussbaum (among others).

the story. But since A1 is an *appraisal* (and not merely a fact at the level of F1-Fn), and since appraisals are under the author's and reader's joint control, the resulting feeling should be not (merely) one of bafflement—that is, the sense that the author is asking us to imagine something as being true *in the story* that simply doesn't make sense—but (also) one of resistance—the sense it is because A1' (the real-world analogue of A1) is not true that there is something amiss with A1.

The neatness of these results suggests that there are indeed two components—superfluity/prohibition on the one hand, and appraisal on the other—that together contribute to the phenomenon of pop-out. We can see this by considering cases where each occurs without the other. When appraisals are merely permitted (that is, neither mandated nor proscribed) by the facts-plus-principles that the reader is operating with, there is no sense of pop-out: the appraisals are treated roughly as if they were basic facts about the fictional world. And where the mandated or proscribed content involves low-level facts rather than appraisals, there is likewise no sense of pop-out: prohibited claims are treated as mistakes, superfluous ones as redundancies.[33]

Moreover, the account predicts that pop-out should disappear when we introduce a supposition clause. This is for two related reasons. First, since the principles of generation governing supposition are maximally permissive (as with absurdist stories, nothing in particular is prohibited or mandated by the "rules" governing the story) there are, *a fortiori*, no prohibited or mandated appraisals, and hence no pop-out. Second, when we engage in supposition, we deliberately suppress our familiar associative patterns. Because supposition requires this sort of distancing, normal patterns of appraisal are suspended, and tendencies to look for some actual-world analogue are correspondingly curtailed. (Moreover, the first may contribute to the second: the absurdity of the proposed content may play a role in preventing the sort of engagement that imagination requires.[34])

Finally, the account sits well with the distinction offered above between the Problem of Imaginative Barriers and the Problem of Imaginative Impropriety. Imaginative barriers arise when the generation principles that the reader has accepted leave no way for A to be true in the story. Imaginative impropriety arises when the reader considers adopting a set of generation principles that she finds problematic. Classic imaginative resistance arises when a reader can't imagine a certain moral claim being true in a story (Imaginative Barriers) because she won't bring herself to adopt the requisite set of generation

---

[33] [33] My account here is indebted in obvious ways to that of Weatherson (2004). Consider also Lewis's discussion of Sherlock Holmes in Lewis 1983c; cf. also Doggett 2004. (See also nn. 25 and 29 above.)

[34] [34] John Holbo (2003a, 2003b) nicely describes these as cases where our imagination "bounces off" the text.

principles governing the use of moral appraisals (Imaginative Impropriety). So classic imaginative resistance arises when we can't because we won't.

7. Applications

The account is best tested through the consideration of particular cases. Consider again the passage from Weatherson's "Freeway" case:

> ... Craig saw that the cause of the bankup had been Jack and Jill, he took his gun out of the glovebox and shot them. People then started driving over their bodies, and while the new speed hump caused some people to slow down a bit, mostly traffic returned to its normal speed. So Craig did the right thing, because Jack and Jill should have taken their argument somewhere else where they wouldn't get in anyone's way. (Weatherson 2004)

My suggestion is that the final sentence pops out because its truth is prohibited by the truth-in-fiction principles that the reader has tacitly been taking to govern the generation of fictional truths in the story, in conjunction with whatever else the reader takes to have been made true in the story. Presumably the latter includes that Craig shot Jack and Jill because they caused the traffic bankup, and that after he shot them, people started to drive over their bodies, allowing traffic to return to its normal speed. For the typical reader, the truth-in-fiction principles that she has been tacitly taking to govern the generation of fictional truths in the story prohibit it from following that, in so doing, Craig did the right thing. But since the passage involves an *appraisal*—a question about whether a particular higher-level concept can be understood as applying to some set of lower-level facts—the reader's attention turns to the actual world. Recognizing the falsity of what she takes to be the actual world analogue of P— that if someone had done something like what Craig did, he would have done the right thing—the reader experiences resistance.

Similar analysis might be offered for the other examples discussed in §5; in each case, the relevant segment pops out because its truth is prohibited by the truth-in-fiction principles that the reader has tacitly been taking to govern the generation of fictional truths in the story, in conjunction with whatever she takes to have been made true in the story so far.[35] But since the claims in question involve appraisals, the reader's attention turns to their actual-world analogues. Since she believes these to be false, resistance arises.[36]

Consider now the mandatory analogues of these cases, which I have suggested should produce pop-out without resistance:

---

[35] [35] Again, modulo worries about the holistic nature of interpretation.
[36] [36] I am thus acknowledging the force of important objections to my original account raised by Matravers 2003; Stock 2003, 2005; and Weatherson 2004.

He told the knock-knock joke for the forty-third time. Everyone laughed uproariously. *But* it was *not* the funniest joke in the history of the world. (Walton 1994, italicized words altered)

She grabbed a jagged five-fingered leaf. Here was the *five-pointed object* they needed! (Yablo 2002, italicized words altered)

Though I think these cases do produce pop-out, it is true that the effect is much less pronounced than in the prohibited cases, and that the effect is even less in the leaf example than in the knock-knock case. The first of these observations has already been explained: redundant pop-outs can easily pop back in, so unless we are alert to their potential appearance—as we are in cases like this one, where we have been thinking about prohibited pop-outs—we may well miss them. (Remember also that the explanation of why redundancy results in pop-out is a pragmatic one—so if we have the sense that there is some reason for the phrase to be expressed in the context of the story, then we will not experience feelings of pop-out; as long as the reader can see a way of understanding the appraisal-involving sentence as articulating a non-obvious implication—as, for example, when the author tells us who committed the crime at the end of a mystery story—then pop-out is not forced.[37]) But the theory also explains the second observation—that the pop-out is less pronounced in the leaf case. Because there is a reading on which the italicized phrase is understood as information-providing (that they were in need of an object that was five-pointed) rather than appraisal-involving (that a particular concept—five-pointedness—applies to this particular circumstance), the conditions for pop-out may not be satisfied. If we replace the second sentence with something like "In doing this she grabbed hold of a five-pointed object," pop-out returns; here, as in our other cases, the sentence is taken as making simultaneous claims about the world of the story and the world outside of the story.[38]

In short, the hypothesis proposed in §6 comports well with the phenomenological profile identified in §5. It looks like passages do exhibit pop-out effects when they involve appraisals that are either mandated or prohibited by the principles of generation that the reader has tacitly been appealing to, and that imaginative barriers arise in the prohibited cases. So far so good. But we still haven't gotten to the bottom of things. For the question remains: why do we accept these principles of generation and not others?

---

[37] [37] Indeed, one way for the author to cue the reader that standard import–export rules have been suspended is to issue a series of apparently obvious claims: "New York is in New York, Paris is in France, London is in England." Gricean rules tell you that the reason the author is reporting these obvious matters is to flag other ways in which the fictional world is not like the actual world. (Thanks to Tyler Doggett and Andy Egan for this point.)

[38] [38] If you don't feel this, make sure that you're not still thinking of the sentence as information-providing.

8. Residual Issues

I don't have a general answer to this question, but I do have a few thoughts to offer in closing. In order to present them, I will first need to step back a bit and say a bit more about what goes on when we engage in the practice of make-believe.

Imagination and pretense involve what I have elsewhere (2003; Ch. 8 above) called *partial mapping*: it is key to the practice of fiction-construction that things in stories may have some but not all of the properties of their actual-world analogues. The three little pigs share with their actual-world counterparts the properties of being pink and four-legged and Q-tailed, but unlike actual pigs, they can speak and scheme and build homes from straw or bricks. Winnie the Pooh shares with his actual-world counterparts the property of being brown and furry and stuffed with fluff, but unlike actual stuffed bears, he can sing and recite poetry and give birthday gifts. Nor are these isolated examples: think of the Three Bears, Babar, the Cat in the Hat, Curious George, Stuart Little, the Owl and the Pussycat, Frog and Toad, the Musicians of Bremen, the Cheshire Cat, Paddington, the Giving Tree, Thomas the Tank Engine, Tubby the Tuba, Humpty Dumpty, Pinocchio, the Velveteen Rabbit, Spongebob Squarepants, the Gingerbread Man—or any of the countless other talking, thinking animals and vegetables and minerals that fill children's literature. It would, I take it, be rather unreasonable to protest that Paddington couldn't *really* be a stuffed bear (in the story) since he walks and speaks and eats marmalade, or that Tubby isn't *really* a tuba, since tubas don't have arms or legs or feelings.

But if we can do this so easily for owls and trains and sponges and cookies, why are we so reluctant to engage in this sort of partial mapping for rightness and goodness and justice?[39] I don't have a complete story to tell—but in examining the answer that I will ultimately propose, it will be helpful to consider a particular example in a bit of detail.

In Chapter 8 of *Alice's Adventures in Wonderland* (L. Carroll 1865), Alice finds herself in a lovely garden where she observes a colorful parade of playing cards:

First came ten soldiers carrying clubs; these were all shaped like the three gardeners, oblong and flat, with their hands and feet at the corners: next the ten courtiers; these were ornamented all over with diamonds, and walked two and two, as the soldiers did. After these came the royal children; there were ten of them, and the little dears came jumping merrily along hand in hand, in couples: they were all ornamented with hearts. Next came the guests, mostly Kings and Queens . . . Then followed the Knave of Hearts, carrying the King's crown on a crimson velvet cushion; and, last of all this grand procession, came THE KING AND QUEEN OF HEARTS.

---

[39] I suspect some of our ease in the former cases stems from our ability—indeed our tendency—to ascribe intentional attributes to almost any entity whose motions are consonant with the motions typical of agents. (Cf. Heider and Simmel 1944.) But I think this is only part of the story.

> When the procession came opposite to Alice, they all stopped and looked at her, and the Queen said... "What's your name, child?" "My name is Alice, so please your Majesty," said Alice very politely; but she added, to herself, "Why, *they're only a pack of cards*, after all. I needn't be afraid of them!" (italics added)

Now, even if we do not have a fully comprehensive mental image of the scenario,[40] it is, I take it, true in the Alice-in-Wonderland fiction that the Queen of Hearts, who is a playing card, has ten heart-sporting children; that spade cards are gardeners whereas club cards are soldiers; that cards ornamented with kings and queens are royalty—and so on. A reader who reported imaginative barriers in the face of such claims would, it seems fair to say, be considered a bit of a bad sport. But note that, in order to understand the Alice story, we must simultaneously exploit a range of conflicting mapping principles each drawing on a different feature of our associational repertoire: people have hands and feet in a roughly diagonal configuration, so the hands and feet of the playing cards are arranged likewise; spades are associated with gardening, so spade-sporting cards are gardeners; children resemble their parents, so heart-sporting cards are the children of the King and Queen of Hearts; kings and queens tend to be friends with other kings and queens, so the King and Queen of Clubs are royal guests. And so on.

Moreover, we do this despite the fact that it introduces all sorts of tensions: If the five of spades is an adult, shouldn't the five of hearts be an adult too? If the seven of spades is a gardener, shouldn't the King of Spades be a gardener too? These inconsistencies do not result in lasting imaginative barriers: we are easily able to circumscribe our attention, focusing on one set of similarities in one context, another in another.[41] Nor is there any sense of imaginative impropriety. One may think that monarchy is a distasteful form of government, or object to parades on aesthetic grounds. But none of this seems to get in the way of imaginatively engaging with the *Alice in Wonderland* story.

Now (as I suggested in a similar context in "Puzzle") one might object by saying that this is a particularly nonsensical example: nothing that is what *we* mean by a "playing card" could do anything like what *we* mean by "stealing some tarts." But then again, nothing that we mean by a "memory" could turn into what we mean by a "silvery thread"; nothing that we mean by a "purple crayon" could draw a world in which the artist then "walks"; and nothing that we mean by a "rainbow" could have a "daughter" who dances and sings and

---

[40] For discussion of the relation between the content of the mental image and the content of what is imagined therewith, see Peacocke 1985; B. Williams 1966/1973. See also Sorensen 2002.

[41] Though it does mean that in ascertaining derived truths, we are not fully at liberty to follow our own initiative.

eats dewdrops.[42] Fictional "counting as" is cheap.[43] As long as the inconsistency does not stare us in the face (and sometimes even when it does), we countenance all sorts of combinations as being true in fiction, and credit ourselves with having imagined them, even though we are in no position to make full sense of what that combination would amount to.[44] It is crucial to realize that if one refuses to grant this, one has basically opted out of the fiction game altogether.[45]

I have suggested that imaginative barriers arise when—given the truth-in-fiction principles that the reader has tacitly been taking to govern the generation of fictional truths in the story—the author makes a claim that is incompatible with whatever else the reader takes to have been made true in the story. This means that the wider the range of principles the reader is considering, the smaller the number of mandated and prohibited appraisals there will be, and the less potential for resistance will arise. But if the range of principles gets too wide, then nothing particular will be mandated or prohibited. And this—for the reasons discussed in §4 above—is tantamount to reader disengagement. I think that what happens in what I above called "can't" cases is that—for some reason—the reader cannot see any non-arbitrary way of adopting some *limited* range of truth-in-fiction principles that could do the requisite work of rendering P (along with already-accepted claims) true in the story—no way for P to be true that does not involve opening the floodgates to the sort of free-for-all that mere supposition involves. And while I suspect that this has to do with our grasp of the concepts at issue—see, for example, Yablo's (2002) discussion of *oval* or Weatherson's (2004) of *table*—I will for the time being take it as a brute fact.

What I want to suggest is that even if this is part of the explanation of what is going on in cases of classic Humean resistance, it is not the full story. Consider a modified version of the previously quoted passage from *Alice in Wonderland*. The passage describes your child's nursery school graduation ceremony (or, if

---

[42] [42] Cf. *Harry Potter and the Goblet of Fire* (Rowling 2000), *Harold and the Purple Crayon* (C. Johnson 1955), and *Ozma of Oz* (Baum 1907) respectively.

[43] [43] At the same time, "counting as" can be *too* cheap. Suppose I were to tell the following story, call it *Frege's Nightmare*: "Once upon a time there was a number—the number two—who was a great Roman orator who conquered Gaul and died on the Ides of March." One might object, quite reasonably, that the sense in which I have thereby told a story in which the number two crossed the Rubicon is attenuated at best. But what makes it true in something more than name only that the knave of hearts stole some tarts in *Alice*, but not that the number two was stabbed by Brutus in *Frege's Nightmare*? I suspect that part of the answer has to do with subtle matters of literary convention and mental imagery and the relation between them. But it is clear that the issue merits further exploration. (Indeed, Weatherson worries that an "in name only" story is all that I have told in the "Tower of Goldbach" (cf. Gendler 2000a (Ch. 9 above); Weatherson 2004; also Stock 2003, 2005); for discussion of this issue from an entirely different angle, see Robertson 2003.) But, to reiterate a point made several times above, to the extent that we are worried about asymmetries rather than absolute prohibitions (see n. 24), the issue is rendered slightly less urgent.

[44] [44] Remember the warnings in nn. 15 and 20.

[45] [45] For more detailed discussion and argumentation, see Gendler 2000 (Ch. 9 above), §6.

you prefer, the movements of a group of refugees, or historically underrepresented minorities):

First came the Cockroaches, their filthy wings folded at their sides: next the Vultures; eager for carrion, clawing at one another for the few remaining morsels. After these came the Maggots; there were ten of them, and the nauseating things inched sluggishly along the floor. Next came the Mosquitoes, whining shrilly in their aggravating and annoying way...and last of all this grand procession, came THE KING AND QUEEN OF DUNG BEETLES.

When the procession came opposite to Alice, they all stopped and gawked at her, and the Queen of the Dung Beetles screeched... "What's your name?" "My name is Alice, so please your Majesty," said Alice, suppressing her revulsion; but she added, to herself, "Why, *they're only a bunch of nursery school children (refugees/Hutus/Jews/homosexuals/Palestinians)*, after all. I needn't be disgusted by them!"

Now, as far as barriers go, this passage should be no harder—indeed, presumably somewhat easier—to engage with imaginatively than the original passage from *Alice*. But—for now-familiar reasons—I take it that it nonetheless evokes a feeling of imaginative impropriety. I will take it as a datum that we find it distasteful to imagine our children—or members of the groups listed above—with our attention directed in these ways.[46]

I think that what goes on in the case of classic Humean Resistance is a complicated combination of what goes on in the five-pointed oval case and what goes on in the refugee parade case. I think what happens is that—to some extent consciously, to some extent unconsciously—the imaginative impropriety associated with viewing something like slavery or torture under anything like a positive light ends up constraining the set of truth-in-fiction principles we are ready to entertain. I think if this were not part of the explanation, then we would much more readily do with terms like "right" or "beautiful" what we do with terms like "cat" (in *The Cat in the Hat*) or "carpet" (in *Aladdin*): engage in the sort of partial mapping where the term retains some but not all of its features, the sort of partial mapping that does not induce pop-out. We would allow that in such cases, "right" means most of what it does in ordinary cases, except that it also applies to the thing that Giselda did in killing her baby just because it was a girl.

Now, *cantians* are committed to saying that in doing this, we lose a handle on the concept of "right"—in the way that to allow an oval to be five-pointed or to allow a table to be a fork is to lose a handle on the concept of "oval" or "table." *Wontians* allow that there are ways that it could be true—merely in the story—

---

[46] [46] Recall Arthur Danto's apt reminder that one of the fundamental functions of artistic engagement is to adopt perspectives that lead us to focus selectively on certain features of our environment: it is "one of the main offices of art less to represent the world than to represent it in such a way as to cause us to view it with a certain attitude and with a special vision" (Danto 1981: 167).

that Giselda did the right thing in killing her baby because it was a girl, or that Craig did the right thing in shooting Jack and Jill, or that Sam's belief in shape-shifting aliens was rational—where "right" or "rational" just means: enough of the things that right or rational means for you to call this a case of rightness or rationality.[47]

If cantianism is correct here, then we've learned something very interesting about a certain class of appraisal-involving terms: that you can't do with them what Lewis Carroll did with the playing cards in *Alice in Wonderland* (or what I did with 5+7=12 in the Goldbach story (Gendler 2000; Ch. 9 above)), thinning them down in ways that lose many of their most important associations while nonetheless proceeding to tell a comprehensible story. But I'm left with the residual feeling that with cantians—as with their more famous namesakes—there's something a bit too rule-bound about this picture of morality and its kin. Couldn't I really—if I were more flexible in my associational commitments—imagine a case where Craig or Giselda did the right thing *just in the story*? Isn't my reluctance to do so a bit like my reluctance to enroll my son in the maggots room instead of the pandas? Isn't it, deep down, in part that I am not prepared to have my nice pure cantian image of rightness distorted by letting it become associated with something ugly and nasty like murder or slavery—even in a story? And isn't it because I'm not willing to let myself imagine this that I can't see a way for it to be true?

My inclination is to think that, to some extent, in some cases at least, the answer is *yes*. If so, then the solution I proposed in "Puzzle" was right in spirit, if not in detail. And so I'm inclined to think, for the reasons just offered.[48]

---

[47] [47] It might seem that there is a third position here—*hardianism*—according to which it is merely hard to imagine the prescribed content. But (see n. 24) I think hardians are just cantians or wontians who make a relative rather than an absolute claim. (For the record, I suspect most wontians are deep-down hardians—and that many cantians are as well.) (Thanks to Tyler Doggett and Andy Egan for the term *hardian*.)

[48] [*] *Acknowledgements*: I am grateful to Jeff Dean for organizing a session at the Nov. 2004 American Society for Aesthetics Meetings where this paper was originally presented, to my commentator Dustin Stokes for his excellent commentary on that early draft, and to the audience at that session for their questions and comments. A very early draft of §§4 and 5 was presented at the Technical University in Budapest in May 2004, and I am grateful to audience members there for helpful questions and discussion. For help with subsequent drafts, warm thanks are due to John Holbo, David Jehle, Shaun Nichols, Kendall Walton, and Brian Weatherson, and especially to Tyler Doggett, Andy Egan, Emily Esch, Jonathan Ichikawa, Zoltán Gendler Szabó, and Kelly Trogdon.

11

Genuine Rational Fictional Emotions

The "paradox of fictional emotions" involves a jointly inconsistent but individually plausible trio of claims. According to the paradox, it is simultaneously true that (a) we have genuine and rational emotional responses towards certain imaginary characters and situations while (b) believing those characters and situations to be purely fictional. But, it is also true that (c) in order for us to have genuine and rational emotional responses towards a character (or situation), we must not believe that the character (or situation) is purely fictional.

In this essay, we offer an account of fictional emotions that rejects the third of these conditions. We argue that in order to have genuine and rational emotional responses towards a character (or situation), it is *not* required that we believe the character (or situation) to be nonfictional. Rather, we contend, our cognitive architecture is such that without the tendency to feel (something relevantly akin to) real emotions in the case of merely imagined situations, we would be largely unable to engage in practical reasoning.

The view presented in this essay has, in many ways, been superseded by the view presented in my more recent essays "Alief and Belief" (Ch. 13) and "Alief in Action (and Reaction)" (Ch. 14). But I include (an abbreviated version of) the essay here because the view that it presents has been discussed and criticized in a number of papers.

***

This essay was co-authored with Karson Kovakovich, and was first published in Matthew Kieran (ed.), *Contemporary Debates in Aesthetics* (New York: Blackwell, 2005), 241–53. It was originally published alongside a companion essay, "The Challenge of Irrationalism and How Not to Meet It," by Derek Matravers (pp. 254–64). It is reprinted with the kind permission of Blackwell.

The text that appears here has been condensed significantly: a number of didactic passages have been removed, and two subsections—one on the ontology of fictional characters, the other surveying a range of responses to the paradox—have been omitted. In addition, section numbers have been introduced, stylistic infelicities have been repaired, and minor typographical errors have been corrected. All of the content that appears in footnotes (except that which is explicitly noted as new) originally appeared as part of the main text; such cases have been noted by the inclusion of "[*In main text in published version*]" at the beginning of the relevant footnote.

1. Introduction

1.1. The Paradox

The "paradox of fictional emotions" involves a jointly inconsistent but individually plausible trio of claims. According to the paradox, regarding certain fictional characters (and situations) F, it is simultaneously true that:

(1) *Response Condition*: We have genuine and rational emotional responses towards F;

(2) *Belief Condition*: We believe that F is purely fictional;

(3) *Coordination Condition*: In order for us to have genuine and rational emotional responses towards a character (or situation), we must not believe that the character (or situation) is purely fictional.

The inconsistency among the three claims is clear: the response and belief conditions together tell us that we can have genuine rational emotions towards F while believing F to be purely fictional; the coordination condition denies that this conjunction is possible. But each of the three claims is also *prima facie* plausible. We do seem to have genuine and rational emotional responses towards purely fictional characters and situations (as when we shed authentic, appropriate tears at the report of Anna Karenina's demise); at the same time, we seem to believe that those characters and situations are purely fictional (we do not expect to read a report of Anna's suicide in the annals of the Leningrad Railroad Authority, nor do we expect to be able to intervene in any way regarding the events described in the novel). Still, there seems to be something irrational, inauthentic, or even impossible about responding emotionally to things we believe to be purely fictional. (How can we rationally feel genuine fear for something we know to be merely imaginary, or authentically respond with anger to something we know could never have happened?)

Since they cannot be true simultaneously, one of the *prima facie* plausible claims must, in fact, be false. Drawing on research by Antonio Damasio and insights of Paul Harris, we will suggest that it is the coordination condition that merits denial: in order to have genuine and rational emotional responses towards a character (or situation), it is *not* required that we believe the character (or situation) to be nonfictional.[1] Rather, we will suggest, our cognitive architecture is such that without the tendency to feel (something relevantly akin to)

---

[1] [*In main text in published version*] In calling an emotion "rational" we are claiming only that it is *not irrational*—that it does not interfere with our capacity to function as agents who make effective use of means–ends reasoning, and that it does not directly involve us in inconsistent belief. In so doing, we neglect a number of important distinctions—between instrumental and intrinsic rationality, between theoretical and practical rationality, and between "act-rationality" and "rule-rationality."

real emotions in the case of merely imagined situations, we would be largely unable to engage in practical reasoning (Damasio 1994, 1999; Harris 2000).

1.2. The Key Questions

For ease of presentation, we will use the term "fictional emotion" to refer to emotional responses that we apparently have towards characters and events that we believe to be fictional,[2] and "actual emotion" to refer to emotional responses that we apparently have towards characters and events that we believe to be actual.[3] So "fictional emotion" as we use the expression refers not to the emotional state of a fictional character (Anna's anguish), but to an actual person's apparent emotional response to such a character (your pity).

We can then state our fundamental questions as follows: what is the significance of the manifest similarities between our fictional and actual emotional reactions, and what is the significance of their manifest differences? Is this configuration of similarity and difference indicative of something problematic in our emotional responses to fiction? And does this pattern of similarity and difference suggest that fictional and actual emotions are two species of the same genus?

We will argue that the manifest similarities between fictional and actual emotions *are* significant, even in light of their differences, that this configuration of responses *is not* a pathological one, given facts about our cognitive architecture, and that it *is* reasonable to employ the expression "genuine, rational emotion" in describing both actual and fictional emotions. While those who deny the response condition are correct to note that our fictional and actual emotions differ in their subject matter and motivational force, this difference is not sufficient to render fictional emotions either inauthentic or irrational. And while those who deny the belief condition are correct to note that the similarities between actual and fictional emotions indicate that we treat their apparent objects in comparable ways, this comparable treatment need not be a reflection of a belief in the actuality of fictional entities. Rather, we will contend, it is the coordination condition that articulates a false constraint on our emotional reactions: it is crucial to our ability to make rational

---

[2] [*In main text in published version*] "Fictional" here is simply contrasted with "nonfictional," so that characters such as Anna Karenina and places such as Oz are fictional insofar as we do not consider them to be concrete denizens or plausible continuations of the actual world. In so doing, we ignore a number of important issues relating to authorial intent, truth in fiction, the semantics of fictional utterances, and the ontology of fictional characters.

[3] [*In main text in published version*] In so doing, we set aside important questions about whether the collection of attitudes and feelings generally referred to as "emotions" forms a natural class, whether there are correctness-conditions for feeling emotions, and whether emotions are—strictly speaking—attitudes directed at particular entities. Instead, we will focus on two classic examples from the literature—pity and fear—each of which is at least a plausible example of an emotional response that, at least in certain cases, seems to be object-directed and correctness-evaluable.

decisions about various courses of action that we respond with genuine emotions to situations that we know to be non-actual.

2. The Positive Account

2.1. Overview

Our view finds its source in recent empirical research (by Antonio Damasio and others) showing that when we make practical decisions about our own futures, our reasoning is action-guiding only in cases where we imaginatively engage with potential consequences to produce emotional responses that are then somatically encoded—that is, that result in particular sorts of bodily changes. (We describe this research in the next subsection.) This suggests that, far from being exceptional, emotional responses to non-actual situations are a fundamental feature of our cognitive repertoire. Moreover, because of the role they play in underpinning practical reasoning (allowing us to act on our preferences by somatically encoding our evaluations of potential outcomes), it is crucial that they resemble actual emotions as precisely as possible. Together, these features suggest that it is legitimate to consider such emotional responses to be both genuine and rational. (We defend this claim in more detail below.) Moreover, we contend, despite their resemblance to actual emotions, fictional emotions do not rest on a confusion in belief about what is merely fictional. As we argue below, we tend initially to interpret all cognitive and sensory input as indicative of the presence of the ordinary source of phenomena of its type. But such instantaneous interpretations are not sufficiently robust to be properly considered beliefs. Together, these considerations suggest both that we should embrace the response and belief conditions, and that we should reject the coordination condition.

2.2. The Damasio Results

Individuals with damage to their ventromedial prefrontal cortex display a characteristic set of behaviors. Most strikingly, though they are able to articulate reasons for pursuing various courses of action, they appear unable to use those reasons as bases for behavior, acting instead in ways that seem erratic and unplanned, and that are often counterproductive and anti-social. In addition, they exhibit a number of patterns that are detectable in laboratory settings. So, for example, while they are easily able to identify whether a photograph is "disturbing," and even to articulate why ("its front paw is caught in a trap"; "the bodies are piled atop one another"), they typically lack autonomic reactions to such emotionally distressing images. This contrasts strikingly with normal patients, who consistently display such responses (Harris 2000: 85, describing Damasio, Tranel, and Damasio 1991).

A similar pattern of deficits reveals itself in a testing paradigm developed by Damasio's team. Experimental subjects are given four decks of cards and a pile of play money, with the goal of maximizing their profit by turning over cards one at a time from any one of the four decks. Cards from the four decks are preassigned values so that for each card from deck A or B that the subjects turn over, they earn a sizable reward, while for each card from deck C or D, they earn a significantly smaller reward. But decks A and B are also associated with high penalties, whereas decks C and D are not, so that playing with decks A and B results in a net loss, whereas playing with decks C and D results in a net gain (Bechara, Damasio, Damasio, and Anderson 1994).

When normal subjects are presented with this task, they initially sample from all decks, but eventually settle on decks C and D (the overall advantageous decks with lower immediate rewards), and their performance continues to improve over time. By contrast, when the task is presented to subjects with damage to the prefrontal cortex, results are strikingly different: they soon settle on decks A and B (the overall disadvantageous decks with higher immediate rewards); moreover, they show no improvement in performance over time.

As normal subjects successively experience the consequences of choosing from the high-risk decks, they begin to exhibit skin conductance responses in anticipation of such selections. Soon afterwards, they begin expressing a "hunch" that these decks are more risky, and begin avoiding them in favor of the lower-risk decks; ultimately, many of them are able to articulate the basis for this avoidance. By contrast, subjects with damage to the prefrontal cortex exhibit no such skin conductance responses in anticipation of their high-risk deck selections, and no tendency to avoid such decks in their own selection process. This is so even when they are able to articulate conceptually the relative risks involved. (Summary based on Harris 2000: 86–7.)

What Damasio, Bechara, and others have concluded on the basis of this research is that autonomic responses play a central role in practical reasoning. Some sort of somatic realization of the potential consequences of a risky action seems crucial to prudent decision-making. Without it, the theoretical advantages of one or another course of action may be apparent, but these will not translate properly into action-guiding behavior.

This research seems to show that our ability to engage in practical reasoning rests on the following sort of process: we imaginatively engage with the potential consequences of various courses of action, thereby activating our emotional response mechanisms, and we encode the results of these simulations somatically; the presence of these "somatic markers" then helps to guide our future behavior. Call these emotions "simulated emotions." It is clear that simulated emotions are a fundamental feature of our cognitive repertoire. It is also clear that there are striking resemblances between *simulated* emotions and *fictional* emotions, so much so that if we can establish that simulated emotions are both genuine and rational, then we will have done most of the work required for establishing the faultiness of the coordination condition.

3. Genuineness

Fictional and simulated emotions differ from actual emotions in at least two crucial ways. Whereas the apparent objects of actual emotions are actual individuals and events, the apparent objects of simulated and fictional emotions are ostensibly non-actual. And whereas actual emotions feed directly into behavior in certain predictable ways (*ceteris paribus*, we move far away from objects that we fear, and intervene on behalf of individuals that we pity), fictional and simulated emotions are not directly tied to action in this fashion.

Famously, Kendall Walton has contended that these differences mean that we do not feel genuine emotional responses to fictional scenarios. Instead, he contends, we experience phenomenally indistinguishable *quasi-emotions* that differ from genuine emotions in the ways just described: in contrast to genuine emotions, they do not require that we be existentially committed to their apparent objects; and they are not intimately connected to motivation and action (Walton 1990; an alternative view is presented in Walton 1997). So, for example, he writes concerning the first requirement: "Grief, as well as pity and admiration, would seem to require at the very least awareness of the existence of their objects. It is arguable that for this reason alone appreciators cannot be said actually to pity Willy [Loman] or grieve for Anna [Karenina] or admire Superman" (1990: 204). And, concerning the second:

Fear is *motivating* in distinctive ways, whether or not its motivational force is attributed to cognitive elements in it.... To deny this, to insist on considering... [a] nonmotivating state to be one of fear of [its purported object] would be to reconceive the notion of fear. Fear emasculated by subtracting its distinctive motivational force is not fear at all. (Walton 1990: 201–2)

Regarding the first quotation, there is the risk of degenerating into terminological debate. If one defines "genuine" (or "actual") emotion so that such emotions "require... awareness of the existence of their objects," then Walton is surely correct. But the substantive question is whether such a restriction effects a natural cut in conceptual space. We think it does not. There is a continuum of cases—from cases where the object of the emotion is an entity that exists only in the past (where I pity someone who has died), to cases where the object of the emotion is a situation that may or may not occur in the future (where I fear a stock market crash), to cases where the object of the emotion is an entity that may or may not exist in the future (where I pity the oldest daughter of my great-grandson), to cases where the object of the emotion is a situation that is explicitly fictional (where I fear the flood that may drown the inhabitants of Alpha Centauri), to cases where the object of the emotion is an entity that is explicitly fictional (where I pity Anna Karenina). We have no inclination to withhold attributions of genuineness from cases involving past or future or merely possible persons or events ("She doesn't *fear* a stock-market crash, she just *quasi-fears* it"). It thus seems that we do not require that the target of a genuine emotion exist in the here and now.

What, then, would incline us to withhold such attributions in the case of explicitly fictional persons and events? The source seems to be either worries about empty names ("She doesn't pity Anna Karenina—there is no Anna Karenina") or related worries about misattribution ("What he fears isn't the bear in the closet—there is no bear there—what he fears is the sound of the wind"). We have already noted that we are setting aside worries of the first sort. And it is interesting to note that worries of the second sort dissipate somewhat when we focus explicitly on the fictionality of our character. When someone (apparently) feels pity for Anna Karenina, knowing full well that Anna is a fictional character, we are not inclined to think that this person has misidentified the target of his or her emotion. In short, unless we stipulate at the outset that attitudes such as fear and pity can take as their targets only certain sorts of entities, then, assuming a standard picture of what exists and what does not, and setting aside legitimate worries about empty names, it seems arbitrary to insist that they are genuine only when their objects exist.

Regarding the second quotation from Walton, it is far from clear that fictional and simulated emotions differ from actual emotions to the degree that Walton seems to be suggesting. Note first that in order for the reasoning process described above to operate effectively, our simulated emotions and our actual emotions must line up as closely as possible: otherwise, the process of considering alternative outcomes would not give us proper information about how we would respond once one of those outcomes became actualized. So simulated emotions and actual emotions should be, in a well-functioning person, as similar as possible. This nonaccidental similarity provides grounds for considering simulated emotions to be genuine, and insofar as fictional emotions exploit similar mechanisms, it provides parallel grounds in that case.[4] Moreover, if Damasio is right, both simulated and fictional emotions produce bodily changes akin to those produced by actual emotions. That the latter feed directly into action whereas the former feed only indirectly into action can be traced, we propose, to a difference in processing, not in motivation (modulo differences in

---

[4] [*In main text in published version*] It is in this regard that part of the truth about fictional emotions is captured by the position known as "factualism," according to which the objects of our emotional responses to fiction are actual people in situations literally or metaphorically akin to those described in the fiction. For versions of this position, see Paskins 1977, S. Johnson 1765, Weston 1975, McCormick 1988.

vivacity of stimulus). An alarm clock set five minutes fast can motivate us to rise, even if we are fully cognizant of the misinformation it gives; we are reluctant to pull the trigger in "Polish roulette," even when we are certain that the gun contains no bullets.[5] So while Walton is surely correct to note that fictional emotions do not feed into behavior in the ways that actual emotions do, it does not follow that they do not have similar motivational structure.

But this line of thought brings out a certain tension in our view. We have been emphasizing the similarities among fictional, simulated, and actual emotions. One elegant explanation of these similarities would be that we momentarily lose track of the non-actuality of the simulated and fictional stimuli when we respond emotionally to them. If so, then perhaps it is the *belief* condition that is at fault (insofar as the response condition holds).[6]

As before, there is a risk of turning a substantive dispute into a terminological one: if "belief" is used thinly enough, then the belief condition may indeed be inapplicable as stated. The substantive question is whether there are other reactions to nonstandard stimuli where we are not inclined to say that the similarity between ordinary and divergent cases rests on a false belief. We think there are many. In cases of optical illusions, for example, we may perceive a bent stick as being straight—or perceive the two lines in the Müller-Lyer illusion as being of different lengths—without *believing* that things are as they seem. If we stand near the edge of a high glassed-in platform, we may recoil slightly, without *believing* that we are at risk of falling. One explanation for this and other such cases is that we respond to nearly all cognitive and sensory input as being indicative of the presence of its ordinary stimulus-source. (So, for example, objects exhibiting the retinal-stimulation pattern of the water-embedded stick are, in ordinary cases, objects that are bent; situations exhibiting the retinal-stimulation pattern of the glassed-in high platform are, in ordinary cases, dangerous.) But precisely because these initial response patterns are so evidence-resistant, there is good reason to think that they are subdoxastic. If a response-pattern cannot be changed in reaction to the presentation of reasoned evidence (we cannot "talk ourselves out of" optical illusions), it seems misleading to categorize it as belief-involving. So the similarities between simulated and actual responses need not be seen as impugning the belief condition.[7]

In sum, there are similarities and dissimilarities between fictional and actual emotions. Whether the differences are sufficient to warrant referring to them with distinct expressions is to some extent a terminological dispute. The

[5] [*Note added in 2009*: I discuss these particular examples further in "Imaginative Contagion" (Ch. 12) and "Alief and Belief" (Ch. 13) below.]

[6] [*In main text in published version*] This is the explanation given by advocates of the position known as the "momentary confusion" or "suspension-of-disbelief" view.

[7] [*Note added in 2009*: The discussion in this paragraph clearly prefigures the discussion of alief in Chs. 13 and 14 below.]

substantive issue concerns what forms these similarities and dissimilarities actually take. It is our contention that the similarities are more striking than the differences.

4. Rationality

In a series of some dozen articles over nearly a quarter of a century, Colin Radford has contended that fictional emotions are irrational. As with Walton, part of our dispute with Radford may be terminological. Radford writes:

What is necessary for the occurrence of these [emotional] responses is missing when the objects which elicit them are (believed to be) fictional. There is then literally, nothing to be concerned about, no one—indeed nothing—to pity. . . . However natural, almost universal, such responses are, we can and do come to see that they are irrational, do we not? (Radford 1989: 96)

These remarks are somewhat perplexing: if "What is necessary for the occurrence of these [emotional] responses is missing" then it is hard to see how such responses could be "almost universal." If, with Walton, Radford is suggesting that the very concept of emotional response precludes our responding emotionally to the non-actual, then our reply is as above. But this does not seem to be his primary worry. Rather, the source of discomfort for Radford seems to be the thought that fictional emotions somehow involve us in competing, even contradictory, commitments. He writes: "we are frightened for ourselves of characters we know to be fictional and are irrational, incoherent, and inconsistent in being thus frightened" (Radford 1995: 75).

By employing the terms "incoherent" and "inconsistent," Radford seems to be suggesting that in feeling fictional emotions, we reveal ourselves to be holding contradictory beliefs. The thought behind such an analysis might be the following: when we respond with genuine emotion to a character, or describe someone as responding with genuine emotion to a character, we reveal that we believe that character to be actual; but when we believe a character to be fictional, we believe that character not to be actual; so when we respond with genuine emotion to a character that we believe to be fictional, we believe that character to be actual and not to be actual. But this reasoning, as we have argued at the end of the last subsection, is flawed: it is a mistake to think that feeling genuine emotions requires a belief, temporary or otherwise, in the actuality of its purported target.

Alternatively, perhaps Radford's worry is that in responding to fictional characters with genuine emotion, we violate a norm that we tacitly hold: that we should respond emotionally only to things that we believe to be actual. The irrationality of our behavior would thus consist in repeatedly violating a principle that we reflectively endorse (in the same way that it would be irrational for someone who had a principled commitment to vegetarianism regularly to eat meat). But it is far from clear that we *do* (or *should*), on reflection, subscribe to such a principle. If, as we have suggested above, simulated emotions play a central role in allowing us to make and act on decisions about our future well-being, then far from impeding our capacity to act as agents who make effective use of means–ends reasoning, they contribute directly to it. If so, it is hard to see why we would want to endorse a principle telling us that we should respond emotionally only to things that we believe to be actual (even if, as a practical matter, this ideal proves unattainable).

Perhaps, then, we would want to endorse a weaker principle according to which we should not respond emotionally to things we explicitly believe to be fictional. After all, one might contend, fictional emotions do not seem to play the same direct role in our capacity for practical reasoning that simulated emotions do, so we should aim not to feel them. But it is not clear that even this weaker line of argument can be successfully maintained. One line of thought, stemming from Aristotle and emphasized more recently by thinkers such as Susan Feagin and Martha Nussbaum, stresses the instrumental role of fictional emotions in the cultivation of moral and intellectual character (Aristotle, *Poetics*; Feagin 1983, Nussbaum 1986, 1990). By engaging emotionally with fictional characters and situations, we broaden our range of simulated encounters, gaining insights about others' experiences that are processed much as if they had been our own. Without such a capacity, actual experience would be our only source of such emotional encounters, severely limiting the range of our reactive possibilities. So fictional emotions may contribute to our capacity for rational action through the role they play in educating our sensibilities. If so, then there is little reason to think that we should endorse a categorical principle according to which we would, ideally, fail to feel such emotions.

Of course, such emotional responses are sometimes out of place. Cases where emotional investments in fictionalia exceed corresponding investments in actualia are exemplary instances of irrationality (as both psychoanalytic theory and common sense remind us). So too are cases where prop-based pretense produces responses that, given ordinary practice in such games of make-believe, are unprompted (as, for example, when a child feels genuine fear that its stuffed animal will catch a cold). But the existence of such cases does not impugn the possibility of rational genuine emotional responses to certain sorts of fictional scenarios. (Though they do reveal that our assessments of rationality and irrationality are, here as elsewhere, governed by conventional norms of appropriateness.)

236

5. Conclusion

As we have formulated it, there are three basic ways to resolve the paradox of fictional emotions, by rejecting the response condition, the belief condition, or the coordination condition.

Those who reject the response condition deny that we have genuine and rational emotional responses to fictional characters or situations. Some hold that we do have emotional responses to fictional characters and situations, but that these responses are either *nongenuine* (quasi-emotion theory) or *irrational* (irrationalism). Others hold that, contrary to appearances, we do *not* have emotional responses to fictional characters and situations; rather, our fictional emotions are actually directed at real-world analogues of their apparent targets (factualism), or are not directed at anything, instead being diffuse, objectless moods (nonintentionalism). We have discussed the first and second of these (*quasi-emotion theory* and *irrationalism*) in some detail in §§3 and 4 above. Regarding both the third (*factualism*) and the fourth (*nonintentionalism*), we note that while they provide plausible explanations for certain cases, they do not seem to have the generality required for a full solution: in many cases, there is no plausible real-world analogue to serve as the requisite surrogate; and in many cases, the emotional response is far too focused to be classified as merely a mood.

Those who reject the belief condition hold that when we respond emotionally to fictional scenarios, we do not *believe* them to be fictional. So the similarity between our emotional responses to actual and non-actual scenarios can be traced to some sort of (albeit temporary) confusion. Although this view brings out the importance of recognizing similarities among actual, simulated, and fictional emotions, as we noted above, it overstates its case in claiming that these similarities arise from a false belief about the fictionality of the scenarios in question.

Those who reject the coordination condition allow that we can respond with genuine, rational emotions to targets that we believe to be fictional. Above, we have offered reasons for holding such a position.[8/9]

---

[8] [*Note added in 2009*: For fascinating discussion of this question in the context of the Indian dramatic and poetic tradition, which makes appeal to the notion of *rasa* (emotion inspired in an audience by a performer), see Ingalls, Masson, and Patwardhan (1990) (or, more compactly, Masson and Patwardhan 1977).]

[9] [1] *Acknowledgements*: For comments on an earlier draft, we are grateful to Gregory Currie, John Hawthorne, and Zoltán Gendler Szabó.

12

Imaginative Contagion

In this essay, I present and discuss a number of cases that exhibit what I call *imaginative contagion*: cases where merely imagining or pretending P has effects that we would expect only believing or perceiving P to have. The examples range from cases involving visual imagination—where merely imagining a figure of a certain size and shape may produce a corresponding afterimage—to cases involving the activation of social categories—where merely imagining being in the presence of others may instigate corresponding behavioral tendencies.

I suggest that imaginative contagion arises because certain features of our mental architecture are *source-indifferent,* in the sense that they process internally and externally generated content in similar ways—even in cases where the content in question is explicitly "marked" elsewhere as reality-insensitive. And I contend that a successful theory of imagination will need to give explicit attention to this fact.

This essay is best read as an immediate predecessor to the two alief papers (Chs. 13 and 14 below).

***

This essay was first published in *Metaphilosophy*, 37/2 (2006), 183–203 and is reprinted here with the kind permission of Wiley-Blackwell. The text that appears here is largely unchanged, though minor stylistic alterations have been made to several footnotes and to brief passages in the main text, and some bibliographic information has been moved from text to footnote and vice versa. As a result of reformatting, several footnote numbers have changed. The original number of each footnote is noted in [square brackets].

0. Overview

Recent philosophical discussions of imagination and pretense have been shaped by a rather sparse diet of examples. The aim of this essay is to expand that diet and to offer some preliminary observations about what we might learn about the nature of imagination as a result.

The bulk of the essay is devoted to presenting a number of cases that involve what I call *imaginative contagion*: cases where merely imagining or pretending that P has effects that we would expect only perceiving or believing that P to have. These range from cases involving visual imagination—where merely imagining a figure of a certain size and shape may produce a corresponding afterimage—to cases involving the activation of social categories—where merely imagining being in the presence of others may instigate corresponding behavioral tendencies. The range and frequency of these cases suggests that a successful theory of imagination will need to give them explicit attention.

Imaginative contagion arises because certain features of our mental architecture are *source-indifferent*, in the sense that they process internally and externally generated content in similar ways—even in cases where the content in question is explicitly "marked" elsewhere as reality-insensitive (that is, even in cases where the subject is explicitly aware of the content as belonging to a pretense rather than a belief, or an image rather than a perception). At some level, of course, the cases presented below are unsurprising: it is common knowledge that watching sad movies may make us sad, and that imagining a vacation may make us more eager to take one. But in most contemporary philosophical theorizing about the imagination, these well-known facts have received minimal attention. In the pages that follow, I will take some preliminary steps towards resolving this omission.

1. Supplementing the Standard Picture

Recent philosophical discussions of imagination and pretense have given a great deal of attention to cases like the following (modified from Leslie 1987; see also Harris 2000). A child pretends that an (empty) teapot is full of water, and "pours" some of the "water" into an empty cup. If one asks the child what would happen if the "full" cup were tipped over, the child will readily assert that (and behave in relevant ways as if):

(a) [the table would be wet] (in the pretense) but

(b) [the table would not be wet] (in reality).

The child's (tacit) recognition of (a) and (b) gives rise to a picture that we might call the *standard model* of pretense. The standard model suggests that successful episodes of pretense exhibit two characteristics: *mirroring* (cf. Gendler 2003; Ch. 7 above) and *quarantining* (cf. Gendler 2003; Ch. 7 above, following Nichols and Stich 2000, 2003; Leslie 1987). *Mirroring* says that if I pretend that P, and if I am tacitly or explicitly attending to my belief that P→Q, then (*ceteris paribus*) I will be inclined to pretend that Q. *Quarantining* says that if I (merely) pretend that P, and (consequently) that Q, I am *not* inclined thereby to believe that P or believe that Q.

Both mirroring and quarantining play important roles in the most detailed theoretical discussion of pretense to date, Shaun Nichols and Stephen Stich's "cognitive theory of pretense." In describing the phenomena for which a theory of pretense needs to account, Nichols and Stich note both that inference mechanisms treat...pretense representations in roughly the same way that the mechanisms treat real beliefs (Nichols and Stich 2000: 125)—that is, that pretense exhibits mirroring—and that the events that [occur] in the context of the pretense have only a quite limited effect on the post-pretense cognitive state of the pretender (Nichols and Stich 2000: 120)—that is, that pretense exhibits quarantining.

Nichols and Stich are careful to hedge these claims: as close attention to these passages reveals, they maintain only that our "inference mechanisms treat... pretense representations in *roughly* the same way that the mechanisms treat real beliefs" (Nichols and Stich 2000: 125, italics added) and that "the events that [occur] in the context of the pretense have *only a quite limited effect* on the post-pretense cognitive state of the pretender" (Nichols and Stich 2000: 120, italics added). And in important recent work Nichols has discussed a number of violations of mirroring—that is, ways that our inference mechanisms treat pretense representations in ways *other* than the ways that they treat belief (Nichols 2004, 2006). But—with the exception of discussions of what I will below call *affective contagion*—there has been little discussion in the philosophical literature of the (albeit limited) effects that the contents of the pretense might have on the post-pretense cognitive state of the pretender. That is, there has been little discussion of violations of quarantining. It is this that will be the focus of my essay.

Let us call a being for whom the standard model is fully instantiated a *perfect pretender*. A perfect pretender is a being whose off-line processing system exactly mirrors its on-line processing system, while remaining completely separate from it. A perfect pretender's inference mechanisms would treat pretense representations in *exactly* the same way its mechanisms treated real beliefs, and events that occurred in the context of the pretense would have *no* effects on the post-pretense cognitive state of the pretender (except insofar as they served as a source for beliefs about what had been pretended). That is, for all P and all Q where the pretender would be inclined to form a belief that Q on the basis of a belief that P, the perfect pretender who makes-believe that P will thereby be inclined to make-believe that Q (so long as the rules governing the pretense episode do not cancel the implication from P to Q). At the same time, the perfect pretender will show no tendency towards a non-pretend belief in either P or Q (except insofar as it has pretense-independent evidence in their favor). The goal of this essay is to bring out some of the ways in which human beings are not perfect pretenders, because our tendency to quarantine is tempered by our susceptibility to imaginative contagion.[1]

2. What Contagion Is (Not)

Though human beings are not perfect pretenders, it is important to remember that they are very good pretenders. Young children are remarkably adept at keeping track of whether something is imaginary or real, and at circumscribing episodes of pretense so that there is little carry-over from one to another. They readily deny that pretend cookies are edible, and show serious dismay if an experimenter tries to bite one with the apparent intent to consume it. They do not expect Teddy to be *really* wet after he has been "bathed" in pretend water, nor do they expect that if the red blocks represent sandwiches in one game, and bars of soap in another, that the sandwiches will somehow be soapy or the soap-bars somehow edible. Children with imaginary friends do not expect them to be visible to others (though they may insist that others join them in acting as if they had independent existence in various ways). And so on.[2]

Adults are similarly effective at separating realms: insofar as they are able to identify a work or character as non-fictional, they generally circumscribe their pretend beliefs about its events or activities accordingly. Normal adults do not believe that Bilbo Baggins *really* handed a magical ring over to his cousin Frodo, or that that Jane Eyre *really* received offers of marriage from St. John Rivers and Mr. Rochester. As Nichols and Stich write: "One obvious way in which the effects of the pretense are limited is that the pretenders do not believe that pretended events, those which occurred only in the context of the pretense, really happened" (Nichols and Stich 2000: 120).

There are, of course, cases where this explicit monitoring fails. Both children and adults do, on occasion, mistake fictional characters for real beings, and imaginary episodes for actual events. We are all subject to hallucinations and their non-sensory analogues. And there are famous examples of effective hoaxes (the radio broadcast of *War of the Worlds*) and numerous instances of fabrication-reality errors (television dramas mistaken for documentaries, April-fool issues taken literally, sympathetic souls defrauded by con-artists). Though interesting in their own right, these cases—where we mistakenly believe that something merely imaginary is real—will not be what concerns me here.

---

[1] [2] Nor is it clear that we would *want* to be perfect pretenders. It is far from clear that perfect pretenders would be in a position to enjoy or learn from fiction, or to engage in action-guiding counterfactual reasoning about the future. (Thanks to Paul Bloom for discussion of these issues.)

[2] For citations on the cases above, and a general review of this experimental literature, see Harris 2000. [*Added in 2009*: For recent work on children's abilities to quarantine imaginary worlds from one another, see Skolnick and Bloom 2006a, 2006b; Weisberg and Bloom 2009.]

Rather, the violations of quarantining that I will focus on are cases where—despite explicitly recognizing something to be fictional (or, in some cases, despite having no explicit commitment to something's being non-fictional)—we nonetheless respond to the content in question in (some of) the ways that we would if the content were reality-reflective. Violations of quarantining, that is, are cases where our explicit commitments fail to govern our reactions or attitudes. In these cases, we do not lose track of whether or not some particular content is reflective of reality: rather, the feature of our mental architecture that produces the content that feeds into action or attitude in this context is actually *indifferent* to input/output relations in the way we thought it was.[3]

Paradigmatic cases of imaginative contagion are cases where—even though we would explicitly assert that we are only make-believing that P, and that we in fact believe something incompatible with P's being true—our reactions or responses under certain conditions are characteristic of a genuine belief that P. In cases of imaginative contagion, even though I explicitly believe that not-P, I am disposed to act or react in ways characteristic of P-believers (or P-perceivers), and non-characteristic of non-P-believers (or non-P-perceivers).

One caveat before continuing. It is important to distinguish cases of imaginative contagion from cases where making-believe that P causes us to act as if P were true *in the circumscribed context of a pretense*. As a number of philosophers have noted, the belief–desire–action structure that characterizes ordinary behavior is—as mirroring would lead us to expect—echoed in the context of pretense.[4] Just as, if I believe that P, then I am disposed to act in ways that would allow me to satisfy my desires (whatever those desires might be) in a world where P (along with my other beliefs) is true,[5] so too, in the context of a pretense episode, if I *make-believe* (or imagine) that P, then I am disposed to pretend-behave in ways that would allow me to satisfy my *make-desires* (or "wishes"; cf. Velleman 2000) in a world where P (along with my other make-beliefs) is true. But this may well lead to genuine action: pretending to do X may be best accomplished by actually doing X'—where X and X' may be (nearly) identical.

Pretend behavior results from allowing (certain) actions to be guided not by beliefs and desires, but by imaginings (make-beliefs) and wishes (make-desires). But those actions, though carried out by the same physical entity that carries out actual actions, are themselves restricted to the context of the pretense. A circumscribed pretend-belief and a circumscribed pretend-desire conjoin to

---

[3] [*Note added in 2009*: Clearly, this foreshadows the notion of alief introduced in Gendler 2008a; Ch. 13 below.]

[4] [3] See e.g. Currie 2002b; Harris 2000; Nichols 2006a; Velleman 2000; Walton 1990. For related discussion of Velleman 2000, see O'Brien 2005.

[5] [4] Cf. Stalnaker 1984/1987, 15; Dennett 1971/1987.

produce a correspondingly circumscribed pretend-action.[6] The action in question is explicitly "marked" as non-actual—it is, to borrow terminology from Alan Leslie (1987), *decoupled* from its ordinary role as an indicator of my status as an intentional agent. Though it uses the same equipment as actual actions (my body, my voice, etc.), the resulting behavior *represents* the content in question, rather than *manifesting* it. If, in the context of pretending to be a witch I say, "I'm going to catch you and put you in a pot and eat you for dinner" and then begin to chase you around the playground, I am not (thereby) *actually* expressing a desire to cook you and eat you for dinner (though I may be expressing an actual desire to catch you)—I am only pretending to do so.

Imaginative contagion is importantly different from this. The cognitive and behavioral manifestations associated with imaginative contagion are *not* marked as explicit episodes of pretense. Instead, they are *actual* responses to imagined content. As a result, they reveal the ways in which we are not perfect pretenders. In the remainder of the essay, I will give some examples of imaginative contagion.

3. Perceptual and Motor Contagion

Imaginative contagion arises when source-indifferent features of our mental architecture process merely imagined input in the same way that non-imaginary input would have been processed, despite our recognition that the content in question is not reality-reflective. There are two sorts of cases where contagion is surprising: (a) cases where we had not recognized that the relevant feature of our mental architecture is source-indifferent in the relevant way (though we may be accustomed to the consequences typically associated with entertaining a certain sort of content); and (b) cases where we had not recognized the consequences of entertaining a certain sort of content (though we may recognize the source-indifference of the relevant feature of our mental architecture).

By way of illustrating the first sort of case, consider two examples, one concerning visual imagining, the other motor imagery.

In the early 1950s, Louis Weiskrantz, then a graduate student in psychology at Oxford, was interested in the issue of figural after-effects.[7] In an effort to determine whether fixation plus focused attention could produce such effects, Weiskrantz "asked subjects to fixate a cross on the screen, and instead of

---

[6] [5] Cf. Harris: "the make-believe situation [is] ... fed into the child's own knowledge and planning system, and the output of this system [is] translated into a pretend action or statement" (Harris 2000: 35). See also the discussions in Currie 2002b, Nichols 2006a.

[7] [6] Figural after-effects are "interesting and lawful changes in spatial location and visuo-spatial metrics that occur after prolonged visual fixation" (Weiskrantz 2002: 569).

actually viewing the stimulus, just continue to fixate and to imagine that the experimentally relevant stimulus was present—which was instructed to be a solid, black square, its size indicated by tiny dots at the corners" (Weiskrantz 2002: 569). While the procedure yielded no results as far as figural afterimages were concerned, it brought to light an extraordinary phenomenon. As Weiskrantz reports:

To my astonishment, one person (a secretary in the Oxford Department who was badgered into being a control subject), after being asked to fixate for over a minute, and to imagine that there was a solid black square in the area indicated by the four tiny faint dots, startled me and herself by reporting afterwards that she had a clear white image of the square—a negative after-image. I repeated this several times, with the same result. To demonstrate that this was no figment of her or my imagination, I made sure the four tiny dots were not producing an after-image, and then measured the size of her after-image projected at various distances, so-called Emmert's Law. And it fitted her "real" after-image determination almost perfectly...I then tried to find anyone who could simulate Emmert's Law, and failed, even with sophisticated subjects. In fact, it is almost impossible to do given the strength of size constancy, and the tendency to scale for constant size independent of viewing distance. (2002: 569–70)

This is a surprising case of imaginative contagion because, even though we are well aware that *seeing* a black square can give rise to a white square-shaped afterimage, many find it surprising to learn that merely forming a vivid mental image of a black square could have the same consequence. That is, we expect the machinery that underpins the formation of afterimages to be source-insensitive (responding only to actual world-induced visual experiences) and not source-insensitive (responding also to imaginary self-induced visual experiences). But it turns out the machinery is—at least in certain cases—source-insensitive.[8]

Similar phenomena can be found in the case of motor routines. As Marc Jeannerod writes, just as "mental images, at least in the visual modality, rely on the same neural substrate as the perceptual images that are generated during normal perception" so too do motor imagery and motor preparation seem to share both a representation vehicle and a neural substrate; there is reason to

---

[8] [7] There is a large related literature on mental imagery that seems to suggest a common neural substrate for perception and visual imagery. For discussion, see Farah 1988, 1989; Finke 1989; Kosslyn 1978, 1994; Kosslyn *et al.* 1993; Shepard 1984; Shepard and Cooper 1982; cf. Pylyshyn 2003; Servos and Goodale 1995. On auditory imagery, see Reisberg 1992; Zatorre *et al.* 1996. [*Added in 2009*: Recent neuroimaging work suggests that although the neural substrates of visual perception and visual imagining are shared in the sense that both involve increased activation of visual cortex, they differ in that visual imagining (in contrast to visual perception) is associated with a *deactivation* of auditory cortex. The authors of the study suggest that "pure visual imagery corresponds to the isolated activation of visual cortical areas with the concurrent deactivation of 'irrelevant' sensory processing that could disrupt the image created by our 'mind's eye'" (Amedi *et al.* 2005: 859).]

think that "motor imagery pertains to motor physiology in the same way as visual imagery pertains to visual physiology" (Jeannerod 1994; see Jeannerod 1997, 2001). In similar fashion, a recent review article on motor imagery concludes: "results from a wide range of studies support the notion that motor imagery and execution involve activation of very similar cerebral structures 'at all stages of motor control' (with the proviso that the final motor output is not expressed during motor imagery)" (Crammond 1997: 54, parentheses added; see also Decety 1996; Papaxanthis *et al.* 2002).[9]

And, indeed, recent work on motor planning has demonstrated what athletes have long known: that simply imagining performing a motor sequence can—under the right circumstances[10]—produce some effects similar to those that would result from its actual performance.[11] Numerous studies have shown that accuracy in motor routines is enhanced by imagined training (Feltz and Landers 1983; Feltz *et al.* 1988). And there is even evidence that muscle strength can be increased in this way. In a recent study by Ranganathan *et al.* (2004), subjects spent fifteen minutes per day for twelve weeks performing "mental contractions" of their little fingers; though subjects in control groups showed no significant changes in strength, for those in the mental exercise group, "abduction strength of the little finger . . . increased almost linearly throughout the training" (p. 948).[12]

Together, these results from visual and motor imagery suggest a degree of source-indifference in domains where it might not have been expected. To be sure, quarantining is the norm: but contagion happens more often, and in more ways, than the standard model would predict.

---

[9] [*Note added in* 2009: Recent neuroimaging work by Jean Decety (Decety and Stevens 2009), Marc Jeannerod (Jeannerod 2006), and others suggests that simulated or imagined action "activates the same cortical structures that are responsible for motor execution" (Markman *et al.* 2009: viii). The implications of this overlap have been a central topic in discussions of, among others, implicit memory and learning (Kosslyn and Moulton 2009), imitation (Hurley and Chater 2005; Meltzoff and Prinz 2002), and social understanding (Decety and Stevens 2009; Goldman 2006; Rizzolatti and Sinigaglia 2006).]

[10] [8] It appears, for example, that totally novel movements cannot be learned merely through mental practice (cf. Mulder *et al.* 2004).

[11] [*Note added in 2009*: For a recent review of some of this work, see Kosslyn and Moulton 2009.]

[12] [9] To be fair, this is an exceptional effect: no one would seriously suggest that imagined sit-ups can trim a bulging belly, or that cardiovascular strength increases significantly as a result of watching the New York Marathon. And, indeed, results were far less impressive in a comparable study of elbow flexion. Cf. Herbert *et al.* 1998. [*Added in 2009*: That said, the phenomenon of contralateral strength training effects, "whereby training one side of the body increases the strength of muscles on the other side of the body," has been well documented in numerous studies (T. Carroll *et al.* 2006: 1514; see also Hortobagyi 2005), beginning with an 1894 report in *Studies from the Yale Psychological Laboratory* (Scripture, Smith, and Brown 1894). The general consensus seems to be that such improvements "reflect increased motoneuron output rather than muscular adaptations" (Carroll *et al.* 2006: 1514).]

4. Affective Contagion

The realm where contagion has been most widely discussed—because it is so noticeable—is in the realm of affect. There are numerous occasions where the mere contemplation of an emotionally charged situation causes the subject to behave as if the situation were probable enough to influence prudent behavior. A child who has been pretending that there is a bear in the closet will tend to hesitate before opening the door.[13] A subject who affixes a label reading "sodium cyanide" to a bottle that she has just filled with sugar will tend to be reluctant to eat from it (Rozin and Nemeroff 1990). Ritual and psychoanalysis both exploit the ways in which symbolic behavior may provide an effective emotional surrogate for that which it represents. And (as the extensive literature on the Paradox of Fictional Emotions attests) a subject who has read *Anna Karenina* or seen *The Shining* will typically respond with pity or fear—despite her explicit recognition that the scenarios depicted are purely fictional.[14]

Indeed, there is good reason to think that the mechanisms that lead to affective contagion play a fundamental role in practical reasoning. Antonio Damasio and his colleagues have repeatedly demonstrated that when normal subjects imaginatively engage with the potential consequences of various courses of action, they activate their emotional response mechanisms and encode the results of these simulations somatically. These autonomic responses seem to play a crucial role in allowing agents to act on their avowed intentions: without some sort of somatic realization of the potential consequences of a risky action, the theoretical advantages of one or another course of action may be apparent to the subject, but they will not play a proper role in action-guiding behavior.[15] In the realm of affect, then, source-indifference is so manifest as to be largely unsurprising. Because it has been so widely discussed, I will not say

---

[13] [10] Philosophical discussions of this phenomenon can be found in Hume 1739/1978: I. iii.13; Ryle 1949: 258; H. H. Price 1960/1969: 308–9. For discussion of recent research, see Harris 2000: 173–80.

[14] [11] See Currie 1990, 1997; Currie and Ravenscroft 2002; Gendler and Kovakovich 2005 (Ch. 11 above); Meskin and Weinberg 2003; Moran 1994. [*Added in 2009*: For reviews of this literature, see Levinson 1997; Neill 2005; and Schneider 2006. Influential anthologies on the topic include Bermúdez and Gardner 2003; Hjort and Laver 1997; Kieran and Lopes 2003; Nichols 2006b; collections of essays include Currie 2004; Levinson 1998. Book-length treatments include N. Carroll 1990; Currie 1990, Currie 1995a; Feagin 1996; J. Robinson 2005; Scruton 1974; Walton 1990; see also Brann 1991.]

[15] Damasio *et al.* 1991; Damasio 1994, 1999; for a discussion of the connection to fictional emotions, see Harris 1990; Gendler and Kovakovich 2005 (Ch. 11 above). Subjects with damage to the ventromedial prefrontal cortex, while they are able to articulate reasons for preferring one over another course of action, are unable to use those reasons as bases for behavior, acting instead in ways that seem erratic, unplanned, counterproductive, and anti-social. They also fail to display autonomic reactions to emotionally distressing images, suggesting that the somatic markers associated with these reactions play a crucial role in practical reasoning. (Cf. Damasio *et al.* 1991; Damasio 1994.)

more here. I note only that though there may well be differences in intensity between emotional responses to real and imagined scenarios, quarantining is decidedly ineffective, and contagion is the norm.

5. Imaginary Companionship

Bystander apathy is a well-documented phenomenon in social psychology. If a subject is presented with another subject in distress, or with some other sort of opportunity to manifest helping behavior, the speed and degree of help that she provides depends on whether she is alone or in a group: if the subject (believes she) is alone, she is more likely to provide more help more quickly than if (she believes) others are also present—indeed, the likelihood and speed of her acting are roughly inversely proportional to the size of the group she (believes she) is in (Latane and Nida 1981).[16]

What is surprising, perhaps, is that bystander apathy can be evoked in situations where the subject is alone, simply by asking the subject to imagine that others are co-present. Indeed, it turns out that bystander apathy can be evoked merely by inducing the subject to think about being in a group in some entirely different context, and then providing her with the opportunity to demonstrate helping behavior. In a series of experiments, Stephen Garcia *et al.* demonstrated that "individuals who merely imagine being in a group . . . exhibit less helping behavior on a subsequent . . . task" (Garcia *et al.* 2002: 845).

In each of the studies, subjects were first prompted to imagine a situation in which they were either alone, in the presence of a few others, or in a large group—for example, by imagining making reservations at a restaurant for a party of two, ten, or thirty, or imagining sitting in an empty or crowded movie theater. They were then asked to indicate how much money they would be willing to donate to their university, or how much of their time they would be willing to contribute to a subsequent experiment. Consistently across the studies, the larger the group a subject imagined in the first stage of the experiment, the less money or time she was willing to pledge in the second stage.

Why might this be? In follow-up studies, Garcia *et al.* found evidence that subjects who imagined being in large groups were more quickly able to identify

---

[16] [13] A wide range of mechanisms have been proposed to explain this phenomenon (see Latane and Darley 1970; Latane and Nida 1981). Given the complexity of human decision-making, and of its behavioral manifestations, it seems likely that multiple reasons are at play. Indeed, it is widely accepted in the literature on bystander apathy that a complex array of psychological predilections underlies this resiliently documented phenomenon. Moreover, the search for an explanation is complicated by the ways in which human reasoning employs heuristics and biases, which means that the ultimate explanatory factor may well be absent in certain cases where the behavior in question is manifest (since people may treat the case as they treat similar cases, even though it lacks precisely the feature that makes apathy an explicable response).

words related to the concept of unaccountability (such as "unaccountable" and "exempt") than words related to neutral terms, whereas no such difference was found in subjects who imagined being in small groups, or those who engaged in no such guided imagining. That is, it appears that imagining being in a large group rendered accessible the cluster of concepts associated with being in such a group, and rendering those concepts accessible made subjects more likely to act in accordance with their associated norms. So even though the subject was in no way confused about whether she was *really* in a large group, or just imagining that she was, the imaginary content (I am in a large group) affected her behavior in somewhat the same way that the actual content (I am in a large group) would. Unlike the perfect pretender, her imaginary representation was not fully quarantined from her action-guiding mechanisms.

Nor is this an isolated phenomenon. If you are watching a funny movie, and you imagine that there is someone else in the room watching it with you, you will smile more broadly than if you imagine yourself to be alone. If you imagine a situation in which you are sad, angry, or afraid, the degree to which your face will display the emotion you feel depends in part on whether you imagine yourself to be solitary or surrounded by others (cf. Fridlund *et al.* 1990; Fridlund 1991). Contrary to what quarantining would seem to suggest, imagining or pretending that one is in the presence of others does—at least to some extent—cause one to behave as if one were.

6. Related Examples

The phenomena just described are simply the tip of an enormous iceberg. Social psychology over the last two decades has systematically explored the multitude of ways that perceptually and evaluatively relevant mental representations may be activated, including through deliberate or accidental encounters with features of the ambient environment, self-generated or externally stimulated contemplative or intention-directed thoughts, and habitual usage. Moreover, "all these possible sources increase the accessibility or ease of use of that representation in an interchangeable, additive fashion" (Bargh, Chen, and Burrows 1996: 232). For a large range of actions, what matters are not your standing reflective considered beliefs, but what you happen to be (explicitly or tacitly) thinking about at the time. In this regard, the mechanisms are importantly source-insensitive: in bringing about access to a particular representational schema, imagination and pretense are as effective as belief and perception.

So, for example, in a series of studies by John Bargh and others, subjects were asked to produce sentences out of collections of words that either contained only neutral terms, or also contained a number of terms associated either with politeness (e.g. respect, honor, considerate, patiently, courteous) or rudeness (e.g. aggressively, bother, disturb, intrude, brazen). Subjects were instructed that, after completing the task, they should come out into the hallway to find the experimenter, who would then give them the next task to complete. When they did so, they emerged to find the experimenter engaged in a conversation with another "subject" (actually a confederate), which continued until the first subject interrupted the conversation (or until ten minutes had passed). Of those who had been primed with the rudeness concept, most interrupted in the allotted time; those in the neutral condition interrupted in less than half of the cases; whereas those in the polite condition interrupted in almost none of the cases (Bargh, Chen, and Burrows 1996: 236).

In another experiment, subjects performed a similar scrambled sentence task. One group confronted sentences containing terms associated with the elderly (e.g. wrinkle, bingo, and retired); the second group's unscrambling task involved only neutral terms. After completing the experiment, subjects were surreptitiously timed as they walked down the hall to the elevator. Subjects primed with the elderly stereotype took significantly longer to walk to the elevator than those who had not been (Bargh, Chen, and Burrows 1996).[17]

Additional research within this paradigm has reinforced and expanded the lessons of these early experiments. In a series of striking studies, Ap Dijksterhuis and others have found that even complex patterns of behavior can be primed in this way. In one set of studies, subjects were instructed to imagine in some detail either a typical professor or a typical soccer hooligan—associated respectively with stereotypes of intelligence and stupidity—and then asked to complete a general knowledge task involving a set of questions selected from the game Trivial Pursuit. Those who had imagined a professor answered significantly more questions correctly than those who had imagined a soccer hooligan, and the longer and more intensely they had imagined the character, the stronger the effect (Dijksterhuis and van Knippenberg 1998).

In a related series of studies, Dijksterhuis, in conjunction with Henk Aarts, went on to show that complex patterns of behavior associated with situational norms can be induced simply by suitably prompting the subject to activate the associated representational schemata. So, for example, showing subjects a picture of a library and asking them to anticipate visiting it is sufficient both to increase the speed with which they access library-associated behavioral terms (silent, quiet, whisper), and to cause them to speak in quieter tones. Likewise in

---

[17] [14] These results may seem difficult to reconcile with neuropsychological evidence suggesting that simple motor actions are impervious to high-level mental processes such as stereotype activation. In an interesting follow-up study, Jane Banfield and others (2003) used a similar priming technique with subjects who then performed an easily segmentable motor task (raising and lowering an egg). "The results showed that relative duration of the gaps in between ballistic actions increased compared with the relative duration of the actions themselves, slowing down part of the action sequence" (Banfield *et al.* 2003: 299). Importantly "the movements themselves were not affected by the elderly stereotype prime" (p. 313); rather "the elderly prime influenced the relative duration of the gaps in between the definable ballistic movements" (p. 313).

the case of an upscale restaurant: if properly primed subjects are shown an image of an elegant dining room and then given a crumbly cracker to eat, they expend significantly greater effort in fastidiously brushing the crumbs from the table top than their unprimed counterparts (Aarts and Dijksterhuis 2003).[18]

7. Resilient Phenomena

The discussion presented above omits much important detail that is surely relevant to any sort of systematic understanding of these perplexing phenomena. So, for example, the situational norm research ("silence of the library") suggests that circumstance-appropriate behavior is evoked only when the presentation of the visual prompt (photograph of the library or restaurant) is accompanied by an actual or imagined intention to visit such a locale, yet in the case of social stimuli (cf. the stereotype research described above) priming effects occur on the basis of mere exposure, and seem to be most profound when the subject is completely unconscious of the prompts to which she has been exposed. More generally, there are important questions that remain unanswered about the role played by conscious perception—some of the effects described are magnified, others mitigated, in the face of awareness by the subject.[19] So contagion in this realm may be limited in certain ways that merit further investigation. Questions also remain about issues concerning affective processing, the nature of motor planning, mental imagery, and so on.[20] Making sense of these details is obviously crucial to a full understanding of the phenomena in question. And it may well turn out that a number of these details are directly relevant to the topic of imaginative contagion.[21]

With full recognition that distribution of and the explanation for these phenomena are themselves topics for a great deal of further inquiry, we can nonetheless acknowledge that the very existence of this class of cases—cases where merely imagining or being exposed to a particular image or circumstance

---

[18] [*Note added in 2009*: Recent work in these laboratories has confirmed and expanded these results. For regularly updated listings of papers, see <http://www.yale.edu/acmelab/publications.html> and <http://www.unconsciouslab.com/index.php?page=Publications>.]

[19] [15] See Lombardi *et al.* 1987; L. S. Newman and Uleman 1990. (Thanks to Paul Bloom for discussion and references.)

[20] [16] Affective "spreading" is quite profound; a large body of research seems to show that "any positively evaluated object (e.g. *water*) facilitates the pronunciation of any other positively evaluated object (e.g. *Friday*) even though the prime and the target share no other semantic features in common" (Bargh 1997: 23, summarizing Bargh, Chaiken *et al.* 1996): given that in general priming effects are weaker if a feature is more common, this suggests that affective processing plays a special role in cognition. In particular, it may be that direct associative connections (directly to the amygdala and bypassing the sensory cortex) can develop between a stimulus and an affective response—and the more conscious processing is removed from the paradigm, the stronger the affective priming effect is.

[21] [17] For discussion of some of these issues, see Uhlmann *et al.* 2008.

seems to have direct effects on subsequent perceptual and behavioral tendencies—is sufficient to raise a number of perplexing puzzles. In particular, the studies described above reveal the following resilient phenomena, involving both *perceptual* and *action-guiding* mindsets:

(a) activating a representational schema associated with a certain stereotype, regardless of how that activation is achieved, may dispose one to attribute its associated features to objects in the ambient environment (perceptual schema/perceptual tendency)

(b) activating a representational or motor schema associated with a certain behavioral repertoire, regardless of how that activation is achieved, may dispose one to act in keeping with that behavioral repertoire (action schema/action tendency)

(c) activating a representational schema associated with a certain stereotype, regardless of how that activation is achieved, may dispose one to comport oneself in accord with that stereotype (perceptual schema/action tendency)[22]

Activation of these schemata, as we have seen, may happen in any number of ways. But importantly for our purposes, one of these ways is by means of spontaneous or guided imagining. This means that imaginative contagion of the sort with which we are concerned is simply a special case of a more general predilection towards source-indifference.

The extant explanation of these phenomena draws on the results of several research programs. The first is the body of research concerning *knowledge structures, priming,* and *construct accessibility,* which together explain the tendencies identified in (a); the second is the body of research concerning *behavioral schemata,* which explains the tendencies identified in (b); the third is the body of research concerning *common coding of perception and action* and on *imitation,* which, in addition to the explanatory resources just mentioned, serves to explain the additional perplexing features of (c). (Since I am clearly not an expert in these areas, and since the literature described below is somewhat controversial, the discussion that follows should be considered somewhat speculative.)

(a) The first cluster of cases to be explained are those in which the activation of a representational schema associated with a certain stereotype disposes the subject to more readily attribute its associated features to objects and entities in the ambient environment. As decades of research have demonstrated, *knowledge structures,* which are large-scale schemata for clustering the

---

[22] [18] There may also be cases where activating a representational schema associated with a certain behavioural repertoire, regardless of how that activation is achieved, disposes one to attribute its associated features to agents in the ambient environment (action schema/perceptual tendency).

otherwise overwhelming diversity of experiences into manageable and predictable sets of features, serve as filters, affecting attention and perception in numerous ways. Whether a particular knowledge structure is in a position to serve as a filter for current experiences depends on the degree to which it is *accessible*—on whether it has been *activated* or "*primed*" by some feature of the current situational context so that it is available to serve its filtering role. Once it has been activated, the knowledge structure in question predisposes the subject to be especially sensitive to features of the world that conform to it.

Psychological research over the last decade has consistently demonstrated that accessibility is conspicuously source-indifferent: the tendency to make use of a given representation is increased regardless of how the representation is activated—whether by perceiving some entity associated with it in the ambient environment, by deliberately bringing to mind it or some entity associated with it, by deliberately trying *not* to bring to mind it or some entity associated with it, by having used it in some unrelated context, and so on.[23] Moreover, activation may occur through chance encounters with associated features of an observed or imagined environment. Once activated, such representations and stereotypes act as filters for the subject's subsequent experience, affecting her perceptual and evaluative tendencies in a manifold of well-documented ways. (For reviews see Bargh, Chaiken *et al.* 1996; Bargh 1997.)

(b) The second cluster of cases to be explained are cases where activating a representational or motor schema associated with a certain behavioral repertoire, such as the behavioral repertoire associated with eating a meal in an elegant restaurant, disposes the subject to act in keeping with it. Here the story is much like the just-related one. Like perceptual schemata, motor routines and behavioral schemata are stored as "packages." Some of those packages represent fairly low-level behavioral routines—unlocking the front door, tying one's shoe, engaging the parking brake—others represent more complex sets of behavioral or *situational norms* (clusters of beliefs concerning appropriate behavior in particular situations or environments)—behaving silently in church, boisterously at a football match, and so on.

---

[23] [19] Cf. Daniel Wegner's research on "ironic processing." As Wegner writes (1994): "merely thinking about a behavior makes it more likely to occur, even if it is unintended" (p. 232)—indeed, precisely because it is intended to be avoided. "The irony of this effect is that the likelihood of this occurrence (under attentional load) is actually greater than if the person had not tried to stop the response ... according to the ironic process model, this occurs because the representation of the unwanted response is more accessible than usual because the person is watching out for its occurrence and has to keep it in mind to do so. For present purposes, the importance of these findings is that the mere act of thinking about a response, even when the thought involved is meant to help prevent the response, has the automatic effect of increasing the likelihood of that response" (p. 232).

As in the previous case, exposure to features of an environment typically associated with one or another situational norm can make salient the behavioral repertoire associated with that set of circumstances, and when that exposure is accompanied by the awakening of some sort of goal-directed behavior (such as a subsequent intention to visit the locale depicted)—it results in norm-appropriate behavior. "The goal to visit an environment activates (albeit implicitly) thoughts about how one should behave in a socially acceptable way, thus triggering the normative behavior associated with the environment automatically" (Aarts and Dijksterhuis 2003: 26). And, as before, the phenomenon manifests a striking degree of source-indifference: "Just as the accessibility or likelihood of use of a concept increases no matter what the particular the source [*sic*] of that accessibility, the likelihood of a behavioral response may increase from thinking about that behavior, regardless of the source of the thought" (Bargh, Chen, and Burrows 1996: 232).

(c) The third and most perplexing cluster of cases are those involving some sort of cross-over—cases where activating a representational schema associated with a certain stereotype leads the subject to comport herself in accord with that stereotype—as in Bargh's "elderly" studies, or Dijksterhuis's "professor/soccer hooligan" experiments. Here, the explanation of the phenomenon might make appeal to a burgeoning body of research concerning the relation between perception and action.

There is a good deal of evidence that perceptual representation of others' actions draws on the subject's own action-related representational structures: it appears, for example, that subjects confronted "with traces of handwritten letters, drawings, or body movements...are often capable of inferring the kinematics or even the dynamics of the movements by which these traces were generated" (Hommel *et al.* 2001: 854; citing various studies by Freyd, Kandel, and others).[24] And watching others perform a familiar motion produces sympathetic nervous responses in the observer (Decety *et al.* 1997; Grèzes and Decety 2001).

In similar vein, a sizable body of research on imitation (including two massive recent anthologies—Hurley and Chater 2005; Meltzoff and Prinz 2002) suggests that imitative action—in which the subject spontaneously copies the

---

[24] [20] Hommel cites this example as evidence for a "common coding" hypothesis concerning perception and action, according to which "the core functional architecture supporting perception and action planning is formed by a common representational domain for perceived events (perception) and intended or to-be-generated events (actions)...stimulus representations underlying perception and action representations underlying action planning are coded and stored...in a common representational medium" (Hommel *et al.* 2001: 849). Imaginative contagion of the sort with which I am concerned can be explained without appeal to this broader theoretical framework, though it is fully compatible with it. (For philosophical discussions of common coding hypotheses, see Noë 2004 and Hurley 2006.)

action of whomever she is observing—may be far more prevalent than is typically recognized. Infants, whose frontal brain areas are not fully developed, display tendencies to imitate a wide range of observed behavior (see Kinsbourne 2006 cited in Hurley 2006), as do adults with damage to their frontal lobes (who imitate the gestures of the experimenter even when explicitly instructed not to and even when the actions in question are inappropriate or ridiculous). Even normal subjects show such tendencies: Subjects who observe someone rubbing his feet or touching his face tend to perform similar actions themselves. This predilection towards imitation—whether or not it is as pronounced as its strongest advocates suggest—may go some way towards explaining the phenomena described in §6 above.[25]

Human beings are remarkably good at quarantining; even in young children, the pretense–reality boundary is a powerful one. But imaginative contagion is more prevalent than most theories have recognized. We are not perfect pretenders, at least in part for a reason articulated by William James more than a century ago: "We may then lay it down for certain that every [mental] representation of a movement awakens in some degree the actual movement which is its object; and awakens it in a maximum degree whenever it is not kept from so doing by an antagonistic representation present simultaneously to the mind" (W. James 1890/1950: 526).[26]

---

[25] [21] One explanation for this tendency for imitation comes from the discovery of "mirror neurons" in macaque monkeys—neurons that fire both when a monkey performs a given action *and* when it perceives a conspecific performing such an action—a discovery that seems to provide direct evidence in favor of the hypothesis that action and perception share some sort of neural substrate (Gallese *et al.* 1996; Gallese and Goldman 1998; Rizzolatti *et al.* 1996). A parallel explanation may hold in the human case, where PET studies consistently reveal similar neuronal firing patterns for executed, observed and imagined actions (Rizzolatti *et al.* 2002).

[26] [1] *Acknowledgements*: For comments on earlier versions of this essay, I am grateful to Martijn Blaauw, Paul Bloom, Tim Crane, Zoltán Gendler Szabó, and René van Woudenberg; I also benefitted from excellent questions from audiences at the Collegium Budapest (2003), and at the Cognition and Imagination Conference at the Vrije Universiteit of Amsterdam (2004).

13

Alief and Belief

In this essay, I introduce and argue for the importance of a cognitive state that I call *alief*. Roughly speaking, an alief is a mental state with associatively linked content that is representational, affective, and behavioral, and that is activated—consciously or unconsciously—by features of the subject's internal or ambient environment. It is a more primitive state than either belief or imagination: it directly activates behavioral response patterns (as opposed to motivating in conjunction with desire or pretended desire).

I contend that alief explains a large number of otherwise perplexing phenomena and plays a far greater role in causing behavior than has typically been recognized by philosophers. I argue further that the notion can be invoked to explain both the effectiveness and the limitations of certain sorts of example-based reasoning, and that it lies at the core of habit-based views of ethics.

This essay and its successor—"Alief in Action (and Reaction)" (Ch. 14)—form a natural pair. They are best read in conjunction with one another. A number of footnotes in each indicate some of the relations between them.

For the reader with limited time, the following selections will give a sense of the larger project:

- Overview of the notion of alief: Ch. 13 §§0 and 1 or Ch. 14 §1

- Explanation of the difference between alief and other mental states: Ch. 13 §2 or Ch. 14 §2

- Applications of the notion of alief: Ch. 13 §3 (automaticity); Ch. 13 §4 (philosophical methodology); Ch. 14 §4 (racism)

***

This essay was first published in the *Journal of Philosophy*, 105/10 (2008), 634–63, and is reprinted with the kind permission of the *Journal of Philosophy*. This essay appears in its original form; changes have been limited to correction of minor typographical errors, the insertion of remarks in footnotes (noted as such), and the reconfiguration of citations to bring reference conventions into line with other essays in the volume. As a result of reformatting citations, footnote numbers have changed. The original number of each footnote is noted in [square brackets].

0. Four Opening Examples

In March 2007, 4,000 feet above the floor of the Grand Canyon, a horseshoe-shaped cantilevered glass walkway was opened to the public. Extending 70 feet from the Canyon's rim, the Grand Canyon Skywalk soon drew hundreds of visitors each day, among them *New York Times* reporter Edward Rothstein, who filed the following dispatch:

A visitor to these stark and imposing lands of the Hualapai Indians on the western rim of the Grand Canyon knows what sensation is being promised at the journey's climax. After driving for a half-hour over bone-jolting dirt roads...you take a shuttle bus from the parking lot...You deposit all cameras at a security desk, slip on yellow surgical booties and stride out onto a horseshoe-shaped walkway with transparent sides and walls that extends 70 feet into space, seemingly unsupported.

Below the floor's five layers of glass (protected from scratches by the booties) can be seen the cracked, sharp-edged rock face of the canyon's rim and a drop of thousands of feet to the chasm below. The promise is the dizzying thrill of vertigo.

And indeed, last week some visitors to this steel-supported walkway anchored in rock felt precisely that. One woman, her left hand desperately grasping the 60-inch-high glass sides and the other clutching the arm of a patient security guard, didn't dare move toward the transparent center of the walkway. The words imprinted on the $20 souvenir photographs taken of many venturesome souls herald completion of a daredevil stunt: "I did it!!!" (Rothstein 2007: 19)

Though some readers may find this story politically or aesthetically disturbing, none—I take it—find it perplexing.[1] While the sarcasm of "venturesome souls" is surely well placed, and the price of the "'I did it!!!'" photo is surely excessive, the basic phenomenon—that stepping onto a high transparent safe surface can induce feelings of vertigo—is both familiar and unmysterious.[2]

How should we describe the cognitive state of those who manage to stride to the Skywalk's center? Surely they *believe* that the walkway will hold: no one would willingly step onto a mile-high platform if they had even a scintilla of doubt concerning its stability. But alongside that belief there is something else going on. Although the venturesome souls wholeheartedly *believe* that the walkway is completely safe, they also *alieve* something very different. The alief has roughly the following content: "Really high up, long, long way down. Not a safe place to be! Get off!!"[3]

---

[1] [2] Indeed, the story is a slight variation on the early modern "problem of the precipice," discussed—among others—by Hume (*Treatise* 1.3.13.10, 148), Pascal (*Pensées*, §44), and Montaigne (1575/1957: 250). For discussion and references, see Traiger 2005: 100–15. I discuss precipice cases in more detail in "Alief in Action" (Ch. 14), §2.1.

[2] [3] The *physiological* explanation, of course, is that there is a mismatch in input between the visual, vestibular, and somatosensory systems. For discussion, see Brandt and Daroff 1980: 195–203 and Brandt 1999/2003.

[3] [4] Throughout my discussion, I am using the term "content" in a somewhat idiosyncratic way, for want of a better term to describe the general notion that I wish to capture. As I am using

In a series of ingenious studies spanning several decades, psychologist Paul Rozin has demonstrated a widespread tendency for well-educated Western adults to exhibit behaviors consonant with a commitment to the existence of "laws of sympathetic magic":[4] that "there can be a permanent transfer of properties from one object . . . to another by brief contact" (*contagion*) and that "the action taken on an object affects similar objects" (*similarity*) (Rozin, Millman, and Nemeroff 1986: 703).

So, for example, subjects are reluctant to drink from a glass of juice in which a completely sterilized dead cockroach has been stirred, hesitant to wear a laundered shirt that has been previously worn by someone they dislike, and loath to eat soup from a brand-new bedpan. They are disinclined to put their mouths on a piece of newly purchased vomit-shaped rubber (though perfectly willing to do so with a sink stopper of similar size and material), averse to eating fudge that has been formed into the shape of dog feces, and far less accurate in throwing darts at pictures of faces of people they like than at neutral faces.[5]

How should we describe the cognitive state of those who hesitate to eat the feces-shaped fudge or wear their adversary's shirt? Surely they *believe* that the fudge has not changed its chemical composition, and that the shirt does not bear cooties[6]—just as they believe that the newly purchased bedpan is sterile and that the fake vomit is actually made of rubber: asked directly, subjects show no hesitation in endorsing such claims. But alongside these beliefs there is something else going on. Although they *believe* that the items in question are harmless, they also *alieve* something very different. The alief has roughly the following content: "Filthy object! Contaminated! Stay away!"

Last month, when I was traveling to the APA Program Committee meeting, I accidentally left my wallet at home. I noticed its absence when I arrived at the

---

the term, content need not be propositional and may include—as the example above makes clear—affective states and behavioral dispositions.

[4] [5] Cf. Frazer 1890/1959 and Mauss 1902/1972 as cited in Rozin, Millman, and Nemeroff 1986.

[5] [7] The descriptions of the cases make it clear that the experimenters go out of their way to avoid the possibility of any sort of confusion. In the fudge study, for example, "subjects were offered a piece of high-quality chocolate fudge, in a square shape, on a paper plate [and then] ate the piece . . . [Next] two additional pieces of the same fudge were presented, each on its own paper plate." Subjects were made explicitly aware that the two pieces came from the same initial source, and that the only difference between them was that "one piece was shaped in the form of a disc or muffin, the other in the shape of a surprisingly realistic piece of dog feces." Despite recognizing that they contained identical ingredients, subjects showed a striking reluctance to consume the feces-shaped piece (Rozin, Millman, and Nemeroff 1986: 705).

[6] [8] For definition of the term, see <http://en.wikipedia.org/wiki/Cooties>. Apparently, a roughly equivalent British term is "lurgies."

check-in desk at the Hartford Airport, and fully expected to be turned away from my flight. Much to my surprise, the desk agent simply wrote the words "No ID" on my boarding pass, and told me to allow for a few extra minutes at security.[7] The various scans showed nothing amiss, so I boarded my plane, flew to Baltimore, and made my way to the meeting site.

Though the Transportation Security Administration may not require identification, restaurants and hotels do require payment, so when I got to Baltimore, I arranged to borrow money from a friend who was also attending the meeting. As he handed me the bills, I said: "Thanks so much for helping me out like this. It's really important for me to have this much cash since I don't have my wallet." Rummaging through my bag as I talked, I continued: "It's a lot of cash to be carrying loose, though, so let me just stash it in my wallet ... "

How should we describe my mental state as my fingers searched for my wallet to house the explicitly wallet-compensatory money? Surely I *believed* that I had left my wallet in New Haven; after all, the reason I was borrowing so much money was because I knew I had no credit cards or cash with me. But alongside that belief there was something else going on. Although I *believed* that my wallet was several hundred miles away as I rooted through my bag, I simultaneously *alieved* something very different. The alief had roughly the following content: "Bunch of money. Needs to go into a safe place. Activate wallet-retrieval motor routine now."

In his debate-framing article "Fearing Fictions," Kendall Walton writes:

Charles is watching a horror movie about a terrible green slime. He cringes in his seat as the slime oozes slowly but relentlessly over the earth destroying everything in its path. Soon a greasy head emerges from the undulating mass, and two beady eyes roll around, finally fixing on the camera. The slime, picking up speed, oozes on a new course straight towards the viewers. Charles emits a shriek and clutches desperately at his chair. (Walton 1978: 5)

How should we describe Charles's cognitive state? Surely he does not *believe* that he is in physical peril; as Walton notes, "Charles knows perfectly well that the slime is not real and that he is in no danger" (Walton 1978: 6). But alongside that belief there is something else going on. Although Charles *believes* that he is sitting safely in a chair in a theater in front of a movie screen, he also *alieves* something very different. The alief has roughly the following content: "Dangerous two-eyed creature heading towards me! H-e-l-p ... ! Activate fight or flight adrenaline now!"

---

[7] [9] Legally, it is *not* required that one carry identification in order to fly. Rather, the Transportation Security Administration requires that airline passengers either "present identification to airline personnel before boarding or be subjected to a search that is more exacting than the routine search that passengers who present identification encounter." Cf. *Gilmore v. Gonzales*, 04-15736 D.C No. CV-02-03444-SI Opinion. (Full text at <http://www.ca9.uscourts.gov/datastore/opinions/2006/01/25/0415736.pdf>.) As a quick internet search for "flying without identification" will reveal, however, there is a gap between the law and the practice: there were, no doubt, additional features of my particular circumstance that led me to be offered this option.

1. Introducing Alief

1.1. Belief–Behavior Mismatch and Belief-Discordant Alief

In each of the cases presented above, it seems clear what the subject believes:[8] that the walkway is safe, that the substance is edible or potable, that the wallet is in New Haven, that the theater is in no danger of being invaded by slime. Ask the subject directly and she will show no hesitation in endorsing such claims as true. Ask her to bet, and this is where she will place her money. Ask her to think about what her other beliefs imply and this is what she will conclude. Look at her overarching behavior and this is what it will point to. At the same time, the belief fails to be accompanied by certain belief-appropriate behaviors and attitudes: something is awry.

When else do we find this sort of belief–behavior mismatch? One sort of case is that of deliberate deception. If I believe that I have a winning hand, but I am trying to mislead you into thinking that I do not, I will behave in ways discordant with my belief. But clearly, this is not a good model for the cases just considered: Charles is not trying to fool the movie-maker; Rozin's subjects are not trying to mislead the experimenters. In contrast to the cases of deliberate deception, the belief–behavior mismatch in our cases is not the result of something other-directed and deliberately controlled.

Perhaps, then, it is akin to a case of self-deception? A self-deceived subject believes, say, that her child has committed some terrible crime, but somehow brings herself to represent the situation—both to herself and to others—as if she believed precisely the opposite, resulting in the requisite belief–behavior mismatch.[9] This is an improvement on the previous model; it corrects the problem

---

[8] [11] Although belief is clearly one of the central notions in epistemology, the question of what belief *is* has been (with important exceptions) underexplored in this context.* One might think a simple characterization would suffice—something like: "To believe a proposition is to hold it to be true" (Blackburn 1996: 40). But, for reasons that David Velleman brings out nicely (Velleman 2000), this won't quite do (at least, not without a careful spelling out of what "hold to be true" amounts to, which just pushes the question one step back). Moreover, the issue is complicated by there being at least two apparently different fundamental notions of belief: what H. H. Price calls the "occurrence" or "traditional" view—that to believe a proposition is to be in a mental state with a particular sort of introspectively available feature, such as "vivacity" or "liveliness" or "solidity" (a view he attributes to, among others, Descartes, Hume, Spinoza, Cardinal Newman, and Cook Wilson)—and what he calls the "dispositional" or "modern" view—that to believe a proposition is to be disposed to act in certain ways (a view he attributes to, among others, Alexander Bain, R. B. Braithwaite, and Gilbert Ryle) (Price 1960/1969). I will have more to say about this matter below. In the meantime—as the astute reader will have suspected by now—I invoke this legacy as much to exculpate as to inform: though I will offer more details in subsequent sections, for the time being, I will leave the notion of belief undefined. (For further discussion, see §2 of "Alief in Action," Ch. 14 below.)

*Of course, there have been extensive discussions of this question in the context of philosophy of mind (for an overview see §1 of Schwitzgebel 2006). But (with some important exceptions) this literature has remained largely insulated from the literature in epistemology.

[9] [12] I discuss the nature of self-deception in Gendler 2008c (Ch. 8 above).

of other-directedness, and—to some extent—the problem of deliberate control. But it still misrepresents the structure of the situation: it's not that the reluctant walker on the Hualapai Skywalk believes that the surface is safe, but has somehow deceived herself into thinking that it is risky; it's not that Rozin's subject believes that the bedpan is sterile, but somehow deceives herself into thinking that there's some reason not to drink from it. The mismatch runs in two directions: unlike in cases of self-deception, the subjects in our cases show no reluctance to explicitly endorse the belief with which their behavior fails to accord. And unlike in cases of self-deception, their behavioral responses do not result from some deliberate or quasi-deliberate process of misrepresentation.

Perhaps, then, the subjects' hesitation to act on their beliefs is the result of some sort of doubt or uncertainty? In setting out for the day, I might dither a bit before leaving my umbrella at home: "it's not going to rain," I might aver—though I am not completely certain that I am right. Though the action-pattern is strikingly similar to some of the cases above, the model is still inadequate. Stepping onto the Skyway, eating the stool-shaped fudge, or staying seated in the theater is not like willing oneself to play Russian roulette: it is not a case of discounting a low-probability outcome and hoping for the best. Charles doesn't leave the theater thinking: "Phew! It's lucky the slime stayed on the screen this time!" Rozin's subject doesn't breathe a sigh of relief that the dart hitting the photograph didn't *actually* harm her friend. I wasn't rooting around on the off-chance that maybe my wallet really *was* in my bag after all.[10]

Perhaps, then, the belief is temporarily forgotten? When I reach for my wallet, perhaps it's that I just don't remember that it isn't with me. When I hesitate before the fudge, perhaps I've just lost track of the fact that it's not dog-shit. When I step timidly on the walkway, perhaps I've just forgotten that it's solid. Perhaps. But I don't think this could be the full story. Rozin's subjects hesitate to eat the soup even if they are vividly and occurrently entertaining the thought "this is a completely sterile bedpan," fully, consciously and with explicit attention to its meaning and implications. I was rooting around in my bag for my wallet at the exact moment that I was vividly and occurrently entertaining the thought "I left my wallet in New Haven," fully, consciously, with explicit attention to its meaning and implications. And certainly the Hualapai Canyon steppers have not *forgotten* that the platform is safe, else they would do something a good deal more dramatic than hesitate before taking the next step.

---

[10] [13] Nor are these cases of what Eric Schwitzgebel calls "in-between beliefs"—attitudes "that are not quite accurately describable as believing that P, nor quite accurately describable as failing to believe that P" (Schwitzgebel 2001:76)—cases such as "gradual forgetting, failure to think things through completely, and variability with context and mood" (Schwitzgebel 2001: 78). They are closer to some of the cases that Price calls "half-beliefs" (H. H. Price 1960/1969: 302–14); I discuss Price's examples in more detail in §2.2 below.

But if it's not a case where the subject is deceiving others, or self-deceived, or uncertain, or forgetful, then why *is* stepping onto the Skywalk different from stepping onto the back porch? The reason, of course, is that each activates a different set of affective, cognitive, and behavioral association-patterns. When the subject steps onto the wooden porch, input to her visual system affirms her explicit conscious belief that the surface is solid and secure; this sets into motion a train of associations and activates a number of motor routines. But since these motor routines coincide with those activated by her explicit intention to walk across a surface that she believes to be solid, there is no belief–behavior mismatch. When she steps onto the glass platform, by contrast, input to her visual system suggests that she is striding off the edge of a cliff. This visual input activates a set of affective response patterns (feelings of anxiety) and motor routines (muscle contractions associated with hesitation and retreat), and the visual–vestibular mismatch produces feelings of dizziness and discomfort, leading to additional activation of motor routines associated with hesitation and withdrawal. (For detailed discussion, see Brandt 1999/2003, Ch. 29.) These motor routines compete with those activated by her explicit intention to walk across a surface that she believes to be solid; the result is the belief–behavior mismatch adverted to above.

Nor do we need anything so dramatic to make the point. The same phenomenon occurs when I set my watch five minutes fast. The effectiveness of the strategy does not depend on my *forgetting* that the watch is inaccurate, or on my *doubting* that it's really 9:40 rather than 9:45, or my *deceiving* myself or others into thinking that it's five minutes later than it is. Rather, as with the glass-bottomed Skywalk, when I look at my watch, input to my visual system suggests that I am in a world where the time is t+5. This visual input activates a set of affective response patterns (feelings of urgency) and motor routines (tensing of the muscles, an overcoming of certain sorts of inertia), leading to the activation of behavior patterns that would not be triggered by my explicit, conscious, vivid, occurrent belief that it is actually only 9:40.[11]

The activation of these response patterns constitutes the rendering occurrent of what I hereby dub a *belief-discordant alief*. The alief has representational-affective-behavioral content that includes, in the case of the Skywalk, the visual appearance as of a cliff, the feeling of fear, and the motor routine of retreat.[12]

---

[11] [15] Examples of such cases are manifold. I think, for example, that many of the cases of motivation by imagination discussed in Velleman 2000 are actually cases of motivation by alief. Likewise, I think that many of the cases of heuristic-based reasoning discussed by Kahneman and Tversky are cases of decision on the basis of alief. (Cf. Kahneman, Slovic, and Tversky 1982; Kahneman and Tversky 2000; Denes-Raj and Epstein 1994, and other work in the "dual processing" tradition.) [*Note added in 2009*: I also discuss a number of these examples in preliminary fashion in "Pretense and Belief" (Ch. 7 above).]

[12] [16] Of course, stepping onto the wooden deck also renders occurrent an alief—indeed many aliefs—but since those aliefs accord with the subject's explicit beliefs, we do not need to make appeal to them in order to explain her subsequent behavior.

Similar appeal to belief-discordant alief can be made in each of the other cases. The visual appearance of the feces-shaped fudge renders occurrent a belief-discordant alief with the content: "dog-shit, disgusting, refuse-to-eat"—an alief that runs counter to the subject's explicit belief that the object before her is composed of a substance that she considers delicious and appealing. The visual–motor input associated with throwing a dart at a representation of a loved one renders occurrent a belief-discordant alief with the content "harmful action directed at beloved, dangerous and ill-advised, don't throw"—an alief that runs counter to the subject's explicit belief that damaging a representation has no effects on the entity represented. The visual–motor input associated with handling cash rendered occurrent my belief-discordant alief with the content: "Bunch of money. Needs to go into a safe place. Activate wallet-retrieval motor routine now"—an alief that ran counter to my explicit belief that my wallet was in Connecticut while I was in Maryland. And so on.

1.2. A Provisional Characterization of Alief

In the remainder of the article, I argue for the importance of recognizing the existence of alief—so-called because *a*lief is *a*ssociative, *a*ction-generating, *a*ffect-laden, *a*rational, *a*utomatic, *a*gnostic with respect to its content, shared with non-human *a*nimals, and developmentally and conceptually *a*ntecedent to other cognitive attitudes.[13/14] I will argue that any theory that helps itself to notions like belief, desire, and pretense needs to include a notion like alief in order to make proper sense of a wide range of otherwise perplexing phenomena. Without such a notion, I will contend, either such phenomena remain overlooked or misdescribed, or they seem to mandate such a radical reconceptualization of the relation between cognition and behavior that traditional notions like belief seem quaint and inadequate. In short, I will argue that if you want to take

---

[13] [17] An alternative term might be *prelief*, but this expression is already spoken for as a way of referring to a state that is intermediate (or indifferent) between pretense and belief (cf. Perner, Baker, and Hutton 1994). And in any case, it lacks the resonance of the chosen term. One might also want to leave room for a notion related to desire in something like the way that alief is related to belief. Had "prelief" been available, one might choose *presire*; since it is not, a suitable expression is *cesire*. (I remain utterly agnostic about what sort of attitude cesire might be.) [*Added in 2009*: Given that alief is in some ways both a cognitive and a conative state, it's not fully clear to me what sort of distinct state cesire would be. Still, it seems prudent to reserve squatting rights.]

[14] [*Note added in 2009*: I enumerate these characteristics in a slightly different way in "Alief in Action" (Ch. 14 below, §1.1). There I say that "To have an alief is, to a reasonable approximation, to have an innate or habitual propensity to respond to an apparent stimulus in a particular way. It is to be in a mental state that is . . . *a*ssociative, *a*utomatic and *a*rational. As a class, aliefs are states that we share with non-human *a*nimals; they are developmentally and conceptually *a*ntecedent to other cognitive attitudes that the creature may go on to develop. Typically, they are also *a*ffect-laden and *a*ction-generating."]

seriously how human minds really work, and you want to save belief, then you need to make conceptual room for the notion of alief.

Because alief is a novel notion, introduced to make sense of a cluster of otherwise baffling cases, most of the essay will proceed by examination of specific examples. The heart of the essay lies in that discussion, and in the claim that consideration of such cases brings to light issues of philosophical importance. At the same time, I will tentatively offer a more abstract characterization of the concept that I am introducing, so that the general claim that I am making can be properly assessed.

The account that follows is explicitly provisional. I have little doubt that I have gotten some of the details wrong—and perhaps a good deal more than the details. But it seems to me better to make an honest mistake by attempting to be precise than to avoid error by refusing to be explicit. With that in mind, I offer the following tentative characterization of a paradigmatic alief:

A paradigmatic *alief* is a mental state with associatively linked content that is representational, affective, and behavioral, and that is activated—consciously or non-consciously—by features of the subject's internal or ambient environment. Aliefs may be either occurrent or dispositional.

Nearly every clause in this characterization merits a quick remark or highlighting:

(1)   Alief is a *mental* state . . .

Since I incline towards physicalism, this means that I think alief is also a physical state. But it is a special sort of physical state—one that occurs in the brain of a conscious subject. And it occurs in her brain as the result of her (or her genetic ancestors') having undergone certain sorts of experiences—experiences that result in the creation of clusters of associations with representational-affective-behavioral content.

(2)   Alief is a mental *state* . . .

Alief is a state and not, say, an attitude. It is (I think) roughly what Aristotle would call a *hexis*.

(3)   . . . with *associatively linked* content . . .

That is, a cluster of contents that tend to be co-activated. The contrast here is with discrete contents that fail to be linked through such an association.

(4)   . . . that is *representational, affective, and behavioral* . . .

In paradigmatic cases, an activated alief has three sorts of components: (a) the representation of some object or concept or situation or circumstance, perhaps propositionally, perhaps non-propositionally, perhaps conceptually, perhaps non-conceptually; (b) the experience of some affective or emotional state;[15] (c) the readying of some motor routine.[16]

(5) *Paradigmatic* alief is a mental state with content that is representational, affective, and behavioral...

Notwithstanding the characterization offered in (4), I do not want to rule out the possibility of there being aliefs that involve the mental activation of a different sort of associative cluster. Perhaps there are cases where the activation occurs at a sufficiently low level to render the notion of representation inapplicable. Perhaps there are states that lack an obvious affective ingredient, or that do not include the clear activation of a motor routine, but that nonetheless sufficiently resemble our paradigm cases that we want to count them as aliefs. Perhaps there are cases where the most noticeable associations are not easily subsumed under the three categories offered—cases that primarily involve the heightening or dampening of certain sorts of attention, or the heightening or dampening of certain perceptual sensitivities.

(6) Alief is a *mental state with...behavioral...content.*

That is: alief does not involve the *execution* of these motor routines; it merely involves their *activation* (alief is a *mental* state). At the same time, this activation renders it more likely that the routine will actually be performed.[17]

---

[15] [18] Our affective processing mechanisms appear to be relatively insensitive to the question of whether the scenario under consideration is real, imagined, supposed, or denied. (To the extent that there is a difference in the intensity of our responses, this can largely be traced to a difference in the intensity of the stimulus.) (Cf. e.g. the literature surveyed in Damasio 1994 and Damasio 1999.) For discussion of this in the context of fictional emotions, see Gendler and Kovakovich 2005 (Ch. 11 above); Harris 2000; Schroeder and Matheson 2006.

[16] [19] This gives rise to a potential worry: that alief is not a fundamental mental state, but instead an amalgam of several more primitive mental states: those of entertaining content R, experiencing affect A, and activating behavioral repertoire B. I reply: the fact that our current vocabulary requires us to describe alief-content using three separate terms doesn't show that the state is an amalgam of three others. Indeed, one might even argue that it is out of these more primitive association patterns ("Mama, warmth and comfort, purse lips to drink") that the less fundamental differentiated attitudes like belief, desire, and imagination are constructed. These are cognitive attitudes that rely on the notion of *representation* (and misrepresentation), a distinction between seeming and being, one that is largely absent from the more primitive state of alief. I discuss this issue further in "Alief in Action" (Ch. 14 below), §1. (Thanks to Andy Egan for raising this concern.)

[17] [20] William James calls the principle that "the mere act of thinking about a behavior increase[s] the tendency to engage in that behavior" the *principle of ideomotor action.* He writes: "We may then lay it down for certain that every [mental] representation of a movement awakens in some degree the actual movement which is its object; and awakens it in a maximum degree whenever it is not kept from so doing by an antagonistic representation present simultaneously to the mind" (W. James 1890/1950). Or again: "Merely thinking about a behavior makes it more likely to occur, even if it is unintended...the mere act of thinking about a response, even when the thought involved is meant to help prevent the response, has the automatic effect of increasing the likelihood of that response" (Bargh, Chen, and Burrows 1996: 232, discussing work on "ironic processing" by Daniel Wegner).

(7)   Alief ... content ... [may be] activated ... *consciously or non-consciously.*

That is: a subject may (occurrently) alieve something with or without being aware of being (put) in such a state.

(8)   Alief ... content ... [may be] activated ... via *features of the subject's internal or ambient environment.*

That is: the activation of an alief may be the result either of (conscious or non-conscious) (quasi-)perception, or of (conscious or non-conscious) non-perceptual thought.[18]

(9)   Aliefs may be either *occurrent or dispositional.*[19]

A subject has an *occurrent alief* with representational-affective-behavioral content R-A-B when a cluster of dispositions to simultaneously entertain R-ish thoughts, experience A, and engage in B are activated—consciously or unconsciously—by some feature of the subject's internal or ambient environment. A subject has a *dispositional alief* with representational-affective-behavioral content R-A-B when there is some (potential) internal or external stimulus such that, were she to encounter it, it would cause her to occurrently alieve R-A-B.[20]

(10)   *Tentative* characterization ...

Despite all that I have said in this section, I continue to waver on whether it would be better to think of the term as two-place (S alieves R) rather than four-place (S alieves R-A-B) relation. Had I opted for the former, I might have introduced the expression as follows:

> S (occurrently) alieves R when S's R-related associations are activated and thereby rendered cognitively, affectively, and behaviorally salient.

In most of the discussion that follows, I will make use of the expression in its four-place version, occasionally noting cases where the two-place version seems more appropriate.[21]

---

[18]   [21] As John Bargh, Mark Chen, and Lara Burrows write: "Recent research has shown that attitudes and other affective reactions can be triggered automatically by the mere presence of relevant objects and events ... without conscious attention or awareness ... [They] then exert their influence on thought and behavior." (Bargh, Chen, and Burrows 1996: 230, citations omitted.)

[19]   [22] For discussion of this distinction in the case of belief, see H. H. Price 1960/1969; Armstrong 1973; Lycan 1986; Searle 1992; Audi 1994. (References thanks to Schwitzgebel 2006.)

[20]   [23] Obviously, there need to be some restrictions on what this causal relation looks like: the connection must be non-deviant, and the encounter must not in itself bring the dispositional alief into existence.

[21]   [*Note added in 2009*: For a few additional remarks on this issue, see "Alief in Action" (Ch. 14 below), §1.2.]

1.3. Examples and Usage

How does the terminology just introduced help us with our opening examples? Consider, for example, Rozin's subject who shows reluctance to put a piece of vomit-shaped rubber in her mouth. When the visual experience as of vomit awakens in the subject the entertainment of vomit-related trains of thought, the affective experience of disgust, and the activation of motor routines associated with behaviors like retreat and avoidance, Rozin's subjects come to *occurrently alieve* the representational-affective-behavioral content: "Vomit! Disgusting! Stay away!"[22] And anyone whose inclinations to feel disgust and avoidance would be activated by encountering a vomit-like visual stimulus (a class which for evolutionary reasons is likely to include nearly everyone) *dispositionally alieves* what Rozin's subjects occurrently alieve.

Of course, occurrently *alieving* "Vomit! Disgusting! Stay away!" is fully compatible with occurrently *believing* that there is no vomit in one's vicinity. An occurrent alief whose content is P may well be accompanied by an occurrent belief whose content includes not-P. Indeed, it is precisely when they are belief-discordant that aliefs tend to be evident to us. It is because Rozin's hesitating subjects occurrently believe something like: "the object in front of me is made of sterilized rubber and poses no risk to my health" that we need to explain their reluctance in terms of their alief. (Actually, I think that alief plays a major role in explaining behavior even when it is belief-concordant. But since the most convincing cases are those involving belief-discordant alief, I will focus primarily on those in making my initial argument.)

One final remark concerning usage. Given that I have opted for the four-place characterization, I need to say that Rozin's subjects occurrently alieve something like "Vomit! Disgusting! Stay away!" while believing that there is no vomit in their vicinity. Had I opted for the two-place characterization, I might have said instead: Rozin's subjects believe that the object before them is a piece of rubber, but they alieve that it is a mound of vomit. This usage seems particularly tempting in cases where the associational clusters are awakened by the presence of a particular object or situation, and where the associations awakened tend to be similar across individuals. Indeed, there is a natural tendency to loosen usage yet further, saying, for example, that visitors to the Skywalk believe that the glass surface is safe, but alieve that it is dangerous; that Rozin's dart-throwers believe that damaging the picture will not harm their loved one, but alieve that it will; that Rozin's shirt-avoiders believe that their enemy's laundered chemise is utterly harmless, but alieve that wearing it is ill-advised; that Charles believes that he is at no risk from the slime, but alieves

---

[22] [24] In fact it is likely that you right now—prompted by the associations set into play through imagining such a case—occurrently alieve something with similar (though decidedly milder) content.

that it is about to attack him. I consider it a live possibility that careful reflection on natural patterns of usage will reveal that I have made the wrong decision in opting for the four-place characterization. But for the time being, I will explore the advantages of employing the term in the way that I have characterized it thus far.

This ends the official introduction of the notion of alief. In the remainder of the essay, I do three things. In §2, I offer some brief additional general remarks about the relation between the state of alief and propositional attitudes such as belief, desire, and pretense. In §3, I offer a series of examples—drawn from recent empirical work in psychology—that played a central role in convincing me that appeal to the notion of alief is crucial if we wish to hold on to a notion like belief that relates to action in anything like the way philosophers have traditionally assumed. In §4, I close with a few speculative remarks about ways that appeal to the notion of alief may help us to make sense of two apparently unrelated phenomena: the tendency of examples to affect us in ways that abstract descriptions do not; and the role of habit in Aristotelian ethics.

2. Alief and Other Attitudes

2.1. Alief, Belief, and Imagination

Why can't alief be assimilated to one of the more familiar cognitive attitudes—belief, for example, or imagining? There are a number of reasons that I think that it cannot, which I will present in the remainder of this section.[23]

Alief differs from both imagining and believing along certain crucial dimensions. If I believe that P, I believe that it is true that P, and my belief is non-defective only if, as a matter of fact, it is true that P. If I suppose or imagine or pretend that P, I suppose or imagine or pretend that it is true that P, but the actual truth or falsity of P is explicitly irrelevant to my successfully supposing or imagining or pretending it to be. Both classes of states, then, involve what David Velleman helpfully calls *accepting* a proposition: to believe or imagine or suppose or pretend that P is to regard P as true (in some way).[24] But though they coincide in this dimension, they differ in another: whereas belief is *reality-sensitive*, supposition and imagination and pretense are explicitly *reality-insensitive*. It is this latter disparity that is typically taken to underlie

---

[23] [25] For additional discussion of the relation between alief and other attitudes, see "Alief in Action" (Ch. 14 below), §2.

[24] [26] He writes: "Regarding-as-true [is]...involved in...believing...[in] supposing or assuming, and in propositional imagining as well...To imagine that *p* is to regard *p* as describing how things are...Imagining is therefore a way of regarding a proposition as true—or, to introduce a term, a way of accepting a proposition" (Velleman 2000: 250). Note that Velleman's use of the term *acceptance* is somewhat different than that of L. Jonathan Cohen (1992) and Michael Bratman (1999b: 15–24).

one important difference between belief on the one hand, and supposition, imagination, and pretense on the other: whereas (modulo certain complications) we can imagine pretty much any content, we can (without acrobatics) believe only what we take to be true.

How does alief fare along these dimensions? Strictly speaking, it lies in another plane altogether. Believing and supposing and imagining and pretending are all (at least on certain uses of the expressions in question) propositional attitudes, whereas alieving (as I am provisionally using the expression) is not. But we can, by employing the "loose" usage adverted to above, make reasonable sense of the notion of alieving that P, and we can ask—keeping in mind that our usage is loose—whether alieving that P involves accepting that P. We will need to be a bit more careful when we ask whether alief is reality-sensitive or reality-insensitive, and whether we are in a position to alieve at will. But again, we will be able to draw certain fairly sharp contrasts between alief and other attitudes.

Let's begin with the question of acceptance. Does alieving that P involve accepting that P? (That is, does being an alief state with the content R-A-B involve regarding it as true in some way that R is part of one's real or imagined environment?[25]) Interestingly, the answer to this question turns out to be *no*, and the way in which it turns out to be *no* reveals something important about the nature of alief. Unlike belief or pretense or imagination or supposition, alief does not involve acceptance. Though the point can be made on conceptual grounds alone, it is helpful to begin with a specific example.

In a 1986 study by Paul Rozin, subjects saw "sugar poured into two bottles, and then applied labels of *sugar* and *sodium cyanide*, each to one of the bottles, making their own choice." Despite having applied the labels themselves, subjects "showed a reluctance to consume sugar from the cyanide labeled bottle" (Rozin, Markwith, and Ross 1990: 383; reporting results from Rozin, Millman, and Nemeroff 1986). So far, the case is a familiar one: while Rozin's subjects believed that both bottles contained sugar, consideration of the second rendered occurrent an alief state with the content "cyanide, dangerous, avoid" associated with the second bottle—and this belief-discordant alief played a role in governing their behavior.[26] Up to this point, there is no reason to posit a case of alief without acceptance: in alieving "cyanide, dangerous, avoid" the subject is regarding as true (perhaps in imagination) that the bottle contains cyanide.

The interesting case comes from a follow-up study four years later. In that study:

---

[25] [27] I am here skating over the difficult question of whether there is a uniform rule for stating what one (loosely) alieves when one (strictly) alieves R-A-B.

[26] [29] As Rozin reports, subjects "knew this response was foolish, but felt the reluctance anyway. This suggests a 'low-level' gut feeling, that can influence behavior in spite of countering cognitions" (Rozin, Markwith, and Ross 1990: 383; cf. also Rozin and Nemeroff (1990)).

Subjects faced two empty brown 500 ml bottles. In the presence of the subject, the experimenter opened a container of "Domino" cane sugar, and poured some into each bottle, so that about ¼ of each bottle was filled. The experimenter informed subjects that she was pouring sugar into each bottle. The experimenter then presented the subject with two typed labels. One had *not sodium cyanide, not poison* written on it, with a red skull and cross bones preceded by the word *not*. The other label had *sucrose, table sugar* typed on it. The subject was invited to put one label on each bottle, in any way he or she chose. The experimenter then set out two different colored plastic cups, one in front of each bottle, and poured unsweetened red (tropical punch) "Kool-Aid" from a glass pitcher into both, until they were about half full. Now, using separate, new plastic spoons for each bottle, the experimenter put a half spoonful of powder from one sugar bottle into the glass standing in front of that bottle, and repeated this with the other glass for the other sugar bottle. (Rozin, Markwith, and Ross 1990)

Subjects then faced the choice of drinking from the cup containing the sugar that had been labeled "sucrose, table sugar" or from the cup containing the sugar that had been labeled "not sodium cyanide, not poison." Though the effect was somewhat less pronounced than in the original study, subjects showed considerable reluctance to drink from the latter.

Here again, while Rozin's subjects believed that both bottles contained sugar, consideration of the second bottle rendered occurrent an alief state with the content "cyanide, dangerous, avoid." But in this case, the label read precisely the opposite: it "had *not sodium cyanide, not poison* written on it, with a red skull and cross bones preceded by the word *not*." So, although these subjects were in an alief state with the content "cyanide, dangerous, avoid," the content they were prompted to imagine was exactly the opposite. They did *not*—as the acceptance condition requires—regard it as true in some way that cyanide is to be found in the vicinity; instead, it was the negated presence of the word "cyanide" that rendered occurrent their cyanide-associated aliefs.

Can we explain this with the resources of only belief and imagining? Clearly, belief cannot do the work: it is implausible to suggest that the subject believed that the bottle she had labeled "not sodium cyanide, not poison" contained cyanide. But what about imagining? Can't we say that the source of the subject's hesitation is that she first imagines that the bottle does contain poison, and that she then somehow negates this, and that this enables her (perhaps in some special Sartrean fashion) to imagine the absence of poison?[27]

Perhaps this is indeed what happens. But how is this supposed to explain the subject's hesitancy to drink the liquid? Is the reason for her hesitancy supposed

---

[27] [30] As in the following joke. Jean-Paul Sartre was sitting in a café when a waitress approached him: "Can I get you something to drink, Monsieur Sartre?" Sartre replied, "Yes, I'd like a cup of coffee with sugar, but no cream." Nodding agreement, the waitress walked off to fill the order, returning a few minutes later. "I'm sorry, Monsieur Sartre," she said, "we are all out of cream—would you like your coffee with no milk instead?" (Taken with slight variation from <http://www.workjoke.com/projoke70.htm>.)

to be that she *had been imagining* that the bottle contained cyanide, though now she is not—and that what she imagined *in the past* (though fails to imagine now) somehow explains her action *at present*? Or that her current imagining that the bottle does not contain cyanide somehow contains within it (in not-fully-*aufgehoben* form) the antithetical imagining that the bottle does contain cyanide? And that somehow this negated semi-imagined content—content that she has, throughout the entire process, been fully consciously aware of explicitly disbelieving—sneaks into the control center for her motor routines and causes her to hesitate in front of the Kool-aid?

Really? Is this really what you think imagining is like? Or have you just described a case of belief-discordant (and imagination-discordant) alief: a case where the subject believes that the bottle does not contain cyanide, imagines that the bottle does not contain cyanide, yet has an occurrent alief with the content: cyanide, dangerous, avoid? Isn't it a lot more natural to describe this as a case of alief-motivated behavior than as a case of motivation by (past or negated) imagination? And if it is alief that is doing the explanatory work here, isn't it plausible that alief is doing the explanatory work in the cases above as well?

For those unconvinced by examples or lines of rhetorical questioning, there is a more general argument for why alief can occur without acceptance. At its core, alief involves the activation of an associative chain—and this is something that can happen regardless of the attitude that one bears to the content activating the associations. (Indeed, since alief may be activated non-consciously, one may bear towards that content no attitude at all.) This means that alief contexts are what we might call *hyperopaque*: they do not permit *salva veritate* substitution even of expressions that the subject explicitly recognizes to be co-referential.[28] Even if I believe that the phrases "not poison" and "safe to consume" pick out co-extensive classes of substances, even if I focus on that belief and hold it vividly before my mind, even if the synonymy of these two terms is crucial to my views about some other matter, still the aliefs activated by the two expressions may be wildly dissimilar.[29] Imagination, by contrast, is not hyperopaque in this way. If I explicitly recognize that P and Q are synonymous, and I imagine P while focusing explicitly on the co-referentiality of P and Q, then in imagining P I imagine Q. Alief just isn't imagination.

The same features that explain alief's hyperopacity and the possibility of alief without acceptance explain why we are not in a position to alieve at will. If I believe that P, and subsequently learn that not-P, I will revise my belief.

[28] [31] Note that they are not hyperopaque in a stronger sense: they *do* permit *salva veritate* substitution of expressions that the subject (loosely speaking) *alieves* to be co-referential. (Thanks to Dave Chalmers for pointing out this stronger reading.)

[29] [32] Likewise (in a slight variation on a Kantian theme), my triskaidekaphobia may be elicited by "13," but not by "7+6." This feature of alief will turn out to be important in the discussion in §4 below.

If I imagine that P, and subsequently learn that not-P, I will make no such revision. But what if I (loosely speaking) alieve that P, and subsequently learn that not-P? What happens then? At first glance, alief seems to behave like imagination and its kin: after all, the cases above are all cases where the subject truly and consciously believes P while actively alieving not-P. But this doesn't quite capture the full story. If I believe that P and imagine that not-P, I am violating no norms. But if I believe that P and alieve that not-P, something is amiss. Learning that not-P may well not cause me to cease alieving that P—but if it doesn't, then I'm violating certain norms of cognitive-behavioral coherence. No such criticism is possible in the analogous case of imagining.

If action is supposed to be responsive to reality, then the well-functioning aliever is one whose aliefs and beliefs largely coincide (or one whose ability to suppress contrary impulse is strong[30]). But alief just isn't reality-sensitive in the way belief is. Its content doesn't track (one's considered impression of) the world. At the same time, it's not reality-insensitive in the way that imagination is. For while we can (for the most part) imagine at will, we do not seem to have the same sort of freedom in alief.[31] We may be relatively unconstrained in which of our dispositional aliefs we render occurrent—at least in the case of those aliefs that can be rendered occurrent through contemplation alone—but we are far from unconstrained in which dispositional aliefs we have in the first place. Our dispositional aliefs depend on the associational patterns that have been laid down in our minds as the result of our experiences and those of our genetic ancestors. We are not in a position to generate such patterns of association merely at will.

So it looks like, just as it is (something close to) *conceptually* impossible to believe at will, it is *practically* impossible to alieve at will. Of course, in both cases we might use all sorts of tricks to bring ourselves to be in a certain sort of mental state—"roundabout routes" involving processes that we ourselves deliberately initiate.[32] But if we use such tricks to cultivate beliefs, we need to cover our tracks;[33] if we use them to cultivate aliefs, we can do so under conditions of full disclosure.

This concludes the brief survey contrasting alief with attitudes like belief and imagining. We now turn to the second issue of this section, the relation between these attitudes and the bringing about of behavior. I will suggest that

---

[30] [33] As William James writes: "To make our nervous system our ally instead of our enemy...we must make automatic and habitual, as early as possible, as many useful actions as we can" (W. James 1890/1950: 122).

[31] [34] It is the reality-sensitivity of belief that is typically taken to explain the impossibility of believing at will. Cf. B. Williams 1970/1973a for a classic articulation of this view. (Thanks to Ted Sider for suggesting that I consider this issue in the context of alief.)

[32] [35] Cf. B. Williams 1970/1973a; for instructions, see Pascal 1669/1966.

[33] [36] For traditional discussions in addition to B. Williams 1970/1973a, see Winters 1979; Bennett 1990; cf. Cook 1987. There has been a recent resurgence of interest in these issues: see e.g. Pettit and Smith 1996; Noordhof 2001; Steup 2008; and essays cited therein.

alief's special structure—its being a mental state with affective, representational, and behavioral content that is activated by features of the environment—means that it poses especially severe problems for behavioral accounts of belief.

2.2. Alief and Behavior

According to what David Velleman has dubbed the "purely motivational view of belief," "all that's necessary for an attitude to qualify as a belief is that it disposes the subject to behave in certain ways that would promote the satisfaction of his desires if its content were true. An attitude's tendency to cause behavioral output is thus conceived as sufficient to make it a belief" (Velleman 2000: 255).[34] Or, again: to believe that P is to be disposed to act in ways that would tend to satisfy one's desires, whatever they are, in a world in which P (together with one's other beliefs) were true (Stalnaker 1984/1987:15; cf. Dennett 1971).

There are at least three sorts of marginal cases where this sort of analysis seems to go awry—two that pose problems for necessity, the third for sufficiency. The first sort are cases where (arguably) a subject believes that P, but where this belief does not bring with it a disposition to act in P-concordant ways because of some feature of the subject. (Think, for example, of an immutable omniscient contemplative God, a permanent paralytic, a subject built to act with utter randomness, a character under an unbreakable spell that causes him to act contrary to his first-order intentions, a hopeless akratic, or an agent who aims always to deceive.) The second are cases where (arguably) a subject believes that P, but where this belief does not bring with it a disposition to act in P-concordant ways because the belief itself has no behavioral implications. (Think, for example, of a subject who believes in causally inert invisible goblins, or of a subject who believes that she inhabits a space that is distorted but Euclidian (rather than undistorted but non-Euclidian).[35]) The third are cases where, although the subject is disposed to act in the requisite ways, she nonetheless fails to believe that P because she lacks beliefs (either locally or globally). (Think, for example, of a super-stoic who acts and has desires but always withholds assent, or of a hyper-Van Fraassenite who extends his constructivist commitments to the realm of the observable.)

Five-finger exercises that they are, these marginal cases don't show that there is anything deeply wrong about the motivational view. All that's needed to

---

[34] [37] Velleman rejects this view, for reasons related to the ones discussed here, but notes that the view has been widely endorsed, by philosophers as diverse as R. B. Braithwaite (1932–3); David Armstrong (1973); W. V. Quine and J. S. Ullian (1978); Robert Stalnaker (1984/1987); Lynn Rudder Baker (1995); and Daniel Dennett (1971, 1995).

[35] [39] If you are worried about verbal reports counting as behavior, add the requisite caveat that they never speak about this particular belief.

avoid them are a few tweaks to the notion of disposition and a reiteration of the irrelevance of mental states. The big guns come loaded with a different sort of ammunition: not with the suggestion that the view is wrong in certain far-fetched contrived cases, but with the assertion that it is problematic through and through because a wide range of attitudes—among them acceptance (Bratman), imagination (Currie, Velleman), and pretense (Doggett and Egan, Velleman)—may motivate P-concordant behavior.[36]

Even here, I think there is room for the defender of a neo-behaviorist account. Restrict yourself to non-deviant subjects, and retreat, say, to betting behavior or high-stakes situations. Once again, you can save the letter of the view that belief and behavior go hand in hand.

To some extent, this strategy works for alief as well. (If it didn't, it would be hard to maintain that the paradigmatic cases above are ones in which the subject believes that P but has an alief whose content centrally includes not-P.) H. H. Price, whose underappreciated discussion of related examples deserves more detailed attention than I have space for here, employs such a strategy. Defending his account of a case of what he calls "half-belief," Price writes:

> It might be suggested that the man who avoids walking under ladders does just *believe* (however unreasonably) that walking under ladders has bad consequences…After all, these people act as if they believed, and they often go to considerable trouble in consequence. They step off the pavement into a muddy street or even into a street full of traffic, to avoid the ladder…Moreover they show the emotional symptoms of belief, for example, discomfort or unrest if there is…no way of avoiding the ladder…Of course, these people will not admit that they…believe these propositions; not even to themselves, and still less in public…But one may hold beliefs…without admitting to oneself that one holds them. (H. H. Price 1960/1969: 310)

Price rejects this account—a proposal, he suggests, to "dispense with the concept of half-belief altogether"—because, while

> no doubt there are some who do wholly believe that their chances of suffering misfortunes are increased if they walk under a ladder…I do not think that this is the usual situation…the ordinary person who avoids walking under ladders does not seriously believe that walking under ladders does any harm, or at any rate he does not believe it with complete seriousness. We notice that if it is very important for him to get to his destination quickly (for example, if he will miss a train if he does not hurry) he does not seem to mind the ladder at all. He sees it—there it is, in front of his nose—but he goes straight under it without hesitation. He himself, if he thinks about his experience afterwards, will be able to notice that he felt no qualms at all about doing the thing which he ordinarily avoids so carefully. (H. H. Price 1960/1969: 310–11)

---

[36] [40] See Bratman 1999; Currie 2002; Velleman 2000; Doggett and Egan 2007. For my own take on these issues, see "On the Relation between Pretense and Belief," "Self-Deception as Pretense," and "Imaginative Contagion" (Chs. 7, 8, and 12 above).

"A half-belief," he concludes, is "something which is 'thrown-off' when circumstances alter... [I]n some contexts to which the proposition is relevant one is in a belief-like state about it, but in other contexts to which it is equally relevant one disbelieves it or disregards it." This is so even though "in both sorts of contexts, the evidence for the proposition... remains the same, and the probability of the proposition is as great, or as little, as it was before" (H. H. Price 1960/1969: 312).

I agree with Price that the ladder case might well proceed as he describes. But I'm not so clear that his analysis will work for the cases presented on the opening pages. Suppose it is very important for me to get to my train, but that the station lies across a chasm fifty feet wide and 1,000 feet deep, bridged by a transparent glass walkway. Even if I "will miss a train if [I do] not hurry," I don't think it's true that I would "not seem to mind the [apparent chasm] at all," crossing it "without hesitation" even though the visual stimulus is "right under my nose." I very much doubt that in "think[ing] about [my] experience afterwards," I would "be able to notice that [I] felt no qualms at all about doing the thing which [I] ordinarily avoid so carefully." (Indeed, in my own case, I'm not sure I could make it across the bridge at all without closing my eyes—which would be, of course, to suspend the occurrent alief by eleminating my encounter with the feature that activates it.)

Suppose we raise the stakes. My child is on the other side of the chasm, and I need desperately to reach him to prevent some dreadful occurrence. Here I suspect I could make it across the bridge—eyes open—to perform the rescue: after all, I believe that he is in danger, and I believe that the bridge is safe. But even here, the hesitation would not fully dissipate. And not because I doubt in any way that the surface is sturdy: I see others walking across it and am about to do so myself. I am 100 percent certain that I will make it safely—as certain as I would be if the chasm were only five feet deep, as certain as I would be if the bridge were made of opaque material. Still, I hesitate; still, I shudder. My behavior reflects something other than my belief. It is my alief in action.

The reason Price's explanation fails for our paradigm cases is that the mechanisms they exploit are not under our rational control. We are not in a position to "throw them off... when circumstances alter." This is not because we are in doubt about what we believe. There is no question in my mind that the fudge has not been transformed into dog feces; there are few things of which I am more certain than that hurling darts at a photo of my baby will do no harm to the baby itself. Still—even in high-stakes situations—there is a hesitation in my belief-concordant actions.[37]

---

[37] [41] Of course, I may become accustomed to performing the alief-averse action, and my hesitation may dissipate. But this is a way of changing alief (by creating new patterns of representational-affective-behavioral association patterns)—not a way of "throwing it off."

The problem with the belief–behavior picture is that at its heart lies a faulty picture of what makes us act.[38] I do not doubt that the account could be made extensionally adequate: limit the cases that count as "behavior" in the relevant sense, fuss with the notion of disposition, make the fate of the world depend on the subject's actions. Belief and behavior can be made to match up, so long as one is free to make relevant alterations from both directions. But deep down, the account misses something very important about human behavior. This is something to which both Aristotle and Hume were especially well attuned (I will return to this in the final section), and which contemporary psychology has begun to explore in detail. It is to cases from the latter domain that I turn in the next section.

3. Automaticity

Recent work on "automaticity" has produced a remarkable series of widely publicized results suggesting that alief plays a larger role in behavior than many had thought. Indeed, one of the main projects in social psychology over the last two decades has been to document systematically the ways that behavior-inducing mental representations may be activated by awakening the associative patterns that have come to be linked with some object, stereotype, protocol, or mental image.[39] A few examples will suffice for giving a sense of their flavor. But it is important for the reader to realize that this is a massive research program and that while it may be possible to come up with alternative explanations for one or another of the examples I discuss, the basic phenomenon I am describing here has been established beyond any reasonable doubt in hundreds of published studies.[40]

Much of the work in this area has been pioneered by John Bargh and his colleagues, who, in a typical task, present subjects with some sort of association-inducing stimulus. This is often a "scrambled sentence" task—a standard

---

[38] [42] A nice recent defense of such an account can be found in Funkhouser and Spaulding (2009) where they defend what they call the "Belief-Desire Thesis: For every intentional action, there is a belief-desire pair that both causes and rationalizes that intentional action." [*Reference updated 2009.*]

[39] [43] I discuss these and related cases in greater detail in Gendler 2006a (Ch. 12 above); some of the material in this section draws on the discussion in that essay. In the earlier essay, I suggested that these cases were examples of a phenomenon that I called "imaginative contagion." I now think that the phenomenon that I identified there is a special case of an alief-like phenomenon. Readers interested in additional examples of these sorts of cases may find them in that essay, and in the works cited therein.

[40] [44] I am gliding over many important distinctions about exactly which sorts of primes tend to generate which sorts of responses: whether they tend to elicit assimilation or contrast, whether they involve goals or non-goals, etc. In a full-fledged account of alief, it will be important to address these subtleties in proper detail.

technique in psychology used to "prime" particular concepts.[41] In one such study, subjects faced one of three conditions: either the collections of words from which they were asked to form sentences contained only neutral terms, or they also contained a number of terms associated either with politeness (e.g. respect, honor, considerate, patiently, courteous) or rudeness (e.g. aggressively, bother, disturb, intrude, brazen). Subjects were instructed that, after completing the task, they should come out into the hallway and find the experimenter, who would then give them the next task to complete. When they emerged, they found the experimenter engaged in a conversation with another "subject" (actually a confederate), a conversation that continued either until the first subject interrupted the conversation, or until ten minutes had passed.

The action-patterns of the three groups differed markedly. Of those who had been primed with the rudeness concept, most interrupted in the allotted time; those in the neutral condition interrupted in less than half of the cases; whereas those in the polite condition interrupted in almost none of the cases (Bargh, Chen, and Burrows 1996: 236).

One *might* maintain that the various groups differ in their beliefs, or that they differ in their desires, or that the subject's interruption of the experimenter is not an action of the sort that belief–desire explanations are designed to cover. I have no doubt that such a story could be told. One might say, for instance, that all three groups share the same desire—to interrupt the experimenter only if doing so would be socially acceptable—but that they differ in their belief about whether it is. (Note that this would involve attributing to the subjects an odd sort of belief—one that is formed as the result of mechanisms that are not themselves sensitive to any subject-independent truth attitudes.[42]) Alternatively, one might try to explain the phenomenon in terms of imagination or pretense. Perhaps engaging in the scrambled sentence task causes the subjects to fantasize that the experimenter is rude or polite—or that they themselves are

---

[41] [45] In such a task, subjects are presented with a list containing a number of five-word sets, and asked to come up with a sentence for each set that contains at least four of the designated words. So, for example, one such set might contain the words "snow, roof, cat, cheerful, red" and the subject might write: "The cat stood in the snow atop the red roof." For original presentation of the scrambled sentence task see Srull and Wyer 1979, 1980. For discussion of priming see (*concept*) Storms 1958; (*term*) Segal and Cofer 1960; (*discussion*) Neely 1997; (*review*) Toth and Reingold 1996.

[42] [47] For either there is no fact of the matter whether interruption in such circumstances is socially acceptable (in which case there is no truth for the mechanisms to be sensitive to), or there is a fact of the matter, which is either dependent on or independent of the subject's attitudes in the situation. If it is independent of those, then the belief-forming mechanism is clearly truth-insensitive, for the three groups using the same mechanism respond in three different ways to the same scenario. (See next note.) And if it is dependent on those attitudes—say: interrupting is socially unacceptable iff the interrupter takes it to be socially unacceptable—then the belief–desire explanation to which we are appealing becomes close to vacuous. (This is not to deny that there are all sorts of interesting instances of self-fulfilling beliefs and assessment-dependent attitudes. But subliminal primes altering perceptions of rudeness are hardly instances of the *Cogito*.)

rude or polite—and, carried away by this fantasy, perhaps they begin to act as if it were true. Perhaps.[43] But why would engaging in the scrambled sentence task cause the subjects to engage in this sort of fantasy (unless, of course, the explanation runs through something like the notion of alief)? And even if we have an answer to that question, why would engaging in such a fantasy make them act as if it were true (again, unless the explanation runs through something like alief)?

Rather, what Bargh and his colleagues have done, I want to argue, is to induce in their different sets of subjects different sorts of occurrent alief. As the result of the pre- or quasi-conscious activation of the cluster of affective tendencies and behavioral repertoires associated with the notion of rudeness, subjects in the third condition find themselves more likely to act in ways in which they would act in the presence of rudeness; as the result of the pre- or quasi-conscious activation of the cluster of affective tendencies and behavioral repertoires associated with the notion of politeness, subjects in the second condition find themselves more likely to act in ways in which they would act in the presence of politeness (Bargh, Chen, and Burrows 1996).[44]

Nor is this an isolated anomaly. Example after example reveals the subtle role of alief in guiding behavior. In another widely publicized Bargh experiment, subjects performed a scrambled sentence task in which one group confronted sentences containing terms associated with the elderly (e.g. wrinkle, bingo, and retired), whereas the second group's unscrambling task involved only neutral terms. After completing the experiment, subjects were surreptitiously timed as they walked down the hall to the elevator. Those primed with the elderly stereotype took significantly longer to walk to the elevator than those who had not been so primed.[45]

---

[43] [48] Actually, there is experimental evidence suggesting that the behavior is not the result of any sort of conscious process. "To assess whether the priming manipulation had resulted in different perception of the experimenter's politeness," Bargh, Chen, and Burrows (1996) "examined the ratings participants made on a scale where they were explicitly asked to rate the experimenter's degree of politeness." They found "no reliable difference in the ratings made in the three priming conditions"—all three groups ranked him as neither especially polite nor especially impolite. They continue: the "fact that the behavioral measure showed quite strong effects of the priming manipulation, whereas the effect on the judgment measurement was nonexistent, argues against the . . . interpretation . . . that the priming manipulation affected consciously made judgments about the experimenter, which then determined behavioral responses to him. The results instead point to a direct effect on behavior that is not mediated by conscious perceptual or judgment processes" (Bargh, Chen, and Burrows, 1996: 235).

[44] [49] Of course, subjects in the first (neutral) condition also have various aliefs rendered occurrent, but none that systematically affects the likelihood of their interrupting the experimenter; they are like the visually induced aliefs associated with stepping onto the back porch (as opposed to the Skywalk); they are present, but we do not need to appeal to them to explain otherwise discordant behavior.

[45] [50] For discussion of how these results can be reconciled with neuropsychological evidence suggesting that simple motor actions are impervious to high-level mental processes such as stereotype activation, see Banfield *et al.* 2003.

It seems implausible (to say the least) that Bargh's elderly-primed subjects *believed* that they had suddenly turned into a bunch of senior citizens who needed to dawdle lest they overtax themselves. It seems slightly less absurd to suggest that Bargh's elderly-primed subjects *imagined* themselves as old—or imagined someone else who is old—and, having so imagined, began to act in some ways as if the imagined content should govern their own actual behavior. But even this is a rather far-fetched explanation.[46] (Among other things, in well-designed scrambled sentence tasks, subjects remain unconscious of the fact that a particular notion is being primed.[47]) Rather, I want to suggest, Bargh's elderly-primed subjects *alieved* something like: "Old. Tired. Be careful walking to that elevator . . . "—and the activation of this behavioral repertoire made them more likely to act in accord with it.

Additional research within this paradigm has reinforced and expanded the lessons of these early experiments. So, for example, showing suitably primed subjects a picture of a library leads them to speak in quieter tones; showing them an image of an elegant dining room—or exposing them to the smell of soap—leads them to eat more neatly (Aarts and Dijksterhuis 2003). Subliminal visual priming with an image of an African-featured face leads subjects to respond more aggressively to certain sorts of provocation (Bargh, Chen, and Burrows 1996). Priming subjects with thoughts of their (achievement-oriented) mother leads them to persist longer at word-find tasks; priming them with thoughts of a friend makes them more likely to help a stranger (Fitzsimmons and Bargh 2003).

Indeed, alief may be activated in even more striking ways. Recently, psychologist Lawrence Williams "hypothesized that a simple experience of physical, spatial distance would trigger feelings of psychological distance and that those feelings, in turn, allow people to enjoy aversive media." Subjects were first asked to plot a pair of points on a Cartesian plane: the points were either quite close to one another (occupying less than ¼ of the plane) or quite far apart.

All the participants then read an embarrassing passage from a novel—in which a woman opens a magazine to find that her ex-boyfriend has written an article about her, called "Loving a Larger Woman"—and rated how much they enjoyed the story. Just as Williams had expected, the participants who drew the dots far apart liked the passage more.

In his next study, after the volunteers drew the dots, they read a book excerpt in which a man beats his brother with a rock after a car crash. When the readers rated their emotional experience, Williams found, people who were told to

---

[46] [51] Though one that I tacitly appealed to in my discussion of this case in "Imaginative Contagion" (Ch. 12 above).

[47] [52] In this particular case, "inspection of the responses" to a similar priming task "revealed that only 1 of the 19 participants showed any awareness of the relationship between the stimulus words and the elderly stereotype" (Bargh, Chen, and Burrows 1996: 237).

draw the dots close together reported feeling more negative emotions (Shulman 2007).[48]

In all of these cases, it is perhaps possible to explain what is going on in familiar terminology. Perhaps Bargh's interruption subjects imagine that there is rudeness afoot in their dominion, and adjust their behavior accordingly. (Really? Even though the priming takes place at the unconscious level?) Perhaps his elevator subjects imagine that they are old and gray and full of sleep, and consequently slow their pace. Perhaps Williams's subjects imagine that they are far away from the stories they hear, and therefore feel their emotional tug less strongly.

Perhaps. Or perhaps what is happening in each of these cases is the activation of a low-level cluster of associations—representational, affective, behavioral—an activation that renders the subject more likely to exhibit behavior of a certain sort. To a reasonable approximation, it looks like all depictive representations—even those that we explicitly disavow as false—feed into our behavioral repertoires, and that it is only through a process of conscious or habit-governed inhibition that representations whose accuracy we endorse come to play a distinctive role in governing our actions.

If so, there is something deeply wrong about the traditional picture of the relation between belief and behavior that we discussed in §2. But of course, the belief-behaviour picture is not the only way philosophers have thought about these matters. In the final section, I briefly examine one competing philosophical strand.

4. Alief, Persuasion, and Habit

Despite certain protestations to the contrary, philosophers have been exquisitely sensitive to the ways in which contemplation of an imaginary particular may have cognitive and motivational effects that differ from those evoked by an abstract description of an otherwise similar state of affairs.[49] (Think of Plato's cave, the ring of Gyges, twin earth, the Chinese room, teletransportation, Thomson's violinist, the veil of ignorance, Mr. Truetemp, the fat man on the bridge, and any of the myriad other examples.) A particularly vivid presentation of this claim can be found in Hume's *Treatise on Human Nature*, where Hume writes:

---

[48] [56] In addition to showing greater enjoyment of embarrassing media and less emotional distress from violent media, distant-dot drawers offered lower estimations of calories in unhealthy food, and weaker reports of emotional attachments to family members (Williams and Bargh 2008).

[49] [57] I discuss this issue in more detail in "Philosophical Thought Experiments, Intuitions and Cognitive Equilibrium" (Ch. 6 above). The discussion in the next three paragraphs draws on the discussion from the opening pages of that essay.

There is a noted passage in the history of Greece, which may serve for our present purpose. Themistocles told the Athenians, that he had form'd a design, which wou'd be highly useful to the public, but which 'twas impossible for him to communicate to them without ruining the execution, since its success depended entirely on the secrecy with which it shou'd be conducted. The Athenians, instead of granting him full power to act as he thought fitting, order'd him to communicate his design to Aristides, in whose prudence they had an entire confidence, and whose opinion they were resolv'd blindly to submit to. The design of Themistocles was secretly to set fire to the fleet of all the Grecian common-wealths, which was assembled in a neighbouring port, and which being once destroy'd wou'd give the Athenians the empire of the sea without any rival. Aristides return'd to the assembly, and told them, that nothing cou'd be more advantageous than the design of Themistocles but at the same time that nothing cou'd be more unjust: Upon which the people unanimously rejected the project. (Hume 1739/1978, II. iii. 6. 4)

Hume goes on to note that his contemporary, the widely read French historian Charles Rollin, found it astounding that the Athenians would reject—merely on grounds of injustice—a strategy so "advantageous" that it would give them "the empire of the sea without any rival." Indeed, Rollin suggests, the episode is "one of the most singular that is any where to be met with," revealing a truly astonishing sense of justice among the Athenian people.

Hume, by contrast, is unmoved:

For my part I see nothing so extraordinary in this proceeding of the Athenians.... [T]ho' in the present case the advantage was immediate to the Athenians, yet as it was known only under the general notion of advantage, without being conceiv'd by any particular idea, it must have had a less considerable influence on their imaginations, and have been a less violent temptation, than if they had been acquainted with all its circumstances: Otherwise 'tis difficult to conceive, that a whole people, unjust and violent as men commonly are, shou'd so unanimously have adher'd to justice, and rejected any consid-erable advantage. (Hume 1739/1978, II. iii. 6. 4)

Hume's story brings out the way in which engagement of the cognitive me-chanisms associated with vivid imagining may lead a subject to reverse a prior commitment, selecting as preferable the option previously rejected, and shun-ning the option previously embraced.[50]

For the reader who has gotten this far, it should be apparent what lesson I want to draw from this case. Ever sensitive to the role of habit and association—"If any thing can intitle the author to so glorious a name as that of an inventor, 'tis the use he makes of the principle of the association of ideas" (Hume 1739/1978: "Abstract," 661–2)—Hume is here pointing out that judgment about a particular case may be driven as much by alief as by belief. Like his K Street counterpart, Hume recognizes the citizen who believes that wealth should be

---

[50] [59] In the essay on thought experiments (Ch. 6 above), I go on to explore how this phenomenon might help explain both the effectiveness and the limitations of philosophical thought experiments.

redistributed across generations alieves that the death tax is unfair; like his Madison Avenue foil, Hume recognizes that a customer who believes that a $9.99 scarf costs nearly ten dollars alieves that it costs only nine. When the citizen votes against the amendment does this show that he really opposes redistribution? Or does it show that action is often governed by alief?

If the latter, then Aristotle is right: In order to live well, we must work to bring our habits in accord with our reflective beliefs:[51]

Men become builders by building and lyre-players by playing the lyre; so too we become just by doing just acts, temperate by doing temperate acts, brave by doing brave acts ... states of character arise out of like activities ... It makes no small difference, then, whether we form habits of one kind or of another from our very youth; it makes a very great difference, or rather all the difference.[52] (Aristotle, *Nicomachean Ethics*, 1103–4)

My conclusion should not be a surprising one. I think that alief governs all sorts of belief-discordant behavior—the cases with which I began the essay, and the ones that I have presented along the way. But if alief drives behavior in belief-discordant cases, it is likely that it drives behavior in belief-concordant cases as well. Belief plays an important role in the ultimate regulation of behavior. But it plays a far smaller role in moment-by-moment management than philosophical tradition has tended to stress.[53]

---

[51] [61] For exploration of this connection in a related context, see the final paragraph in Cook 1987. Cf. also Burnyeat 1980; Pollard 2006.

[52] [62] Somewhat simplistically, one might say that Aristotelian ethics is an ethics of alief, whereas Kantian ethics is an ethics of belief. I hope to explore this issue in more detail in further work.

[53] [*] *Acknowledgements*: I am grateful to the Yale faculty lunch group for comments on a very early draft of this essay, and to audiences at Princeton University (Mar. 2007), the Central APA Chicago (Apr. 2007), and the *Mind & Language* Pretense Conference at University College London (June 2007) for excellent questions, comments, objections, and suggestions regarding the talk that served as its immediate predecessor. For more recent discussion and comments, I thank John Bargh, Paul Bloom, Richard Brooks, Carolyn Caine, David Chalmers, Greg Currie, Paul Davies, Andy Egan, Roald Nashi, Elliot Paul, Eric Schwitzgebel, Ted Sider, Jason Stanley, Zoltán Gendler Szabó, and Jonathan Weinberg.

14

Alief in Action (and Reaction)

In this essay, I offer further discussion of the cognitive state that I call *alief*, which was introduced in "Alief and Belief" (Ch. 13). An alief is, to a reasonable approximation, an innate or habitual propensity to respond to an apparent stimulus in a particular way.

I contend that recognizing the role that alief plays in our cognitive repertoire provides a framework for understanding reactions that are governed by non-conscious or automatic mechanisms, which in turn brings into proper relief the role played by reactions that are subject to conscious regulation and deliberate control.

More specifically, I argue that thinking about the mind in terms of alief brings out the connection between a number of otherwise apparently discrepant issues—including fictional emotions, heuristics-based errors, and residual racism—and renders unmysterious a number of otherwise perplexing phenomena—for example, certain superstitions. And I contend that by directing philosophical attention to responses that are governed by habit and instinct, it encourages a new appreciation of a number of important insights from the ancient and early modern traditions, particularly those related to self-regulation and morality.

This essay and its predecessor—"Alief and Belief" (Ch. 13)—form a natural pair and are best read together. Because I have tried to make each piece self-standing, there is inevitably some overlap between them. But I have tried to keep this to a minimum.

Suggestions for how partial readings of the two essays can be fruitfully combined can be found on the opening page of the previous chapter.

***

This essay was first published in *Mind and Language*, 23/5 (2008), 552–85, and is reprinted here with the kind permission of Wiley-Blackwell. The essay appears in its original form; changes have been limited to correction of minor typographical errors, the insertion of remarks in footnotes (noted as such), and the reconfiguration of citations to bring reference conventions into line with other essays in the volume. As a result of reformatting, some footnote numbers have changed. The original number of each footnote is noted in [square brackets].

> Certain complex actions are of direct or indirect service under certain states of the mind, in order to relieve or gratify certain sensations, desires, &c.; and whenever the same state of mind is induced, however feebly, there is a tendency through the force of habit and association for the same movements to be performed, though they may not then be of the least use.
>
> Charles Darwin, "The principle of serviceable associated Habits"
> (Darwin 1898: 28)

0. Introduction

A frog laps up the metal birdshot pellet past its tongue. A puppy bats at the "young dog" in the mirror in front of him. A sports fan watching a televised rerun of a baseball game loudly encourages her favorite player to remain on second base. A cinema-goer watching a horror film "emits a shriek and clutches desperately at his chair." A man suspended safely in an iron cage above a cliff "trembl[es] when he surveys the precipice below him." An avowed anti-racist exhibits differential startle responses when Caucasian and African faces are flashed before her eyes.

In each of these cases, an experience or behavior is elicited that violates an apparent norm. At least in some sense of "should," the dog *should* yelp only at an actual dog, the cinema-goer *should* exhibit fear only in the face of actual danger, the anti-racist *should* react similarly to members of different racial groups. (Whether this is the same sense of *should* is an issue that I will return to later in the essay.) Moreover, in each of these cases, there is no easy way for the agent to override the norm-violating tendency. "Frogs continue to snap at (and ingest) bee-bees even when they have plenty of evidence that the bee-bees they're snapping at aren't flies" (Fodor 1999).[1] The sports fan will feel the temptation to shout at the screen even if she emphatically reminds herself that she is watching a rerun. And the caged "man ... cannot forbear trembling ... tho' he knows himself to be perfectly secure from falling, by his experience of the solidity of the iron, which supports him" (Hume 1739/1978: 148).

My goal in this essay is to offer a general account of these sorts of recalcitrant norm-discordant responses. In each of these cases, I will contend, the reactions in question are best understood as resulting from a mental state that I will call *alief*. An alief is, to a reasonable approximation, an innate or habitual propensity to respond to an apparent stimulus in a particular way. Recognizing the role that alief plays in our cognitive repertoire brings out the connection between a number of otherwise apparently discrepant issues, and renders unmysterious a number of otherwise perplexing phenomena. By providing a framework for understanding reactions that are governed by non-conscious or automatic

---

[1] [1] Indeed, as Fodor remarks, it's not "just that frogs sometimes go for bee-bees ... they are prepared to go on going for bee-bees *forever* " (Fodor 1999: 241).

mechanisms, it brings reactions that are subject to conscious regulation and deliberate control into proper relief. And by directing philosophical attention to responses that are governed by habit and instinct, it encourages a new appreciation of a number of important insights from the ancient and early modern traditions.

0.1. Overview

The essay has four main sections. In the first and second, I offer a general account of alief. I present a number of examples of alief, enumerate its key characteristics, and explain the ways in which alief is like and unlike classic mental states like belief, desire, and imagination. I also distinguish among various kinds of alief, bringing out the ways that aliefs resulting from innate propensities do and do not differ from aliefs resulting from acquired habits, and considering the implications this has for the account that I am offering.

In the third, I turn to a discussion of norm-concordant and norm-discordant aliefs. When a subject's environment is stable, typical, and desirable, and the subject is attentive to its relevant features, her salient occurrent aliefs will be largely in accord with her occurrent reality-reflective attitudes (that is, beliefs and their teleofunctional analogues). But when a subject's environment is unstable, atypical, or undesirable, or when a subject is reality-inattentive in certain ways, her salient occurrent aliefs will come apart from her occurrent reality-reflective attitudes. Sometimes this discord is deliberate and welcome: daydreaming, roller-coasters, and therapy all exploit our capacity for belief-discordant alief. But sometimes this discord is inadvertent and unwelcome: superstition, phobias, and bad habits are all supported by the same capacity. In the third section, I discuss these issues.

In the final section, I turn to the topic of how we might regulate and respond to discordant alief in cases where discord is unwelcome. As beings who are simultaneously embodied and capable of rational agency, the challenge is one that we face repeatedly. This has not gone unnoticed. It is the challenge that the ancients explored when they considered the problem of *harmonizing the parts of the soul*,[2] and that the moderns discussed when they examined the *conflict*

---

[2] [3] Examples include the following: Plato: *Gorgias* 492d–494e; *Republic*, Bks. 4–10, esp. 434d–445b, 601b–606e and 611a–612a; *Timaeus* 34b–37c, 41a–44d, 69a–72d; *Phaedrus* 245c–256e (all in Plato 1997, ed. Cooper). Aristotle: *Nicomachean Ethics*, Bks. 1. 13 and 7. 1–10, 10. 6–8; *On the Soul*, Bk. 1. 1, 3 (esp. 3. 9) (all in Aristotle 1984, trans. Barnes). Alcinous: *Handbook*, chs. 23–5 (in Alcinous 1993). Galen: *On the doctrines of Hippocrates and Plato*, esp. Bks. 3–6 (in Galen and De Lacy 162–176 CE 2005). Plutarch: *On the generation of the soul in the Timaeus* (in Plutarch 1976). Plotinus: e.g. *Enneads* 1. 1, 1. 2, 4. 3 (in Plotinus 1984). (Many thanks to Charles Brittain and Verity Harte for guidance on these sources.) It is also a major theme in Confucian ethics. The ancient (3rd c. BCE) Chinese philosopher Xunzi (sometimes transliterated "Hsun-tzu"), for example, advocates the view that the sage is one whose second nature is in accord with virtue. (Thanks to Eric Schwitzgebel for alerting me to the Chinese literature.)

between reason and the passions.[3] And it is one that contemporary cognitive and social psychology (among other disciplines) have been exploring under many rubrics—both behavioral and neurological. Crudely put, there are two strategies for regulating alief. One—stressed by Aristotle among others (especially in the *Nicomachean Ethics*)—involves the cultivation of alternative habits through deliberate rehearsal. The other—stressed by Descartes among others (especially in the *Passions of the Soul*)—involves the refocusing of attention through directed imagination. Both of these strategies have important analogues in the contemporary literature on racism. In the final section of the essay, I offer some preliminary remarks on this topic.

0.2. Two Caveats

Two final caveats. This project is provisional in several senses. First: I make no claim to alief's being a fundamental mental category, one that will be part of our "final theory" of how the mind makes sense of the world. Rather, I am making a parity argument: that any theory that makes appeal to notions like belief, desire, and pretense in order to explain behavior needs to make appeal to (something like) alief in order to make sense of a wide range of otherwise perplexing phenomena. Introducing the notion of alief into our descriptive repertoire provides a useful alternative way of answering "why?" questions when confronted with a behavior or tendency that we seek to explain. It provides an alternative that falls somewhere in between a classic reason-based explanation (of the sort offered by belief/desire accounts) and a simple physical-cause explanation (of the sort offered by accounts that appeal to physical or chemical descriptions). Without the availability of such a notion in our present framework, we are likely to misattribute mental states (for example, by crediting or blaming a subject for a belief when only an alief is present, or by suggesting that her belief is somehow partial or weak), overlook important similarities (for example, by failing to recognize the resemblances among domains such as fictional emotions, superstition, heuristics-based errors, and residual racism), neglect certain continuities (for example, between our own mental states and those of non-human animals with whom we are evolutionarily continuous), and lack explanations for certain evaluations (for example, for *why* it might seem disrespectful to treat an image of someone in a way that we would not want to treat the person herself, even though she is obviously distinct from the image). Of course, these issues may not arise in an alternative explanatory

---

[3] [4] For numerous examples, see S. James 1999 (which also includes discussions of Aristotle and Aquinas). Cf. also, among others, Baier 1991; Hirschman 1977; and the papers collected in Jenkins, Whiting, and Williams 2005. (Many thanks to Ken Winkler for help with these references.)

framework—one that does not make use of notions like belief, desire, and pretense; but that is not my concern here.

Second: I am fully open to the possibility that, even given the first caveat, I have misdrawn the boundaries of the mental state that I am interested in, either by characterizing it too narrowly or by classing together cases that ought to be treated as distinct. If so, I have no doubt that critics will help to characterize more precisely the notion that I am grasping at.

1. Introducing Alief

What explains the tendency of a person who has set her watch five minutes fast to rush, even when she is explicitly aware of the fact that the time is not what the watch indicates it to be? What explains her reluctance to eat fudge shaped to look like dog feces, to drink lemonade served in a sterilized bedpan, to throw darts at a picture of a loved one—even when she explicitly acknowledges that the behaviors are harmless (Rozin *et al.* 1986)? What makes her hesitant to sign a "pact" giving her soul away to the devil—even if she is an atheist, and even if the pact says explicitly at the bottom "this is not a real pact with the devil; it is just a prop in a psychology experiment" (Haidt, personal communication)? What explains the tendency of the Hitchcock expert to experience suspense as the shower scene proceeds, even though she has written a book detailing *Psycho* frame by frame? What explains the tendency of a chef who has recently rearranged his kitchen to walk towards the old knife drawer to get his cleaver, even as talks about how happy he is with the new set-up? What explains the propensity of subjects whose aim is to select a red ball to go with frequency (choosing from a bag with 9 red and 91 white balls) rather than probability (choosing from a bag with 1 red and 9 white balls)—even when the comparative likelihoods are prominently displayed (Denes-Raj and Epstein 1994)?

Is it relevantly similar to what explains the tendency of the frog to snap at the BB, and the puppy to bat at the image of the dog—even when they have ample evidence that the lure and the BB aren't edible, and that the dog-image isn't a fellow canine? What explains the tendency of the cinema-goer to cower and of the baseball fan to exhort—even as they assure their interlocutor that the images before them are nothing more than patterns of pixels on a screen? What explains the tendency of the man in the cage to tremble—even as he acknowledges that the precipice is of no danger to him? And what explains the tendency of the avowed anti-racist to respond differentially to Blacks and Caucasians—even as she reiterates her commitment to their equality?

It is natural to think that different explanations are called for in the different cases. Some are due to instinct, some to habit. Some are due to the operation of "system I,"[4] others to forgetfulness. Some are due to vivid imagining, others to false belief. Some are due to superstition, others to hypocrisy. Call the outlook that underlies this cluster of explanations—along with the assumption that different explanations are needed for the different cases—the *classic cognitivist picture*.

For reasons that will become easier to articulate once I present my proposed alternative, I think the classic cognitivist picture is an unhelpful way to make sense of the cases I am interested in. It is insufficiently sensitive to certain key differences among belief, imagination, habit, and instinct, and—correspondingly—insufficiently sensitive to certain important similarities among cases that it classes as falling under those categories. Some of these explanations it proposes are simply wrong—those that credit the subjects with false belief, for example. Others are merely incomplete—such as those that appeal to vivid imagining. Yet others draw distinctions that—for the purposes of recognizing important patterns of similarity—are best overlooked in the context (I have in mind those that appeal to habit and instinct). But contrast, the picture that lies behind the explanation that I propose—that, at base, all of these cases involve instances of norm-discordant behavior arising as the result of the mental state that I call *alief*[5]—helps us attend to certain important similarities among the cases, and to be sensitive to important differences among other cognitive states.[6]

The value of the account I offer lies in its reframing of the explanatory terrain, enabling us to notice similarities where there had appeared to be only differences, and differences where there appeared to be only similarities. In making this claim, I am not claiming that alief has a localized substrate, or that it is associated with distinctive neural firing patterns, or that it can be selectively inhibited, or whatever other criterion you think is required for something to be included in our "mature science" of the mind. Rather, I am claiming that it is of explanatory utility: it helps us make sense of things.

---

[4] [*Note added in 2009*: For a brief overview of dual-processing theory (System I/System II), see Ch. 6, §2 above.]

[5] [5] My resort to neologism gives rise to the utterly reasonable question—raised explicitly by Sylvain Bromberger (personal communication)—of why I should have been so fortunate to have discovered a category of thought that has evaded the eyes of philosophers for two millennia. As the discussion below will make apparent, however, I make no claim to novelty: at most, I am claiming to have noticed a certain commonality across some lines of thought that might otherwise have appeared disparate. A related worry—raised by J. Brendan Ritchie (personal communication)—is why we lack a folk psychological notion for alief, given that we have such notions for attitudes like belief, desire, imagination, and perception. I have no convincing response to this worry, though the discussion in section 2.1.1 below may go some way towards offering an answer.

[6] [6] This fact—that having a blanket term for a phenomenon can be philosophically useful by making us attentive to certain patterns—is itself due to the phenomenon for which I now offer a blanket term. For some very preliminary thoughts on this matter, see Gendler 2007 (Ch. 6 above).

1.1. Overview

So what is alief? To have an alief is, to a reasonable approximation, to have an innate or habitual propensity to respond to an apparent stimulus in a particular way. It is to be in a mental state that is (in a sense to be specified) *associative*, *automatic*, and *arational*. As a class, aliefs are states that we share with non-human *animals*; they are developmentally and conceptually *antecedent* to other cognitive attitudes that the creature may go on to develop. Typically, they are also *affect-laden* and *action-generating*.[7]

Examples will follow, but in the meantime, a bit of clarification about each of the features just identified:

- *Associative*: Aliefs encode patterns of responses to particular (internally or externally prompted) mental images.

- *Automatic*: Though a subject may be consciously aware of her aliefs, aliefs operate without the intervention of conscious thought.

- *Arational*: Though aliefs may be useful or detrimental, laudable or contemptible, they are neither rational nor irrational.

- *Shared by human and non-human animals*: Any creature capable of responding differentially to features of its environment that impinge upon its sensory organs has aliefs.

- *Conceptually antecedent to other cognitive attitudes that the creature may go on to develop*: Aliefs are more primitive than beliefs or desires. While it may be possible to paraphrase the content of aliefs using the language of belief and desire, alief cannot be factorized into belief and desire.[8]

- *Action-generating*: Aliefs typically activate behavioral proclivities (though these may not translate into full-blown actions), and can do so directly, without the mediation of classic conative attitudes like desire.[9]

- *Affect-laden*: Aliefs typically include an affective component.

---

[7] Thanks to Paul Bloom, Emily Esch, Elliot Paul, and Ralph Wedgwood for pushing me to clarify the relations among these characteristics.

[8] [8] As Paul Davies notes (personal communication): "Given some very conservative assumptions about the evolution of the human brain, it is overwhelmingly plausible that mental capacities that produce alief-like states evolved prior to the relatively fussy capacities we have for belief and imagination, and these latter states should be conceptualized as probable effects or evolutionary byproducts of the former. So...the suggestion that alief might be assimilated to belief and imagination... is not merely implausible: It is naïve."

[9] [9]This may or may not differentiate alief from other attitudes. On many pictures of belief, belief motivates only in conjunction with desire. But there are other views of belief—Nagel's (1970) for example—according to which desire contributes to belief in motivating action "only in the sense that *whatever* may be the motivation for someone's intentional pursuit of a goal, it becomes in virtue of his pursuit *ipso facto* appropriate to ascribe to him a desire for that goal" (Nagel 1970: 29). (Thanks to Jessica Moss for discussion of these issues.)

In short, adult humans have aliefs, but so do puppies and frogs. So do babies, and so do birds and bees.[10] Indeed, it's because of the birds and the bees and the babies—that is, because of sexual reproduction and the role that it plays in underpinning certain facts about evolution—that we shouldn't be surprised that, as human animals, we share a great deal of our cognitive apparatus with other, non-human animals. Rather, it would be surprising if the opposite were the case. Much of animal behavior—both human and non-human—is the result of innate or habitual propensities to respond to apparent stimuli in particular ways. What differentiates humans (and some non-human animals) from (other) non-human animals is that some of their behavior is the result of something else.

This completes my overview of the notion of alief. In the next section, I offer some clarification on how I propose to use the expression.

1.2. Examples and Usage

Traditional propositional and objectual attitudes are two-place affairs. A subject believes (that) *b* or desires (that) *d* or hopes (that) *h* or fears (that) *f*. But alief, as I propose to use the term, involves a relation between a subject and an entire associative repertoire, one that paradigmatically includes not only representational (or "registered") content, but also affective states, behavioral propensities, patterns of attentiveness, and the like.[11] There is no natural way of articulating this, but—as a reasonable (if cumbersome) approximation—we can say that a subject in a paradigmatic state of alief is in a mental state whose content is representational, affective, and behavioral: she alieves *r, a, d*. Though this usage is approximate—and in that sense, misleading—it helps to emphasize the ways in which thinking in terms of alief differs from thinking in terms of the traditional cognitive and conative attitudes.

---

[10] [10] It appears, for example, that both birds and bees are subject to what is sometimes called the "asymmetric dominance" or "decoy" effect (cf. Ariely 2008). "Contrary to the theory of rational preference...honeybees (*Apis mellifera*) and gray jays (*Perisoreus canadensis*) are,...like humans,...influenced by the addition of an option to a rational choice set...Their relative preference between two original options change[s] with the introduction of a third...option" that is dominated by one but not the other of the original choices (Shafir *et al.* 2002: 180). A similar effect has been reported in hummingbirds (*Selasphorus rufus*) and starlings (*Sturnus vulgaris*) (Bateson 2002; Bateson *et al.* 2002, 2003; Hurly and Oseen 1999). (For a dissenting interpretation of some of these results, see Schuck-Paim *et al.* 2004.)

[11] [11] For additional discussion, see "Alief and Belief" (Ch. 13), §§1.2 and 1.3. For the distinction between registering and representing content, see Prinz 2004. The notion of representation here is a thin one: because they involve mechanisms that are wholly insensitive to the difference between seeming and being, or between appearance and reality, aliefs lack certain sorts of correctness conditions. Their representational content is akin to that of Aristotle's *phantasia* (being-appeared-to). (Thanks to Emily Esch, Jessica Moss, Elliot Paul, and J. Brendan Ritchie for discussion here, though I suspect I have not fully appreciated all of their suggestions.)

Examples will make this usage clearer. Consider again the frog going for the BB, the puppy batting at the mirror, and the suspended man trembling in the cage. In each of these cases the norm-discordant behavioral tendency can be explained by an alief with content that might be expressed, among other ways, as follows. The frog alieves (all at once, in a single alief): small round black object up ahead; appealing in a foody sort of way; move tongue in its direction. The puppy alieves (again, all at once): dog-shaped dog-motiony creature in front of me; attractive and threatening in a my-size-conspecific sort of way; engage in (play-)fighting. The suspended man alieves (all at once): high up above the ground right now; dangerous place to be; tremble. Likewise for each of the additional cases presented above: in each of them, the subject's behavioral tendencies can be explained by appeal to an alief with representational, affective, and behavioral content.

Though paradigmatic alief is at least a four-place relation, it is tempting to slip into the more natural two-place usage. It is natural to say that the frog alieves that the BB is a fly, or that it is edible, or that it is worth jumping towards.[12] Or that the moviegoer alieves that there is an axe-murderer in front of him, or that he is in danger, or that there are good grounds for shrieking and cowering. Or that the sports fan alieves that his team is playing right now, or that the batter is in need of his support, or that his cheer will help his team win.

This "loose" usage may be handy in some contexts. Its naturalness makes it easy to employ (an approximation of) the concept of alief, and employing (an approximation of) the concept of alief helps us to break free from the grip of the classic cognitivist picture. Moreover, although *paradigmatic* instances of alief involve the activation of associative repertoires that saliently include representational, affective, and behavioral content, there may be cases where we wish to ascribe alief where the salient content falls primarily in only one or two of these domains. In the text that follows, I will be careful to use the expression in its canonical fashion when care is required. When care is not required, I will allow myself to slip into a more familiar two-place attitude structure.

2. Alternative Explanations

The time has come to explain why I think the family of alternative explanations offered by the classic cognitivist account provides an unhelpful way of mapping the cognitive territory. That is, the time has come to say what I think is

---

[12] [12] Note, however, that when we make this move, we open ourselves to the classic teleosemantic worries. (For discussion, see Millikan 1995.)

unhelpful about the natural response that we're done if we say that, in the case of the frog and the puppy, the norm-discordant response is due to instinct; that in the case of the chef, it is due to habit; that in the case of the cinema-goer and the baseball fan, it is due to vivid imagining; that in the case of the man in the cage, it is due to false belief; and that in the case of the avowed anti-racist, it is due to hypocrisy—and why I instead want to say that in each of the cases, the response is (also or instead) helpfully understood as being due to alief.[13]

Before continuing, two caveats that may forestall certain objections. First, it is clear that the disputed subject matter does not admit of easy classification: there is no periodic table of the attitudes, or Linnaean taxonomy of mental states. So some disputes that seem substantive may turn out to be merely terminological. Though the line is not as sharp as it may seem initially—after all, terminological habits may have cognitive effects—I will nonetheless try to be careful about this in the discussion that follows.

Second: I am not denying that habit, instinct, vivid imagining, false belief, and hypocrisy can give rise to norm-discordant behavioral tendencies. Indeed, understood properly, I think that in *all* of the cases we are considering the relevant behavioral tendencies *do* arise from habit and instinct. And, understood properly, I think that in the case of the cinema-goer and the baseball fan it *is* vivid imagining that activates the relevant habitual propensity. Moreover, on certain spellings-out of the avowed anti-racist case—for example, a case where the subject is vividly aware of her discordant tendencies and makes no effort to extinguish them—the relevant state might indeed *be* one of hypocrisy. And there are even versions of the caged man story in which it *would* be correct to say that the subject has two sets of conflicting alief-driven behavioral tendencies, each norm-concordant with respect to one of his beliefs, and norm-discordant with respect to the other (though there is also a version where he does not).

In short, to say that a behavioral response is due to instinct, or habit, or imagining, or false belief, or hypocrisy does not *preclude* its being due to a norm-discordant alief. Moreover, there may be contexts where one of the other terms provides an especially useful description of one of the cases in question. My claim is simply that it is *also* useful to have recourse to the notion of alief, and that to describe the cases without recourse to such a notion will lead us to say things that are incomplete, or misleading, or false. In the remainder of this section, I will explain what I mean by this and why I think it is so.

---

[13] [*Note added in 2009*: For additional discussion of the relation between alief and other attitudes, see "Alief and Belief" (Ch. 13 above), §2.]

2.1. Appeals to Belief

Let's begin with the example of the trembling man suspended safely in the cage.[14] Here is how Hume describes the case:[15]

> consider the case of a man, who, being hung out from a high tower in a cage of iron cannot forbear trembling, when he surveys the precipice below him, tho' he knows himself to be perfectly secure from falling, by his experience of the solidity of the iron, which supports him. (Hume 1739/1978: 146)[16]

Hume prefaces his story by describing it as a "familiar instance." And, as I have learned from Saul Traiger, "precipice thought experiments were common fare in a philosophical debate about reason and the passions in Hume's predecessors" (Traiger 2005: 100). Montaigne, for example, notes that "if you place a sage on the edge of a precipice he will shudder like a child"[17] (Montaigne 1575/1957: 250). And Pascal and Malebranche both consider such cases. (I discuss their versions below.)

Such cases have a common structure. As a follower of Plato might put it, the "rational part of the soul" pulls in one direction; the "spirited" or "appetitive"

---

[14] [13] Hume presents the case in his underappreciated chapter on "unphilosophical probability" (1739/1978: I. iii. 13), which is studded with striking psychological insights. In discussing the "second unphilosophical species of probability," for instance, he foreshadows Kahneman and Tversky's *availability heuristic* (Tversky and Kahneman 1973/1982). Hume writes: "A lively impression produces more assurance than a faint one; because it has more original force to communicate to the related idea, which thereby acquires a greater force and vivacity. A recent observation has a like effect; because the custom and transition is there more entire, and preserves better the original force in the communication. Thus a drunkard, who has seen his companion die of a debauch, is struck with that instance for some time, and dreads a like accident for himself: But as the memory of it decays away by degrees, his former security returns, and the danger seems less certain and real" (Hume 1739/1978, Book I. iii. 13. 2). In discussing the "fourth species"—a "species of probability, deriv'd from analogy, where we transfer our experience in past instances to objects which are resembling, but are not exactly the same with those concerning which we have had experience"—he discusses not only the case of the man suspended in the cage, but also an example of racial stereotyping.

[15] [14] Interpreting the case in the Humean context is complicated, given Hume's associationism, and his correspondingly idiosyncratic conception of belief. I will set these issues aside in the discussion that follows. My humility in advancing any sort of interpretation has been reinforced by the insights gained from reading the following articles and books: Hearn 1970; Falkenstein 1997; Passmore 1952; Loeb 2002. (Many thanks to Ken Winkler for guidance concerning this literature.)

[16] [15] Note that the explanation cannot be due to the actual danger of the situation. Exactly the same response would be evoked if one were actually on the ground, subjected to an optical illusion as of being suspended. Indeed, much the same response would be evoked even if one *knew* that one was on the ground, being subjected to such an optical illusion.

[17] [16] Or again: "Put a philosopher in a cage of small bars of thin iron suspended at the top of the towers of Notre Dame de Paris, he will see for obvious reasons that it is impossible for him to fall, and yet (unless he is used to the roofer's trade) he will not be able to keep the vision of that height from frightening and astonishing him . . . Set a plank between those two towers, of a size such as is needed for us to walk on it: there is no philosophical wisdom of such firmness as to give us the courage to walk on it as we would do if it was on the ground" (Montaigne, Essays II, ch. 12 (in Montaigne 2003: 155).

part pulls in another. Or, as the early moderns would say, "reason" inclines the subject one way, "passion" inclines him another. While there are many ways of understanding such cases, here are two that I think are deeply misleading. As Traiger writes:

Philosophers "deployed precipice examples to support one of the following claims: (1) Affective mechanisms can *lead to beliefs* which we must embrace, but which are incompatible with the beliefs we are led to by causal reasoning. (2) Affective mechanisms *make it impossible to form beliefs* that would have been arrived at through reasoning in the absence of the affective response." (Traiger 2005: 101; emphasis added)

On both interpretations, the precipice case is taken to be one that tells us something about the trembling man's *beliefs*. On the first view, the man's tendency to tremble shows that he believes (on one sort of ground) that he is in danger of falling, while his tendency to avow his safety shows that he believes (on another sort of ground) that he is not in danger of falling.[18] Call the assumption that lies behind this view: that *behavior reveals belief*. On the second view, the man's tendency to tremble shows that—even in the face of his avowals to the contrary—he does not truly believe that he is safe.[19] Call the assumption that lies behind this view: that *hesitation precludes belief*.

It is easy to see how these two strategies would play out in our other cases. In the case of the cinema-goer, the first strategy would say that the viewer's tendency to shriek and cower shows that he believes (on one sort of ground) that he is in danger of being attacked by the creature on the screen, while his contrary tendency to remain in the room shows that he believes (on another sort of ground) that he is in no such danger. The second strategy would say that the cinema-goer lacks beliefs about his safety, because the tension between his reasoning and affective mechanisms makes it impossible to form the relevant beliefs. In the case of Rozin's subjects, the first strategy says that the subject believes both that throwing a dart at a picture of a loved one will harm the loved

[18] [17] Cf. Louis Loeb: "Suppose the man has observed that whenever he sees a precipice and has not been suspended, he has fallen . . . Suppose the man has observed that whenever he is suspended, he has not fallen. Suppose that for the first time the man both sees a precipice and is suspended. He will have the inclination to *believe* both that he will fall and that he will not fall . . . Here we have the presence of contrary beliefs" (Loeb 2002: 107; emphasis added). Matters are a bit complicated here, since at times Loeb appears to be using "belief" in a Humean sense (according to which beliefs differ from other (non-committal) mental states only in their degree of vivacity). But it seems clear from the context that at least the final sentence is *in propria persona*.

[19] [18] Cf. Eric Schwitzgebel: "Many Caucasians in academia sincerely profess that all races are of equal intelligence. Yet I suppose that many of these same people would also be less quick to credit the intelligence of a black student than a white or Asian student, feel some (perhaps suppressible) twinge of reluctance before hiring a black person for a managerial job requiring mental acuity, expect slightly less from a conversation with a black custodian than a white one—and, in short, reveal through their actions a pervasive if subtle racism. Such people, you will perhaps agree, don't fully and completely believe in the intellectual equality of the races, as genuine and unreserved as their rebukes of racism might be" (Schwitzgebel, MS).

one and that it will not. The second would tell us that the subject lacks a belief about the harmfulness of throwing a dart at a photograph. And so on. For ease of reference below, let's call the first of these two attitudes the subject's attitude towards the *real content* (e.g. safety) and the second his attitude towards the *merely apparent content* (e.g. danger).

Both of these readings characterize the competing tendencies—the man's tendency to aver that he is safe or that throwing the dart is harmless (his response to the real content), and his tendency to tremble or hesitate (his response to the merely apparent content)—as being on a par. On the first view, each of the competing tendencies is seen as sufficient to credit the subject with the relevant belief; on the second, the latter tendency (trembling or hesitation) is seen as sufficient to undermine crediting the subject with the belief associated with the former (safety). I will argue that the inclination to treat these tendencies as on a par reflects a picture of the relation between belief and behavior that is both deeply natural and deeply mistaken. I will address the issue of naturalness first, and the issue of mistakenness second.

My discussion will proceed as follows. First, I will offer a diagnosis of why the behavioral account is so appealing, tracing its attractiveness to the "feeling of naturalness" that attaches to it. I will argue that it is a mistake to take this feeling as an indicator of appropriate attribution, since there are many cases where we feel the pull to attribute belief but where such attribution is clearly mistaken. Second, I will argue that there is a distinct role that the notion of belief needs to play in our cognitive repertoire if it is to bear the relation to knowledge and rationality that philosophers require of it. In particular, in order for an attitude to count as a belief, the attitude needs to be responsive to changes in the world, and in our evidential relation to it. I will argue that the attitude present in the cases presented above does not satisfy these criteria.

2.1.1. THE ATTRACTION OF THE BEHAVIORAL ACCOUNT

The tendency to "infer" intention from action is deep-seated and automatic. We are all inclined to attribute intentions, beliefs, emotions, and personality traits to Heider and Simmel's (1944) moving triangles[20] ("The big triangle wants to get out the door"; "The little triangle keeps trying to block him")—even if on reflection we do not think that geometric line-figures apparently moving across a screen could want or think or try. We are all inclined to experience ATMs and computers and cars as having mental states ("The machine won't believe that I don't want a receipt"; "My car always wants to turn left when I leave the driveway")—even if on reflection we do not think that inanimate objects

---

[20] [19] Cf. Heider and Simmel 1944. Note that the "we" here includes infants and non-human primates: "Numerous studies have since demonstrated this automatic attribution of high-level mental states to animate motion in adults in a wide range of cultures, young infants, and even chimpanzees" (Blakemore and Decety 2001).

could be bearers of beliefs and desires. And the tendency emerges at higher levels as well, perhaps as the result of the same mechanisms, perhaps as the result of different ones. (Even with respect to ourselves, we are inclined to take an interpretative intentional stance, reading our own "beliefs" off of our behavior. Post-hypnotic and left-brain/right-brain confabulation provide the most extreme examples; cognitive dissonance provides another.) (For related discussion, cf. Dennett 1987; Carruthers 2006, 2009.)

To put the point somewhat coyly and self-referentially: when subjects encounter patterns of motion that resemble genuine intentional actions, they have the habitual propensity to respond as if they were in the presence of an agent with beliefs and desires. (For those already convinced of the utility of the notion of alief, we might say: they come to have occurrent aliefs that they are in such a circumstance.) When the soda machine repeatedly returns the patron's dollar, the patron has the habitual propensity to respond as if the soda machine was an intentional agent who believes the dollar to be fake. (We might say: the patron alieves that the machine believes the dollar is fake.) When Heider and Simmel's subjects observe an animated triangle moving in a certain way, they have the habitual propensity to respond as if the triangle were an intentional agent looking for a door. (We might say: Heider and Simmel's subjects alieve that the triangle desires to find the door.) When a subject in a cognitive dissonance experiment observes that she has ended up with the red ball instead of the blue one, she finds herself in a situation normally associated with her preferring the red ball to the blue one. So her habitual propensities associated with her preferring the red ball to the blue one are activated. (We might say that she comes to occurrently alieve: nice red ball, appealing, happily retain possession.) And so on.

Let's get back to the larger dialectic. These examples are meant to discount one possible argument in favor of the parity accounts. What they show is that our natural inclination to treat something as indicative of belief regularly misfires, so that the presence of this natural inclination cannot be taken as decisive evidence for the correctness of the attribution.

Of course, there are also theoretical reasons that one might embrace such an equivalence. One might hold, for example, that there is a conceptual connection between belief and behavior, so that "All that's necessary for an attitude to qualify as a belief is that it disposes the subject to behave in certain ways that would promote the satisfaction of his desires if its content were true. An attitude's tendency to cause behavioral output is thus conceived as sufficient to make it a belief" (Velleman 2000: 255).[21]

---

[21] [20] Velleman rejects this account, but goes on to give a long list of philosophers who he contends have endorsed (some version of) it. These include: Braithwaite 1932–3; Armstrong 1973; Quine and Ullian 1978; Stalnaker 1984/1987; Baker 1995; and Dennett 1971, 1995.

As stated, this can't be right: belief–desire explanations are supposed to explain (or "rationalize") *intentional* actions—not mere behaviors. But of course, that's precisely what is at issue in the cases we are considering. There is no question that the subjects' attitudes towards the merely apparent content dispose them "to behave in certain ways that would promote the satisfaction of [their] desires if [that] content were true." But are those behaviors intentional in the relevant sense? Presumably this is not something that can be read off the behaviors themselves. And to the extent that reflective verbal report can distinguish the cases, it tells against the intentional reading. (Did you *really* believe that there was really an ax-murderer approaching you? that throwing the dart at the photograph would harm your loved one? that the metal bars were not strong enough to hold you?)

2.1.2. THE MISTAKE BEHIND THE BELIEF INTERPRETATION

It remains to be established that the belief interpretation is misguided in cases such as precipice (where the attribution is most tempting). I will base this argument on the role that belief needs to play in our cognitive repertoire. The defense can be made without offering a full-fledged account of belief.[22] All that is needed is to note that—whatever belief is—it is normatively governed by the following constraint: belief aims to "track truth" in the sense that belief is subject to immediate revision in the face of changes in our all-things-considered evidence.[23] When we gain new all-things-considered evidence—either as the result of a change in our evidential relation to the world, or as a result of a change in the (wider) world itself—the norms of belief require that our beliefs change accordingly. I used to believe that stomach ulcers were caused primarily by stress and diet; but when Warren and Marshall's research on the *Helicobacter pylori* bacterium became widely known, I revised my belief to reflect this information.[24]

---

[22] [21] Here are some features beliefs are supposed to have: Belief "tracks truth." It is "responsive to evidence." It is intimately connected with notions like knowledge and rationality. It gives rise to Moore's paradox, and its strength can be ascertained using Ramsey's methods. "Believing *p* is, roughly, treating *p* as if one knew *p*" (Williamson 2000: 46–7). Or, for those whose philosophical temperament inclines them towards Pittsburgh rather than Oxford: Belief falls "within...the space of reasons"; "A belief...is an actualization of capacities of a kind, the conceptual, whose paradigmatic mode of actualization is in the exercise of freedom that judging is. This freedom, exemplified in responsible acts of judging, is essentially a matter of being answerable to criticism in the light of rationally relevant considerations" (McDowell 1998: 434).

[23] [22] For classic discussion, cf. B. Williams 1970/1973a. For recent discussion, see Velleman 2000; Owens 2003; Wedgwood 2002; and Velleman and Shah 2005. Cf. also Hieronymi 2008 and A. M. Smith 2005.

[24] [23] It is an interesting fact—though one that will have to wait for another paper—that the medical community was apparently quite reluctant to accept these data as decisive. This introduces an important complication, namely, that numerous features may affect what a subject takes to be evidentially relevant, and that motivated attention to or ignoring of (apparent) evidence plays a major role in the formation even of belief in this narrower sense.

Williamson's "N.N."—"who has not yet heard the news from the theatre where Lincoln has just been assassinated"—believes that Lincoln is President; but as soon as he learns that Lincoln has been shot, he will make the corresponding adjustment in his belief (Willamson 2000: 23).[25]

In each of the cases we have been considering, only *one* of the competing tendencies is evidence-sensitive in this way. The man suspended in the cage *believes* that he is safe because if he were to gain evidence to the contrary, his attitude would change accordingly. So too with Rozin's subjects, the baseball fan, the cinema-goer, and the rest. One—and only one—of the two behavior-generating attitudes can turn on a dime (or a sixpence) in this way, even in the face of apparent sensory evidence to the contrary. This gives reason to treat the two as not being on a par.

Indeed, a slightly too simple argument can be made on the following grounds: Beliefs change in response to changes in evidence; aliefs change in response to changes in habit. If new evidence won't cause you to change your behavior in response to an apparent stimulus, then your reaction is due to alief rather than belief.[26] (Of course, there are strategies for changing aliefs as well— but these run through sub-rational mechanisms. See also §3 below.)

2.1.3. CONCLUSION: ALIEF IS NOT BELIEF

In conclusion, I think precipice examples show neither that "affective mechanisms can lead to beliefs which we must embrace, but which are incompatible with the beliefs we are led to by causal reasoning" nor that "affective mechanisms make it impossible to form beliefs that would have been arrived at through reasoning in the absence of the affective response" (Traiger 2005: 101). Rather, what precipice examples show is that affective mechanisms associated with habitual propensities to behave in particular ways may be predictably triggered by certain apparent stimuli. These alief-generated behaviors are naturally "read" as indicative of belief (or as preclusive of belief to the contrary). But this is a mistake. The behavioral account rests on an overextension of a heuristic: it depends on treating something that is a *general indicator* of belief as if

---

[25] [24] Aliefs will be slower to change. As Hume notes, "After the death of any one, 'tis a common remark of the whole family ... that they can scarce believe him to be dead, but still imagine him to be in his chamber or in any other place, where they were accustomed to find him" (Hume 1739/1978: I. iii. 9). Cf. also Kübler-Ross's five stages of grief, where "acceptance" may be understood as the stage at which one's beliefs that a loved one has died come to be matched by the relevant aliefs.

[26] [26] As stated, this principle is too strong, for there are certainly cases of subjects who hold evidence-recalcitrant *beliefs*. (Theists and atheists each consider the other to be an example. More mundanely, think about flat earthers, Roswellians, or your political opponents.) Cases of evidence-recalcitrant belief tend to be cases where the subject somehow *distorts* the evidence that is available to her through selective attention or sophisticated weighting. But this is a preliminary response at best: the matter requires further thought. (Thanks to Elliot Paul for pressing me on this issue.)

it were a *necessary and sufficient correlate* of belief. The assumption that behavior invariably indicates belief arises from aliefs that are mistaken for beliefs.

2.2. Appeals to Imagination and Pretense

Here is a natural response to many of the cases I have been discussing. The subject believes one thing (say, that affixing his signature to the piece of paper will have no practical consequences) but imagines or pretends another (say, that affixing his signature to the piece of paper will result in his soul belonging to the devil). The content that he imagines or pretends conjoins with a (perhaps imaginary) desire to act in accord with that imagined content, resulting in the observed behavioral repertoire. (For recent discussion, cf. Currie 2002b and responses thereto.)

Again, it is easy to see how this would go in other cases. The cinema-goer believes that she is safe, but imagines that she is in danger; Rozin's subjects believe that ingesting the food or throwing the dart is harmless, but imagine that doing so is harmful; the frequency/probability subject believes that she has a better chance of pulling out a red ball if she draws from the bag with the greater proportion of reds to whites, but imagines that she has a better chance if she draws from the bag with the greater frequency of reds. And so on. Here, for example, is Pascal on the precipice case: "Put the world's greatest philosopher on a plank hanging over a precipice, but wider than it needs to be. Although his reason will convince him of his safety, his *imagination* will prevail" (Pascal 1669/1966: 10, italics added).

As I indicated above, I do think imagining is (in some of the cases) part of the story. But not in the way traditional accounts suggest. This can be brought out by contrasting what goes on in our cases with what goes on both in cases of voluntary pretense and in cases of involuntary imagining as traditionally understood.

Suppose I am engaged in a classic game of pretense, where I pretend that a banana is a telephone.[27] I hold the banana to my ear, and say "Hello: I'd like to order 100 large pizzas." Here my action is the result of an imagined belief (this is a telephone) and an imagined desire (I'd like to order 100 pizzas): together these combine to produce the behavior in question. But here each of the pieces—the belief, the desire, and the action—can plausibly be prefixed with "make-": I make-believe that I am holding a telephone; I make-desire that I wish to order a pizza; and I make-behave that I am doing so.[28] My action in "ordering" the "pizza" is a controlled and deliberate one that I can regulate at will. And it is one that takes place within a circumscribed realm of the merely pretend; my

---

[27] [27] Discussion in this paragraph draws on ideas from Gendler 2006a (Ch. 12 above).

[28] [28] Children are enormously adept at these sorts of games; for review, cf. Harris 2000. For evidence regarding their ability to quarantine between games, cf. Skolnick and Bloom 2006a.

voice and body serve as props in a game of make-believe in much the same way that the banana does. So though it uses the same equipment as actual actions (my body, my voice, etc.), the resulting behavior *represents* the content in question, rather than *manifesting* it; clearly this is not what is going on in our cases above. Moreover, in such cases the action in question is "flagged"—both by the performer and by the perceiver—as merely symbolic. Both children and adults show a marked ability to distinguish such "decoupled" actions from their ordinary counterparts. (For review, cf. Harris 2000. I discuss these matters in more detail in Gendler 2003, 2006a, Chs. 7 and 12 above.)

So deliberate pretense is not a good model for our cases. But what about externally prompted involuntary imagining? Here the answer is more complicated. I *do* think that imagination plays an important role in (some cases of) alief—but when it does so, it does so by violating one of the norms of imagination. Imagination, like Las Vegas, is governed by a norm of *quarantining*: what happens in imagination stays in imagination. Our actual, real-world, non-pretend actions aren't supposed to be guided by things that happen in *that* part of the mind.[29] But of course, this is exactly what happens in (some) cases of norm-discordant alief-generated action: a behavioral repertoire that is activated by merely imagined content manifests itself in observable actions or proclivities.[30]

So the behavioral response in precipice examples *can*, in an important sense, be traced to the imagination. But this does not mean that alief and imagination are the same. Some cases of imagining—at least in principle—do not give rise to these sorts of behavioral propensities. And some cases of alief-generated behavioral response—consider the frog and the puppy—are not the result of imagining. Imagination gives rise to behavior via alief. What happens in imagination may have (non-pretend) effects beyond imagination—but it does so when the process of imagining activates a subject's innate or habitual propensity to respond to an apparent stimulus in a particular way.

2.3. Appeals to Habit and Instinct

The time has come to address another natural objection. Even if the cases do all involve—as I have argued—an innate or habitual propensity to respond to an apparent stimulus in a particular way, what justification is there for treating these etiologically distinct cases as relevantly similar? The frog and the puppy and the vertigo-sufferers are responding as they are hard-wired to respond, whereas in many of the other cases, the source is merely habitual. Moreover,

---

[29] Cf. Nichols and Stich 2000.

[30] Popular psychology, of course, is replete with strategies that exploit this leakage, as any self-help section will reveal: there is even a journal entitled the *Journal of Imagery Research in Sport and Physical Activity*. For related discussion, see Gendler 2006a (Ch. 12 above).

in some of the cases the response is highly impermeable to deliberate regulation, whereas in others, direct control seems possible.

These differences are indeed important. And they are ones to which philosophers worrying about (what I would call) alief were quite sensitive. Here, for example, is Malebranche, discussing the precipice case, invoking a sharp distinction between innate and merely habitual propensities (and offering a fine characterization of an alief-state as he does so):

There are traces in our brains that are naturally tied to one another, and even to certain emotions of the spirits, because this is necessary to the preservation of life; and their connection cannot be broken, or at least cannot be easily broken, because it is good that it always be the same. For example, the trace of a great elevation that one sees below oneself... is naturally tied to the one that represents death to us, and to an emotion of the spirit that disposes us to flight and to the desire to flee. The connection never changes, because it is necessary that it be always the same, and it consists in a disposition of the brain fibers that we have from birth. (Malebranche 1712/1997: 106)

By contrast, he continues:

All the connections that are not natural can and should be broken, because different circumstances of time and place are bound to change them, so that they can be useful to the preservation of life... Thus, it is necessary for the conservation of all animals that there be certain connections of traces that can be easily formed and destroyed, and that there be others that can be broken only with difficulty, and finally, still others that can never be broken. (Malebranche 1712/1997: 106)

That is, "connections of traces"—aliefs—differ in their etiology, and in their corresponding degree of malleability.

There is no doubt that etiology matters for some things: perhaps sunburn can only be produced by the sun. But it seems unmotivated in this case to distinguish propensities that result (directly) from the experiences and actions of a particular individual from those that result (indirectly) from the experiences and actions of her ancestors, merely on those grounds. Certainly we make no such distinction in the case of beliefs and other mental states, else the debate between Locke and Leibniz would have taken a very different form.[31]

A parallel response can be made to the argument that innate propensities are fixed while habitual propensities are malleable. For it is not so clear either that this difference obtains in a relevant sense, or that malleability is what really matters. Recent studies of plasticity suggest that in both cases, the development of alternative propensities proceeds through bypass, not erasure. As a widely cited 2008 *New York Times* article admonishes, "don't bother trying to kill off old habits; once those ruts of procedure are worn into the hippocampus, they're

---

[31] Interesting related discussion can be found in the writings of William James, George Herbert Mead, and John Dewey, each of whom is highly sensitive to the important similarities between what Mead called "inherited and acquired habits" (G. H. Mead 1938: 68).

there to stay."[32] And, as the discussion in §4 will make clear, the processes by which we go about regulating unwanted discordant alief are the same, regardless of whether the aliefs are innate or acquired.[33]

That said, I remain open to the possibility that there are distinct subspecies of alief: innate and habitual, perhaps—or controllable and uncontrollable. All that matters to my argument is that these subspecies be more similar to one another than they are to other candidate states. And of this I remain convinced.

3. Norm-concordant and Norm-discordant Aliefs

Aliefs activate behavioral propensities. So (in conjunction with desire) do beliefs (and their teleofunctional analogues). Sometimes these behavioral propensities pull in opposite directions; sometimes they coincide. When they pull in opposite directions, the subject's belief-discordant behavioral tendencies are governed by what I have been calling *norm-discordant aliefs*. When they coincide, the subject's belief-concordant behavioral tendencies may be consciously regulated by her beliefs, or they may be governed by what I will call *norm-concordant aliefs*.

The main focus of this essay is on norm-discordant aliefs, and on the ways in which these sorts of aliefs are problematic. But it will also be worth saying a bit about cases where norm-discordant aliefs are desirable,[34] and also about cases—which, in the well-lived life, are the rule rather than the exception—in which behavior is governed by norm-concordant alief.

Given the nature of alief and belief, it is inevitable that there will be cases where alief-generated propensities and belief-generated propensities activate contrary behavioral repertoires. The reason is simple: Aliefs involve habitual responses to apparent actual stimuli, but things may not be as they seem, the world may change, and one's norms may demand that the way things are is

---

[32] [32] <http://www.nytimes.com/2008/05/04/business/04unbox.html?em&ex=1210910400&en=3259989c860445c2&ei=5070>. Cf. Tim Wilson *et al.*: "When an attitude changes from A_1 to A_2, what happens to A_1?... The authors argue that a new attitude can override, but not replace, the old one, resulting in dual attitudes. Dual attitudes are defined as different evaluations of the same attitude object: an automatic, implicit attitude and an explicit attitude... Even if an explicit attitude changes, an implicit attitude can remain the same" (Wilson *et al.* 2000).

[33] [33] Cf. Descartes: "Although the movement of each gland seems to have been joined by nature to each of our thoughts from the beginning of our life, one can nevertheless join them to others by habituation... So when a dog sees a partridge, it is naturally inclined to run toward it, and when it hears a gun fired the noise naturally incites it to run away. But nevertheless setters are commonly trained so that the sight of a partridge makes them stop and the noise they hear... when the bird is fired on, makes them run up to it... [In such a way] even [men] who have the weakest souls could acquire a most absolute dominion over all their passions if one employed enough training and skill in guiding them" (Descartes 1649/1989, para. 50).

[34] [34] Thanks to Daniel Bonavec for encouraging me to think about these sorts of cases.

not the way things ought to be. Aliefs by their nature are insensitive to the possibility that appearances may misrepresent reality, and are unable to keep pace with variation in the world or with norm-world discrepancies. By contrast, beliefs, are (modulo error) responsive to the way things are: not merely to the way things tend to be or to the way things seem to be. Actions generated by beliefs are generated by a mental state that is proportioned to all-things-considered evidence and subject to rational and normative revision; actions generated by aliefs are generated by a mental state that is not. (See §2.1.2 above.) So it should come as no surprise that human animals are rife with (the tendency to manifest) belief-discordant aliefs, and that our non-human counterparts are rife with (the tendency to manifest) teleofunctional-discordant aliefs.[35]

Since teleofunctions and beliefs (in conjunction with right desires) generally activate propensities to act and react in ways that we (think we) should, discordant aliefs must, by definition, generally activate propensities to act and react in ways that we (think we) shouldn't. To put things a bit too simply: except in certain exceptional cases (discussed in the next paragraph), teleofunctionally discordant aliefs predispose (human and non-human) animals to behave in ways that violate their (local) self-interest, and belief-discordant aliefs predispose (human) animals to behave in ways that violate their intention to regulate their behavior according to some norm.[36]

That said, there are cases where local self-interest seems unharmed—even aided—and where freedom seems unimpeded, even enhanced, by the presence of norm-discordant alief. Theater, cinema, novel-reading, video games, board

---

[35] [35] As Hume notes: "In almost all kinds of causes there is a complication of circumstances, of which some are essential, and others superfluous; some are absolutely requisite to the production of the effect, and others are only conjoin'd by accident. Now we may observe, that when these superfluous circumstances are numerous, and remarkable, and frequently conjoin'd with the essential, they have such an influence on the imagination, that even in the absence of the latter they carry us on to the conception of the usual effect, and give to that conception a force and vivacity, which make it superior to the mere fictions of the fancy. We may correct this propensity by a reflection on the nature of those circumstances: but 'tis still certain, that custom takes the start, and gives a bias to the imagination" (Hume 1739/1978: 147).

[36] [36] There is an important strand of Western philosophical thought according to which action governed by norm-discordant alief is not just undesirable, but unfree. Here, for example, is Milton, channeling Kant:

> Since thy original lapse, true Liberty
> Is lost, which always with right Reason dwells
> Twinn'd, and hath from her no divided being:
> Reason in man obscur'd, or not obeyed,
> Immediately inordinate desires
> And upstart Passions catch the Government
> From Reason, and to servitude reduce
> Man till then free.
> (Milton 1667/1980, Book XII, 83–90)

"True liberty" on such a picture "always with right Reason dwells Twinn'd" and when "upstart Passions catch the Government from Reason" man is "to servitude reduce[d]."

games, poetry, metaphor, circumlocution, daydreaming, therapy, roller-coasters, and bungee jumping all exploit—in various ways—our tendency to respond to merely apparent stimuli in habitual ways. Circumscribed indulgence of these associative chains is crucial to a richly lived human life.[37] Further discussion of this issue will take us too far afield, but I hope to discuss these matters in greater detail in future work.[38]

Typically, though, teleofunctionally concordant aliefs predispose (human and non-human) animals to behave in ways that accord with their (local) self-interest, and belief-concordant aliefs predispose (human) animals to behave in ways that accord with their intention to regulate their behavior according to some norm. According to the ancient ideal, a well-functioning soul is one where, so to speak, alief and belief are in accord.[39] Plato writes:

> One who is just ... regulates well what is really his own and rules himself. He puts himself in order, is his own friend, and harmonizes the three parts of himself ... He binds together those parts and any others there may be in between, and from having been many things, he becomes entirely one, moderate and harmonious. Only then does he act. (*Republic*, 443 DE in Plato 380 BCE/1992)

The ideal that a person will act only after he has put "himself in order ... harmonize[d] the ... parts of himself ... and ... become[] entirely one, moderate and harmonious" is what lies at the heart of the aspiration that belief, desire, and action form a neat inter-derivable triangle. For only in such a case will belief be readable off of action and (presumed) desire. But, as the opening examples and subsequent discussion have brought out, this ideal is (inevitably) unrealized. In the final section, I consider some of the implications of this internal disharmony.

4. Regulating Unwanted Discordant Alief

As beings who are simultaneously embodied and capable of rational agency, the challenge of bringing our aliefs into line with our commitments is one that we face repeatedly. Given that we all have norm-discordant aliefs that we disavow, and whose influence on our actions we wish to reduce, what can be done? In this final section, I offer some preliminary remarks on this question.

---

[37] [37] Indeed, one of the deficits characteristic of those on the autistic spectrum is an inability or unwillingness to indulge in this way. This may be connected in interesting ways with a corresponding propensity not to engage in games of spontaneous pretense.

[38] [38] Some of these topics are discussed under the rubric of what Paul Rozin has dubbed "benign masochism." See e.g. Rozin 1999. (Thanks to Paul Bloom for alerting me to this literature.)

[39] [39] I have been helped in my thinking about these questions by Cooper (1999); Ferrari (2007); Lorenz (2006); Moss (2005, 2008); A. W. Price (1994); and Reeve (1988). Cf. also the essays collected in Barney, Brittain, and Brennan (forthcoming).

4.1. Traditional Strategies

Both the ancient and early modern traditions are replete with strategies for bringing our aliefs into line with our considered commitments. The recommendations fall under two main rubrics: the first stresses the value of cultivating norm-concordant habits through actual rehearsal; the second brings out how (otherwise occurrent) norm-discordant aliefs can be regulated through the refocusing of attention (especially by directed imagination), thereby redrawing the lines of internal association.[40] Here is Aristotle discussing the first:[41]

[W]e learn a craft by producing the same product that we must produce when we have learned it, becoming builders, e.g. by building, and harpists by playing the harp; so, also, then we become just by doing just actions, temperate by doing temperate actions, brave by doing brave actions...a state [of character] arises from [the repetition of] similar activities...It is not unimportant, then, to acquire one sort of habit or another, right from our youth; rather, it is very important, indeed all-important. (*Nicomachean Ethics*, 1103^{a}30–1103^{b}25 in Aristotle 1984)[42]

One way, then, to cultivate aliefs in line with our reflective commitments is to make a conscious effort to behave in the ways that our commitments dictate, so that these patterns of behavior become familiar and habitual. (Of course, the discordant aliefs may also remain—hence the warning that it is "not unimportant... indeed, all-important... to acquire one sort of habit or another, right from our youth"—but they will be so outweighed by the concordant aliefs that something close to harmony will be achieved.)

We can also make use of the resources of the imagination. Descartes, for example, "notes that an effective way of countering an undesirable passion is to imagine a new and different state of affairs, or response to the state of affairs." Such "voluntary, imaginative practice" may ultimately "reshape our internal bodily 'dispositions' so that they produce specific passions under the appropriate, rationally endorsed circumstance" (Schmitter 2006; cf. Descartes 1649/

---

[40] [*Note added in 2009*: For an overview of work connecting this pair of strategy-families with recent neuroimaging results, see Ochsner and Gross 2005.]

[41] [40] On one natural reading of Aristotle's view, moral virtue is a matter of alief: it is a *hexis*—"a tendency or disposition, induced by our habits, to have appropriate feelings." Cf. Kraut 2001/2007. (There are, however, passages in the *Ethics* that appear to give more weight to consciously regulated mechanisms such as "choice" (*prohairesis*) and "action" (*praxis*) (for example, *NE* II. 5 (1106^{a}3) and *NE* II. 6 (1106^{b}26–36) in Aristotle 1984). For related discussion, see Irwin 1975 and Sorabji 1980.) (Thanks to Ralph Wedgwood and Jessica Moss for this corrective.)

[42] [41] Here is Descartes in a similar vein: "We cannot continually pay attention to the same thing; and so, however clear and evident the reasons may have been that convinced us of some truth in the past, we can later be turned away from believing it by some false appearance unless we have so imprinted it on our mind by long and frequent meditation that it has become a settled disposition with us. In this sense the scholastics are right when they say that virtues are habits" (Letter to Elizabeth, 15 Sept. 1645, *CSM* III 267/AT 295; in Descartes 1645/1991: 267). (Thanks to Elliot Paul for this reference.)

1989, *passim*). And Malebranche holds that "[a]ctively deploying the imagination ... can generate the entire train of sensations and emotions typical of that passion we deem appropriate." Using these techniques, we "can ... resist the pernicious influences of the imagination caused by recalcitrant passions." By "training ourselves to associate some thought with whatever arouses our passion, we can redirect the accompanying bodily movements as we see fit. Doing so repeatedly produces a habituation that changes our dispositions for actions and passions" (Schmitter 2006, §7; cf. Malebranche 1712/1997).

In the final sections of this essay, I will examine analogues of these strategies in a particular contemporary context—that of reorienting unwanted racist alief.

4.2. Reorienting Racist Alief

The literature on (what I would call) racist alief is large and highly consistent,[43] at least in its broad outlines.[44] While it appears that there is a small portion of American Whites who "do not experience the automatic activation of any negative evaluation from memory on encountering a Black person" and some portion who "have no qualms about their experiencing such negativity or about expressing it" (Fazio *et al.* 1995: 1025), many American Whites seem to be what Jack Dovidio and Schmel Gaertner (following Joel Kovel) call "aversive racists"—people who consciously endorse egalitarian values, but who have negative feelings towards the relevant racial group that are "typically excluded from awareness" (Gaertner and Dovidio 1986: 62; cf. Wilson *et al.* 2000; Dovidio and Gaertner 2004). Even among those who are explicitly and sincerely committed to anti-racism, then, the legacy of having lived in a society structured by hierarchical and hostile racial divisions retains its imprint. So, for example, White subjects primed with images of Black faces tend to be faster to identify an ambiguous image as a gun, and more likely to misidentify a (non-gun) tool as a gun (Payne 2001). Otherwise identical résumés bearing stereotypical black names (e.g. Jamal, Lakisha) are less likely to result in interviews than résumés bearing stereotypical White names (Emily, Greg) (Bertrand and Mullainathan 2003). In both Black and White Americans, fMRI scanning shows greater amygdale activity—associated with detection of threat—in subjects presented with images of out-group (different race) as opposed to in-group (same race) members (Amadio *et al.* 2003). And so on (Devine *et al.* 2002; cf. also Payne 2006).

---

[43] [43] Many thanks to Carolyn Caine for excellent research assistance on this section.

[44] [44] For classic discussion, see Allport 1954. For an overview of some of the philosophical issues involved, with useful bibliography, see Kelly and Roedder 2008. Cf. also (among others) Alcoff 2006; Blum 2002; Levine and Pataki 2004; and Sullivan 2006. I focus here on the case of race; parallel literatures exist concerning other sorts of bias.

Some of the tendencies of aversive racism can be countered at the level of belief through deliberate control, or through indirect manipulation.[45] Conscious application of stereotype-generated information can be regulated, for example, by providing external motivation for subjects to act in nonprejudiced ways, by encouraging subjects to be aware of egalitarian norms and standards, or by setting goals for subjects that require them to acquire unique information about group members.[46] But what about the *unconscious* or *quasi-conscious* *activation* of stereotypical responses—that is, what about racist alief? How, if at all, can this be regulated?

Whatever techniques are available, they will need to be strong enough to balance the effects of enormously deep-seated habits.[47] For, as Patricia Devine writes:

There is strong evidence that stereotypes are well established in children's memories before children develop the cognitive ability and flexibility to question or critically evaluate the stereotype's validity or acceptability (Allport 1954; Katz 1976; Porter 1971; Proshansky 1966).[48] As a result, personal beliefs (i.e., decisions about the appropriateness of stereotypic ascriptions) are necessarily newer cognitive structures (Higgins & King 1981). An additional consequence of this developmental sequence is that stereotypes have a longer history of activation and are therefore likely to be more accessible than are personal beliefs... Inhibiting stereotype-congruent or prejudice-like responses and intentionally replacing them with nonprejudiced responses can be likened to the breaking of a bad habit... [E]limination of a bad habit requires essentially the same steps as the formation of a habit. (Devine 1989: 6)[49]

In the twenty years that have elapsed since Devine wrote these words, a great deal of research has been devoted to the topic of implicit prejudice, and to the question of whether—and if so, how—automatic activation of stereotypical

---

[45] As Descartes notes, it is often possible to deliberately control our passions through indirect means. "If someone wills to dispose his eyes to look at an extremely distant object, this volition makes the pupils dilate... But if he thinks only of dilating the pupil, he may well have the volition but he will not thereby dilate it... Our passions cannot likewise be directly excited or displaced by the action of our will, but they can be indirectly by the representation of things which are usually joined with the passions we will to have and opposed to the ones we will to reject" (Descartes 1649/1989, paras. 44–5).

[46] Cf. Kawakami *et al.* 2000 citing (on the first) Devine, Monteith, Zuwerink, and Elliot 1991; Monteith 1993, 1996; Monteith, Devine, and Zuwerink 1993; Monteith, Sherman, and Devine 1998); (on the second) Macrae, Bodenhausen, and Milne 1997; (and on the third) Erber and Fiske 1984; Fiske and Neuberg 1990; Neuberg and Fiske 1987. Cf. also Kawakami *et al.* 2005.

[47] Remember Aristotle's admonition that "It is not unimportant... to acquire one sort of habit or another, right from our youth; rather, it is very important, indeed all-important" (*NE* II. 2, 1103^{b}21–5 in Aristotle 1984). For qualifications, see the caveats in n. 41.

[48] For recent work on this issue, see Baron and Banaji 2006.

[49] Devine continues: "An important assumption to keep in mind in the change process, however, is that neither the formation of an attitude from beliefs nor the formation of a decision from attitudes or beliefs entails the elimination of earlier established attitudinal or stereotype representations... [A]lthough low-prejudiced persons have changed their beliefs concerning stereotyped group members, the stereotype has not been eliminated from the memory system. In fact, it remains a well-organized, frequently activated knowledge structure" (Devine 1989: 15).

responses can be controlled.[50] The literature on this topic is enormous and the examples that follow are but two of (literally) hundreds that could have been selected. I invoke them here because I think this is an area ripe for philosophical reflection, one where ancient and early modern discussions of the regulation of the passions resonate profoundly.

Three studies carried out by Kerry Kawakami *et al.* (2000) give a flavor of one line of response that echoes Aristotle's admonition that "we learn a craft by producing the same product that we must produce when we have learned it" (*NE* 1103 in Aristotle 1984). In each study, "participants were presented with two types of tasks, one involving training and the other relating to the assessment of stereotypic activation. The goal of the training task was to allow participants to practice responding "NO" to stereotypic traits following category representations and "YES" to nonstereotypic associations." The assumption behind this was that "by repeatedly and consistently implementing this simple act of negating certain category–stereotype combinations while responding positively to other category–nonstereotype combinations, the presentation of the category [would] no longer automatically activate associated stereotypes." Experimental evidence bore out this hypothesis: subjects who had undergone this training showed reduced stereotype activation—measured using two different sorts of standard psychological metrics—effects that lasted for at least twenty-four hours following the training (Kawakami *et al.* 2000).[51/52]

Related work by Irene Blair provides an example of a case involving mental imagery techniques akin to those suggested by Descartes:

Prior research has shown that mental imagery increases the accessibility of the imagined event (e.g., Carroll, 1978; Gregory, Cialdini, & Carpenter, 1982). By the same token, Blair *et al.* argued that counterstereotypic mental imagery ought to increase the accessibility of counterstereotypic associations, and thereby decrease automatic stereotypes. In four separate tests, the participants were asked to spend approximately 5 min creating a mental image of a (counterstereotypic) strong woman and then complete a measure of their

---

[50] [50] Research in this area is so lively that it would be pointless to attempt a survey here. But for those seeking a compact overview, three helpful starting points are Stangor 2000; Dovidio *et al.* 2005; and Devine 2001. For additional bibliographies on particular topics, see <http://www.understandingprejudice.org/readroom/>.

[51] [51] Similar effects can be seen to result from the contemplation of admired Black exemplars; cf. Dasgupta and Greenwald 2001. For related discussion, see Pizarro and Bloom 2003. Cf. also Rudman, Ashmore, and Gary 2001.

[52] [55] Cf. also Kawakami *et al.* 2000: "It is possible that one of the reasons why people who are low in prejudice demonstrate lower levels of automatic stereotype activation associated with Blacks (Kawakami et al., 1998; Lepore & Brown, 1997) is that these individuals have learned to automate through experience their explicit desires to be egalitarian (Moskowitz et al., 1999)—specifically, because they have developed a strong associative link between this goal and specific target categories . . . [G]radually, by consistently and frequently inhibiting the activation of cultural stereotypes and possibly also concurrently developing and using new associations that are consistent with their egalitarian beliefs, their cognitive representations may actually change" (p. 885).

automatic gender stereotypes. In each test, the participants who had engaged in the counterstereotypic mental imagery produced substantially weaker automatic stereotypes, compared to participants who, (a) engaged in neutral mental imagery, (b) did not engage in any imagery, (c) imagined a weak woman, (d) imagined a strong man, or (e) attempted to suppress their stereotypes during the task. (Blair 2002: 249, describing Blair, Ma, and Lenton 2001)

4.3. The Cost of Disharmony

What are the costs of disharmony in cases where our ideals and social reality come apart? In this final section, I offer a few sobering remarks on this matter.

The Implicit Association Test (IAT) is a widely used test in experimental social psychology. The test asks subjects to categorize a series of words and images presented on a computer screen into one of two disjunctively specified categories, and measures the amount of time it takes for them to make these classifications. So, for example, subjects might be presented with a sequence of Black and White faces and positive and negative words (e.g. "happy" and "harmful") and asked to classify them either into the categories White-or-positive and Black-or-negative, or—alternatively—into the categories White-or-negative or Black-or-positive.[53] Hundreds of studies have shown that subjects—on aggregate—are faster to make classifications into the categories White-or-positive and Black-or-negative than into their converses, suggesting that the former categories are represented as more "natural" or easily accessed.

There is some controversy about whether the relevant IAT measures anti-Black evaluative bias, or whether it merely measures the social knowledge of the cultural association between Blacks and a cluster of negative attributes (cf. Karpinski and Hilton 2001; Olson and Fazio 2004). But the notion of alief finesses this distinction. From the perspective of alief, it doesn't matter whether the IAT measures your degree of access to information that you endorse (as the "evaluative bias" reading contends), or your degree of access to information that you may reject (as the "mere social knowledge" reading contends).[54] What the IAT unquestionably reveals—as its name indicates—are *implicit associations*. And in the case in question, the social knowledge itself involves implicit associations between certain racial categories and highly valenced affective content.

---

[53] [52] You can take the test yourself at <https://implicit.harvard.edu/implicit/> or <http://www.understandingprejudice.org/iat/>. For discussion, see Nosek, Greenwald, and Banaji 2006.

[54] [53] Cf. Eberhardt 2005: "'Bias' calls forth a sense of moral condemnation in a matter that 'social knowledge' does not ... [P]eople may feel less urgently the need to remedy responses thought to reflect social knowledge as opposed to bias ... [But] as researchers highlight the often unconscious and unintentional character of bias, they undermine the moral foundation of the dichotomy between bias and knowledge" (p. 184).

So what about a subject who holds these associations in the form of an easily and regularly accessed alief, though she aims to be non-racist in her daily interactions? In what ways is her desire to regulate her actions in terms of her (non-racist) beliefs undermined by her very knowledge of the cultural categories of American race?

In an ingenious series of studies, psychologist Jennifer Richeson has demonstrated the cognitive cost of racist alief (cf. Richeson and Shelton 2007; Trawalter and Richeson 2006; Richeson, Trawalter, and Shelton 2005; Richeson and Shelton 2003). In each experiment, subjects who had previously completed an IAT concerning racial attitudes interacted either with a same-race or different-race confederate. Following the interaction, subjects completed an ostensibly unrelated task—a Stroop color-naming task[55]—which is standardly used to measure executive control. Richeson reports her findings as follows:

Consistent with the prediction that interracial contact stress will undermine subsequent executive control, White individuals, on average, performed more poorly on the Stroop task after contact with a Black experimenter than they did after contact with a White experimenter. Furthermore, the greater the...relative ease with which [these subjects] associate[d]...negative words with...Black American racial categories...the poorer their Stroop performance after interracial interactions...[T]his...suggests that, like other stressors, interracial interactions can be cognitively costly. (Richeson and Shelton 2007: 316–17, drawing from several paragraphs)

Subsequent neuroimaging traced the difference between the groups to differential activation of areas in the prefrontal cortex associated with executive function and self-regulation. That is, subjects whose occurrent aliefs were out of line with their conscious goal of acting in a non-discriminatory fashion expended significant cognitive effort to suppress the response-tendencies activated through these associations.

This research suggests that living in a society that violates one's normative ideals has unavoidable cognitive consequences. For either you will need to deliberately restrict your attention or experiences so as not to encode certain sorts of genuine regularities (for example, by deliberately preventing yourself from acquiring and attending to the fact that, in contemporary American society, certain racial categories are associated with certain sorts of highly valenced affective content). Or you will need to engage in alief-driven rationalization, changing your normative ideals to accord with the relevant sorts of experienced regularity (for example, by coming to endorse the legitimacy of these stereotypical associations). Or you will experience the cognitive costs of disharmony, redeploying cognitive energy to suppress the pull of your

---

[55] [54] On the unlikely chance that you are not familiar with this effect, see <http://en.wikipedia.org/wiki/Stroop_effect>. Richeson provides a nice summary of the task in the opening paragraphs of Richeson and Shelton 2007.

belief-discordant aliefs (for example, by expending executive control in cases of interracial interaction to suppress your aliefs, thereby temporarily depleting your cognitive resources). This is the trichotomy of norm-discordant alief.

Where ideals and reality come apart, reason and the passions will inevitably conflict. And the costs of this disharmony can be paid only through cognitive compromise. Such is our fate as embodied beings capable of rational reflection living in an imperfect world.[56]

[56] [unnumbered] *Acknowledgements*: My thinking about the matters discussed in this essay has been profoundly influenced by the groundbreaking discussions of belief and related attitudes by Michael Bratman, Patricia Churchland, Paul Churchland, Donald Davidson, Daniel Dennett, Fred Dretske, Jerry Fodor, H. H. Price, Ruth Garrett Millikan, Steven Stich, and Bernard Williams, and by more recent work of Andy Egan, Sally Haslanger, Richard Holton, Susan Hurley, David Owens, Eric Schwitzgebel, Michael Smith, David Velleman, and Ralph Wedgwood. Evidence of their influence should be evident throughout to those familiar with the work of these thinkers. For specific discussion of the issues addressed in this essay, I am grateful to John Bargh, John Bengson, Paul Bloom, Daniel Bonavec, Charles Brittain, Richard Brooks, Carolyn Caine, David Chalmers, Troy Cross, Greg Currie, Paul Davies, Michael Della Rocca, Gil Diesendruck, Andy Egan, Emily Esch, Sam Guttenplan, Verity Harte, Shelly Kagan, Jill North, Elliot Paul, J. Brendan Ritchie, Eric Schwitzgebel, Matthew Noah Smith, Zoltán Gendler Szabó, Ralph Wedgwood, Kara Weisman, and Ken Winkler, and to audiences at Princeton University (Mar. 2007), the Central APA Chicago (Apr. 2007), the *Mind & Language* Pretense Conference at University College London (June 2007) (with commentator Greg Currie), Connecticut College (Nov. 2007), MIT (Nov. 2007), the University of Texas at Austin Graduate Philosophy Conference (Apr. 2008) (with commentator Daniel Bonavec), the Yale Philosophy Faculty Discussion Group (May 2008), and Paul Bloom's Mind and Development Lab Meeting (May 2008), at which excellent questions, comments, objections, and suggestions were raised in response to talks and presentations where some of these ideas were explored.

Bibliography

Aarts, Henk, and Dijksterhuis, Ap (2003). "The Silence of the Library: Environment, Situational Norm, and Social Behavior," *Journal of Personality and Social Psychology*, 84/1: 18–28.

Alcinous (1993). *The Handbook of Platonism*, trans. John Dillon (Oxford: Oxford University Press).

Alcoff, Linda M. (2006). *Visible Identities: Race, Gender, and the Self* (Oxford: Oxford University Press).

Alexander, Joshua, and Weinberg, Jonathan M. (2007). "Analytic Epistemology and Experimental Philosophy," *Philosophy Compass*, 2/1: 56–80.

Allén, Sture (ed.) (1989). *Possible Worlds in Humanities, Arts and Sciences: Proceedings of Nobel Symposium*, 65 (New York: de Gruyter).

Alloy, Lauren B., and Abramson, Lyn Y. (1979). "Judgment of Contingency in Depressed and Nondepressed Students: Sadder but Wiser?," *Journal of Experimental Psychology*, 108/4: 441–85.

————(1988). "Depressive Realism: Four Theoretical Perspectives," in L. B. Alloy (ed.), *Cognitive Processes in Depression* (New York: Guilford), 223–65.

Allport, Gordon (1954). *The Nature of Prejudice* (Reading, Mass.: Addison Wesley).

Alston, William, and Bennett, Jonathan (1988). "Locke on People and Substances," *Philosophical Review*, 97: 25–46.

Amadio, D., Harmon-Jones, E., and Devine, P. (2003). "Individual Differences in the Activation and Control of Affective Race Bias as Assessed by Startle Eyeblink Response and Self-report," *Journal of Personality and Social Psychology*, 84/4: 738–53.

Amedi, Amir, Malach, Rafael, and Pascual-Leone, Alvaro (2005). "Negative BOLD Differentiates Visual Imagery and Perception," *Neuron*, 48/5: 859–72.

Ames, Roger T., and Dissanayke, Wimal (eds.) (1996). *Self and Deception: A Cross-cultural Philosophical Enquiry* (Albany: SUNY Press).

Anderson, Elizabeth (2006). *Which Game Would You Rather Play?* Available from <http://left2right.typepad.com/main/2006/02/what_game_would.html>.

Ariely, Dan (2008). *Predictably Irrational: The Hidden Forces that Shape Our Own Decisions* (New York: HarperCollins).

Aristotle (1984). *The Complete Works of Aristotle*, ed. J. Barnes, 2 vols. (Princeton: Princeton University Press).

Armstrong, David M. (1973). *Belief, Truth, and Knowledge* (Cambridge: Cambridge University Press).

Atkinson, D. (2003). "Experiments and Thought Experiments in Natural Science," *Boston Studies in the Philosophy of Science*, 232: 209–26.

Audi, Robert (1994). "Dispositional Beliefs and Dispositions to Believe," *Noûs*, 28: 419–34.

Baier, Annette (1991). *A Progress of Sentiments: Reflections on Hume's Treatise* (Cambridge, Mass.: Harvard University Press).

Baillargeon, R., Scott, R., and He, Z. (2010). "False-belief Understanding in Infants," *Trends in Cognitive Sciences*, 14: 110–18.

Baker, Lynn Rudder (1995). *Explaining Attitudes: A Practical Approach to the Mind* (Cambridge: Cambridge University Press).

Banfield, Jane F., Pendry, Louise F., Mewse, Avril J., and Edwards, Martin G. (2003). "The Effects of an Elderly Stereotype Prime on Reaching and Grasping Actions," *Social Cognition*, 21/4: 299–319.

Bargh, John A. (1997). "The Automaticity of Everyday Life," in Robert S. Wyer (ed.), *The Automaticity of Everyday Life: Advances in Social Cognition*, vol. 10 (Mahwah, NJ: Lawrence Erlbaum Associates), 1–62.

——(2005). "Bypassing the Will: Towards Demystifying Behavioral Priming Effects," in Hussen, Uleman, and Bargh (2005), 37–58.

——Chaiken, W., Raymond, P., and Hymes, C. (1996). "The Automatic Evaluation Effect: Unconditional Automatic Attitude Activation with a Pronunciation Task," *Journal of Experimental Social Psychology*, 32/1: 104–28.

——and Chartrand, Tanya (1999). "The Unbearable Automaticity of Being," *American Psychologist*, 54/7: 462–79.

——Chen, Mark, and Burrows, Lara (1996). "Automaticity of Social Behavior: Direct Effects of Trait Construct and Stereotype Activation on Action," *Journal of Personality and Social Psychology*, 71/2: 230–44.

Barnes, Annette (1997). *Seeing through Self-deception* (Cambridge: Cambridge University Press).

Barney, R., Brittain, C., and Brennan, R. (eds.) (forthcoming). *Plato and the Divided Self* (Cambridge: Cambridge University Press).

Baron, A. S., and Banaji, M. R. (2006). "The Development of Implicit Attitudes: Evidence of Race Evaluations from Ages 6 and 10 and Adulthood," *Psychological Science*, 17/1: 53–8.

Bateson, Melissa (2002). "Context-Dependent Foraging Choices in Risk-Sensitive Starlings," *Animal Behaviour*, 64/2: 251–60.

——Healy, S. D., and Hurly, T. A. (2002). "Irrational Choices in Hummingbird Foraging Behaviour," *Animal Behavior*, 63/3: 587–96.

————(2003). "Context-Dependent Foraging Decisions in Rufous Hummingbirds," *Proceedings: Biological Sciences*, 270/1521: 1271–6.

Baum, L. Frank (1907). *Ozma of Oz*. Available through Project Gutenberg at <http://www.gutenberg.org/etext/486>.

Bayne, T., and Pacherie, E. (2005). "In Defence of the Doxastic Conception of Delusions," *Mind and Language*, 20/2: 163–88.

Bealer, George (1998). "Intuition and the Autonomy of Philosophy," in DePaul and Ramsey (1998), 201–40.

Bechara, A., Damasio, A. R., Damasio, H., and Anderson, S. W. (1994). "Insensitivity to Future Consequences following Damage to Human Prefrontal Cortex," *Cognition*, 50: 7–15.

Bennett, Jonathan (1990). "Why is Belief Involuntary?," *Analysis*, 50/2: 87–107.

Bentham, Jeremy (1789/1961). *An Introduction to the Principles of Morals and Legislation* (Garden City, NY: Doubleday).

Bermúdez, José Luis, and Gardiner, Sebastian (eds.) (2003). *Art and Morality* (London: Routledge).

Bernecker, Sven, and Dretske, Fred (2000). *Knowledge: Readings in Contemporary Epistemology* (Oxford: Oxford University Press).

Bertrand, M., and Mullainathan, S. (2003). "Are Emily and Greg More Employable than Lakisha and Jamal? A Field Experiment on Labor Market Discrimination," *NBER Working Papers from National Bureau of Economic Research*, No. 9873.

Bishop, Michael (1999). "Why Thought Experiments are not Arguments," *Philosophy of Science*, 66: 534–41.

Blackburn, Simon (1996). *The Oxford Dictionary of Philosophy* (New York: Oxford University Press).

Blair, I. V. (2002). "The Malleability of Automatic Stereotypes and Prejudice," *Personality and Social Psychology Review*, 6/3: 242–61.

——Ma, J. E., and Lenton, A. P. (2001). "Imagining Stereotypes Away: The Moderation of Implicit Stereotypes through Mental Imagery," *Journal of Personality and Social Psychology*, 81: 828–41.

Blair, R. J. R. (1995). "A Cognitive Developmental Approach to Morality: Investigating the Psychopath," *Cognition*, 57/1: 1–29.

Blakemore, S. J., and Decety, Jean (2001). "From the Perception of Action to the Understanding of Intention," *Nature Reviews Neuroscience*, 2/8: 561–7.

Blum, Lawrence A. (2002). *I'm not a Racist, but . . . : The Moral Quandary of Race* (Ithaca, NY: Cornell University Press).

Bogdan, R. J. (ed.) (1986). *Belief: Form, Content, and Function* (Oxford: Clarendon Press).

Bonomi, Andrea, and Zucchi, Sandro (2003). "A Pragmatic Framework for Truth in Fiction," *Dialectica*, 57/2: 103–20.

Borge, Steffen (2003). "The Myth of Self-deception," *Southern Journal of Philosophy*, 41/1: 1–28.

Bouldin, Paula, and Pratt, Chris (2001). "The Ability of Children with Imaginary Companions to Differentiate between Fantasy and Reality," *British Journal of Developmental Psychology*, 19/1: 99–114.

Bourchier, Alison, and Davis, Alyson (2000a). "Individual and Developmental Differences in Children's Understanding of the Fantasy–Reality Distinction," *British Journal of Developmental Psychology*, 18/3: 353–68.

————(2000b). "The Influence of Availability and Affect on Children's Pretence," *British Journal of Developmental Psychology*, 18/1: 137–56.

Bourgeois, Warren (1995). *Persons: What Philosophers Say about You* (Waterloo, Ont.: Wilfrid Laurier University Press).

Braithwaite, R. B. (1932–3). "The Nature of Believing," *Proceedings of the Aristotelian Society*, 33: 129–46.

Brandt, Thomas (1999/2003). *Vertigo: Its Multisensory Syndromes*, 2nd edn. (London: Springer-Verlag).

————and Daroff, R. B. (1980). "Multisensory Physiological and Pathological Vertigo Syndromes," *Annals of Neurology*, 7/3: 195–203.

Brann, E. T. H. (1991). *The World of the Imagination* (Lanham, Md.: Rowman & Littlefield).

Bransford, J. D., and Johnson, M. K. (1972). 'Contextual Prerequisites for Understanding: Some Investigations of Comprehension and Recall', *Journal of Verbal Learning and Verbal Behavior*, 4/2: 717–26.

Bratman, Michael (1987/1999). *Intention, Plans, and Practical Reason* (Cambridge, Mass.: Harvard University Press; re-issued 1999 by CSLI Publications).

————(1999). "Practical Reasoning and Acceptance in a Context," in id., *Faces of Intention: Selected Essays on Intention and Agency* (Cambridge: Cambridge University Press), 15–34.

Brendel, E. (2004). "Intuition Pumps and the Proper Use of Thought Experiments," *Dialectica*, 58/1: 89–108.

Brown, James Robert (1986). "Thought Experiments since the Scientific Revolution," *International Studies in the Philosophy of Science*, 1/1: 1–15.

————(1991a). *The Laboratory of the Mind: Thought Experiments in the Natural Sciences* (London and New York: Routledge).

————(1991b). "Thought Experiments: A Platonic Account," in Horowitz and Massey (1991), 119–28.

————(1993a). "Author's Response/to Norton [1993]," *Metascience*, NS 3: 38–40.

————(1993b). "Why Empiricism Won't Work," in Hull, Forbes, and Ohrulik (1993), 271–9.

————(1995). "Critical Notice: Roy Sorensen's *Thought Experiments*," *Canadian Journal of Philosophy*, 25: 135–42.

————(2004a). "Peeking into Plato's Heaven," *Philosophy of Science*, 71/5: 1126–38.

————(2004b). "Why Thought Experiments Transcend Experience," in Hitchcock (2004), 23–43.

Bruell, Marc J., and Woolley, Jacqueline D. (1998). "Young Children's Understanding of Diversity in Pretense," *Cognitive Development*, 13/3: 257–77.

Burnyeat, Myles (1980). "Aristotle on Learning to be Good," in A. O. Rorty (ed.), *Essays on Aristotle's Ethics* (Berkeley: University of California Press), 69–92.

Butts, Robert E., and Pitt, Joseph C. (1978). *New Perspectives on Galileo* (Dordrecht: Reidel).

Byrne, Ruth (2005). *The Rational Imagination: How People Create Alternatives to Reality* (Cambridge, Mass.: MIT Press).

——and Johnson-Laird, Philip (n.d.). *Mental Models Website* <http://www.tcd.ie/Psychology/other/Ruth_Byrne/mental_models/>.

Camp, Elisabeth (2009). "Two Varieties of Literary Imagination: Metaphor, Fiction, and Thought Experiments," *Midwest Studies in Philosophy*, 33/1: 107–30.

Cargile, James (1987). "Definitions and Counter-Examples," *Philosophy*, 62/240: 179–93.

Carrier, Martin (1993). Review of Horowitz and Massey (eds.), *Thought Experiments in Science and Philosophy*, in *Erkenntnis*, 39: 413–19.

Carroll, J. S. (1978). "The Effect of Imagining an Event on Expectations for the Event: An Interpretation in Terms of the Availability Heuristic," *Journal of Experimental Social Psychology*, 14: 88–96.

Carroll, Lewis (1865). *Alice's Adventures in Wonderland*. Available through Project Gutenberg at <http://www.gutenberg.org/etext/11>.

Carroll, Noël (1990). *The Philosophy of Horror* (New York: Routledge).

Carroll, Timothy J., Herbert, Robert D., Munn, Joanne, Lee, Michael, and Gandevia, Simon C. (2006). "Contralateral Effects of Unilateral Strength Training: Evidence and Possible Mechanisms," *Journal of Applied Physiology*, 101/5: 1514–22.

Carruthers, Peter (2006). *The Architecture of the Mind: Massive Modularity and the Flexibility of Thought* (Oxford: Oxford University Press).

——(2009). "How We Know Our Own Minds: The Relationship between Mind-reading and Metacognition," *Behavioral and Brain Sciences*, 32/2: 121–38.

——and Smith, Peter K. (eds.) (1996). *Theories of Theories of Mind* (Cambridge: Cambridge University Press).

Cavell, Stanley (1979). *The Claim of Reason: Wittgenstein, Skepticism, Morality, and Tragedy* (Oxford: Clarendon Press).

Ceci, Stephen J., and Bruck, Maggie (1993). "Suggestibility of the Child Witness: A Historical Review and Synthesis," *Psychological Bulletin*, 113: 403–39.

——and Friedman, R. D. (2000). "Suggestibility of Children: Scientific Research and Legal Implications," *Cornell Law Review*, 86: 33–108.

Chaiken, Shelly, and Trope, Yaacov (eds.) (1999). *Dual-Process Theories in Social Psychology* (New York: Guilford Press).

Cheng, P. W., and Holyoak, K. J. (1985). "Pragmatic Reasoning Schemas," *Cognitive Psychology*, 17/4: 391–416.

————Nisbett, R. E., and Oliver, L. M. (1986). "Pragmatic versus Syntactic Approaches to Training Deductive Reasoning," *Cognitive Psychology*, 18/3: 293–328.

Chisholm, Roderick (1970). "Identity through Time," in Kiefer and Munitz (1970), 163–82.

Clagett, Marshall (1959). *The Science of Mechanics in the Middle Ages* (Madison, Wis.: University of Wisconsin Press).

Clavelin, Maurice (1974). *The Natural Philosophy of Galileo*, trans. A. J. Pomerans (Cambridge, Mass.: MIT Press).

Clement, John (1983). "A Conceptual Model Discussed by Galileo and Used Intuitively by Physics Students," in D. Gentner and A. L. Stevens (eds.), *Mental Models* (Hillsdale, NJ: Lawrence Erlbaum Associates), 325–39.

Cockburn, David (ed.) (1991). *Human Beings* (Cambridge: Cambridge University Press).

Cohen, L. Jonathan (1992). *An Essay on Belief and Acceptance* (Oxford: Clarendon Press).

Cook, J. T. (1987). "Deciding to Believe without Self-deception," *Journal of Philosophy*, 84/8: 441–6.

Cooper, J. (1999). *Reason and Emotion: Essays in Ancient Moral Psychology and Ethical Theory* (Princeton: Princeton University Press).

Cooper, Lane (1935). *Aristotle, Galileo, and the Tower of Pisa* (Ithaca, NY: Cornell University Press).

Cornoldi, Cesare, Logie, Robert H., Brandimonte, Maria A., Kaufmann, Geir, and Reisberg, Daniel (eds.) (1996). *Stretching the Imagination: Representation and Transformation in Mental Imagery* (New York and Oxford: Oxford University Press).

Cosmides, Leda (1989). "The Logic of Social Exchange: Has Natural Selection Shaped how Humans reason? Studies with the Wason Selection Task," *Cognition*, 31/3: 187–276.

Crammond, Donald (1997). "Motor Imagery: Never in Your Wildest Dream," *Trends in Neurosciences*, 20/2: 54–7.

Crandall, C. S., and Greenfield, B. (1986). "Understanding the Conjunction Fallacy: A Conjunction of Effects?," *Social Cognition*, 4: 408–19.

Cummins, Robert (1998). "Reflections on Reflective Equilibrium," in DePaul and Ramsey (1998), 113–27.

Currie, Gregory (1990). *The Nature of Fiction* (Cambridge: Cambridge University Press).

——(1995a). *Image and Mind: Film, Philosophy, and Cognitive Science* (Cambridge: Cambridge University Press).

——(1995b). "Imagination and Simulation: Aesthetics Meets Cognitive Science," in Davies and Stone (1995b), 151–69.

——(1997). "The Paradox of Caring: Fiction and the Philosophy of Mind," in Hjort and Laver (1997), 63–77.

——(1998). "Pretence, Pretending and Metarepresenting," *Mind and Language*, 13/1: 35–55.

——(2000). "Imagination, Delusion and Hallucinations," *Mind and Language*, 15/1: 168–83.

——(2002a). "Desire in Imagination," in T. S. Gendler and J. Hawthorne (eds.), *Conceivability and Possibility* (New York: Oxford University Press), 201–21.

——(2002b). "Imagination as Motivation," *Proceedings of the Aristotelian Society*, 102: 201–16.

——(2004). *Arts and Minds* (Oxford and New York: Oxford University Press).

——(2007). "Framing Narratives," *Royal Institute of Philosophy Supplement*, 82 (supplement 60), 17–42.

——and Ravenscroft, Ian (2002). *Recreative Minds: Imagination in Philosophy and Psychology* (Oxford and New York: Oxford University Press).

Damasio, Antonio (1994). *Descartes' Error: Emotion, Reason, and the Human Brain* (New York: Putnam).

——(1999). *The Feeling of what Happens: Body and Emotion in the Making of Consciousness* (New York: Harcourt/Harvest).

——Tranel, D., and Damasio, H. (1991). "Somatic Markers and the Guidance of Behavior: Theory and Preliminary Testing," in H. S. Levin, H. M. Eisenberg, and A. L. Benton (eds.), *Frontal Lobe Function and Dysfunction* (New York and Oxford: Oxford University Press), 217–29.

Damerow, Peter, Freudenthal, Gideon, McLaughlin, Peter, and Jürgen, Renn (1992). *Exploring the Limits of Preclassical Mechanics: A Study of Conceptual Development in Early Modern Science: Free Fall and Compounded Motion in the Work of Descartes, Galileo, and Beeckman* (New York: Springer Verlag).

Dancy, Jonathan (ed.) (1997). *Reading Parfit* (Oxford: Blackwell).

Danto, Arthur (1981). *The Transfiguration of the Commonplace* (Cambridge: Cambridge University Press).

Darwin, Charles (1898). *The Expression of the Emotions in Man and Animals* (New York: D. Appleton).

Dasgupta, N., and Greenwald, A. G. (2001). "On the Malleability of Automatic Attitudes: Combating Automatic Prejudice with Images of Admired and Disliked Individuals," *Journal of Personality and Social Psychology*, 81/5: 800–14.

Daurignac, Elsa, Houdé, Olivier, and Jouvent, Roland (2006). "Negative Priming in a Numerical Piaget-like Task as Evidenced by ERP," *Journal of Cognitive Neuroscience*, 18/5: 730–6.

Davidson, Donald (1970/1985). "How is Weakness of the Will Possible?," in *Essays on Actions and Events* (Oxford: Clarendon Press), 289–305.

——(1982). "Paradoxes of Irrationality," in Wollheim and Hopkins (1982), 289–305.

——(1985). "Deception and Division," in LePore and McLaughlin (1985), 138–48.

Davies, David (2007). "Thought Experiments and Fictional Narratives," *Croatian Journal of Philosophy*, 7/19: 29–45.

Davies, Martin, Coltheart, Max, Langdon, Robyn, and Breen, Nora (2001). "Monothematic Delusions: Towards a Two-Factor Account," *Philosophy, Psychiatry, and Psychology*, 8/2–3: 133–58.

——and Stone, Tony (eds.) (1995a). *Folk Psychology* (Cambridge, Mass.: Blackwell).

————(1995b). *Mental Simulation* (Cambridge, Mass.: Blackwell).

Davies, Stephen, Higgins, Kathleen M., Hopkins, Robert, Stecker, Robert, and Cooper, David E. (eds.) (2009). *Blackwell Companion to Aesthetics*, 2nd edn. (Oxford: Blackwell).

de Waal, Franz (1996). *Good Natured: The Origins of Right and Wrong in Humans and Other Animals* (Cambridge, Mass.: Harvard University Press).

Decety, Jean (1996). "The Neurophysiological Basis of Motor Imagery," *Behavioural Brain Research*, 77/1–2: 45–52.

——and Grézes, Julie (1999). "Neural Mechanisms Subserving the Perception of Human Actions," *Trends in Cognitive Sciences*, 3/5: 172–8.

————Costes, N., Perani, D., Jeannerod, Marc, Procyk, E., Grassi, F., and Fazio, F. (1997). "Brain Activity during Observation of Actions: Influence of Action Content and Subject's Strategy," *Brain*, 120/10: 1763–77.

——and Stevens, J. A. (2009). "Action Representation and its Role in Social Interaction," in Markman, Klein, and Suhr (2009), 3–20.

DeMey, Tim (2006). "Imagination's Grip on Science," *Metaphilosophy*, 37/2: 222–39.

Denes-Raj, Veronika, and Epstein, Seymour (1994). "Conflict between Intuitive and Rational Processing: When People Behave against their Better Judgment," *Journal of Personality and Social Psychology*, 66/5: 819–29.

Dennett, Daniel (1971). "Intentional Systems," *Journal of Philosophy*, 68/4: 87–106.

——(1987). *The Intentional Stance* (Cambridge, Mass.: MIT Press).

——(1995). "Do Animals Have Beliefs?," in Roitblat and Meyer (1995), 111–18.

DePaul, Michael (1988). "Argument and Perception: The Role of Literature in Moral Inquiry," *Journal of Philosophy*, 85/10: 552–65.

——(1993). *Balance and Refinement: Beyond Coherence Methods of Moral Inquiry* (New York: Routledge).

——and Ramsey, William (eds.) (1998). *Rethinking Intuition* (Savage, Md.: Rowman & Littlefield).

Descartes, René (1649/1989). *The Passions of the Soul*, trans. S. H. Voss (Indianapolis, Ind.: Hackett).

——(1998). *The Philosophical Writings of Descartes*, trans. J. Cottingham, R. Stoothoff, and D. Murdoch, 3 vols. (Cambridge: Cambridge University Press).

Devine, P. G. (1989). "Stereotypes and Prejudice: Their Automatic and Controlled Components," *Journal of Personality and Social Psychology*, 56/1: 5–18.

——Monteith, M. J., Zuwerink, J. R., and Elliot, A. J. (1991). "Prejudice with and without Compunction," *Journal of Personality and Social Psychology*, 60/6: 817–30.

——Plant, E. A., Amodio, D. M., Harmon-Jones, E., and Vance, S. L. (2002). "The Regulation of Explicit and Implicit Race Bias: The Role of Motivations to Respond without Prejudice," *Journal of Personality and Social Psychology*, 82/5: 835–48.

——(ed.) (2001). "Special Section: Implicit Prejudice and Stereotyping: How Automatic Are They?," *Journal of Personality and Social Psychology*, 81/5.

Diamond, A., and Kirkham, N. (2005). "Not Quite as Grown-up as We Like to Think: Parallels between Cognition in Childhood and Adulthood," *Psychological Science*, 16/4: 291–7.

Diamond, Cora (1991). "The Importance of Being Human," in Cockburn (1991), 35–62.

Dijksterhuis, Ap, and Bargh, John A. (2001). "The Perception–Behavior Expressway: Automatic Effects of Social Perception on Social Behavior," in Zanna (2004), 1–40.

——and Van Knippenberg, Ad (1998). "The Relation between Perception and Behavior, or How to Win a Game of Trivial Pursuit," *Journal of Personality and Social Psychology*, 74/4: 865–77.

Dijksterhuis, Eduard Jan (1961/repr. 1986). *The Mechanization of the World Picture: Pythagoras to Newton*, trans. C. Dikshoorn (Princeton: Princeton University Press).

Doggett, Tyler (2004). "Moral Properties and Moral Imagination" (Ph.D. diss., MIT).

——and Egan, Andy (2007). "Wanting Things You Don't Want," *Philosophers' Imprint*, 7/9: 1–17, <http://hdl.handle.net/2027/spo.3521354.0007.009>.

Dominowski, R. L. (1995). "Content Effects in Wason's Selection Task," in Newstead and Evans (1995), 41–65.

Doris, John (2002). *Lack of Character: Personality and Moral Behavior* (New York: Cambridge University Press).

Dovidio, John F., and Gaertner, S. L. (2004). "Aversive Racism," in Zanna (2004), 1–52.

————(eds.) (1986). *Prejudice, Discrimination, and Racism* (Orlando, Fla.: Academic Press).

——Glick, P. G., and Rudman, L. (eds.) (2005). *On the Nature of Prejudice: Fifty Years after Allport* (Malden, Mass.: Blackwell).

Drake, Stillman (1978). *Galileo at Work: His Scientific Biography* (Chicago: University of Chicago Press).

——(1989). *History of Free Fall: Aristotle to Galileo* (Toronto: Wall & Thompson).

——(1990). *Galileo: Pioneer Scientist* (Toronto: University of Toronto Press).

——and Drabkin, I. E. (trans.) (1969). *Mechanics in Sixteenth-Century Italy: Selections from Tartaglia, Benedetti, Guido Ubaldo, and Galileo* (Madison: University of Wisconsin Press).

Driver, Julia (2008a). "Attributions of Causation and Moral Responsibility," in Sinnott-Armstrong (2008d), *Moral Psychology*, 423–39.

——(2008b). "Imaginative Resistance and Psychological Necessity," *Social Philosophy and Policy*, 25/1: 301–13.

Earman, John, Janis, Allen I., Rescher, Nicholas, and Massey, Gerald J. (eds.) (1993). *Philosophical Problems of the Internal and External Worlds: Essays on the Philosophy of Adolf Grünbaum* (Pittsburgh, Pa.: University of Pittsburgh Press).

Eberhardt, J. L. (2005). "Imaging Race," *American Psychologist*, 60/2: 181–90.

Eco, Umberto (1979). *The Role of the Reader* (London: Hutcheson).

——(1990). *The Limits of Interpretation* (Bloomington: Indiana University Press).

Egan, Andy (2009). "Imagination, Delusion, and Self-deception," in T. Bayne and J. Fernandez (eds.), *Delusion and Self-deception: Affective and Motivational Influences on Belief Formation* (New York: Psychology Press).

Elga, Adam (2005). "On Overrating Oneself... and Knowing It," *Philosophical Studies*, 123/1–2: 115–24.

Elster, John (ed.) (1986). *The Multiple Self* (New York: Cambridge University Press).

Epley, N., and Dunning, David (2000). "Feeling 'Holier than Thou': Are Self-serving Assessments Produced by Errors in Self or Social Psychology?," *Journal of Personality and Social Psychology*, 79/6: 861–75.

——Morewedge, C. K., and Keysar, B. (2004). "Perspective Taking in Children and Adults: Equivalent Egocentrism but Differential Correction," *Journal of Experimental Social Psychology*, 40: 760–8.

Epstein, Seymour (1990). "Cognitive-experiential Self-theory," in Pervin (1990), 165–92.

——Donovan, S., and Denes-Raj, V. (1999). "The Missing Link in the Paradox of the Linda Conjunction Problem: Beyond Knowing and Thinking of the Conjunction Rule, the Intrinsic Appeal of Heuristic Processing," *Personality and Social Psychology Bulletin*, 25: 204–14.

——Pacini, R., Denes-Raj, V., and Heier, H. (1996). "Individual Differences in Intuitive-experiential and Analytical-rational Thinking Styles," *Journal of Personality and Social Psychology*, 71: 390–405.

Erber, R., and Fiske, S. (1984). "Outcome Dependency and Attention to Inconsistent Information," *Journal of Personality and Social Psychology*, 47/709–26.

Estes, D., Wellman, Henry, and Woolley, Jacqueline (1989). "Children's Understanding of Mental Phenomena," in Reese (1989), 41–87.

Evans, Jonathan St. B. T. (1998). "Matching Bias in Conditional Reasoning: Do We Understand It after 25 Years?," *Thinking and Reasoning*, 4: 45–82.

——(2003). "In Two Minds: Dual-processing Accounts of Reasoning," *Trends in Cognitive Sciences*, 7/10: 454–9.

——(2008). "Dual-processing Accounts of Reasoning, Judgment, and Social Cognition," *Annual Review of Psychology*, 59: 255–78.

——Barston, J. L., and Pollard, P. (1983). "On the Conflict between Logic and Belief in Syllogistic Reasoning," *Memory and Cognition*, 11: 295–306.

——and Frankish, Keith (2009). *In Two Minds: Dual Processes and Beyond* (Oxford: Oxford University Press).

——and Over, D. E. (1996). "Rationality in the Selection Task: Epistemic Utility versus Uncertainty Reduction," *Psychological Review*, 103/2: 356–63.

Eysenck, Michael W. (ed.) (1994). *The Blackwell Dictionary of Cognitive Psychology* (Cambridge, Mass.: Blackwell).

Falkenstein, Lorne (1997). "Naturalism, Normativity, and Scepticism in Hume's Account of Belief," *Hume Studies*, 23: 29–72.

Farah, Martha (1988). "Is Visual Imagery Really Visual? Overlooked Evidence from Neuropsychology," *Psychological Review*, 95/3: 307–17.

——(1989). "The Neural Basis of Mental Imagery," *Trends in Neurosciences*, 12/10: 395–9.

——(2000). *The Cognitive Neuroscience of Vision* (Oxford: Blackwell, 2000).

Fauconnier, Gilles (1994). *Mental Spaces* (repr. New York: Cambridge University Press).

——and Sweetser, Eve (1996). *Spaces, Worlds and Grammar* (Chicago: University of Chicago Press).

——and Turner, Mark (1998). "Conceptual Integration Networks," *Cognitive Science*, 22/2: 133–87.

Fazio, R. H., Jackson, J. R., Dunton, B. C., and Williams, C. J. (1995). "Variability in Automatic Activation as an Unobtrusive Measure of Racial Attitudes: A Bona Fide Pipeline?," *Journal of Personality and Social Psychology,* 69/6: 1013–27.

Feagin, Susan (1983). "The Pleasures of Tragedy," *American Philosophical Quarterly,* 20: 95–104.

——(1996). *Reading with Feeling: The Aesthetics of Appreciation* (Ithaca, NY: Cornell University Press).

Feltz, D. L., and Landers, D. M. (1983). "The Effects of Mental Practice on Motor Skill Learning and Performance: A Meta-analysis," *Journal of Sport Psychology,* 5/1: 25–57.

————and Becker, B. J. (1988). *A Revised Meta-analysis of the Mental Practice Literature on Motor Skill Learning* (Washington, DC: National Academy Press).

Ferrari, G. R. F. (2007). "The Three-Part Soul," in id. (ed.), *The Cambridge Companion to Plato's Republic* (Cambridge: Cambridge University Press).

Finke, Ronald A. (1989). *Principles of Mental Imagery* (Cambridge, Mass.: MIT Press).

Fiske, S., and Neuberg, S. (1990). "A Continuum of Impression Formation from Category-Based to Individuating Processes: Influences of Information and Motivation on Attention and Interpretation," in Zanna (2004), 1–74.

Fitzsimons, G., and Bargh, J. A. (2003). "Thinking of You: Nonconscious Pursuit of Interpersonal Goals Associated with Relationship Partners," *Journal of Personality and Social Psychology,* 84: 148–64.

Fodor, Jerry (1999). "A Theory of Content," repr. in W. G. Lycan (ed.), *Mind and Cognition: An Anthology* (Malden, Mass.: Blackwell).

Foot, Philippa (1978). "The Problem of Abortion and the Doctrine of the Double Effect," in *Virtues and Vices and Other Essays in Moral Philosophy* (Berkeley: University of California Press; Oxford: Blackwell), 19–35.

Foss, B. (ed.) (1966). *New Horizons in Psychology* (Harmondsworth: Penguin Books).

Foster, John, Robinson, Howard (eds.) (1985). *Essays on Berkeley* (Oxford: Oxford University Press).

Frazer, J. G. (1890/1959). *The New Golden Bough: A Study in Magic and Religion* (abridged) (New York: Macmillan).

Fridlund, Alan J. (1991). "Sociality of Solitary Smiling: Potentiation by an Implicit Audience," *Journal of Personality and Social Psychology,* 60/2: 229–40.

——Sabini, J. P., Hedlund, L. E., Schaut, J. A., Shenker, J. I., and Knauer, M. J. (1990). "Social Determinants of Facial Expressions during Affective Imagery: Displaying to the People in Your Head," *Journal of Nonverbal Behavior,* 14: 113–37.

Funkhouser, Eric (2005). "Do the Self-deceived Get what They Want?," *Pacific Philosophical Quarterly,* 86/3: 295–312.

——and Spaulding, S. (2009). "Imagination and Other Scripts," *Philosophical Studies,* 143/3: 291–314.

Gaertner, S. L., and Dovidio, John F. (1986). "The Aversive Form of Racism," in Dovidio and Gaertner (1986), 61–89.

Gaita, Raymond (ed.) (1990). *Value and Understanding: Essays for Peter Winch* (London and New York: Routledge).

Galen and De Lacy, P. (162–176, CE/2005). *On the Doctrines of Hippocrates and Plato*, trans. and ed. P. De Lacey, 2nd edn., augmented and revised (Berlin: Akademie Verlag).

Galilei, Galileo (1590/1960). *On Motion*, trans. I. E. Drabkin (Madison: University of Wisconsin Press).

——(1638/1914/repr. 1954). *Dialogues concerning Two New Sciences*, trans. H. Crew and A. De Salvio (New York: Dover).

——(1638/1974/rev. 1989). *Two New Sciences, including Centers of Gravity and Force of Gravity and Force of Percussion*, trans. S. Drake (Toronto: Wall & Thompson).

Gallese, V., Fadiga, L., Fogassi, L., and Rizzolatti, G. (1996). "Action Recognition in the Premotor Cortex," *Brain*, 119/2: 593–609.

——and Goldman, A. (1998). "Mirror Neurons and the Simulation Theory of Mind-reading," *Trends in Cognitive Sciences*, 2/12: 493–501.

Garcia, S. M., Weaver, K., Moskowitz, G. B., and Darley, J. M. (2002). "Crowded Minds: The Implicit Bystander Effect," *Journal of Personality and Social Psychology*, 83/4: 843–53.

Gendler, Tamar Szabó (1998a). "Exceptional Persons: On the Limits of Imaginary Cases," *Journal of Consciousness Studies*, 5/5–6: 592–610.

——(1998b). "Galileo and the Indispensability of Scientific Thought Experiment," *British Journal for the Philosophy of Science*, 49: 397–424.

——(1999). Review of Eric Olson, *The Human Animal*, in *Philosophical Review*, 108/1: 112–15.

——(2000a). "The Puzzle of Imaginative Resistance," *Journal of Philosophy*, 97/2: 55–81.

——(2000b). *Thought Experiment: On the Powers and Limits of Imaginary Cases* (New York: Garland).

——(2002a). "Critical Study of Carol Rovane's *The Bounds of Agency: An Essay in Revisionary Metaphysics*," *Philosophy and Phenomenological Research*, 64/1: 229–40.

——(2002b). "Personal Identity and Thought-Experiments," *Philosophical Quarterly*, 52/206: 34–54.

——(2002c). "Thought Experiments," in L. Nadel (ed.), *Encyclopedia of Cognitive Science*, iv (New York and London: Nature/Routledge), 388–94.

——(2003). "On the Relation between Pretense and Belief," in Kieran and Lopes (2003), 125–41.

——(2004). "Thought Experiments Rethought—and Reperceived," *Philosophy of Science*, 71: 1152–64.

——(2005). "Thought Experiments in Science," in D. Borchert (ed.), *Encyclopedia of Philosophy*, 10 vols. (Detroit: Macmillan), ix. 452–6.

——(2006a). "Imaginative Contagion," *Metaphilosophy*, 37/2: 183–203.

——(2006b). "Imaginative Resistance Revisited," in Nichols (2006b), 149–73.

——(2007). "Philosophical Thought Experiments, Intuitions, and Cognitive Equilibrium," *Midwest Studies in Philosophy*, 31/1: 68–89.

——(2008a). "Alief and Belief," *Journal of Philosophy*, 105/10: 634–63.

——(2008b). "Alief in Action (and Reaction)," *Mind and Language*, 23/3: 552–85.

——(2008c). "Self-deception as Pretense," *Philosophical Perspectives*, 21: *Philosophy of Mind*: 232–58.

——(2009). "Imaginative Resistance," in Davies, Higgins, Hopkins, Stecker, and Cooper (2009), 351–4.

——and Hawthorne, John (eds.) (2002). *Conceivability and Possibility* (New York and Oxford: Oxford University Press).

————(2005). "The Real Guide to Fake Barns: A Catalogue of Gifts for Your Epistemic Enemies," *Philosophical Studies*, 124: 331–52.

————(2006). *Perceptual Experience* (Oxford and New York: Oxford University Press).

——and Kovakovich, Karson (2005). "Genuine Rational Fictional Emotions," in Kieran (2005), 241–53.

——Siegel, Susanna, and Cahn, Stephen M. (eds.) (2008). *The Elements of Philosophy: Readings from Past and Present* (New York and Oxford: Oxford University Press).

Gentner, Dedre, and Stevens, Albert L. (eds.) (1983). *Mental Models* (Hillsdale, NJ: Lawrence Erlbaum).

German, Tim P., and Leslie, Alan M. (2001). "Children's Inferences from 'Knowing' to 'Pretending' and 'Believing,'" *British Journal of Developmental Psychology*, 19: 59–83.

Giere, Ronald (ed.) (1992). *Cognitive Models of Science: Minnesota Studies in the Philosophy of Science*, 15 (Minneapolis: University of Minnesota Press).

Gigerenzer, Gerd, and Hug, K. (1992). "Domain-Specific Reasoning: Social Contracts, Cheating, and Perspective Change," *Cognition*, 43: 127–71.

——and Regier, T. P. (1996). "How Do We Tell an Association from a Rule?," *Psychological Bulletin*, 119/1: 23–6.

——Todd, Peter M., and the ABC [Center for Adaptive Behavior and Cognition] Research Group (2000). *Simple Heuristics that Make Us Smart* (New York: Oxford University Press).

Gilbert, Daniel T. (1991). "How Mental Systems Believe," *American Psychologist*, 46/2: 107–19.

——(1999). "What the Mind's Not," in Chaiken and Trope (1999), 3–11.

——and Gill, Michael J. (2000). "The Momentary Realist," *Psychological Science*, 2/5: 394–8.

——Tafarodi, Romin W., and Malone, Patrick S. (1993). "You Can't Not Believe Everything You Read," *Journal of Personality and Social Psychology*, 65/2: 221–33.

Gilovich, Tom, Griffin, D., and Kahneman, Daniel (eds.) (2002). *Heuristics and Biases: The Psychology of Intuitive Judgment* (Cambridge: Cambridge University Press).

God via Samuel, Gad, and Nathan *et al.* (913–722 BCE(?)). *The Second Book of Samuel*: Authorized Version of the Bible (London, 1611).

Goel, Vinod, Buchel, C., Frith, C., and Dolan, R. J. (2000). "Dissociation of Mechanisms Underlying Syllogistic Reasoning," *Neuroimage*, 12: 504–14.

——and Dolan, R. J. (2003). "Explaining Modulation of Reasoning by Belief," *Cognition*, 87: B11–B22.

Goldie, Peter (2005). "Imagination and the Distorting Power of Emotion," *Journal of Consciousness Studies*, 12/8–10: 127–39.

Goldman, Alvin (1976). "Discrimination and Perceptual Knowledge," *Journal of Philosophy*, 73/20: 771–91.

——(1995). "Empathy, Mind, and Morals," in Davies and Stone (1995b), 185–209.

——(2006). *Simulating Minds* (Oxford and New York: Oxford University Press).

——(2007). "Philosophical Intuitions: Their Target, Their Source, and Their Epistemic Status," *Grazer Philosophische Studien*, 74: 1–25.

Gollwitzer, Peter M., and Kinney, Ronald F. (1989). "Effects of Deliberative and Implemental Mind-sets on Illusion of Control," *Journal of Personality and Social Psychology*, 56/4: 531–42.

Golomb, Claire, and Kuersten, Regina (1996). "On the Transition from Pretence Play to Reality: What are the Rules of the Game?," *British Journal of Developmental Psychology*, 14: 203–17.

Gooding, David C. (1990). *Experiment and the Making of Meaning* (Dordrecht: Kluwer Academic Publishers).

——(1992). "The Procedural Turn; or Why Do Thought Experiments Work?," in R. Giere (ed.), *Cognitive Models of Science: Minnesota Studies in the Philosophy of Science* (Minneapolis: University of Minnesota Press).

——(1993). "What is *Experimental* about Thought Experiments?," in Hull, Forbes, and Ohrulik (1993), 280–90.

——(1994). "Imaginary Science," *British Journal for the Philosophy of Science*, 45/4: 1029–45.

Gordon, Robert (1995). "Simulation without Introspection or Inference from Me to You," in Davies and Stone (1995b), 53–67.

Gould, Stephen J. (1991). *Bully for Brontosaurus: Reflections on Natural History* (New York: Norton).

Greene, Joshua, Sommerville, R. B., Nystrom, L. E., Darley, J. M., and Cohen, J. D. (2001). "An fMRI Investigation of Emotional Engagement in Moral Judgment," *Science*, 293: 2105–8.

Gregory, W. L., Cialdini, R. B., and Carpenter, K. M. (1982). "Self-relevant Scenarios as Mediators of Likelihood Estimates and Compliance: Does Imagining Make It So?," *Journal of Personality and Social Psychology*, 43/1: 89–99.

Grèzes, Julie, and Decety, Jean (2001). "Functional Anatomy of Execution, Mental Simulation, Observation and Verb Generation of Actions: A Meta-analysis," *Human Brain Mapping*, 12: 1–19.

Griggs, R. A., and Cox, J. R. (1982). "The Elusive Thematic Materials Effect in the Wason Selection Task," *British Journal of Psychology*, 73: 407–20.

Hacking, Ian (1993). "Do Thought Experiments Have a Life of Their Own?," in Hull, Forbes, and Ohrulik (1993), 302–8.

Haidt, Jonathan (2001). "The Emotional Dog and its Rational Tail: A Social Intuitionist Approach to Moral Judgment," *Psychological Review*, 108: 814–34.

——and Joseph, C. (2004). "Intuitive Ethics: How Innately Prepared Intuitions Generate Culturally Variable Virtues," *Daedalus*, 133/4: 55–66.

Hanley, Richard (2004). "As Good as It Gets: Lewis on Truth in Fiction," *Australasian Journal of Philosophy*, 82/1: 112–28.

Harman, Gilbert (1998/1999). "Moral Philosophy Meets Social Psychology: Virtue Ethics and the Fundamental Attribution Error," *Proceedings of the Aristotelian Society*, 99: 315–31.

——(1999/2000). "The Nonexistence of Character Traits," *Proceedings of the Aristotelian Society*, 100: 223–6.

Harris, Paul L. (1994). "Understanding Pretence," in Lewis and Mitchell (eds.) (1994), 235–59.

——(2000). *The Work of the Imagination* (Oxford: Blackwell).

——Brown, Emma, Marriott, Crispin, Whittall, Semantha, and Harmer, S. (1991). "Monsters, Ghosts and Witches: Testing the Limits of the Fantasy–Reality Distinction in Young Children," *British Journal of Developmental Psychology*, 9/1: 105–23.

——and Kavanaugh, R. D. (1993). "Young Children's Understanding of Pretense," *Monographs of the Society for Research in Child Development*, 58/1: 1–107.

————and Meredith, M. C. (1994). "Young Children's Comprehension of Pretend Episodes: The Integration of Successive Actions," *Child Development*, 65: 16–30.

——Lillard, Angeline, and Perner, Josef (1994). "Commentary: Triangulating Pretence and Belief," in Lewis and Mitchell (1994), 287–93.

Harvey, Nigel (1992). "Wishful Thinking Impairs Belief–Desire Reasoning: A Case of Decoupling Failure in Adults?," *Cognition*, 45/2: 141–62.

Hauser, Marc D. (2006). *Moral Minds: How Nature Designed Our Sense of Right and Wrong* (New York: HarperCollins).

Hearn, T. (1970). "General Rules in Hume's Treatise," *Journal of the History of Philosophy*, 8: 405–22.

Heider, F., and Simmel, M. (1944). "An Experimental Study of Apparent Behavior," *American Journal of Psychology*, 57/2: 243–59.

Herbert, R. D., Dean, C., and Gandevia, S. C. (1998). "Effects of Real and Imagined Training on Voluntary Muscle Activation during Maximal Isometric Contractions," *Acta Physiologica Scandinavica*, 163/4: 361–8.

Hesse, Mary (1966). *Models and Analogies in Science* (Notre Dame: University of Notre Dame Press).

Hieronymi, Pamela (2008). "Responsibility for Believing," *Synthese*, 161/3: 357–73.

Higgins, E. T., and King, G. (1981). "Accessibility of Social Constructs: Information-Processing Consequences of Individual and Contextual Variability," in N. Cantor and J. F. Kihlstrom (eds.), *Personality, Cognition, and Social Interaction* (Hillsdale, NJ: Erlbaum), 69–121.

Hinton, G. E. (1990). "Mapping Part–Whole Hierarchies into Connectionist Networks," *Artificial Intelligence*, 46/1: 47–75.

Hirschman, A. O. (1977). *The Passions and the Interests* (Princeton: Princeton University Press).

Hitchcock, Christopher (ed.) (2004). *Contemporary Debates in Philosophy of Science* (Oxford: Blackwell).

Hjort, Mette, and Laver, Sue (eds.) (1997). *Emotion and the Arts* (New York and Oxford: Oxford University Press).

Hogan, Patrick Colm (1996). *On Interpretation: Meaning and Inference in Law, Psychoanalysis and Literature* (Athens, Ga.: University of Georgia Press).

Holbo, John (2003a). "Imaginative Resistance," at <http://homepage.mac.com/jholbo/ homepage/pages/blog/giant%20thoughts/resistance.html>, accessed 5/2/2004.

——(2003b). "The Varieties of Imaginatively Resistant Experience," at <http:// homepage.mac.com/jholbo/homepage/pages/blog/giant%20thoughts/resistance2. html>, accessed 5/2/2004.

Holton, Richard (2000/1). "What is the Role of the Self in Self-Deception?," *Proceedings of the Aristotelian Society*, 101: 53–69.

Hommel, Bernhard, Müsseler, Jochen, Aschersleben, Gisa, and Prinz, Wolfgang (2001). "The Theory of Event Coding/TEC: A Framework for Perception and Action Planning," *Behavioral and Brain Sciences*, 24/5: 849–937.

Horowitz, Tamara (1998). "Philosophical Intuitions and Psychological Theory," *Ethics*, 108/2: 367–85.

——and Massey, Gerald J. (eds.) (1991). *Thought Experiments in Science and Philosophy* (Savage, Md.: Rowman & Littlefield Publishers).

Hortobagyi, T. (2005). "Cross Education and the Human Central Nervous System," *IEEE Engineering in Medicine and Biology Magazine*, 24/1: 22–8.

Houdé, Olivier, Zago, Laure, Mellet, Emmanuel, Moutier, Sylvain, Pineau, Arlette, Mazoyer, Bernard, and Tzourio-Mazoyer, Nathalie (2000). "Shifting from the Perceptual Brain to the Logical Brain: The Neural Impact of Cognitive Inhibition Training," *Journal of Cognitive Neuroscience*, 12/5: 721–8.

Hull, David, Forbes, M., and Ohrulik, K. (eds.) (1993). *Proceedings of the Philosophy of Science Association*, 2 (East Lansing, Mich.: Philosophy of Science Association).

Hume, David (1739/1978). *A Treatise on Human Nature*, ed. L. A. Selby-Bigge (Oxford: Clarendon Press).

——(1757/1985). "Of the Standard of Taste," repr. in *David Hume: Essays: Moral, Political and Literary* (Indianapolis, Ind.: Liberty Fund), 226–49.

Humphreys, Paul (1993). "Seven Theses on Thought Experiments," in Earman, Janis, Rescher, and Massey (1993), 205–27.

Hurley, Susan L. (2006). "Active Perception and Perceiving Action: The Shared Circuits Hypothesis," in Gendler and J. Hawthorne (2006), 205–59.

——and Chater, Nicholas (eds.) (2005). *Perspectives on Imitation: From Cognitive Neuroscience to Social Science* (Cambridge, Mass.: MIT Press).

Hurly, T. A., and Oseen, M. D. (1999). "Context-dependent, Risk-sensitive Foraging Preferences in Wild Rufous Hummingbirds," *Animal Behaviour*, 58/1: 59–66.

Hussen, R., Uleman, J., and Bargh, J. (eds.) (2005). *The New Unconscious* (Oxford: Oxford University Press).

Ingalls, Daniel H. H. Sr. (ed. and trans.), with Jeffrey Moussaieff Masson and M. V. Patwardhan (trans.) (1990). *The* Dhvanyāloka *of Ānandavardhana with the* Locana *of Abhinavagupta* (Cambridge, Mass.: Harvard University Press).

Irvine, Andrew D. (1991). "On the Nature of Thought Experiments in Scientific Reasoning," in Horowitz and Massey (1991), 149–65.

Irwin, T. H. (1975). "Aristotle on Reason, Desire, and Virtue," *Journal of Philosophy*, 72/17: 567–78.

Jacobson, Anne Jaap (ed.) (2000). *Feminist Interpretations of David Hume* (University Park, Pa.: Pennsylvania State University Press).

James, S. (1999). *Passion and Action: The Emotions in Seventeenth-Century Philosophy* (New York and Oxford: Oxford University Press).

James, William (1890/1950). *The Principles of Psychology* (New York: Dover Reprints).

Janis, Allen I. (1991). "Can Thought Experiments Fail?," in Horowitz and Massey (1991), 113–18.

Jeannerod, Marc (1994). "The Representing Brain: Neural Correlates of Motor Intention and Imagery," *Behavioral and Brain Sciences*, 17/2: 187–245.

——(1995). "Mental Imagery in the Motor Context," *Neuropsychologia*, 33/11: 1419–32.

——(1997). *The Cognitive Neuroscience of Action* (Oxford: Blackwell).

——(2001). "Neural Simulation of Action: A Unifying Mechanism for Motor Cognition," *Neuroimage*, 14/1: S103–S109.

——(2006). *Motor Cognition: What Actions Tell to the Self* (Oxford and New York: Oxford University Press).

Jenkins, Joyce, Whiting, Jennifer, and Williams, Christopher (eds.) (2005). *Persons and Passions: Essays in Honor of Annette Baier* (Notre Dame, Ind.: University of Notre Dame Press).

Johnson, Crockett (1955). *Harold and the Purple Crayon* (New York: Harper).

Johnson, Samuel (1765). "Mr. Johnson's Preface to his Edition of Shakespeare's Plays," in *The Plays of William Shakespeare*, ed. S. Johnson (London: J. and R. Tonson and others), sig. A3ʳ–D4ʳ.

Johnson-Laird, P. N., and Byrne, Ruth (2002). "Conditionals: A Theory of Meaning, Pragmatics, and Inference," *Psychological Review*, 109/4: 646–78.

Johnston, Mark (1987). "Human Beings," *Journal of Philosophy*, 84/2: 59–83.

——(1988). "Self-deception and the Nature of Mind," in McLaughlin and Rorty (1988), 63–91.

——(1989). "Fission and the Facts," in Tomberlin (1989), 369–97.

——(1992). "Reasons and Reductionism," *Philosophical Review*, 101/3: 589–618.

——(1997). "Human Concerns without Superlative Selves," in Parfit (1997), 149–79.

Kahneman, Daniel, Slovic, Paul, and Tversky, Amos (eds.) (1982). *Judgment under Uncertainty: Heuristics and Biases* (Cambridge: Cambridge University Press).

——and Tversky, Amos (eds.) (2000). *Choices, Values, and Frames* (Cambridge: Cambridge University Press).

Kamm, Frances Myra (1998). "Moral Intuitions, Cognitive Psychology, and the Harming-versus-not-Aiding Distinction," *Ethics*, 108/3: 463–88.

Kant, Immanuel (1785/1981). *Grounding for the Metaphysics of Morals*, trans. J. W. Ellington (Indianapolis, Ind.: Hackett).

Karpinski, A., and Hilton, J. L. (2001). "Attitudes and the Implicit Association Test," *Journal of Personality and Social Psychology*, 81/5: 774–88.

Katz, P. A. (1976). "The Acquisition of Racial Attitudes in Children," in id. (ed.), *Towards the Elimination of Racism* (New York: Pergamon Press), 125–54.

Kawakami, Kerry, Dion, K. L., and Dovidio, John F. (1998). "Racial Prejudice and Stereotype Activation," *Personality and Social Psychology Bulletin*, 24/4: 407–16.

——Dovidio, John F., and Dijksterhuis, Ap (2003). "The Effect of Social Category Priming on Personal Attitudes," *Psychological Science*, 14/4: 315–19.

——Moll, J., Hermsen, S., and Russin, A. (2000). "Just Say No (to Stereotyping): Effects of Training in the Negation of Stereotypic Associations on Stereotype Activation," *Journal of Personality and Social Psychology*, 78/5: 871–88.

——and van Kamp, S. (2005). "Kicking the Habit: Effects of Nonstereotypic Association Training and Correction Processes on Hiring Decisions," *Journal of Experimental Social Psychology*, 41/1: 68–75.

Kelly, Daniel, and Roedder, Erica (2008). "Racial Cognition and the Ethics of Implicit Bias," *Philosophy Compass*, 3/3: 522–40.

Kiefer, H. E., and Munitz, M. (eds.) (1970). *Language, Belief, and Metaphysics* (New York: State University of New York Press).

Kieran, Matthew (ed.) (2005). *Contemporary Debates in Aesthetics and the Philosophy of Art* (New York: Blackwell).

——and Lopes, Dominic M. (eds.) (2003). *Imagination, Philosophy, and the Arts* (London: Routledge).

Kinsbourne, Marcel (2006). "Imitation as Entrainment: Brain Mechanisms and Social Consequences," in Hurley and Chater (2006), 163–72.

Kipling, Rudyard (1899). "The White Man's Burden," *McClure's*, 12 Feb. 1899.

Kirby, Kris N. (1994). "Probabilities and Utilities of Fictional Outcomes in Wason's Four-Card Selection Task," *Cognition*, 51: 1–28.

Klayman, J. (1995). "Varieties of Confirmation Bias," *Psychology of Learning and Motivation*, 32: 385–418.

Knobe, Joshua (2003). "Intentional Action and Side Effects in Ordinary Language," *Analysis*, 63: 190–3.

——and Nichols, Shaun (eds.) (2008). *Experimental Philosophy* (New York: Oxford University Press).

Koenigs, Michael, Young, Liane, Adolphs, Ralph, Tranel, Daniel, Cushman, Fiery, Hauser, Marc, and Damasio, Antonio (2007). "Damage to the Prefrontal Cortex Increases Utilitarian Moral Judgements," *Nature*, 446/7138: 908–11.

Komatsu, Lloyd K. (1992). "Recent Views of Conceptual Structure," *Psychological Bulletin*, 112/3: 500–26.

Korsgaard, C. M. (1989). "Personal Identity and the Unity of Agency: A Kantian Response to Parfit," *Philosophy and Public Affairs*, 18/2: 101–32.

Kosslyn, Stephen M. (1978). "Measuring the Visual Angle of the Mind's Eye," *Cognitive Psychology*, 10/3: 356–89.

——(1994). *Image and Brain: The Resolution of the Imagery Debate* (Cambridge, Mass.: MIT Press).

——Alpert, N. M., Thompson, W. L., Maljkovic, V., Weise, S. B., Chabris, C. F., Hamilton, S. E., Rauch, S. L., and Buonanno, F. S. (1993). "Visual Mental Imagery Activates Topographically Organized Visual Cortex: PET Investigations," *Journal of Cognitive Neuroscience*, 5/3: 263–87.

——and Moulton, S. T. (2009). "Mental Imagery and Implicit Memory," in Markman, Klein, and Suhr (2009), 35–52.

——Thompson, William L., and Ganis, Giorgio (2006). *The Case for Mental Imagery* (New York and Oxford: Oxford University Press).

Koyré, Alexandre (1939/1979). *Galileo Studies*, trans. J. Mepham (Atlantic Highlands, NJ: Humanities Press).

——(1960/1968). "Galileo's Treatise De motu gravium: The Use and Abuse of Imaginary Experiment," repr. in *Metaphysics and Measurement: Essays in Scientific Revolution* (Cambridge, Mass.: Harvard University Press, 1968), 44–88.

Kraemer, D. J. M., Macrae, C. N., Green, A. E., and Kelley, W. M. (2005). "Sound of Silence Activates Auditory Cortex," *Nature*, 434: 158.

Kraut, Richard (2001/2007). "Aristotle's Ethics," in *Stanford Encyclopedia of Philosophy*, ed. E. N. Zalta, <http://plato.stanford.edu/archives/spr2008/entries/aristotle-ethics/>.

Kuhn, Thomas (1964). "A Function for Thought Experiments," repr. in *The Essential Tension* (Chicago: University of Chicago Press, 1977), 240–65.

Kujundzic, Nebojsa (1993). "How Does the Laboratory of the Mind Work?," *Canadian Philosophical Review*, 32: 573–9.

Kunda, Ziva (1990). "The Case for Motivated Reasoning," *Psychological Bulletin*, 108/3: 480–98.

Lamarque, Peter, and Olsen, Stein Haugom (1994). *Truth, Fiction and Literature: A Philosophical Perspective* (New York and Oxford: Oxford University Press).

Latane, B. and Darley, J. M. (1970). *The Unresponsive Bystander: Why Doesn't He Help?* (New York: Appleton-Century-Crofts).

——and Nida, S. (1981). "Ten Years of Research on Group Size and Helping," *Psychological Bulletin*, 89/2: 308–24.

Laymon, Ronald (1991). "Thought Experiments of Stevin, Mach, and Gouy: Thought Experiments as Ideal Limits and as Semantic Domains," in Horowitz and Massey (1991), 167–92.

Lazar, Ariela (1999). "Deceiving Oneself or Self-deceived? On the Formation of Beliefs 'under the Influence'," *Mind*, 108/430: 265–90.

LeDoux, Joseph (1996). *The Emotional Brain: The Mysterious Underpinnings of Emotional Life* (New York: Simon & Schuster/Touchstone).

Lehrer, Keith (1990). *Theory of Knowledge* (Boulder, Col.: Westview Press).

LePore, Ernest, and McLaughlin, Brian (eds.) (1985). *Actions and Events: Perspectives on the Philosophy of Donald Davidson* (Oxford: Basil Blackwell).

Lepore, L., and Brown, R. (1997). "Category and Stereotype Activation: Is Prejudice Inevitable?," *Journal of Personality and Social Psychology*, 72: 275–87.

Leroux, Gaëlle, Spiess, Jeanne, Zago, Laure, Rossi, Sandrine, Lubin, Amélie, Turbelin, Marie-Renée, Mazoyer, Bernard, Tzourio-Mazoyer, Nathalie, Houdé, Olivier, and Joliot, Marc (2009). "Adult Brains Don't Fully Overcome Biases that Lead to Incorrect Performance during Cognitive Development: An fMRI Study in Young Adults Completing a Piaget-like Task," *Developmental Science*, 12/2: 326–38.

Leslie, Alan M. (1987). "Pretense and Representation: The Origins of a 'Theory of Mind'," *Psychological Review*, 94/4: 412–26.

——(1994). "Pretending and Believing: Issues in the Theory of ToMM," *Cognition*, 50: 211–38.

Leslie, Sarah-Jane (2008). "Generics: Cognition and Acquisition," *Philosophical Review*, 117/1: 1–47.

Levin, H. S., Eisenberg, H. M., and Benton, A. L. (eds.) (1991). *Frontal Lobe Function and Dysfunction* (New York and Oxford: Oxford University Press).

Levine, M. P., and Pataki, T. (eds.) (2004). *Racism in Mind* (Ithaca, NY and London: Cornell University Press).

Levine, Sydney (2009). "An Experimental Philosophy Approach to Imaginative Resistance (unpublished manuscript).

Levinson, Jerrold (1997). "Emotions in Response to Art: A Survey of the Terrain," in Hort and Laver (1997), 20–36.

——(1998). *Aesthetics and Ethics: Essays at the Intersection* (Cambridge: Cambridge University Press).

Levy, Neil (2005). "Imaginative Resistance and the Moral/Conventional Distinction," *Philosophical Psychology*, 18/2: 231–41.

Lewis, Charlie, and Mitchell, Peter (eds.) (1994). *Children's Early Understanding of Mind* (Hove, East Sussex: Lawrence Erlbaum Associates).

Lewis, David (1976). "Survival and Identity," in Rorty (1976); repr. in D. Lewis (1983a), 55–72.

——(1983a). *Philosophical Papers*, i (New York and Oxford: Oxford University Press).

——(1983b). Postscripts to "Survival and Identity," in D. Lewis (1983a), 73–7.

——(1983c). "Truth in Fiction," in D. Lewis (1983a), 261–80.

Lewis, Michael, and Saarni, Carolyn (eds.) (1993). *Lying and Deception in Everyday Life* (New York: Guilford).

Liao, Shen-yi, and Gendler, Tamar Szabó (2010). "Pretense and Imagination," *Wiley Interdisciplinary Reviews: Cognitive Science* (forthcoming).

Lichtenberg, Judith (1994). "Moral Certainty," *Philosophy*, 69: 181–204.

Lillard, Angeline (1993). "Young Children's Conceptualization of Pretense: Action or Mental Representational State?," *Child Development*, 64/2: 372–86.

——(1994). "Making Sense of Pretence," in Lewis and Mitchell (1994), 211–34.

Lipton, Peter (1993). Review of Horowitz and Massey (eds.), *Thought Experiments in Science and Philosophy*, in *Ratio*, NS 6: 82–6.

Lockard, J., and Paulhaus, D. (eds.) (1988). *Self-deception: An Adaptive Mechanism?* (Englewood Cliffs, NJ: Prentice Hall).

Locke, John (1710/1975). *An Essay concerning Human Understanding*, ed. Peter H. Niddich (Oxford: Clarendon Press).

Loeb, Louis E. (2002). *Stability and Justification in Hume's Treatise* (New York and Oxford: Oxford University Press).

Loftus, Elizabeth (1996). *Eyewitness Testimony: With a new preface by the author* (1979; Cambridge, Mass.: Harvard University Press).

Lombardi, W. J., Higgins, E. T., and Bargh, John A. (1987). "The Role of Consciousness in Priming Effects on Categorization: Assimilation versus Contrast as a Function of Awareness of the Priming Task," *Personality and Social Psychology Bulletin*, 13/3: 411–29.

Lombrozo, Tania (2006). "The Structure and Function of Explanations," *Trends in Cognitive Sciences*, 10/10: 464–70.

Lorenz, H. (2006). *The Brute Within: Appetitive Desire in Plato and Aristotle* (New York and Oxford: Oxford University Press).

Lycan, William G. (1986). "Tacit Belief," in Bogdan (1986), 61–82.

McAllister, James (1996). "The Evidential Significance of Thought Experiment in Science," *Studies in History and Philosophy of Science*, 27/2: 233–50.

——(2004). "Thought Experiments and the Belief in Phenomena," *Philosophy of Science*, 71/5: 1164–75.

McCormick, P. J. (1988). *Fictions, Philosophies, and the Problems of Poetics* (Ithaca, NY: Cornell University Press).

McDowell, John (1997). "Reductionism and the First Person," in Dancy (1997), 230–50.

——(1998). "Lecture I: Sellars on Perceptual Experience," *Journal of Philosophy*, 59/9: 431–50.

Mach, Ernst (1883/1960). *The Science of Mechanics*, trans. T. McCormack (6th edn., La Salle, Ill.: Open Court Publishers).

——(1897/1976). "On Thought Experiments," in Mach (1926/1976), 134–47.

——(1926/1976). *Knowledge and Error* (Dordrecht: Reidel). Original edition, *Erkenntnis und Irrtum*, 5th edn.

McKay, Ryan T., and Dennett, Daniel C. (2009). "The Evolution of Misbelief," *Behavioral and Brain Sciences*, 32/6: 493–510, with commentaries 510–41, and authors' response 541–61.

Mackie, J. L. (1976). *Problems from Locke* (Oxford: Clarendon Press).

McLaughlin, Brian P., and Rorty, Amélie Oksenberg (eds.) (1988). *Perspectives on Self-deception* (Berkeley: University of California Press).

Macrae, C. N., Bodenhausen, G. V., and Milne, A. B. (1997). "Saying No to Unwanted Thoughts: Self-focus and the Regulation of Mental Life," *Journal of Personality and Social Psychology*, 74: 578–89.

Malebranche, Nicolas (1712/1997). *The Search after Truth*, ed. and trans. T. M. Lennon and P. J. Olscamp (Cambridge: Cambridge University Press).

Margolis, Eric, and Laurence, Stephen (eds.) (1999). *Concepts: Core Readings* (Cambridge, Mass.: MIT Press).

Markman, K. D., Klein, W. M. P., and Suhr, J. A. (eds.) (2009). *Handbook of Imagination and Mental Simulation* (New York: Taylor and Francis).

Marshall, Graeme (1990). "Intelligibility and the Imagination," in Gaita (1990), 13–31.

Martin, D. J., Abramson, Lyn Y., and Alloy, Lauren B. (1984). "Illusion of Control for Self and Others in Depressed and Nondepressed College Students," *Journal of Personality and Social Psychology*, 46: 125–36.

Martin, Michael (ed.) (1985). *Self-deception and Self-understanding* (Lawrence, Kans.: University Press of Kansas).

Martin, Raymond (1995). "Fission Rejuvenation," *Philosophical Studies*, 80/1: 17–40.

——and Barresi, John (1999). *Naturalization of the Soul: Self and Personal Identity in the Eighteenth Century* (London: Routledge).

Massey, Gerald J. (1991). "Gedankenexperimente: Where Science and Philosophy Meet." Manuscript.

Masson, J. Moussaieff, and Patwardhan, M. V. (1977). "The Dhvanyāloka and the Dhvanyālokalocana: A Translation of the Fourth Uddyota, Pt. I," *Journal of the American Oriental Society*, 97: 285–304.

Matravers, Derek (2003). "Fictional Assent and the (So-called) 'Puzzle of Imaginative Resistance'," in Kieran and Lopes (2003), 91–106.

——(2005). "The Challenge of Irrationalism and How Not to Meet It," in Kieran (2005), 254–64.

Mauss, M. (1902/1972). *A General Theory of Magic*, trans. by R. Brain (New York: W. W. Norton).

Mead, George Herbert (1938). *The Philosophy of the Act* (Chicago: University of Chicago Press).

Mead, Rebecca (1999). "Fuller Explanation Department: Tom Wolfe Decodes the Naughty Riddle that has His Readers Stumped," *New Yorker*, 25 Jan. 1999, p. 26.

Medin, Douglas L., and Goldstone, Robert L. (1994). "Concepts," in Eysenck (1994), 77–83.

——and Smith, Edward E. (1984). "Concepts and Concept Formation," *Annual Review of Psychology*, 35/1: 113–38.

Mele, Alfred R. (1987a). "Recent Work on Self-deception," *American Philosophical Quarterly*, 24: 1–17.

——(1987b). *Irrationality: An Essay on Akrasia, Self-deception, and Self-control* (Oxford and New York: Oxford University Press).

——(1997). "Real Self-deception," *Behavioral and Brain Sciences*, 20/1: 91–102, with commentaries 103–27, and author's response 127–34.

——(1999). "Twisted Self-deception," *Philosophical Psychology*, 12/2: 117–37.

——(2001). *Self-deception Unmasked* (Princeton and Oxford: Princeton University Press).

Meltzoff, Andrew N., and Prinz, Wolfgang (eds.) (2002). *The Imitative Mind: Development, Evolution, and Brain Bases* (Cambridge, Mass.: MIT Press).

Meskin, Aaron, and Weinberg, Jonathan M. (2003). "Emotions, Fiction, and Cognitive Architecture," *British Journal of Aesthetics*, 43/1: 18–34.

Mill, John Stuart (1843/1963–91). *A System of Logic*, in *The Collected Works of John Stuart Mill*, ed. J. M. Robinson, 33 vols. (Toronto: University of Toronto Press).

——(1861/2001). *Utilitarianism* (Indianapolis, Ind.: Hackett).

——(1963–91). *The Collected Works of John Stuart Mill*, ed. J. M. Robinson, 33 vols. (Toronto: University of Toronto Press).

Millikan, Ruth Garrett (1995). "Compare and Contrast Dretske, Fodor, and Millikan on Teleosemantics," in ead. (ed.), *White Queen Psychology and Other Essays for Alice* (Cambridge, Mass.: MIT Press).

Mills, Eugene (1993). "Dividing without Reducing: Bodily Fission and Personal Identity," *Mind*, 102/405: 37–51.

Milton, John (1667/1980). *Paradise Lost* (New York: W. W. Norton).

Mitchell, Robert W. (1986). "A Framework for Discussing Deception," in id. and N. S. Thompson (eds.), *Deception: Perspectives on Human and Non-human Deceit* (Albany, NY: SUNY Press), 3–40.

Montaigne, Michel de (1575/1957). *Essays*, trans. D. Frame (Stanford: Stanford University Press).

——(2003). *Apology for Raymond Sebond*, trans. R. Ariew and M. Grene (Indianapolis, Ind.: Hackett).

Monteith, M. J. (1993). "Self-regulation of Prejudiced Responses: Implications for Progress in Prejudice-reduction Efforts," *Journal of Personality and Social Psychology*, 65/33: 469–85.

——(1996). "Contemporary Forms of Prejudice-related Conflict: In Search of a Nutshell," *Personality and Social Psychology Bulletin*, 22: 461–73.

——Devine, P. G., and Zuwerink, J. R. (1993). "Self-directed versus Other-directed Affect as a Consequence of Prejudice-related Discrepancies," *Journal of Personality and Social Psychology*, 64: 198–210.

——Sherman, J., and Devine, P. (1998). "Suppression as a Stereotype Control Strategy," *Personality and Social Psychology Review*, 1: 63–82.

Moran, Richard (1989). "Seeing and Believing: Metaphor, Image, and Force," *Critical Inquiry*, 16: 87–112.

——(1992). "Art, Imagination, and Resistance." Talk given before the American Society for Aesthetics.

——(1994). "The Expression of Feeling in Imagination," *Philosophical Review*, 103/1: 75–106.

Moskowitz, G. B., Gollwitzer, P. M., Wasel, W., and Schaal, B. (1999). "Preconscious Control of Stereotype Activation through Chronic Egalitarian Goals," *Journal of Personality and Social Psychology*, 77: 167–84.

Moss, Jessica (2005). "Shame, Pleasure, and the Divided Soul," *Oxford Studies in Ancient Philosophy*, 29: 137–70.

——(2008). "Appearances and Calculations: Plato's Division of the Soul," *Oxford Studies in Ancient Philosophy*, 34: 35–68.

Most, Steven, Scholl, Brian, Clifford, Erin, and Simons, Daniel (2005). "What You See Is What You Set: Sustained Inattentional Blindness and the Capture of Awareness," *Psychological Review*, 112/1: 217–42.

Mothersill, Mary (2003). "Make-believe Morality and Fictional Worlds," in Bermúdez and Gardiner (2003), 74–94.

Mulder, Theo, Zijlstra, S., Zijlstra, W., and Hochstenbach, J. (2004). "The Role of Motor Imagery in Learning a Totally Novel Movement," *Experimental Brain Research*, 154/2: 211–17.

Murphy, Gregory (2002). *The Big Book of Concepts* (Cambridge, Mass.: MIT Bradford).

Nagel, Jennifer (2008). "Knowledge Ascriptions and the Psychological Consequences of Changing Stakes," *Australasian Journal of Philosophy*, 86: 279–94.

——(forthcoming). "The Psychological Basis of the Harman-Vogel Paradox," forthcoming in *Philosophers' Imprint*.

Nagel, Thomas (1970). *The Possibility of Altruism* (Princeton: Princeton University Press).

——(1971). "Brain Bisection and the Unity of Consciousness," *Synthese*, 22/3: 396–413. Reprinted with new pagination in Perry (1975b), 227–45.

Narayan, Uma (1988). Bibliography, in McLaughlin and Rorty (1988), 553–8.

Neely, J. H. (1997). "Semantic Priming and Retrieval from Lexical Memory," *Journal of Experimental Psychology: General*, 106: 226–54.

Neill, Alex (2005). "Art and Emotion," in J. Levinson (ed.), *The Oxford Handbook of Aesthetics* (New York and Oxford: Oxford University Press), 421–35.

Neisser, Ulrich (1963). "The Multiplicity of Thought," *British Journal of Psychology*, 54/1: 1–14.

Nersessian, Nancy (1984). *Faraday to Einstein: Constructing Meaning in Scientific Theories* (Dordrecht and Boston: Kluwer).

——(1992). "How Do Scientists Think? Capturing the Dynamics of Conceptual Change in Science," in Giere (1992), 3–44.

——(1993). "In the Theoretician's Laboratory," in Hull, Forbes, and Ohrulik (1993), 291–301.

Neuberg, S. L., and Fiske, S. T. (1987). "Motivational Influences on Impression Formation: Outcome Dependency, Accuracy-driven Attention, and Individuating Processes," *Journal of Personality and Social Psychology*, 53/3: 431–44.

Newman, John Henry, Cardinal (1909). *An Essay in Aid of a Grammar of Assent* (New York: Longmans, Green, and Co.).

Newman, L. S., and Uleman, J. S. (1990). "Assimilation and Contrast Effects in Spontaneous Trait Inference," *Personality and Social Psychology Bulletin*, 16/2: 224–40.

Newstead, S. E., and Evans, Jonathan St. B. T. (eds.) (1995). *Perspectives on Thinking and Reasoning* (Hove, Sussex: Psychology Press).

Nichols, Shaun (2003). "Imagination and the Puzzles of Iteration," *Analysis*, 63: 182–7.

——(2004). "Imagining and Believing: The Promise of a Single Code," *Journal of Aesthetics and Art Criticism*, 62/2: 129–39.

——(2006a). "Just the Imagination: Why Imagining Doesn't Behave like Believing," *Mind and Language*, 21/4: 459–74.

——(ed.) (2006b). *The Architecture of the Imagination* (New York and Oxford: Oxford University Press).

——and Knobe, Joshua (2007). "Moral Responsibility and Determinism: The Cognitive Science of Folk Intuitions," *Noûs*, 41/4: 663–85.

——and Stich, Stephen (2000). "A Cognitive Theory of Pretense," *Cognition*, 74/2: 115–47.

————(2003). *Mindreading* (Oxford and New York: Oxford University Press).

Nickerson, R. S. (1998). "Confirmation Bias: A Ubiquitous Phenomenon in Many Guises," *Review of General Psychology*, 2: 175–220.

Noë, Alva (2004). *Action in Perception* (Cambridge, Mass.: MIT Press).

Noonan, Harold (1989). *Personal Identity* (London and New York: Routledge).

Noordhof, Paul (2001). "Believe what You Want," *Proceedings of the Aristotelian Society*, 101: 247–65.

Norton, John (1991). "Thought Experiments in Einstein's Work," in Horowitz and Massey (1991), 129–48.

——(1993). "Seeing the Laws of Nature: Review of James Robert Brown, *The Laboratory of the Mind*," *Metascience*, NS 3: 33–8.

——(1996). "Are Thought Experiments just what You Thought?," *Canadian Journal of Philosophy*, 26: 333–66.

——(2004a). "On Thought Experiments: Is there More to the Argument?," *Philosophy of Science*, 71/5: 1139–51.

——(2004b). "Why Thought Experiments do not Transcend Empiricism," in Hitchcock (2004), 44–66.

Nosek, B. A., Greenwald, A. G., and Banaji, M. R. (2006). "The Implicit Association Test at Age 7: A Methodological and Conceptual Review," in J. A. Bargh (ed.), *Social Psychology and the Unconscious: The Automaticity of Higher Mental Processes* (New York: Psychology Press), 265–92.

Nozick, Robert (1981). *Philosophical Explanations* (Cambridge, Mass.: Belknap/Harvard University Press).

——(1993). *The Nature of Rationality* (Princeton: Princeton University Press).

Nussbaum, Martha (1986). *The Fragility of Goodness* (New York: Cambridge University Press).

——(1990). *Love's Knowledge: Essays on Philosophy and Literature* (Oxford: Oxford University Press).

O'Brien, Lucy (2005). "Imagination and the Motivational View of Belief," *Analysis*, 65/1: 55–62.

Oaksford, Mike, and Chater, Nick (1994). "A Rational Analysis of the Selection Task as Optimal Data Selection," *Psychological Review*, 101/4: 608–31.

——(1996). "Rational Explanation of the Selection Task," *Psychological Review*, 103/2: 381–91.

Ochsner, Kevin, and Gross, James (2005). "The Cognitive Control of Emotion," *Trends in Cognitive Sciences*, 9/5: 242–9.

Olson, Eric (1997). *The Human Animal: Personal Identity without Psychology* (Oxford and New York: Oxford University Press).

Olson, M. A., and Fazio, R. H. (2004). "Reducing the Influence of Extrapersonal Associations on the Implicit Association Test: Personalizing the IAT," *Journal of Personality and Social Psychology*, 86/5: 653–67.

Onishi, K. H., and Baillargeon, R. (2005). "Do 15-Month-Old Infants Understand False Beliefs?," *Science*, 308: 255–8.

Owens, David J. (2003). "Does Belief Have an Aim?," *Philosophical Studies*, 115/3: 283–305.

Palmieri, Paolo (2003). "Mental Models in Galileo's Early Mathematization of Nature," *Studies in History and Philosophy of Science*, 34/2: 229–64.

——(2005a). "Galileo's Construction of Idealized Fall in the Void," *History of Science*, 43/4: 343–89.

——(2005b). "Spuntar lo scoglio più duro': Did Galileo ever Think the Most Beautiful Thought Experiment in the History of Science?," *Studies in History and Philosophy of Science*, 36/2: 223–40.

——(2008). *Reenacting Galileo's Experiments: Rediscovering the Techniques of Seventeenth-Century Science* (Lewiston, NY and Lampeter: Edwin Mellen Press).

Papaxanthis, Charalambos, Schieppati, Marco, Gentili, Rodolphe, and Pozzo, Thierry (2002). "Imagined and Actual Arm Movements Have Similar Durations when Performed under Different Conditions of Direction and Mass," *Experimental Brain Research*, 143/4: 447–52.

Parfit, Derek (1971). "Personal Identity," *Philosophical Review*, 80/1: 3–27. Reprinted with new pagination in Perry (1975b), 199–223.

——(1984/1987). *Reasons and Persons* (Oxford and New York: Oxford University Press).

Pascal, Blaise (1669/1966). *Pensées*, trans. A. J. Krailsheimer (Baltimore, Md.: Penguin Books).

Paskins, B. (1977). "On Being Moved by Anna Karenina and *Anna Karenina*," *Philosophy*, 52: 344–7.

Passmore, John (1952). *Hume's Intentions* (Cambridge: Cambridge University Press).

Pavel, Thomas (1986). *Fictional Worlds* (Cambridge, Mass.: Harvard University Press).

Payne, K. (2001). "Prejudice and Perception: The Role of Automatic and Controlled Processes in Misperceiving a Weapon," *Journal of Personality and Social Psychology*, 81/2: 181–92.

——(2006). "Weapon Bias: Split-second Decisions and Unintended Stereotyping," *Current Directions in Psychological Science*, 15/6: 287–91.

Peacocke, Christopher (1985). "Imagination, Experience, and Possibility: A Berkeleian View Defended," in Foster and Robinson (1985), 19–35.

Pears, David (1984). *Motivated Irrationality* (Oxford: Clarendon Press).

Peijnenburg, Jean, and Atkinson, David (2003). "When Are Thought Experiments Poor Ones?," *Journal for General Philosophy of Science*, 34/2: 305–22.

Perner, Josef (1991). *Understanding the Representational Mind* (Cambridge, Mass.: MIT/Bradford).

——Baker, Sarah, and Hutton, Deborah (1994). "Prelief: The Conceptual Origins of Belief and Pretence," in Lewis and Mitchell (1994), 261–86.

Perry, John (1975a). "The Problem of Personal Identity," in Perry (1975b), 3–30.

——(ed.) (1975b). *Personal Identity* (Berkeley and Los Angeles: University of California Press).

Pervin, L. (ed.) (1990). *Handbook of Personality Theory and Research* (New York: Guilford).

Pettit, Philip, and Knobe, Joshua (2009). "The Pervasive Impact of Moral Judgment," *Mind and Language*, 24/5: 586–604.

——and Smith, Michael (1996). "Freedom in Belief and Desire," *Journal of Philosophy*, 93/9: 429–49.

Piaget, Jean (1929). *The Child's Conception of the World* (London: Routledge and Kegan Paul).

——(1945/1962). *Plays, Dreams, and Imitation in Childhood*, trans. C. Gattegno and F. M. Hodgson (New York: W. W. Norton).

Pitino, Rick, and Reynolds, Bill (1997). *Success is a Choice: Ten Steps to Overachieving in Business and Life* (New York: Broadway Books).

Pizarro, David A., and Bloom, Paul (2003). "The Intelligence of the Moral Intuitions: Comment on Haidt," *Psychological Review*, 110/1: 193–6.

Plato (380 BCE/1992). *The Republic*, trans. G. M. A. Grube and C. D. C. Reeve (2nd edn., Indianapolis, Ind.: Hackett).

Plato (1997). *Complete Works*, ed. J. Cooper (Indianapolis, Ind.: Hackett).

Platt, R. D., and Griggs, R. A. (1993). "Facilitation in the Abstract Selection Task: The Effects of Attentional and Instructional Factors," *Quarterly Journal of Experimental Psychology*, 46A/4: 591–613.

Plotinus (1984). *The Enneads*, trans. A. H. Armstrong (Loeb Classical Library; Cambridge, Mass.: Harvard University Press).

Plutarch (1976). *Moralia, XIII, Part 1. Platonic Essays*, trans. H. Cherniss (Loeb Classical Library; Cambridge, Mass.: Harvard University Press).

Pollard, Bill (2006). "Explaining Actions with Habits," *American Philosophical Quarterly*, 43: 57–68.

Popper, Karl (1959/1992). *The Logic of Scientific Discovery*, trans. K. Popper (New York: Routledge).

Porro, C. A., Facchin, P., Fusi, S., Dri, G., and Fadiga, L. (2007). "Enhancement of Force after Action Observation: Behavioural and Neurophysiological Studies," *Neuropsychologia*, 45/13: 3114–21.

Porter, Judith D. R. (1971). *Black Child, White Child: The Development of Racial Attitudes* (Cambridge, Mass.: Harvard University Press).

Price, A. W. (1994). *Mental Conflict* (New York: Routledge).

Price, H. H. (1960/1969). *Belief* (London: George Allen & Unwin).

Priest, Graham (1997). "Sylvan's Box: A Short Story and Ten Morals," *Notre Dame Journal of Formal Logic*, 38/4: 573–82.

Prinz, Jesse (2004). *Gut Reactions: A Perceptual Theory of Emotion* (Oxford: Oxford University Press).

Pronin, Emily (2007). "Perception and Misperception of Bias in Human Judgment," *Trends in Cognitive Sciences*, 11/1: 37–43.

——Gilovich, T. D., and Ross, L. (2004). "Objectivity in the Eye of the Beholder: Divergent Perceptions of Bias in Self versus Others," *Psychological Review*, 111: 781–99.

Proshansky, H. M. (1966). "The Development of Intergroup Attitudes," in L. W. Hoffman and M. L. Hoffman (eds.), *Review of Child Development Research*, 2 (New York: Russell Sage Foundation), 311–71.

Prudovsky, Gad (1989). "The Confirmation of the Superposition Principle: On the Role of a Constructive Thought Experiment in Galileo's *Discorsi*," *Studies in History and Philosophy of Science*, 20/4: 453–68.

Pust, Joel (2000). *Intuitions as Evidence* (New York: Garland Press).

Pylyshyn, Zenon (2003). *Seeing and Visualizing: It's not what You Think* (Cambridge, Mass.: MIT Press).

Quine, W. V. (1972). Review of Milton K. Munitz, *Identity and Individuation*, in *Journal of Philosophy*, 69/16: 488–97.

——and Ullian, J. S. (1978). *The Web of Belief* (2nd edn., New York: Random House).

Radford, Colin (1989). "Replies to Three Critics," *Philosophy*, 64: 93–7.

——(1995). "Fiction, Pity, Fear, and Jealousy," *Journal of Aesthetics and Art Criticism*, 53/1: 71–5.

Ranganathan, Vinoth K., Siemionow, Vlodek, Liu, Jing Z., Sahgal, Vinod, and Yue, Guang H. (2004). "From Mental Power to Muscle Power—Gaining Strength by Using the Mind," *Neuropsychologia*, 42/7: 944–56.

Rawls, John (1971, rev. 1999). *A Theory of Justice* (Cambridge, Mass.: Harvard University Press).

Reese, Hayne W. (ed.) (1989). *Advances in Child Development and Behavior*, 22 (San Diego: Academic Press).

Reeve, C. D. C. (1988). *Philosopher-Kings: The Argument of Plato's Republic* (Princeton: Princeton University Press).

Reisberg, Daniel (ed.) (1992). *Auditory Imagery* (Hillsdale, NJ: Lawrence Erlbaum Associates).

——(1996). "The Non-ambiguity of Mental Images," in Cornoldi *et al.* (1996), 127–31.

Rescher, Nicholas (1991). "Thought Experiments in Presocratic Philosophy," in Horowitz and Massey (1991), 31–41.

Rey, Georges (1983), "Concepts and Stereotypes," *Cognition*, 15/1–3: 237–62.

——(1985). "Concepts and Conceptions: A Reply to Smith, Medin and Rips," *Cognition*, 19/3: 297–303.

Richeson, J. A., and Shelton, J. N. (2003). "When Prejudice Does not Pay: Effects of Interracial Contact on Executive Function," *Psychological Science*, 14/3: 287–90.

—— ——(2007). "Negotiating Interracial Interactions: Costs, Consequences, and Possibilities," *Current Directions in Psychological Science*, 16/6: 316–20.

——Trawalter, S., and Shelton, J. N. (2005). "African Americans' Racial Attitudes and the Depletion of Executive Function after Interracial Interactions," *Social Cognition*, 23: 336–52.

Rizzolatti, G., Fadiga, L., Fogassi, L., and Gallese, V. (2002). "From Mirror Neurons to Imitation: Facts and Speculations," in Meltzoff and Prinz (2002), 247–66.

—— ——Gallese, V., and Fogassi, L. (1996). "Premotor Cortex and the Recognition of Motor Actions," *Cognitive Brain Research*, 3/2: 131–41.

——and Sinigaglia, C. (2006). *Mirrors in the Brain: How Our Minds Share Actions and Emotions*, trans. F. Anderson (New York and Oxford: Oxford University Press).

Robertson, Teresa (2003). "(In the Fiction/Myth) the Number Seventeen Crosses the Rubicon," *Southwest Philosophy Review*, 19/1: 125–34.

Robinson, Denis (1985). "Can Amoeba Divide without Multiplying?," *Australasian Journal of Philosophy*, 63/3: 299–319.

Robinson, Jenefer (2005). *Deeper than Reason: Emotion and its Role in Literature, Music, and Art* (Oxford and New York: Oxford University Press).

Robinson, John (1988). "Personal Identity and Survival," *Journal of Philosophy*, 85/6: 319–28.

Rogers, S., Cook, I., and Meryl, A. (2005). "Imitation and Play in Autism," in F. R. Volkmar, R. Paul, A. Klin, and D. Cohen (eds.), *Handbook of Autism and Pervasive Developmental Disorders* (3rd edn., New York: John Wiley and Sons), 382–405.

Roitblat, Herbert, and Meyer, Jean-Arcady (eds.) (1995). *Comparative Approaches to Cognitive Science* (Cambridge, Mass.: MIT Press).

Ronen, Ruth (1994). *Possible Worlds in Literary Theory* (New York and Cambridge: Cambridge University Press).

Rorty, Amélie Oksenberg (ed.) (1976). *The Identities of Persons* (Berkeley: University of California Press).

——(ed.) (1980). *Essays on Aristotle's Ethics* (Berkeley: University of California Press).

——(1988). "The Deceptive Self: Liars, Layers, and Lairs," in McLaughlin and Rorty (1988), 11–29.

Rothstein, Edward (2007). "Skywalk Review: Great Space, Glass Floor—through, Canyon Views," *New York Times*, 19 May 2007.

Rovane, Carol (1990). "Branching Self-consciousness," *Philosophical Review*, 99/3: 355–95.

——(1994). "Critical Notice: Peter Unger's *Identity, Consciousness, and Value*," *Canadian Journal of Philosophy*, 24: 119–33.

——(1998). *The Bounds of Agency* (Princeton: Princeton University Press).

Rowling, J. K. (2000). *Harry Potter and the Goblet of Fire* (New York: Scholastic).

Rozin, Paul (1999). "Preadaptation and the Puzzles and Properties of Pleasure," in D. Kahneman, E. Diener, and N. Schwartz (eds.), *Well Being: The Foundations of Hedonic Psychology* (New York: Russell Sage), 109–33.

——Markwith, Maureen, and Ross, Bonnie (1990). "The Sympathetic Magical Law of Similarity, Nominal Realism and Neglect of Negatives in Response to Negative Labels," *Psychological Science*, 1/6: 383–4.

——Millman, Linda, and Nemeroff, Carol J. (1986). "Operation of the Laws of Sympathetic Magic in Disgust and Other Domains," *Journal of Personality and Social Psychology*, 50/4: 703–12.

——and Nemeroff, Carol J. (1990). "The Laws of Sympathetic Magic: A Psychological Analysis of Similarity and Contagion," in J. Stigler, G. Herdt, and R. A. Shweder (eds.), *Cultural Psychology: Essays on Comparative Human Development* (Cambridge: Cambridge University Press), 205–32.

Rubiner, Michael (1996). "Endpaper: Greetings," *New York Times Magazine*, 14 Jan. 1996, p. 60.

Rudman, L. A., Ashmore, R. D., and Gary, M. L. (2001). "'Unlearning' Automatic Biases: The Malleability of Implicit Prejudice and Stereotypes," *Journal of Personality and Social Psychology*, 81/5: 856–68.

Ryan, Marie-Laure (1991). *Possible Worlds, Artificial Intelligence, and Narrative Theory* (Bloomington: Indiana University Press).

Ryle, Gilbert (1949/1984). *The Concept of Mind* (Chicago: University of Chicago Press).

Sackheim, Harold A., and Gur, Ruben C. (1978). "Self-deception, Self-confrontation, and Consciousness," in Schwartz and Shapiro (1978), 139–97.

Sawyer, Robert J. (2005). *Mindscan* (New York: Tom Doherty Associates).

Schechtman, Marya (1990). "Personhood and Personal Identity," *Journal of Philosophy*, 77/2: 77–92.

——(1996). *The Constitution of Selves* (Ithaca, NY: Cornell University Press).

Schmitter, Amy M. (2006). "17th and 18th Century Theories of Emotions," in *The Stanford Encyclopedia of Philosophy* (Summer 2006 edition), ed. E. N. Zalta, <http://plato.stanford.edu/archives/sum2006/entries/emotions-17th18th/>.

Schneider, S. (2006). "The Paradox of Fiction," in *The Internet Encyclopedia of Philosophy*, <http://www.iep.utm.edu/f/fict-par.htm>.

Schroeder, T., and Matheson, C. (2006). "Imagination and Emotion," in Nichols (2006b), 19–39.

Schuck-Paim, C., Pompilio, L., and Kacelnik, A. (2004). "State-dependent Decisions Cause Apparent Violations of Rationality in Animal Choice," *PLoS Biology*, 2/12: 2305–15.

Schwartz, Gary E., and Shapiro, David (eds.) (1978). *Consciousness and Self-regulation: Advances in Research and Theory*, ii (New York and London: Plenum Press).

Schwitzgebel, Eric (2001). "In-between Believing," *Philosophical Quarterly*, 51/202: 76–82.

——(2006). "Belief," in *The Stanford Encyclopedia of Philosophy* (Fall 2006 Edition), ed. E. N. Zalta, <http://plato.stanford.edu/archives/fall2006/entries/belief/>.

——(MS). "Acting Contrary to Our Professed Beliefs," at <http://www.faculty.ucr.edu/~eschwitz/>, acc. 12 Feb. 2008.

Scott-Kakures, Dion (2002). "At 'Permanent Risk': Reasoning and Self-Knowledge in Self-Deception," *Philosophy and Phenomenological Research*, 65: 576–603.

Scripture, E. W., Smith, T. L., and Brown, E. M. (1894). "On the Education of Muscular Control and Power," *Studies from the Yale Psychological Laboratory*, 2: 114–19.

Scruton, Roger (1974). *Art and Imagination* (South Bend, Ind.: St. Augustine's Press).

Searle, John R. (1992). *The Rediscovery of the Mind* (Cambridge, Mass.: MIT Press).

Segal, S. J., and Cofer, C. N. (1960). "The Effect of Recency and Recall on Word Association," *American Psychologist*, 15: 451 (Abstract).

Segre, Michael (1989). "Galileo, Viviani and the Tower of Pisa," *Studies in History and Philosophy of Science*, 20/4: 435–51.

Semino, Elena (1997). *Language and World Creation in Poems and Other Texts* (New York: Longman).

Servos, P., and Goodale, M. A. (1995). "Preserved Visual Imagery in Visual Form Agnosia," *Neuropsychologia*, 33/11: 1383–94.

Shafir, S., Waite, T. A., and Smith, B. H. (2002). "Context-dependent Violations of Rational Choice in Honeybees (Apis mellifera) and Gray Jays (Perisoreus canadensis)," *Behavioral Ecology and Sociobiology*, 51/2: 180–7.

Shah, Nishi (2003). "How Truth Governs Belief," *Philosophical Review*, 112/4: 447–82.

——and Velleman, J. David (2005). "Doxastic Deliberation," *Philosophical Review*, 114/4: 497–534.

Shepard, Roger N. (1984). "Ecological Constraints on Internal Representation: Resonant Kinematics of Perceiving, Imagining, Thinking, and Dreaming," *Psychological Review*, 91/4: 417–47.

——(1994). "Mind and World: From Newton, Einstein, and Darwin to Principles of Mind (unpublished William James Lectures, Harvard University).

——and Cooper, Lynn A. (1982). *Mental Images and Their Transformations* (Cambridge: MIT Press).

——and Metzler, J. (1971). "Mental Rotation of Three-Dimensional Objects," *Science*, 171: 701–3.

Shoemaker, Sydney (1963). *Self-knowledge and Self-identity* (Ithaca, NY: Cornell University Press).

——and Swinburne, Richard (1984). *Personal Identity: Great Debates in Philosophy* (Oxford: Basil Blackwell).

Show, don't tell (2009). Wikipedia, The Free Encyclopedia 2009, <http://en.wikipedia.org/w/index.php?title=Show,_don%27t_tell&oldid=292377338>, acc. 17 Oct. 2009.

Shulman, Polly (2007). "Priming the Mind," *Science: Science Careers* (Mar. 2007).

Silver, Lee M. (1997). *Remaking Eden: How Genetic Engineering and Cloning Will Transform the American Family* (New York: Avon Books).

Sinnott-Armstrong, Walter (2008a). "Abstract + concrete = paradox," in Knobe and Nichols (2008), 209–30.

——(2008b). "Consequentialism," in *The Stanford Encyclopedia of Philosophy* (Fall 2008 Edition), ed. E. N. Zalta.

——(2008c). "Framing Moral Intuitions," in Sinnott-Armstrong (2008d), 47–76.

——(ed.) (2008d). *Moral Psychology* (Cambridge, Mass.: MIT Bradford).

Skolnick, Deena, and Bloom, Paul (2006a). "The Intuitive Cosmology of Fictional Worlds," in Nichols (2006b), 73–86.

————(2006b). "What Does Batman Think about SpongeBob? Children's Understanding of the Fantasy/Fantasy Distinction," *Cognition*, 101: B9–B18.

Sloman, S. A. (1996). "The Empirical Case for Two Systems of Reasoning," *Psychological Bulletin*, 119: 3–22.

Smetana, J. G., and Braeges, J. L. (1990). "The Development of Toddlers' Moral and Conventional Judgments," *Merrill-Palmer Quarterly*, 36/3: 329–46.

Smith, Angela M. (2005). "Responsibility for Attitudes: Activity and Passivity in Mental Life," *Ethics*, 115: 236–71.

Smith, Edward E., and Medin, Douglas L. (1981). *Categories and Concepts* (Cambridge, Mass.: Harvard University Press).

Smolensky, Paul (1988). "On the Proper Treatment of Connectionism," *Behavioral and Brain Sciences*, 11: 1–23.

Snowdon, P. F. (1991). "Personal Identity and Brain Transplants," in Cockburn (1991), 109–26.

Sorabji, Richard (1980). "Aristotle on the Role of Intellect in Virtue," in Rorty (1980), 201–20.

Sorensen, Roy (1992a). *Thought Experiments* (New York and Oxford: Oxford University Press).

——(1992b). "Thought Experiments and the Epistemology of Laws," *Canadian Journal of Philosophy*, 22/1: 15–44.

——(2002). "The Art of the Impossible," in Gendler and Hawthorne (2002a), 337–68.

Sosa, Ernest (2007a). "Experimental Philosophy and Philosophical Intuition," *Philosophical Studies*, 132/1: 99–107.

——(2007b). "Intuitions: Their Nature and Epistemic Efficacy," *Grazer Philosophische Studien*, 74/1: 51–67.

——and Kim, Jaegwon (2000). *Epistemology: An Anthology* (Oxford: Basil Blackwell).

Southgate, V., Senju, A., and Csibra, G. (2007). "Action Anticipation through Attribution of False Belief by 2-Year-Olds," *Psychological Sciences*, 18: 587–92.

Srull, Thomas K., and Wyer, Robert S. (1979). "The Role of Category Accessibility in the Interpretation of Information about Persons," *Journal of Personality and Social Psychology*, 37/10: 1660–72.

————(1980). "Category Accessibility and Social Perception," *Journal of Personality and Social Psychology*, 38/6: 841–56.

Stalnaker, Robert (1984/1987). *Inquiry* (Cambridge, Mass.: MIT Bradford).

Stangor, C. (ed.) (2000). *Stereotypes and Prejudice: Key Readings* (Key Readings in Social Psychology; Philadelphia, Pa.: Psychology Press).

Stanovich, Keith E. (1999). *Who is Rational? Studies of Individual Differences in Reasoning* (Hillsdale, NJ: Lawrence Erlbaum Associates).

——(2009). "Distinguishing the Reflective, Algorithmic, and Autonomous Minds: Is it Time for a Tri-process Theory?," in J. Evans and K. Frankish (eds.), *In Two Minds: Dual Processes and Beyond* (Oxford: Oxford University Press), 55–88.

——and West, Richard F. (2000). "Individual Differences in Reasoning: Implications for the Rationality Debate," *Behavioral and Brain Sciences*, 23: 645–726.

————(2008). "On the Relative Independence of Thinking Biases and Cognitive Ability," *Journal of Personality and Social Psychology*, 94/4: 672–95.

Steup, Matthias (2008). "Doxastic Freedom," *Synthese*, 161/3: 375–92.

Stevin, Simon (1955). *The Principal Works of Simon Stevin*, i: *General Introduction and Mechanics*, ed. E. J. Dijksterhuis (Amsterdam: C.W. Swets and Zeitlinger).

Stich, Stephen (1990). *The Fragmentation of Reason* (Cambridge, Mass.: MIT Press).

Stock, Kathleen (2003). "The Tower of Goldbach and other Impossible Tales," in Kieran and Lopes (2003), 107–24.

——(2005). "Resisting Imaginative Resistance," *Philosophical Quarterly*, 55/221: 607–24.

Stokes, Dustin (2006). "The Evaluative Character of Imaginative Resistance," *British Journal of Aesthetics*, 46/4: 387–405.

Storms, L. H. (1958). "Apparent Backward Association: A Situational Effect," *Journal of Experimental Psychology*, 55: 390–5.

Sullivan, Shannon (2006). *Revealing Whiteness: The Unconscious Habits of Racial Privilege* (Bloomington and Indianapolis, Ind.: University of Indiana Press).

Sunstein, Cass (1993). "On Analogical Reasoning," *Harvard Law Review*, 106: 741–91.

——(1996). "Political Conflict and Legal Agreement," *Tanner Lectures on Human Values*, 18: 137–250.

——(2005). "Moral Heuristics" (with discussion and replies), *Behavioral and Brain Sciences*, 28/4: 531–73.

Swain, Stacey, Alexander, Joshua, and Weinberg, Jonathan M. (2008). "The Instability of Philosophical Intuitions: Running Hot and Cold on Truetemp," *Philosophy and Phenomenological Research*, 76/1: 138–55.

Tanner, Michael (1994). "Morals in Fiction and Fictional Morality/II," *Proceedings of the Aristotelian Society, Supplementary Volumes*, 68: 51–66.

Taylor, Shelley E., and Brown, Jonathan D. (1988). "Illusion and Well-being: A Social Psychological Perspective on Mental Health," *Psychological Bulletin*, 103/2: 193–210.

Tetlock, Philip, and Belkin, Aaron (eds.) (1996). *Counterfactual Thought Experiments in World Politics* (Princeton: Princeton University Press).

Thomas, Nigel J. T. (n.d.). *Imagination, Mental Imagery, Consciousness, and Cognition: Scientific, Philosophical, and Historical Approaches*. Available from <http://www.imagery-imagination.com/>.

Thomason, Sarah (1991). "Thought Experiments in Linguistics," in Horowitz and Massey (1991), 247–57.

Thomson, Judith Jarvis (1971). "A Defense of Abortion," *Philosophy and Public Affairs*, 1/1: 47–66.

——(1985). "The Trolley Problem," *Yale Law Journal*, 94: 1395–1415.

——(1986). *Rights, Restitution, and Risk: Essays in Moral Theory* (Cambridge: Harvard University Press).

——(1997). "People and Their Bodies," in Dancy (1997), 202–29.

Thorndike, E. L. (1922). "The Effect of Changed Data upon Reasoning," *Journal of Experimental Psychology*, 5/1: 33–8.

Todd, Cain Samuel (2009). "Imaginability, Morality, and Fictional Truth: Dissolving the Puzzle of 'Imaginative Resistance'," *Philosophical Studies*, 143/2: 187–211.

Tomberlin, James E. (ed.) (1989). *Philosophical Perspectives*, 3 (Atascadero, Calif.: Ridgeview Publishing Co.).

Toth, J. P., and Reingold, E. M. (1996). "Beyond Perception: Conceptual Contributions to Unconscious Influences of Memory," in Underwood (1996), 41–84.

Traiger, Saul (2005). "Reason Unhinged: Passion and the Precipice from Montaigne to Hume," in Jenkins, Whiting, and Williams (2005), 100–15.

Travers, P. L. (1934/1962). *Mary Poppins* (New York: Harcourt, Brace & World).

Trawalter, S., and Richeson, J. A. (2006). "Regulatory Focus and Executive Function after Interracial Interactions," *Journal of Experimental Social Psychology*, 42/3: 406–12.

Trogdon, Kelly (2004). "Moral Imaginative Resistance." Unpublished manuscript available at <http://www.nyu.edu/gsas/dept/philo/gradconf/papers/Trogdon.pdf>.

Tse, Dorothy, Largston, Rosamund F., KayeKama, Masaki, Bethus, Ingrid, Spooner, Patrick A., Wood, Emma R., Witter, Menno P., and Morris, Richard G. M. (2007). "Schemas and Memory Consolidation", *Science*, 316/5821: 76–82.

Turner, Mark (1996). "Conceptual Blending and Counterfactual Argument in the Social and Behavioral Sciences," in Tetlock and Belkin (1996), 291–5.

Tversky, Amos, and Kahneman, Daniel (1973/1982). "Availability: A Heuristic for Judging Frequency and Probability," *Cognitive Psychology*, 4: 207–32; repr. in Kahneman, Slovic, and Tversky (1982), 163–78.

————(1981). "The Framing of Decisions and the Rationality of Choice," *Science*, 211: 453–8.

————(1983). "Extensional versus Intuitive Reasoning: The Conjunction Fallacy in Probability Judgment," *Psychological Review*, 90: 293–315.

Uhlmann, E. L., Pizarro, David A., and Bloom, Paul (2008). "Varieties of Social Cognition," *Journal for the Theory of Social Behaviour*, 38/3: 293–322.

————Tannenbaum, D., and Ditto, P. H. (2009). "The Motivated Use of Moral Principles," *Judgment and Decision Making*, 4: 479–91.

Underwood, G. (ed.) (1996). *Implicit Cognition* (Oxford: Oxford University Press).

Unger, Peter (1975). *Ignorance* (Oxford: Oxford University Press).

——(1990). *Identity, Consciousness, and Value* (New York and Oxford: Oxford University Press).

Vahid, Hamid (2006). "Aiming at Truth: Doxastic vs. Epistemic Goals," *Philosophical Studies*, 131/2: 303–35.

Vazquez, C. (1987). "Judgment of Contingency: Cognitive Biases in Depressed and Nondepressed Subjects," *Journal of Personality and Social Psychology*, 52/2: 419–31.

Velleman, J. David (1996). "Self to Self," *Philosophical Review*, 105/1: 39–76.

——(1999). "Love as a Moral Emotion," *Ethics*, 109/2: 338–74.

——(2000). "On the Aim of Belief," in *The Possibility of Practical Reason* (Oxford and New York: Oxford University Press), 244–81.

——and Shah, Nishi (2005). "Doxastic Deliberation," *Philosophical Review*, 114/4: 497–534.

Vranas, Peter (2005). "The Indeterminacy Paradox: Character Evaluations and Human Psychology," *Noûs*, 39: 1–42.

Walker-Andrews, Arlene S., and Kahana-Kalman, Ronit (1999). "The Understanding of Pretence across the Second Year of Life," *British Journal of Developmental Psychology*, 17/4: 523–36.

Walton, Kendall (1978). "Fearing Fictions," *Journal of Philosophy*, 75/8: 5–27.

——(1990). *Mimesis as Make-believe* (Cambridge, Mass.: Harvard University Press).

——(1993). "Metaphor and Prop Oriented Make-believe," *European Journal of Philosophy*, 1/1: 39–57.

——(1994). "Morals in Fiction and Fictional Morality/I," *Proceedings of the Aristotelian Society, Supplementary Volumes*, 68: 27–50.

——(1997). "Spelunking, Simulation and Slime: On Being Moved by Fiction," in Hort and Laver (1997), 37–49.

——(2006). "On the (So-called) Puzzle of Imaginative Resistance," in Nichols (2006b), 137–48.

Wason, P. C. (1960). "On the Failure to Eliminate Hypotheses in a Conceptual Task," *Quarterly Journal of Experimental Psychology*, 12: 129–40.

——(1966). "Reasoning," in Foss (1966), 135–51.

Weatherson, Brian (2003a). "Furniture in Fiction and Fictional Furniture," at <http://philosophyweblog.blogspot.com/mfp.htm>.

——(2003b). "What Good are Counterexamples?," *Philosophical Studies*, 115/1: 1–31.

——(2004). "Morality, Fiction, and Possibility," *Philosophers' Imprint*, <http://hdl.handle.net/2027/spo.3521354.0004.003>.

Wedgwood, Ralph (2002). "The Aim of Belief," *Philosophical Perspectives*, 16 (Language and Mind): 267–97.

Wegner, Daniel M. (1994). "Ironic Processes of Mental Control," *Psychological Review*, 101: 34–52.

——(2002). *The Illusion of Conscious Will* (Cambridge, Mass.: MIT Press).

Weinberg, Jonathan M., Nichols, Shaun, and Stich, Stephen (2008). "Normativity and Epistemic Intuitions," in J. Knobe and S. Nichols (eds.), *Experimental Philosophy* (New York: Oxford University Press), 17–45.

——Crowley, Steve, Gonnerman, Chad, Swain, Stacey, and Vandewalker, Ian (MS). "Intuition and Calibration." Version of 9/18/2005 available at <http://www.indiana.edu/~eel/>.

——and Meskin, Aaron (2006). "Puzzling over the Imagination: Philosophical Problems, Architectural Solutions," in Nichols (2006b), 175–204.

——Nichols, Shaun, and Stich, Stephen (2001). "Normativity and Epistemic Intuitions," *Philosophical Topics*, 29: 429–60.

Weisberg, Deena Skolnick, and Bloom, P. (2009). "Young Children Separate Multiple Pretend Worlds," *Developmental Science*, 12/5: 699–705.

——and Goodstein, Joshua (2009). "What Belongs in a Fictional World?," *Journal of Cognition and Culture*, 9: 69–78.

Weiskrantz, Louis (2002). "Prime-sight and Blindsight," *Consciousness and Cognition*, 11: 568–81.

Wellman, Henry, and Estes, D. (1986). "Early Understanding of Mental Entities: A Reexamination of Childhood Realism," *Child Development*, 57: 910–23.

Werth, Paul (1999). *Text-worlds: Representing Conceptual Space in Discourse* (New York: Longman).

Weston, P. (1975). "How Can We Be Moved by the Fate of Anna Karenina? II," *Proceedings of the Aristotelian Society, Supplementary Volumes*, 49: 67–93.

Whiting, Jennifer (1986). "Friends and Future Selves," *Philosophical Review*, 95/4: 547–80.

Wiggins, David (1980). *Sameness and Substance* (Cambridge, Mass.: Harvard University Press).

Wilkes, Kathleen V. (1988). *Real People: Personal Identity without Thought Experiments* (Oxford: Clarendon Press).

Wilkins, Minna Cheves (1928). "The Effect of Changed Material on the Ability to Do Formal Syllogistic Reasoning," *Archives of Psychology*, 102: 1–84.

Williams, Bernard (1956/1973). "Personal Identity and Individuation," repr. (with new pagination) in Williams (1973), 1–18.

——(1966/1973). "Imagination and the Self," repr. (with new pagination) in Williams (1973), 26–45.

——(1970/1973a). "Deciding to Believe," repr. (with new pagination) in Williams (1973), 136–51.

——(1970/1973b). "The Self and the Future," repr. (with new pagination) in Williams (1973), 46–63.

——(1973). *Problems of the Self* (Cambridge: Cambridge University Press).

Williams, Christopher (2000). "False Delicacy," in Jacobson (2000), 239–62.

Williams, L. E., and Bargh, J. A. (2008). "Keeping One's Distance: The Influence of Spatial Distance Cues on Affect and Evaluation," *Psychological Science*, 19/3: 302–8.

Williamson, Timothy (2000). *Knowledge and its Limits* (Oxford: Oxford University Press).

——(2005). "Armchair Philosophy, Metaphysical Modality, and Counterfactual Thinking," *Proceedings of the Aristotelian Society*, 105: 1–23.

Wilson, T. D., Lindsey, S., and Schooler, T. Y. (2000). "A Model of Dual Attitudes," *Psychological Review*, 107/1: 101–26.

Winters, Barbara (1979). "Believing at Will," *Journal of Philosophy*, 76/5: 243–56.

Wolf, Susan (1986). "Self-interest and Interest in Selves," *Ethics*, 96/4: 704–20.

Wolfe, Tom (1998). *A Man in Full* (New York: Farrar, Strauss, and Giroux).

Wollheim, Richard, and Hopkins, Jasper (eds.) (1982). *Philosophical Essays on Freud* (Cambridge: Cambridge University Press).

Wolterstorff, Nicholas (1980). *Works and Worlds of Art* (Oxford: Clarendon Press).

Wood, Allen (1988). "Self-deception and Bad Faith," in McLaughlin and Rorty (1988), 207–27.

Woolley, J. (1995). "Young Children's Understanding of Fiction vs. Epistemic Mental Representations: Imagination and Belief," *Child Development*, 66: 1011–1021.

Yablo, Stephen (2002). "Coulda, Woulda, Shoulda," in Gendler and Hawthorne (2002a), 441–92.

Young, Andrew W. (2000). "Wondrous Strange: The Neuropsychology of Delusional Beliefs," *Mind and Language*, 15/1: 47–73.

Zanna, M. P. (ed.) (2004). *Advances in Experimental Social Psychology* (San Diego, Calif.: Academic Press).

Zatorre, Robert J., and Halpern, Andrea R. (2005). "Mental Concerts: Musical Imagery and Auditory Cortex," *Neuron*, 47/1: 9–12.

——— Perry, D. W., Meyer, E., and Evans, A. C. (1996). "Hearing in the Mind's Ear: A PET Investigation of Musical Imagery and Perception," *Journal of Cognitive Neuroscience*, 8: 29–46.

Index of Names

Aarts, Henk 165n26, 249, 250, 253, 278
Abramson, Lyn 176n49, 177
Ahn, Woo-Kyoung vii
Akadémiai Óvoda of Budapest vii
Alcauskas, Katherine viii
Alcinous 284n2
Alcoff, Linda 305n44
Alexander, Joshua 127n23
Alloy, Lauren 176n49, 177
Allport, Gordon 305n44, 306
Alston, William 59n15
Amadio, Dean 305
Amedi, Amir 244
American Council for Learned Societies vi
Ames, Roger T. 160n12
Anderson, Elizabeth 132n29
Anderson, S.W. 231
Ariely, Dan 289n10
Aristotle 27n10, 33n17, 58n14, 81n13, 236, 263, 275, 281, 284n2, 285, 285n3, 289n11, 304, 304n41, 306n47, 307
Armstrong, David 265n19, 272n34, 295n21
Ashmore, R.D. 307n51
Atkinson, David 23n3
Audi, Robert 265n19

Baier, Annette 285n3
Baillargeon, Renee 142n6
Baker, Lynn Rudder 272n34, 295n21
Baker, Sarah 192n19, 262n13
Banaji, Mahzarin R. 306n48, 308n53
Banfield, Jane F. 249n17, 277n45
Bargh, John A. vii, 165n26, 248, 249, 250n20, 252–3, 264n17, 265n18, 275–9, 279n48, 281n53, 310n56

Barnes, Annette 158–9, 169n35, 284n2
Barney, Rachel 303n39
Baron, A.S. 306n48
Barresi, John 63n23
Bateson, Melissa 289n10
Baum, L. Frank 224n42
Bayne, Tim 159n9
Bealer, George 23n3, 127n19
Bechara, Antoine 149, 231, 231
Bengson, John 310n56
Bennett, Jonathan 59n15, 271n33
Bentham, Jeremy 128
Bernecker, Sven 98n1
Berry, Catherine viii
Bertrand, M. 305
Betegh, Gabor 178n54
Bishop, Michael 44n4
Blaauw, Martijn 254n26
Blackburn, Bonnie viii
Blackburn, Simon 259n8
Blair, Irene V. 307–8
Blair, R. James R. 198n27
Blakemore, Sarah-Jayne 294n20
Bloom, Paul vii, viii, 142n7, 192n19, 241n2, 250n19, 254n26, 281n53, 288n7, 298n28, 303n38, 307n51, 310n56
Blum, Lawrence A. 305n44
Bobzien, Susanne 178n54
Bodenhausen, G.V. 306n46
Bodnar, István 178n54
Bonavec, Daniel 310n56
Boney, Monique vii
Bonomi, Andrea 217n31
Borge, Steffen 158, 178n54
Bouldin, Paula 141
Bourchier, Alison 144
Bourgeois, Warren 54n2
Bourner, Daniel viii
Boyd, Richard 41n30
Braeges, J.L. 198n27

Braithwaite, R.B. 259n8, 272n34, 295n21
Brandt, Thomas 256n2, 261
Brann, Eva T.H. 246n14
Bransford, J.D. 37n22
Bratman, Michael 165n25, 267n24, 273, 273n36, 310n56
Brendel, E. 23n3
Brennan, R. 303n39
Brittain, Charles vii, 284n2, 303n39, 310n56
Brittain, Harriet vii
Brooks, Heidi vii
Brooks, Richard vii, 281n53, 310n56
Brown, E.M. 245n12
Brown, James Robert 21, 23n3, 25n4, 26n6, 41n30, 42–46, 51n10, 52n12, 132n30, 176n49, 178n54
Brown, Jonathan D. 176n49
Brown, R. 307n52
Bruck, Maggie 149n15
Bruell, Marc J. 142n6
Burge, Tyler 154n17
Burnyeat, Myles 281n51
Burrows, Lara 165n26, 248–249, 253, 264n17, 265n18, 276–8
Butts, Robert E. 26n6
Byrne, Ruth 52n11, 121n5, 139n4

Caine, Carolyn viii, 132n30, 178n54, 281n53, 305n43, 310n56
Camp, Elisabeth 201n32
Camper, Naomi Gendler viii
Carey, Susan vii
Cargile, James 26n6
Carpenter, K.M. 307
Carrier, Martin 23n3
Carroll, J.S. 307
Carroll, Lewis 222–3, 226
Carroll, Noël 246n14

349

Index of Names

Index of Names

Subject Index

Affect
  See Emotions
Affective contagion
  See Contagion, affective
Alief
  and aversive racism 305–10
  and behavior 14–16,
    255–81, 282–311
  belief-concordant 266, 274,
    281, 301–3
  belief-discordant 14–16,
    122n7, 259–62, 266,
    268, 270, 281, 301–3,
    303–10
  characterized 14, 261–5,
    282, 288–9
  contrasted with belief 14,
    122n7, 266–75, 290–8
  contrasted with habit and
    instinct 290–1,
    299–301
  contrasted with hypocrisy
    290–1
  contrasted with imagination
    and pretense 255,
    267–72, 290–1, 298–9
  contrasted with instinct
    290–1, 299–301
  contrasted with self-
    deception 259–60
  discussed v,14–16, 38n24,
    50n9, 90n18, 116,
    123n10, 144n8, 179,
    200n30, 234n7, 242n3,
    255–310
  examples of 255–281
    passim, 282–310 *passim*
  norm-concordant and norm-
    discordant 301–3
  See also Alief, belief-
    concordant; Alief,
    belief-discordant
  regulation of 15–16, 303–10
    See also Harmony and
    Disharmony
    of the Soul

Association-Dependence
  Test 78, 91–4
Attention
  redirection of 3, 37, 132,
    191–2, 285, 304–5, 309
  selective 171n41, 192,
    297n26
Attitudes
  explicit 3, 9, 15–16, 35–6,
    48n6, 141, 143–4, 148,
    150–1, 165, 168n32,
    239, 242–3, 248, 260–2,
    270, 279, 286, 301n32,
    305–6, 307n52
  implicit 3, 7, 13, 15–16,
    35–6, 48n6, 148, 150–1,
    168n32, 197–200, 206,
    236, 239, 248, 301n32,
    305–6, 307n52, 308
  projective vs. receptive 11,
    139, 163, 171, 175, 178
  See also Alief; Belief;
    Imagination;
    Make-belief; Pretense
Authoritative breakdown,
  puzzle of
  See Imaginative resistance
    and Puzzle of
    Authoritative Break-
    down
Autism 139, 303n37
Automatic behavior
  See Behavior, automatic and
    habitual
Automaticity 15, 165, 248–50,
    252–3, 275–9
Aversive racism
  See Racism, aversive and
    non-aversive

Behavior
  automatic and habitual v, 13,
    14–15, 123, 138–9, 164,
    170, 262–3, 271n30,
    275–9, 282–4, 288–9,
    291, 295, 297 300

belief-desire based 135,
    146–7, 242, 272, 275–6,
    285, 295–8
reasons vs. causes explana-
    tions of 285–6
self-deceptive 155–78
See also Alief and behavior;
    Belief -behavior
    mismatch; Imagination
    and action
Belief
  aims of 183, 212
  and justification 3, 25,
    43–4, 46–7, 128n25
  and bimagination 159n8
  as a receptive attitude
    162–5, 267–72
  See also Attitudes,
    projective vs. receptive;
    Belief, will-indepen-
    dence of
  attempts to characterize
    162–5, 259n8, 265n19,
    272–3
  -behavior mismatch 259–61
  See also Alief and behavior;
    Behavior, automatic
    and habitual; Behavior,
    self-deceptive;
    Imagination and action
  -behavior picture 272–5,
    292–8
  See also Alief and behavior;
    Behavior, belief-desire
    based; Belief-behavior
    mismatch; Imagination
    and action
  -concordant alief
  See Alief, belief-
    concordant
  contradictory or
    inconsistent 140,
    228n1, 235
  contrasted with alief 14,
    122n7, 256–8, 266–73,
    290 8

Made in the USA
Middletown, DE
16 May 2017